State Fragility
Around
the World

Fractured Justice and
Fierce Reprisal

State Fragility Around the World

Fractured Justice and Fierce Reprisal

Laurie A. Gould
Department of Criminal Justice and Criminology
Georgia Southern University

Matthew Pate
Senior Research Fellow
Violence Research Group School of Criminal Justice
University at Albany

CRC Press
Taylor & Francis Group
Boca Raton London New York

CRC Press is an imprint of the
Taylor & Francis Group, an **informa** business

CRC Press
Taylor & Francis Group
6000 Broken Sound Parkway NW, Suite 300
Boca Raton, FL 33487-2742

Printed on acid-free paper
Version Date: 20160113

International Standard Book Number-13: 978-1-4665-7767-1 (Hardback)

Library of Congress Cataloging-in-Publication Data

Names: Gould, Laurie A., author. | Pate, Matthew, author.
Title: State fragility around the world : fractured justice and fierce
reprisal / Laurie A. Gould and Stephen Matthew Pate.
Description: Boca Raton : Taylor & Francis, 2016. | Includes bibliographical
references and index.
Identifiers: LCCN 2015038862 | ISBN 9781466577671 (alk. paper)
Subjects: LCSH: Failed states.
Classification: LCC KZ4029 .G68 2016 | DDC 321--dc23
LC record available at http://lccn.loc.gov/2015038862

Visit the Taylor & Francis Web site at
http://www.taylorandfrancis.com

and the CRC Press Web site at
http://www.crcpress.com

Dedication

To those who must live in the shadow of tyranny; and to those for whom the necessities of survival demand continuing struggle; and to those souls for whom violence, sickness, and fear are the immutable cadence of life.

Contents

Preface

A strong nation, like a strong person, can afford to be gentle, firm, thoughtful, and restrained. It can afford to extend a helping hand to others. It's a weak nation, like a weak person, that must behave with bluster and boasting and rashness and other signs of insecurity.

—Jimmy Carter

Inasmuch as it is tempting to talk about "the book we wrote," a more honest appraisal acknowledges that this volume is only possible because many gifted thinkers laid the groundwork for it. The foundation for this study is built on centuries of social thought. It also rests on the disenchantment of postmodernity, but not just the postmodernity that rebukes grand theory. Rather, it is a postmodern sensibility that understands the expanse and implications of prior and constituent theories.

To this point, our construction here is one of relationships—relationships that are dynamic, recursive, and adaptive. We seek to treat the world for what it is: a network of interconnected individuals and circumstances, whose actions in the collective guide the evolution of the system they comprise. Our predicate assumptions about society blend tenets of methodological individualism with its often (and in our view errantly) opposed mirror, methodological holism, much in the way that Robert Prechter's (1999) socionomic theory does.

The seeds of this idea have a long scholarly pedigree (Parker 2006). Werner Stark (1962) traces the lineage to Wilhelm Dilthey's concept of *Wirkungszusammenhang* (the "productive nexus or system"). Human lives and indeed history itself in Dilthey's construction are to be understood in terms of "productivity before any causal or teleological analysis is applied" (Makkreel 2012). As Rudolf Makkreel (2012) further clarifies, "The carriers of history, whether they be individuals, cultures, institutions, or communities, are productive systems capable of producing value, meaning, and, in some cases, realizing purposes. Each is to be considered structurally as centered in itself."

For Dilthey (1989), the German historical school was incorrect in its conceptualization of individuals as mere subordinates to larger social institutions such as the family and the state. Moreover, and perhaps more importantly for present concerns, Dilthey held that the historical school was incorrect in its assumption that "the positive laws of institutions define the full reality of life" (Makkreel 2012). As Dilthey (1989, p. 132 as cited by Makkreel 2012) observes, the authority of the state "encompasses only a certain portion ... of the collective power of the populace" and even when state power exerts a certain preponderance it can do so only "through the cooperation of psychological impulses."

In the cooperative nexus, "methodological individualism... and... methodological collectivism emerge as two of the basic thought-forms, logically prior to the third ... [a] sublation of the former. This third form... posits self and society as... aspects of the same thing... ontologically equivalent: it is traced from Vico to Summer and Cooley" (Martins 1964, pp. 77–78). This then gets us to a point philosophically where we can start to discuss society as a system—a system composed of and amenable to the whims of both the desultory and the determined; yet a system greater than the mere additive sum of those whims.

Within the first pages of this volume, the reader will be thrown into the middle of broad dissensus. Not only will the demarcation line of state "failure" be hotly debated, so too will the more basic concept of the "state." With such foundational ideas up for discussion, the remainder of the enterprise may appear a tad impudent or unwise. Even so, we forge ahead, plowing deep into the weeds of humanity. While the reader may not join us in all (or perhaps even any) of our conclusions, we present this work just as we have long held it to be—a collection of ideas, a collection of questions, a collection of observations.

Laurie A. Gould and Matthew Pate

References

Dilthey, W. 1989. In R. A. Makkreel and F. Rodi (Eds) *Selected Works, Volume 1. Introduction to the Human Sciences*. Princeton, NJ: Princeton University Press.

Makkreel, R. 2012. Wilhelm Dilthey. In E. N. Zalta (Ed.) *The Stanford Encyclopedia of Philosophy*. Summer 2012 edn. http://plato.stanford.edu/archives/sum2012/entries/dilthey/>

Martins, H. G. 1964. The fundamental forms of social thought. *British Journal of Sociology* 15(1): 77–78.

Parker, W. 2006. Methodological individualism vs. methodological holism: Neoclassicism, institutionalism and socionomic theory. *Congress of the International Association for Research in Economic Psychology and the Society for the Advancement of Behavioral Economics*. Paris, France. July 5–8, 2006. http://www.socionomics.org/pdf/neoclassicism_institutionalism.pdf

Prechter, R. 1999. *The Wave Principle of Human Behavior and the New Science of Socionomics*. Gainsville, GA: New Classics Library.

Stark, W. 1962. *The Fundamental Forms of Social Thought*. New York: Fordham University Press.

Acknowledgment

Deep thanks go out to our friends and families who have graciously tolerated the creation of one more manuscript. Your support gives us the fortitude to complete projects such as these. We want to extend particular thanks to our friend and mentor, Graeme Newman, as well as Georgia Southern University and the University at Albany. We also wish to express a very special thank you to Jack Lightfoot, whose countless hours of assistance helped make this volume possible. Lastly, we want to thank Kathleen, Vern, and all the furry ones for their continuing love and patience.

Introduction: The State as a System

1

Just as a man would not cherish living in a body other than his own, so do nations not like to live under other nations, however noble and great the latter may be.

—Mahatma Gandhi

In its popular framing, state failure is a dystopian horror with burned-out cities, rampant crime, famine, drought, civil war, corruption, and plagues. These are the places where nongovernmental organizations (NGOs) send aid and nervous television reporters huddle amid the smoldering rubble. State failure is a topic that lends itself to colorful metaphor and vivid gory description. Often, these broad-brush depictions succinctly capture the essence of a place, but the economy of such generalizations typically comes at the expense of important and revelatory detail. Those overlooked details are the focus of this book.

In his work on the globe's most imperiled societies, John Heilbrunn (2006, p. 136) writes of failed states as "a Hobbesian world of poverty and violence." Heilbrunn's description captures two of the most salient aspects of failure. While the overconcentration of wealth is an important issue in almost all nations, the extremes of poverty are especially apparent in many failed states. So, too is the omnipresent specter of violence. Be it open war, revolution, criminogenic chaos, or state-sponsored treachery, the consequences of violence are often more apparent in failed states.

While it would be easy to identify several places on Earth that embody many or all of the above-listed cataclysms, not all failure fits neatly into Heilbrunn's very well-informed circumscription. State failure is as varied a condition as the regions to which that description might be applied. Appropriating Tolstoy's line from *Anna Karenina*, "All happy families resemble one another; each unhappy family is unhappy in its own way," Jack Goldstone et al. (2005, p. 12) observe, "All stable nations resemble one another; each unstable nation is unstable in its own way."

Such contentions owe to the fact that state failure is not one universal condition. While Goldstone's pithy observation is true in a narrow sense, failed states often have more in common with one another than such a tight framing might imply. Some of the present inability to discern the patterns of failure stems from the fact that the extant scholarship on state fragility has yet to provide an enduringly solvent operationalization of the concept.

As Stuart Eizenstat et al. (2005, p. 136) succinctly capture it, "The terms, 'weak,' 'failing' and 'failed' are frustratingly imprecise." To this list, one might also add "collapsed," "collapsing," "fragile," "unstable," or any number of similar descriptors of a state imperiled. In this definitional mélange, some consensus emerges around a handful of indisputably failed nations, but much beyond the rim of that agreement the terms *failure* and *fragility* lose their explanatory heft.

In short, that is the starting point for this volume. The core argument presented in the following pages acknowledges the tremendous variability of failed and fragile states. More importantly, however, the included case studies and other analyses suggest the existence of functional and structural attributes common across most state systems. Indeed, it is the adoption of a systems perspective that allows the careful observer to find very clear patterns and predictable trajectories within the population of less-viable nations. Nowhere do we see this more clearly than in the ways that criminality and criminal justice are treated.

Of course, assessing the role that crime and justice play in society takes us back to the foundational theories of modern social science, the work of Emile Durkheim in particular. Durkheim is especially of consequence given the role that violence tends to play in failed and fragile states. Because he understood that a stable social order requires widely shared and deeply held values, anything that undermines that consensus also facilitates violence. As Vincenzo Ruggiero (2006, p. 49) explains, Durkheim held the loosening of this social bond to be the harbinger of ascending egoism, personal ambition, and "spreading social malaise."

Of all the stability indicators one might consider, the insights that a society's economic order provides are among the deepest. Economies are defined by an opposition of interests (Durkheim 1897/1951). They exist in perpetual change. Durkheim argues that the economic sphere of social life appears to evade the moderating action of moral regulation (Ruggiero 2006). When combined with the aforementioned array of self-interested motivations, a stage is set for calamity.

Anthony Giddens (1978, p. 45) makes an important point in his observation that the "causative factor is not the material circumstances themselves, but the instability which they introduce into social life." This stems from the fact that desires loosed from a previous moral order have no natural circumscription. When the traditional "God-given" economic order is no longer viewed as relevant, anomic winds sweep through society; and those with the means and proclivity to do so may impose a new order couched in their own immoderate desires (Giddens 1978).

In this reordering, the individual is further subordinated and devalued. With respect to war (and applicably to other forms of state violence), Durkheim (1937/1996, p. 117) states that this process pushes "into the background all feelings of sympathy for the individual" and that "a rigid authoritarian discipline is imposed on all violations."

Therefore, it is reasonable to assume a similar dynamic with regard to crime and criminal justice. Any ascendant ordering/disordering brings with it new ideas as to the most effective methods of demonstrating the value in compliance. Perhaps these ideas are mere extensions or refinements of traditional modalities. Perhaps they are whole-cloth innovation. Russian gulags and French guillotines suggest themselves as accessible examples. So too does the U.S. Bill of Rights—the broader point being that perturbations to the social order evoke adaptive responses. This is exemplified in the processes by which a state treats the issues of crime and criminality.

To this point, Durkheim invokes a useful biological/natural systems metaphor—one that will play heavily into the analyses presented in this volume—in his discussion of mechanical and organic solidarity. For present purposes, one passage in that discussion is most relevant. Durkheim (1893/1960, p. 353) observes, "Cancer and tuberculosis increase the diversity of biological organic tissues without bringing forth a new specialization of biological functions." Applied to matters of social responses to crime, much the same might be said. Durkheim also demonstrated an awareness of this fact. He understood that endogenous change in society could promote solidarity, especially with respect to the division of labor. Durkheim believes that this increasing consensus is conditioned on the changes being spontaneous and not forced on the collective (Ruggiero 2006). As Durkheim (1893/1960, p. 377) states, "By spontaneity we must understand not simply the absence of violence, but also of everything that can even indirectly shackle the free unfolding of the social force that individuals carry in themselves." Uneven definitions of crime and criminality clearly fit within this view. Ruggiero (2006, p. 53) clarifies the underlying mechanism, "If we follow Durkheim's logic, we may link criminality, including political violence, to contingent social morality, connecting it to the social structure, rather than to universal moral codes."

Because state failure and fragility can manifest in many ways and to varied extents, it is logical that criminal justice in failed and fragile states might look very different from more stable and functioning states. This too provides a stepping-off point for the present volume. While the products and processes of criminal justice in fragile states are often very different from those in nations of the stable world, they nonetheless strongly exhibit the aforementioned patterning and predictability. By extension, a deeper understanding of these institutions and practices informs what we know not only about criminal justice, but also about the institution of state more generally.

At the outset, it should be noted that a bright-line bifurcating those nation-states that have failed from those that are stable is an elusive and perhaps vain pursuit. While many scholars have advanced theories aimed toward this purpose, an immutable taxonomy of relative state fragility and collapse has yet to be articulated. Even so, many theories of failure and fragility have been advanced, for example, Mark Beissinger and Crawford Young (2002), Stuart E. Eizenstat and Francis Fukuyama (2004), Jeffrey Herbst (2000), Jennifer Milliken (2003), Robert Rotberg (2003, 2004), and William Zartman (1995).

Furthermore, Michele Foucault (1977, p. 220) poses an even more fundamental question with his outright dismissal of the state as a useful explanation for social phenomena, "Maybe after all the state is no more than a composite reality and a mythicized abstraction, whose importance is a lot more limited than any of us think." He goes on to say, "Maybe what is really important… is not so much the statization of society, as the governmentalization of state." Foucault raises a number of important issues in this passage, the most intriguing of which emanates from his perspective on the nature of power in society. In contrast to thinkers such as Nico Poulantzas (2008), Robert Dahl (1961), and Benno Teschke (2003) whose writings reflect a Weberian understanding of power—defined by questions as to who has power and what do they do with it—Foucault instead starts with the assumption that "power as such does not exist" but that it should be viewed as a dense net of omnipresent relations—it comes from below and is everywhere (Nohr 2012).

Foucault (1983, p. 217) argues that power "produces, it produces reality; it produces domains and objects and rituals of truth." As Foucault (1977, p. 213) further states, "It is often difficult to say who holds power in a precise sense, but it is easy to see who lacks power." In this framing, the relationship between those who govern and those who are governed is mediated by knowledge-power apparatuses (i.e., governmentalizations) that transform the relation away from a power over death to a conditional promise of life. As he observes, "[P]ower would no longer be dealing with legal subjects over whom the ultimate dominion was death, but with living beings, and the mastery it would be able to exercise over them would be applied at the level of life itself" (Foucault 1977, pp. 142–143). He goes on to clarify the finality of the power actuation, "[I]t was the taking charge of life, more than the threat of death, that gave power its access even to the body" (Foucault 1977, p. 143).

To be certain, however, autocrats, despots, warlords, and their kin often retain and reassert their willingness to demonstrate power relations in terms of life or death; and insofar as "rituals of truth" are concerned, there are few more profound than the criminalization of behavior and the social processes that emanate from that criminalization. Which acts become criminalized in a given society has a great deal to do with consistency of the broader social narrative and the degree to which that narrative is clearly communicated, deemed relevant, and maintained by social structures. In periods of transition or upheaval, as is often the case in fragile states, these tasks may be difficult if not impossible.

This then leads us to a discussion of two core Durkheimian concepts: the social fact and anomie. In brief, social facts serve as guides to society's expectations. As Durkheim (1895/1982, p. 56) states, "A social fact is identifiable through the power of external coercion which it exerts or is capable of exerting upon individuals." Social facts attach to the individual through the course of socialization. These rules become internalized in the consciousness of the individual. Extended beyond the self, they form the complex of obligations to obey societal rules (norms, mores, folkways, and laws).

According to Durkheim (1893/1933, p. 129), a duality emerges from this process, "There are in each of us... two consciences: one which is common to our group in its entirety... the other, on the contrary, represents that in us which is personal and distinct, that which makes us an individual." "It is not without reason, therefore, that man feels himself to be double: he actually is double.... this duality corresponds to the double existence that we lead concurrently; the one purely individual and rooted in our organisms, the other social and nothing but an extension of society" (Durkheim 1914/1973, p. 162).

Flowing from this, each individual must understand his or her role in the larger enterprise. As part of that understanding, a transition must occur, "Because society surpasses us, it obliges us to surpass ourselves, and to surpass itself, a being must, to some degree, depart from its nature—a departure that does not take place without causing more or less painful tensions" (Durkheim 1914/1973, p. 163).

As atomized individuals, we are, in Durkheim's construction, little more than a collection of boundless appetites and desires. Because attainment of infinite satisfactions is axiomatically impossible, a condition emerges that Durkheim terms *anomie*. He first articulates the concept in the classic sociological text, *Le Suicide*, "The more one has, the more one wants, since satisfactions received only stimulate instead of filling needs" (Durkheim 1897/1951, p. 248). He further states, "Unlimited desires are insatiable by definition and insatiability is rightly considered a sign of morbidity. Being unlimited, they constantly and infinitely surpass the means at their command; they cannot be quenched. Inextinguishable thirst is constantly renewed torture" (Durkheim 1897/1951, p, 247). "It is this anomic state that is the cause, as we shall show, of the incessantly recurrent conflicts, and the multifarious disorders of which the economic world exhibits so sad a spectacle" (Durkheim 1893/1933, p. 5).

Durkheim contends that broad anomic tension may occur after a sudden change in the social, political, or economic spheres of society. When such changes take place, they "inevitably curtail society's collective conscience in regards to norms and values... during this time of structural transition, individuals are not sure of the moral laws that constrain them" (Kayaoglu 2007, p. 101). Durkheim's central argument is that these loosened attachments to the social rules cause social disorder.

When the government loses its ability to exercise the necessary controls needed to quell violence, a gap in institutional control is created that provides the motivation and opportunity to engage in criminogenic activities while increasing social disorganization (Rothe and Collins 2010). We can extend this reasoning by recognizing that incipient disorder can create a feedback loop where loosened attachments to social rules spur disorder, which may in turn provide positive stimulus to further flout the conventional social boundaries.

Building on this dynamic, without the fetter of the old rules, anomically driven appetites may broaden perceived opportunities contained in erstwhile proscribed (and perhaps unthinkable) activities. As will be discussed in future sections of this volume, perceived opportunity when twined with crippling poverty plays a critical role in helping to explain lawlessness in places such as Somalia.

Somalia has experienced anomic social conditions and social disorganization (perhaps on unprecedented levels) that have limited legitimate employment opportunities for most of the citizenry. As such, people turn to illicit activities, such as piracy and human trafficking, as a means to derive an income. This illustrates the nexus between motivation (e.g., poverty) and involvement in criminal activities that are far more lucrative when compared with available legitimate employment opportunities. We see proof of this with rampant piracy in the Gulf of Aden. This illicit activity provides ample opportunities for attack and its location is ideal because Somali pirates are able to attack in narrow chokepoints in international waters and then quickly return to Somali waters (Tuerk 2012).

The instability in places such as this is also a breeding ground for more global problems, namely, terrorism. Within the political science literature, there are several theoretical explanations for the relationship between instability and terrorism, including the Clash of Civilizations thesis, the Democratic Peace thesis, and the poverty–terrorism nexus (Cox and Drury 2007). As we have argued previously (Gould and Pate 2011), a number of methodological issues must be rectified when attempting to resolve the plight of different nations (Bennett and Lynch 1990; Cavadino and Dignan 2006; Gertz and Myers 1992; Lynch 1993; Mauer 1995; Weiss and South 1998). While the legal and criminal justice systems of all countries vary according to their culture, Newman (1999, p. 2) maintains, "[A]t the close of the twentieth century, all countries of the world are inextricably tied together by commerce, past colonization and historical circumstance."

Implicit in this arrangement is the concept of risk. The distribution of social resources (however construed) implies imbalance. With imbalance comes risk as parties vie for greater control over whatever resource is at issue.* Beck (1992) maintains that risks will become increasingly pervasive in everyday life. This leads us then to what many scholars term the *risk society*. O'Malley (1998, p. xi) describes the risk society as "a society which is organized in significant ways around the concept of risk and which increasingly governs its problems in terms of discourses and technologies of risk." The risk society has developed largely in response to economic insecurities as well as the threat of a global disaster (e.g., terrorism and nuclear war). The global nature of the economy has further contributed to insecurities by producing an economic climate where virtually no one has job security (Beck 1998). These changes have greatly impacted societies across the globe through the permanent marginalization of certain segments of the population.

Terrorism can also be linked to the economic inequality and marginalization brought about by globalization. As Benjamin and Simon (2002, p. 175) note, "deligitimation of regimes and the emergence of religious violence are unquestionably linked to the failure of leaders to cope with massive region-wide socioeconomic problems." In this, we see multiple influential dynamics: economic imperatives; attempts to control territory and natural resources; assertions of cultural, ethnic, class, or social hegemony; individual power aspirations; levels of labor surplus; relative modernity and technological development; public infrastructure; and so forth. What many of these dynamics share is an embeddedness with respect to issues of power relations. Given the greater interconnectedness of global capital, technology, transportation, and communication, one must at least entertain Foucault's (1977) base contention that the state is an outmoded rubric for understanding social relations. While this idea is counter to one of this volume's core narrative themes, such cautions have an inarguable merit. When one considers that states are an historically malleable construct, with some lasting centuries and others faltering at birth, scholars would do well to keep the seeming inevitability of impermanence in mind.

In fact, since the rise of the nation-state, failure has been more the rule than the exception. As Jeffrey Herbst (2004, p. 303) notes, "There's nothing novel about the phenomenon of state failure." Herbst is correct in this characterization. Charles Tilly (1986) elaborates this point by reminding us that the majority of states that have arisen since AD 1500 have gone on to fail. Furthermore, size, influence, records of conquest, and economic, political, and social hegemony appear to be no bar against failure. Just as all humans have an inescapable trajectory from cradle to grave, so too do nation-states. Surely as it is built, so does Rome fall.

---

* It should be noted that the term *resources* is used here in its most generic and all-inclusive sense. A social resource may be economic, material, political, geographic, information, justice, or any other distributable commodity to which society has assigned some value.

In his study of modern Europe, Tilly (1986, p. 38) further observes, "The substantial majority of the units which got so far as to acquire recognizable existence as states... still disappeared. And of the handful that survived or emerged into the nineteenth century as autonomous states, only a few operated effectively—regardless of what criterion we employ." Echoing the work of both Tilly (1986) and Malcolm Anderson (1996), Herbst (2004) highlights the pull of both external (i.e., conquest) and internal (i.e., disintegration) forces on European states during the nineteenth and twentieth centuries. As states have consolidated, fractured, and tested the limits of history, a relatively stable, modern Eurasia has emerged. Since the fall of the Soviet Union, that stability has been weakened.

To motivate this point, the first case study presented will give detailed consideration to the former Soviet Republic of Georgia. As both Georgia and imperiled states in Africa such as the Sudan and Somalia (also treated as case studies) demonstrate, a rising umbrage against arbitrarily drawn Cold War borders, postcolonial struggles, old ethnic and cultural rivalries, as well as persistently volatile hegemonic interests have been inflamed anew.

Tilly (1990) also discusses the "continuous aggressive competition for trade and territory among changing states of unequal size, which made war the driving force in European history." Again, with the dissolution of the Soviet Union, war in the Balkans, wars in the Middle East, the Arab Spring, multiple African civil wars, revolutions in the Pacific rim as well as innumerable smaller revolts, rebellions, and skirmishes across the globe, it appears that Tilly's observation has a much broader applicability.

Just as old rivalries have reignited, the end of the age of empire ushered in another important dynamic—the ever-increasing number of states (from approximately 55 in 1900 to more than 200 in 2015). To the larger point, it would be difficult to overstate the impact of the postcolonial legacy in those regions exhibiting the greatest number of failed and fragile states. While the allegiances of modern Europe and Western Asia have shifted, so too have those of the nations within the various spheres of European, Russian, Chinese, and American influence.

In his concise review of six leading state failure studies, John Heilbrunn (2006) describes how colonialism set in place a confluence of poisoned dynamics that undermined the forces of stability in several African states. In the first instance, indigenous rulers were overthrown in favor of (often corrupt and abusive) European administrators. To ensure the solidity of European rule, domestic trade and financial networks were subordinated to the priorities of the colonial administrations. Concomitantly, various resource streams were concentrated in urban areas, thus economically, socially, and politically marginalizing large segments of the outlying population. In response, the postcolonial reconstruction of state often takes on a more authoritarian form with strongmen and warlords predominating across much of the continent.

Similarly, the marginalization of large segments of the population also laid the foundation for postcolonial fracturing and challenges to geographic boundaries set by the Europeans.

Perhaps more important to current geopolitics is Heilbrunn observation that this pattern has been replicated in Central Asia. As he states, "[Dynastic nepotism has become a practice in Kazakhstan and Azerbaijan. Indeed, these practices suggest the neo-patrimonial pattern that is evolving in Central Asia may be a precursor to the instability that followed African independence" (Heilbrunn 2006, p. 138). Events over the last 20 years certainly lend support to this perspective.

In this sea of fragility, it is important to recognize the wide variation among the states involved. As the Organization for Economic Co-operation and Development (2014) observes, fragility can manifest in many different situational contexts. Of special note is the fact that fragile states are not always impoverished or bereft of resources. As the Organization for Economic Co-operation and Development (2014, p. 15) concludes "from the one-party state of North Korea to war-torn Syria and relatively stable Bosnia and Herzegovina. Close to half—23 of 51—are middle-income states and economies, and many of them are rich in natural resources."

By extension, there are innumerable ways for a state to cease delivering the core social, economic, and political products necessary for a stable, if not prosperous society; but even loosely characterizing failure in terms of service provision provokes some scholarly debate (Eriksen 2011). Moreover, the broader discussion requires the adoption of terminology that may be taken as an indicator of implied value judgments.

When describing those states that exist in relatively greater peace, quiescence, or affluence, terms such as *successful* and *stable* suggest themselves. While these descriptors have a certain appeal on face, they also hold the potential to move the discussion from one of "is" to one of "ought." The use of "failure" connotes similar judgments. Owing to the nature of language, it would make the present enterprise much more cumbersome to distinguish with full (and arguably deserved) detail all the differences this volume explores. Therefore, the authors choose, by inelegant convention, terms that have an intuitive, albeit subjective tenor.

As Stein Eriksen (2011, p. 231) observes, "[T]he gap between ideals and empirical reality is treated as justification for interventions which aim to close this gap, and make empirical reality conform to the model. It might well be the case that such a state is desirable and that good reasons can be given to justify this."

If one assents that many of the conditions found to be concomitant with "failure" (i.e., social chaos, disruption of critical services, widespread fear, disease, violence, cessation of meaningful governance, etc.) are not desirable environments for human existence, then such is/ought implications are perhaps more acceptable. In the face of genocide, extrajudicial disappearances, torture, unchecked epidemics, starvation, human trafficking, terrorism, and warlord rule, it is arguably natural to adopt this kind of framing. Even so, as Eriksen suggests, this drifts into the chasm between ideals and empirical reality. While this is perhaps unavoidable, such assessments are not the central purview of this volume. Rather, the primary objective could be better described as a search for a defensible set of criteria by which to evaluate relative state stability or success and to understand what role criminality and criminal justice play in this dynamic process. To begin this process, it is instructive to consider how other scholars have chosen to demarcate the line between stability and fragility.

Perhaps the most broadly accepted paradigm for the analysis of failure revolves around the study of a given government's relative provision of state products. The essential question in this framing is whether a state is capable of doing those things one expects of a stable and functioning government. The constituent questions might interrogate whether the regime in power is capable of protecting the nation from invasion, protracted riots, or civil war. This perspective also questions to what degree there is predictable delivery of medical care. Are there unchecked epidemics or can one obtain medical care easily? Other aspects of this approach ask about the consistency and availability of utility services and infrastructure. Is potable water available to most citizens? Do citizens have access to electricity?

Exemplifying this type of inquiry is William Zartman (1995, p. 5), who contends a state has failed "when the basic functions of the state are no longer performed." Similarly, Robert Rotberg (2003), another authoritative voice on state failure, defines the condition as the inability of states to provide positive political goods to their inhabitants. In this light, questions pertaining to civil liberties, access to courts, police protection, and the right of confronting the government become more central. One might also add questions of governmental transparency, freedom of expression, and freedom of the press.

Writing in the Weberian tradition of defining state, Stephen Krasner (2004) and Robert Jackson (1991) each propose definitions that rely not on measures of relative service provision, but territorial control and the state's monopoly on violence. Famously, Charles Tilly (1985) observes that states make war, and "war makes states." As will be discussed throughout this volume, where failed states are concerned, the "enemy" in these wars is often found within. Gary King and Langche Zeng (2001, p. 623) advance a similarly couched definition, "State failure refers to the collapse of the authority of the central government to impose order, as in civil wars, revolutionary wars, genocides, politicides, and adverse or disruptive regime transitions. States that sponsor terrorism or allow it to be organized within their borders are all failed states."

While an inability to impose order is certainly one configuration of a distorted coercive capacity, it should be noted that criminal justice structures and domestic military operations can be very strong in failed states. In fact, despotic administration of criminal justice is a regular feature in many failed and fragile states. Throughout this volume, several case studies are presented that amplify the extent to which regimes use criminal justice or quasi-criminal justice processes to subordinate oppositional interests. Internally, this manifests as a process whereby a society's elite essentially use a "protection racket" scheme to consolidate their power and bind lower-level influentials to them. Individual freedoms are surrendered in exchange for social order and property interests. This process serves to "legitimate" both the authority and coerciveness of the elites.

Legitimacy is a topic that regularly appears in discussions of state fragility. Monty Marshall and Benjamin Cole, writing for the Center for Systemic Peace, provide one of the more comprehensive circumscriptions of state fragility. Their work hinges in large part on the import of perceived governmental legitimacy. Marshall and Cole's research represents an attempt to reconcile the work of many different state fragility scholars. In summarizing points of consensus, they state, "What is common among these [approaches] is a recognition that assessing a state's ability to ensure the support of its people depends on its performance in multiple spheres, spanning the qualities and dynamics of governance, societal conflict, and systemic development." They further observe that the optimal functioning of a state system is dependent on each "unit" within the system carrying out the tasks expected of competent governance, coordinating with and working with other parts of the system and perhaps most critically, "[working] to foster legitimacy and compliance through their just and fair actions" (Marshall and Cole 2009, p. 24).

Of course, the balance of social, political, and economic interests is a quantity that is always in flux. To this point, Robert Bates clarifies an important distinction between states that are in a period of revolution and those that have failed, "Note the distinction… both lead to violence; but revolution creates a new order, whereas state failure yields disorder." Bates is correct that revolution and failure imply two separable trajectories. It should be noted, however, that they are neither mutually exclusive, nor is one a necessary precondition for the other. Bates bases his observation in part on the works of Marx and Engles (1994/1848) as well as de Tocqueville (1966/1866), who argue that revolution leads to the establishment of the aforementioned "new order." Similarly, Heilbrunn (2006, p. 135) argues that the reconstruction of a state is "inevitable after conflict and collapse."

Through the long lens of historical perspective, these sentiments are largely correct, but in the violence and chaos of the revolutionary interregnum, that ascendant new order may require many painful years to emerge. The global events of the last century suggest that revolution may also lead to a complete breakdown in the function of state. While semantically a new "order," failure is, as Bates suggests, a condition of inherent disorder. Following Bates' (2008) lead further, it is necessary to understand the difference between revolution and civil war. He clarifies that not all revolutions originate out of failed states. Rather, they may foment as a reaction to stable, yet objectionable conditions imposed by the dominant regime. In the face of civil war, the regime may in fact become yet stronger, more stable, and dominant as opposition forces are fully subordinated.

Similarly, Nicos Poulantzas' commentary on the nature of state crises reasserts the point that conceptualizing revolution, civil war, and social homeostasis as discrete, mutually exclusive conditions is not entirely useful. Moreover, crises of state are not necessarily just episodic perturbations of an inevitable and inescapable order. As Poulantzas (2008, p. 295) states, "The economic and bourgeois-sociological conception of a crisis... views crisis as a dysfunctional moment that ruptures an otherwise harmonious functioning of the 'system,' a moment that will pass when equilibrium is re-established."

Consideration of Poulantzas' thoughts also reveals a paradox common among failed states. Just because a strong central order has been established does not mean that the rest of the state system functions well or that the population lives in safe, humane, or desirable conditions. Quite the opposite appears to be more common. Indeed, history is rife with examples of strongmen and warlords whose iron grasp is held tight against a starving public.

The broader discussion at hand also hinges on a much larger sphere of dissensus. Just as no universal agreement on the definitive criteria for state failure exists, an even more fundamental question remains as to the attributes, characteristics, and functions that are necessary before a given geographical, political, or social entity can be pronounced "a state." As Timothy Mitchell (1999) notes, the very idea of the state bifurcates along two axes: the material force and the ideological construct. The two axes, when combined produce a paradox. As Mitchell (1999, p. 169) explains, "The network of institutional arrangement and political practice that forms the material substance of the state is diffuse and ambiguously defined at its edges, whereas the public imagery of the state as an ideological construct is more coherent."

Extending this line of reasoning (and as a response to Foucault's discourse on power relations), Mitchell (1999, p. 169) elaborates, "[H]ow does one define the state apparatus and locate its limits? At what point does power enter channels fine enough and its exercise become ambiguous enough that one recognizes the edge of this apparatus? Where is the exterior that enables one to identify it as an apparatus?"

Following Mitchell's inquiry, identifying that point where the apparatus has collapsed becomes yet more problematic. In a consideration of "stateness" with respect to failure or fragility, Jennifer Milliken and Keith Krause (2002, p. 753) observe, "The modern state, since it emerged out of the ashes of the medieval order, has always been a work in progress... it is against this backdrop that the current discourse of 'failed' or 'collapsed' states must be understood."

States (irrespective of the prevailing condition of the moment) are intrinsically fluid organisms. Steven Best (1995, p. xi) speaks directly to this point with his observation, "History is the temporal context of human evolution within socionatural conditions; it is the continuous present that instantly recedes into the past and from which we project the future." While this perspective is useful in broader discussions of global history, the present concern requires an admittedly more arbitrary line in the metaphorical sand. To begin with, it must be acknowledged that a twofold conundrum exists. Lacking a scholarly consensus for the precise moment at which a given geopolitical constituency has attained "stateness," it becomes yet more difficult to demarcate the place where that condition has been surrendered to some other force. As an outgrowth of these attempts to understand the institution of state in all its myriad configurations, the need for a more fluid analytical vocabulary suggests itself. This new vocabulary must be able to circumscribe the dimensions of state, not as a static enterprise, but as the dynamic entity that all states are.

If one considers a state to be an iterative system of interactions that responds to inputs within the context of established structures, then the necessary new analytical vocabulary becomes clearer. Moreover, openness to alternative methodological paradigms may also be important. As Hubert Blalock and Paul Wilken (1979, p. 2) contend, researchers need "to accommodate our methodology to [the] admitted complexity [of society] and to accept whatever limitations are implied by the presence of a large number of unknowns in any theoretical system." They go on to argue, "If reality is complex we must learn to develop complex theories to deal with it… we must also study the implications of these complexities for testing and evaluating these theories."

Herbert Simon (1965, pp. 63–64) in his seminal piece, The Architecture of Complexity, provides an enduring definition of complex systems. He states that they are "made up of a large number of parts that interact in a non-simple way." Further, he explains, "the whole is more than the sum of the parts, not in an ultimate metaphysical sense, but in the important pragmatic sense that, given the properties of the parts and the laws of interaction, it is not a trivial matter to infer the properties of the whole" (Simon 1965, p. 64).

Marshall and Cole (2009) help motivate this point in their characterization of the state as a complex system. They observe that societal systems are formed through four processes: self-actuation, self-organization, self-regulation, and self-correction. As they further state, these systems "incorporate multiple, networked and interdependent levels, integrated in cohesive schemes of subsidiarity within which authority is allocated to the level most appropriate to its effects. The analytics focus on the complex relations between dynamics (human agency and environmental forces) and statics (physical and social attributes, conditions, and structures)" (Marshall and Cole 2009, p. 2).

Marshall and Cole (2009, p. 13) also observe that a state should be "self-actuating." They offer that a state is self-actuating when "the social impetus for establishing state authority to regulate group affairs comes principally from within the social group rather than imposed from outside. This... also [suggests] that stable (central) state authority should be compatible with and complementary to traditional sources of local authority."

The second criterion is the capacity to self-organize. One way to access the concept of self-organization would be to recall the Nobel Prize–winning economist Thomas Schelling's (1978) classic example of seating patterns in an auditorium. As he observes, patrons arranging themselves in a theater are driven by individualized motivations, but from that constellation of micro-level motives, more macro-level patterns of seat use develop—patterns that are independent of the individualized motives. Complexity scientists often speak of this phenomenon as "emergence." A corollary to this is the concept of "punctuated equilibrium." Without wandering into a treatise on evolutionary biology, the essential feature of this phenomenon is that complex systems generally exist in a stasis (or epoch of relative stability) with occasional perturbations that "punctuate" that stasis (Gould and Eldrege 1977). However, it is important to note that the concept of a steady state need not imply a quiescence or peaceful state. Failed and fragile states ably demonstrate this fact.

When applied to social systems, the criterion of self-regulation can be thought of as the mechanism that keeps the organized, self-defined group a coalesced whole. With special regard to hierarchical systems (as formally governed states are), Gafiychuk et al. (1997, p. 357) provide some instructive insight. They observe that hierarchical systems can be divided into constituent subsystems. These subsystems contain elements that are similar in their properties. As they go on to explain, subsystems can be "ordered according to their mutual interactions: The behavior of an element at each level is determined by the aggregated state of a certain large group of elements belonging to the nearest lower level, while each element of a lower level is directly governed by a given element of the higher level." Even without the use of metaphor, which is the common modus of importing these concepts from physical to social sciences, the applicability to states and their populations is clear.

In further elaborating the mediating function of verticality, Gafiychuk et al. (1997, p. 358) state, "The characteristic feature of hierarchical systems is the nonlocal interference among elements at the same level, as mediated by the higher levels. The term nonlocal means... the state of some elements depends on the state of some surrounding neighbors. Higher levels... feel only the averaged state of the proceeding levels." As a consequence, localized lower-order variations "reflect the states of elements at higher levels over larger scales." As they continue, larger components influence (govern) elements at the lower level in a region "whose domain substantially exceeds the size of the initial perturbation" (Gafiychuk et al. 1997, p. 358).

In some stead, this explains the final criterion, self-correction. Larger-order structures in society serve as limit functions over lower-order structures. In the context of conflict, an army may wish to move to new territory, but it may be constrained by a higher-order element such as inadequate roadways or fuel supplies, both of which are infrastructural elements whose size and influence may exceed the military's control. Larger-order structures may also fail to provide a limit function, thus allowing some element to wash over the established edges; thereby swirling the society into chaos, or pushing it into a new and different epoch of stability. The course taken is highly dependent on localized conditions and the strength of the larger-order structures. Directly to this point, Gafiychuk et al. (1997, p. 358) assert, "These characteristics make such hierarchical systems fragile with respect to perturbations in the environment." In a sentence, they circumscribe most of the successes and miseries of the human era. The inability to adapt when environmental conditions change explains why some empires fall and others rise.

Readers may also recall the aphorism "that which does not kill me, makes me stronger." Claudio Cioffi-Revilla (2005) observes something similar about the fate of nations. He asserts that phase transitions into more complex forms of social organization were likely to occur after repeated incidents of successful management of external and internal crises. Societies emerging from the metaphorical cauldron of fire become more complex organisms having navigated said crises. This then gives rise to a question about those that fail to chart such troubled waters: Do societies that fail in the face of danger lose complexity? The seeming inability of many failed states to provide core goods would suggest as much, assuming that such provisions were in evidence before the tumult.

While a discussion of social phenomenon in terms of a complex adaptive system is arguably outside the mainstream of scholarly thought, it is nonetheless a very robust paradigm from which to explore the processes of state. In their awareness of the work by Gafiychuk et al., Marshall and Cole (2009, p. 2) further remind us that any fitting analytical scheme must be equipped to deal with processes that exist at every level of society; and that researchers should be prepared to take "...into account the interconnectedness of three fundamental dimensions of societal-systems: governance, conflict, and development (based on the accumulation of both physical and human capital)." Where many theoretical paradigms falter is at exactly this juncture. They may well explain phenomena that are macrosocial or microsocial but lack the capacity for scaling the divide. A complex systems approach obviates this concern.

With regard to Marshall and Cole's (2009) first fundamental dimension of societal systems, governance, any exploration of state failure necessarily considers this realm. As above, many researchers predicate their definitional structure on measures of governance, but governance as an atomized construct does not fully describe the present discussion. Rather, as Marshall and Cole (2009) suggest, only with respect to the interconnected nature of governance with issues of conflict and development does the deeper value emerge.

To a somewhat greater degree, conflict as a stand-alone concept is useful, but here too, system context is critically important, especially as this volume interrogates the global variety of criminality and criminal justice processes. As the following chapters document, conflict—particularly class, race, and religiously based conflict—is a prime mover in the world's more fragile and failing states.

We also argue that the societies of the world are shaped by another constantly moving hand: technology. Moreover, that the influence of technological change is as potent a driver as any other mechanism of social change. In this introduction, we have briefly discussed the peril of shifting economic orders and how a reordering of this aspect of society can be fraught with danger. The economic order of a given society is predicated on a number of variables, one of which is the influence and pace of technological change.

In testimony before the U.S. House of Representatives Committee on Science and Technology Subcommittee on Research and Science Education, Daniel Sarewitz (2010, p. 7) speaks to the role of public policy in this equation:

> Science and innovation policies often aim... to transform existing technological systems to achieve particular societal outcomes... Yet modern societies have very little understanding of how to catalyze and steer these sorts of complex system changes... well-intentioned efforts can often lead to unanticipated consequences whose benefits are very difficult to assess.

What Sarewitz foreshadows in this incisive testimony is that any potential societal "benefit" of technological innovation may be conditioned on the latent consequences surrounding it. Again, we see society's capacity to self-correct at play.

Industrial development may provide thousands of jobs, but the economic benefit of those new jobs may be offset by smog-darkened skies and poisoned water supplies. Similarly, increased production capacity may cause great trade imbalances that destabilize otherwise solid political alliances. Of course, this new capacity might just as easily open new trading markets and lead to a period of widespread prosperity.

There are, however, other consequences of rapid economic change and industrial growth. Turning back to Foucault's (1977) themes, the increased need for industrial workers may "necessitate" more strident techniques of public regulation, which then influence perceptions of crime and criminality. The greater point here resides in the fact that shifts in one-quarter of society invariably produce (often unanticipated) shifts in another. Such shifts also represent an impingement on or facilitation of specialized interests within society.

As our analysis unfolds, readers will be repeatedly asked to consider whose values and interests are represented in the various modalities of the criminal justice process. The struggle to assert the primacy of one contingent's priorities to the peril of another is arguably the story of human civilization. The terms under which such hegemony is achieved have occupied the curiosity and imagination of historians and social scientists since the dawn of scholarly analysis.

Within the last two centuries, the criminal as a political commodity has gained notable attention, particularly as those in the modern conflict and critical traditions explore the relationship between economic standing and criminalization. For example, Loic Wacquant (1993, p. xviii) characterizes the prison not simply as an instrument of the criminal justice system designed to punish law violators, but instead as a "core political institution." Dario Melossi (2008, p. 5) concurs with this position and notes, "because one of the main powers of the State is the power to punish, penality is particularly apt to be used to define the powers and boundaries of sovereignty."

That a relationship exists between the various forms of repression, subjugation, and formal punishment makes intuitive sense. With regard to regimes in fragile or failing states, Ruddell and Urbina (2004, p. 87) observe, "political leaders may use incarceration as a method of controlling protests, opposition to the regime, or persons who would not ordinarily fit under the definition of a criminal in a nation with a justice system that had high levels of legitimacy and was politically independent." These sentiments when taken together suggest a pattern for what we should expect to find in terms of a relationship between the various configurations of criminal justice and the relative fragility of a given state.

Even a cursory glance across the landscape of history supports this position. Whether it is the systematic redaction of inconvenient individuals from Soviet history books, genocide at the hands of African warlords, the United States' "war on drugs," or the silent nocturnal disappearances familiar to many throughout the world, the veil of criminality has a long provenance as a way for those in power to remain so.

It has often been noted that a state's criminal justice infrastructure (the police in particular) are the primary venue through which most people come into contact with their government. Such interfacing moments are strongly conditioned both by individual-level and system-level inputs. As Thorsten Sellin (1938, p. 21) frames it, "Social values which receive the protection of the criminal law are ultimately those which are treasured by dominant interest groups." Alan Liska (1987, p. 12) likewise asserts, "Law making is assumed to reflect the interests of the powerful; those activities are criminalized that threaten their interests." Minority threat theory expands on the conflict perspective by arguing that law violations by racial and ethnic minorities can be perceived as particularly threatening to those in power, and will therefore be met with greater force (Liska 1987, p. 77). This last point has a special prescience with regard to events in the developing world.

In brief, the minority threat perspective theorizes that growth in the relative size of a given minority population along with the perception of increased competition for social and political resources will be regarded as threatening by those in positions of greater social power (Blalock and Wilken 1979). Regarding responses to crime specifically, this perspective argues that dominant groups will support coercive measures to keep minority populations sufficiently oppressed and their relative social power circumscribed so as to permit the dominant interests in society to remain in that position (Ruddell 2005; Turk 1969).

Of course, societies and cultures around the world respond to crime in many different ways (Christie 1993; Newman 1999; Ruddell 2005). Therefore, it is appropriate that we inquire as to the nature and extent of social forces that motivate and support these observed variations. From its outset, modern social science has theorized that formal social controls have a purpose beyond the mere control of crime (Durkheim 1900/1983). Many studies drawing from the work of Georg Rusche (1933/1978), as well as Rusche and Otto Kirchheimer (1939/1968), assert that dominant groups within a society will invoke formal social controls when they perceive threats to their economic and power interests. As Jonathon Simon (1997, p. 1036) observes, this manifests as "governing through crime."

Several studies throughout the mid- and late-twentieth century build on this idea. Hall (1952) tracks changes in the legal interpretation of property crime from the first emergence of capitalism. Chambliss (1964) shows how vagrancy laws are interpreted to match the interests of persons in control of the labor supply. Gusfield (1963), Dickson (1968), and Graham (1972) study the influence of powerful groups on the manipulation of criminal statutes. Perhaps the most influential studies specific to the economic context of corrections are Michel Foucault's (1977) *Discipline and Punish* and Nils Christie's (1993) *Crime Control as Industry*.

Of the studies in this tradition, Hubert Blalock and Wilken (1979) *Toward a Theory of Minority-Group Relations* has been among the most fecund analyses of relative minority population size and its value for predicting social control. In the context of American society, Blalock contends that as the relative percentage of nonwhites increases, they are perceived to constitute a political and economic threat to the white majority. The growing minority "forces" members of the white majority to compete for jobs and other economic resources. Further, as the minority population grows, it competes with the majority for political power. Moreover, the increased relative number of minority members, irrespective of other realms of influence, can be interpreted by the dominant group as a form of threat. Discrimination and systematized differential treatment, according to this perspective, is an attempt by the majority to subvert minority efforts to exercise power.*

Blalock's central contentions have robustly withstood many subsequent scholarly considerations. Researchers have found that social controls are often formulated and directed so as to systematically exclude or impede minority participation in an attempt to lessen the economic competition between races (Jackson and Carroll 1981; Jacobs and Wood 1999); Taylor (1998) concludes that the relative size of the black population significantly affects white levels of anti-black prejudice and the perceived economic threat from blacks.

A variant of this perspective, the "political threat" hypothesis, holds that as the relative size of the minority population increases, dominant groups will increasingly perceive the minority as a threat to political power and in response intensify politically actualized control to maintain power relations (Brown and Warner 1992; Jacobs and Carmichael 2002; Myers 1990). Still others have expanded on Blalock with a third formulation centered on the threat of black crime. This perspective theorizes that social control increases as a result of higher rates of black-on-white crime (Liska and Chamlin 1984; Chamlin and Liska 1992; Eitle et al. 2002).

The value of these studies for this book is less about the animus between any particular groups and more about the dynamic that may emerge as a consequence of perceived encroachment by marginal groups on what society's dominant groups hold as rightfully theirs. As this volume unfolds, the reader will repeatedly greet ideas predicated on two primary ideas: First, societies (and indeed humankind) should be regarded as a complex adaptive system. This (these) system(s) function not as atomized entities, but as hierarchies and components, each amenable to influences both from within and externally. These systems respond to whatever influences history provides. These responses either maintain the system status or adapt to a new equilibrium (chaotic violence being as sustainable as productive quiescence).

---

* This perspective has been employed by scholars studying myriad aspects of power distribution and social control. Among the lynching and informal social control studies from this perspective are: Reed (1972), Corzine et al. (1983), Green et al. (1996), and Inverarity (1976). Research on incarceration includes: Meyers (1990), Title and Curran (1988), Ignatieff (1978), Jankovic (1977), and Rusche and Kirchheimer (1939). Economic control studies include: Piven and Cloward (1971), Jennings (1983), and Schram and Turbett (1983); as well as Issac and Kelly (1981). Respective differences aside, a litany of studies support the conclusion that the size of the minority population in some way influences formal social control (Bobo 1983; Chamlin 1989; Fossett and Kiecolt 1989; Giles and Hertz 1994; Giles and Evans 1986; Glaser 1994; Huckfeldt and Kohfeld 1989; Jacobs 1979; Matthews and Prothro 1966; Taylor 1998; Wright 1977).

In either instance, a given society's response to perturbations does not exist in a vacuum. The response is itself a stimulus to some other constituency; and thus the cycle continues. Secondly, within these systems, groups will attempt to assert dominance over one another. Differences will be construed along every possible dimension of human social structure. At many points, these differences will be exploited and used for provincial gains. At the core of this resides a matrix of power relations. The degree to which one seat of power exerts hegemony over another is key to our understanding of what it is to be a state; and what it is to steer that construction.

As this volume unfolds, the reader may be inclined to construct a dichotomy of sorts: states that are failed and states that are not. Tempting as this may be, we argue that waypoints along a continuum rather than discrete bins is a more profitable method to reconcile the fate of nations. In the research culminating in this book, we attempted to devise a number of analytically and statistically complicated schemes to justify one binning or another. Ultimately though, we are forced to recognize that the desire for such cataloging does much damage to that which is ultimately a very fluid, often tangled and imperfect constellation of information. Moreover, our presentation of a static ranking would place an expiration date on this volume that we also believe to be unwise. We have elected instead to give the reader a thematically driven tour of global politics with an emphasis on fragility, conflict, and the formal processing of those deemed recalcitrant.

To these ends, we begin Chapter 2 with an examination of justice delivery in failing states. This chapter begins with the simple proposition that governments should be the protectors of human rights. As history well documents, this is often not the case. Through the power of coercion, governments can not only define and manage criminality, but also control and suppress dissent. Through this latter office, they erode legitimacy and slip into an authoritarian abyss. This often manifests as extrajudicial killings, enforced disappearances, and the use of torture. We see this time and again in fragile and failing states. To motivate this point, we will consider these and other corrupted justice processes in several countries.

A corollary to justice delivery, Chapter 3 asks how punishment differs between fragile and more stable states. Where Chapter 2 explores how certain states have corrupted the interface between state and citizen, this chapter takes up a theme suggested by Dario Melossi (2008, p. 5), "[B]ecause one of the main powers of the State is the power to punish, penality is particularly apt to be used to define the powers and boundaries of sovereignty." In our own research (Gould and Pate 2011), we have noted that fragile governments use both incarceration and physical punishments (i.e., capital punishment and corporal punishment) at much higher rates, compared with more stable environs. This phenomenon is especially visible in places dealing with domestic strife, civil war, and similar internal conflicts. Research suggests that human rights are more likely to be violated when internal conflict is high; and in times of extreme political unrest (e.g., civil war), governments tend to increase their use of torture and political imprisonment (Carey 2010). As before, we will examine this trend through a series of brief case studies.

In Chapter 4, we address one of the most common topics in modern geopolitics: terrorism. One need not know much about fragile states to recognize their seeming hospitality to terrorism. Building on ideas presented in the first three chapters, we interrogate the process through which states lose their monopoly on nonnegotiable coercive force. In particular, we consider how anomic tides are often developmentally linked to terrorist activities. Following the complex adaptive systems framework, we explore how terrorist groups (or what some may perceive as such) may actually serve as limited ordering principles in lands where no other order finds much purchase. Extended treatment is given to the Islamic State.

In Chapter 5, the full flower of state failure on the international stage comes into focus. In this consideration, we see that failure cannot be viewed as an atomized and local phenomenon. In "ungoverned spaces" as Anne Clunan and Harold Trinkunas (2010) term them, a culture of lawlessness or permissiveness may exist that makes them ripe for use by human traffickers, drug smugglers, arms traders, and those involved with gray market finance. Of course, these enterprises may also operate in more regulated places through the co-optation of corrupt government officials (Andreas 2011). Irrespective of localized context, these activities do not exist as ends unto themselves, but as a part of a larger global chain in which more stable and affluent nations play a key role. Indeed, without the markets and infrastructure supplied by these countries, demand for illicit products would likely plummet. To illustrate these points, we will examine how illegal drug trafficking deeply affects Mexico and Afghanistan. We will also show how secretive finance and banking practices in very affluent countries, such as the Principality of Liechtenstein, facilitate these activities.

Chapter 6 explores the differential impact of state failure on men and women. Women in failed states have an elevated risk of violence and are often doubly victimized, both by society and in the home. In addition to a greater likelihood of violence, women face many traditional, religious, and other social barriers to full public participation in the majority of the failed states. As will be discussed, gender disparities are not only a mark of great social lapse, but they are also robust predictors of other types of violence. We highlight the work of scholars such as Mary Caprioli (2000) who explores the relationship between gender equality and willingness to use military force.

In Chapter 7, we consider the plight of the Republic of Georgia, a state on the verge of failure. In this chapter and in Chapter 8, we use detailed case studies to examine the path to fragility and failure. A casualty of Cold War politics and the fall of the Soviet Union, Georgia has weathered separatist movements, the so-called Rose Revolution, hostile relations with Russia, and innumerable challenges to its nascent independence.

The case studies presented in Chapter 8 are a record of tragedy. The spiraling descent of Somalia, Sudan, and South Sudan could be circumscribed with one thought: This is what happens when everything goes wrong. No individual and no nation wants to be a cautionary tale, but that is exactly what these failed states offer us. Along virtually every axis of stability, Somalia is found wanting. Sudan and South Sudan fare better, but just barely. These states are the epitome of postcolonial legacy and post-Cold War disinterest. For much of the past century, these states have been little more than pawns in someone else's poisoned game. Despite natural resources (and in some cases, because of them), strategic locations, and a host of other potential assets, a broad failure to thrive is laid bare for all to see. Stopping short of presenting an entire volume dedicated to their plight, we give them an especially detailed consideration. Their sad history goes to the heart of this volume—they are a microcosm of all that can fail.

In Chapter 9, the conclusion to this study, we take stock of the cases and conditions considered thus far; however, stopping short of the predictable summary, we attempt to frame fragility in terms that are more familiar to the urban criminologist. We also offer a few suggestions with regard to improving the lot of failing and fragile states. Lastly, we present the role of nation-building, postcolonial legacy, and global economic priorities with respect to their capacity to influence stability.

References

Anderson, M. 1996. *Frontiers: Territory and State Formation in the Modern World.* Cambridge: Polity Press.

Andreas, P. 2011. Illicit globalization: Myths, misconceptions, and historical lesson. *Political Science Quarterly* 126(3): 403–425.

Bates, R. H. 2008. State failure. *Annual Review of Political Science* 11: 1–12.

Beck, U. 1992. *Risk Society: Towards a New Modernity.* (M. Ritter, Trans.) London: Sage.

Beck, U. 1998. *Democracy without Enemies.* Cambridge: Policy Press.

Beissinger, M. R. and C. Young (Eds). 2002. *Beyond State Crisis? Postcolonial Africa and Post-Soviet Eurasia in Comparative Perspective.* Washington, DC: The Woodrow Wilson Center Press.

Benjamin, D. and S. Simon. 2002. *The Age of Sacred Terror: Radical Islam's War Against America.* New York: Random House.

Bennett, R. R. and J. P. Lynch. 1990. Does a difference make a difference: Comparing cross-national crime indicators. *Criminology* 28(3): 153–181.

Best, S. 1995. *The Politics of Historical Vision: Marx, Foucault and Habermas.* New York: The Guilford Press.

Blalock, H. and P. Wilken. 1979. *Intergroup Processes: A Micro-Macro Perspective.* New York: Free Press.

Brown, C. and B. Warner. 1992. Immigrants, urban politics, and policing in 1900. *American Sociological Review* 57(3): 293–305.

Caprioli, M. 2000. Gendered conflict. *Journal of Peace Research* 37: 51–68.

Carey, S. 2010. The use of repression as a response to domestic dissent. *Political Studies* 58: 167–186.

Cavadino, M. and J. Dignan. 2006. Social structure and crime control revisted: The declining significance of intergroup threat. *Penal Systems: A Comparative Approach*. Thousand Oaks, CA: Sage.

Chambliss, W. 1964. A sociological analysis of the law of vagrancy. *Social Problems* 12: 67–77.

Chamlin, M. and A. Liska. 1992. Social structure and crime control revisted: The declining significance of intergroup threat. In A. E. Liska (Ed.) *Social Threat and Social Control*, pp. 103–112, Albany, NY: Sunny Press.

Christie, N. 1993. *Crime Control as Industry*. London: Routledge.

Cioffi-Revilla, C. 2005. A canonical theory of origins and development of political complexity. *Journal of Mathematical Sociology* 29 Spring: 133–153.

Clunan, A. and H. Trinkunas. 2010. *Ungoverned Spaces: Alternatives to State Authority in an Era of Softened Sovereignty*. Stanford, CA: Stanford Security Studies.

Cox, D. G. and A. C. Drury. 2007. Democratic sanctions: Connecting the democratic peace and economic sanctions. *Journal of Peace Research* 43(6): 709–722.

Dahl, R. 1961. *Who Governs?: Democracy and Power in an American City*. New Haven, CT: Yale University Press.

Dickson, D. 1968. Bureaucracy and morality: An organizational perspective on a moral crusade. *Social Problems* 16(2): 143–156.

Durkheim, E. 1893/1933. *The Division of Labor in Society* (W. D. Halls, Trans.) New York: The Free Press.

Durkheim, E. 1893/1960. *The Division of Labor in Society*. (G. Simpson, Trans.) New York: The Free Press.

Durkheim, E. 1895/1982. *The Rules of the Sociological Method*. (W. D. Halls, Trans.) New York: The Free Press.

Durkheim, E. 1897/1951. *Suicide: A Study in Sociology*. (J. Spaulding and G. Simpson, Trans.) New York: The Free Press.

Durkheim, E. 1900/1983. Two laws of penal evolution. In S. Lukes and A. Scull (Eds) *Durkheim and the Law*, pp. 102–132, Oxford: Martin Robertson.

Durkheim, E. 1914/1973. *The Dualism of Human Nature and Its Social Conditions*. Chicago, IL: University of Chicago Press.

Durkheim, E. 1937/1996. *Professional Ethics and Civic Morals*. (C. Brookfield, Trans.) Glencoe, IL: The Free Press.

Eitle, D., S. D'Alessio and L. Stolzenberg. 2002. Racial threat and social control: A test of the political, economic, and threat of crime hypotheses. *Social Forces* 81(2): 557–576.

Eizenstat, S. E. and F. Fukuyama. 2004. *State-Building: Governance and World Order in the 21st Century*. Ithaca, NY: Cornell University Press.

Eizenstat, S., J. Porter, and J. Weinstein. 2005. Rebuilding weak states. *Foreign Affairs* 84(1): 134–146.

Eriksen, S. 2011. 'State failure' in theory and practice: The idea of the state and the contradictions of state formation. *Review of International Studies* 37: 229–247.

Foucault, M. 1977. *Discipline and Punish: The Birth of the Prison*. (A. Sheridan Trans.) London: Penguin Books.

Foucault, M. 1983. The subject and power. In H. L. Dreyfus and P. Rabinow (Eds) *Michel Foucault: Beyond Structuralism and Hermeneutics*, pp. 208–226, Chicago, IL: University of Chicago Press.

Gafiychuk, V. V., I. A. Lubashevskii, and R. E. Ulanowicz. 1997. Distributed self-regulation in ecological and economic systems. *Complex Systems* 11: 357–372.

Gertz, M. G. and L. B. Myers. 1992. Impediments to cross-national research: Problems of reliability and validity. *International Journal of Comparative and Applied Criminal Justice* 16(1): 57–65.

Giddens, A. 1978. *Durkheim*. Modern Masters series. New York: Harper Collins.

Goldstone, J., R. Bates, T. Gurr, M. Lustik, M. Marshall, J. Ulfelder, and M. Woodward. 2005. A global forecasting model of political instability. Annual Meeting of the American Political Science Association. Washington, DC.

Gould, S. and N. Eldredge. 1977. Punctuated equilibria: The tempo and mode of evolution reconsidered. *Paleobiology* 3(2): 115–151.

Gould, L. and M. Pate. 2011. Penality, power and polity: Exploring the relationship between political repression and modalities of punishment. *International Criminal Justice Review* 21(4): 443–461.

Graham, J. M. 1972. Amphetamine politics on Capitol Hill. *Society* 9(3): 14–22.

Gusfield, J. 1963. *Symbolic Crusade. Status Politics and the American Temperance Movement*. Urbana, IL: University of Illinois Press.

Hall, J. 1952. *Theft, Law and Society*. Indianapolis, IN: Bobbs-Merrill.

Heilbrunn, J. 2006. Paying the price of failure: Reconstructing failed and collapsed states in Africa and Central Asia. *Perspectives on Politics* 4(1): 135–150.

Herbst, J. 2000. *States and Power in Africa*. Princeton, NJ: Princeton University Press.

Herbst, J. 2004. Let them fail: State failure in theory and practice. In R. I. Rotberg (Ed.) *When States Fail: Causes and Consequences*, pp. 302–318, Princeton, NJ: Princeton University Press.

Jackson, P. and L. Carroll. 1981. Race and the war on crime: The sociopolitical determinants of municipal police expenditures in 90 non-southern US cities. *American Sociological Review* 46(3): 290–305.

Jackson, R. 1991. *Quasi-States: Sovereignty, International Relations and the Third World*. Cambridge: Cambridge University Press.

Jacobs, D. and K. Wood. 1999. Interracial conflict and interracial homicide: Do political and economic rivalries explain white killings of blacks or black killings of whites? *American Journal of Sociology* 105: 157–190.

Jacobs, D. and J. Carmichael. 2002. Subordination and violence against state control agents: Testing political explanations for lethal assaults against the police. *Social Forces* 80(4): 1223–1251.

Kayaoglu, T. 2007. The extension of Westphalian sovereignty: State-building and the abolition of extraterritoriality. *International Studies Quarterly* 51(3): 649–676.

King, G. and L. Zeng. 2001. Improving forecasts of state failure. *World Politics* 53(4): 623–658.

Krasner, S. 2004. Sharing sovereignty: New institutions for collapsed and failing states. *International Security* 29(2): 85–120.

Liska, A. 1987. A critical examination of macro perspectives on crime control. *Annual Review of Sociology* 13: 67–88.

Liska, A. and M. Chamlin. 1984. Social structure and crime control among macrosocial units. *The American Journal of Sociology* 90: 383–395.

Lynch, J. P. 1993. A cross-national comparison of the length for serious crimes. *Justice Quarterly* 10(4): 639–659.

Marshall, M. G. and B. R. Cole. 2009. *Global Report 2009 Conflict, Governance, and State Fragility*. Arlington, VA: Center for Systemic Peace.

Marx, K. and F. Engels. 1994/1848. *The Communist Manifesto*. Berkeley, CA: Center for Socialist History.

Mauer, M. 1995. The international use of incarceration. *The Prison Journal* 75(1): 113–123.

Melossi, D. 2008. Foreword. In G. Rusche, O. Kirchheimer, and D. Melossi (Eds) *Punishment and Social Structure*, pp. ix–xxxvi, New York: Transaction.

Melossi, D. 2008. *Controlling Crime, Controlling Society: Thinking about Crime in Europe and America*. Malden, MA: Polity Press.

Meyers, M. 1990. Black threat and incarceration in postbellum Georgia. *Social Forces* 69: 373–393.

Milliken, J. 2003. *State Failure, Collapse and Reconstruction: Issues and Response*. Oxford: Blackwell.

Milliken, J. and K. Krause. 2002. State failure, state collapse, and state reconstruction: Concepts, lessons and strategies. *Development and Change* 33(5): 753–774.

Mitchell, T. 1999. Society, economy and the state effect. In G. Steinmetz (Ed.) *State/Culture: State-Formation After the Cultural Turn*, pp. 76–97, Ithaca, NY: Cornell University Press.

Newman, G. 1999. *Global Report on Crime and Justice*. New York: Oxford University Press.

Nohr, A. 2012. The governmentalization of the state: Two questions of power. *E-International Relations*. http://www.e-ir.info/2012/09/06/the-governmentalization-of-the-state-two-questions-of-power/#_ftn11.

O'Malley, P. 1998. Risk, power and crime prevention. In P. O'Malley (Ed.) *Crime and the Risk Society*, pp. 71–96, Dartmouth: Aldershot.

Organization for Economic Co-Operation and Development. 2014. *Fragile States 2014: Domestic Revenue Mobilisation in Fragile States*. Paris: OECD.

Poulantzas, N. 2008. The political crisis and the crisis of the state. In J. Martin (Ed.) *The Poulantzas Reader: Marxism, Law and the State*, pp. 294–322, New York: Verso.

Rotberg, R. 2003. *State Failure and State Weakness in a Time of Terror*. Washington, DC: Brookings Institution Press.

Rotberg, R. 2004. *When States Fail: Causes and Consequences*. Princeton, NJ: Princeton University Press.

Rothe, D. and V. Collins. 2010. An exploration of system criminality and arms trafficking. *International Criminal Justice Review* 21(1): 22–38.

Ruddell, R. 2005. Social disruption, state formation and minority threat: A cross-national study of imprisonment. *Punishment & Society* 7: 7–28.

Ruddell, R. and M. Urbina. 2004. Minority threat and punishment: A cross-national analysis. *Justice Quarterly* 21(4): 903–931.

Ruggiero, V. 2006. *Understanding Political Violence: A Criminological Analysis*. Milton Keynes: Open University Press.

Rusche, G. 1933/1978. Labor market and penal sanction. *Crime and Justice* 10: 2–8.

Rusche, G. and O. Kirchheimer, 1968. *Punishment and Social Structure*. New York: Russell & Russell. (Original work published 1939.)

Sarewitz, D. 2010. Testimony before U. S. house of representatives committee on science and technology subcommittee on research and science education. Arizona State University. Consortium for Science, Policy and Outcomes. Report 10–14.

Sellin, T. 1938. *Culture Conflict and Crime*. New York: Social Science Research Council.

Simon, H. 1965. The architecture of complexity. In L. von Bertalanffy and A. Rapoport (Eds) *General Systems Yearbook*, pp. 63–64, New York: Springer.

Simon, J. 1997. Governing Through Crime. In G. Fisher and L. Friedman (Eds) *The Crime Conundrum: Essays on Criminal Justice*, pp. 171–190, Boulder, CO: Westview Press.

Stein, S. E. 2011. 'State failure' in theory and practice: The idea of the state and the contradictions of state formation. *Review of International Studies* 37: 229–247.

Taylor, M. C. 1998. How white attitudes vary with the racial composition of local populations. *American Sociological Review* 63(4): 512–535.

Teschke, B. 2003. *The Myth of 1648: Class, Geopolitics, and the Making of Modern International Relations*. London: Verso.

Tilly, C. 1985. War-making and state-making as organized crime. In P. Evans, D. Rueschemeyer, and T. Skocpol (Eds) *Bringing the State Back*, pp. 169–191, Cambridge: Cambridge University Press.

Tilly, C. 1986. Reflections on the history of European state-making. In C. Tilly (Ed.) *The Formation of National States in Western Europe*, pp. 3–84, Princeton, NJ: Princeton University Press.

Tilly, C. 1990. *Coercion, Capital and European States: AD 990–1992.* Cambridge, MA: Harvard University Press.

de Tocqueville, A. 1966/1866. *The Ancien Regime and the French Revolution.* New York: Collins.

Turk, A. 1969. *Criminality and Legal Order.* Chicago, IL: Rand McNally.

Tuerk, H. 2012. *Reflections on the Contemporary Law of the Sea.* Boston, MA: Martinus Nijhoff.

Wacquant, L. 1993. Urban outcasts: Stigma and division in the black American ghetto and the French urban periphery. *International Journal of Urban and Regional Research* 17: 366–383.

Weiss, R. and N. South. 1998. *Comparing Prison Systems: Toward a Comparative and International Penology.* Amsterdam: Gordon and Breach.

Zartman, W. 1995. *Collapsed States: The Disintegration and Restoration of Legitimate Authority.* Boulder, CO: Lynne Rienner.

Circumventing the System: Justice Delivery in Fragile States

2

All human beings, whatever their cultural or historical background, suffer when they are intimidated, imprisoned or tortured.

—**The Dalai Lama**

There is no greater tyranny than that which is perpetrated under the shield of the law and in the name of justice.

—**Montesquieu**

These quotations illustrate a fundamental aspect of life: we are all entitled to basic human rights and we all suffer when any individual's rights are violated. Ultimately, the responsibility to guard these rights falls to individual nations; and while this responsibility is compartmentalized, there is broad and international consensus regarding what constitutes core, inalienable human rights. Writing about the 1948 United Nations Declaration of Human Rights, French philosopher Jacques Maritain (1951, p. 76) observes, "Despite the diversity of interests, histories, cultures, politics, and ideologies, nations from every part of the planet were able to agree on a list of universal human rights."

There are 30 articles contained within the declaration, each detailing important rights to which we are all entitled. Some of the rights mentioned in the declaration include

...the right to life, liberty and security of person (Article 3); No one shall be held in slavery or servitude; slavery and the slave trade shall be prohibited in all their forms (Article 4); No one shall be subjected to torture or to cruel, inhuman or degrading treatment or punishment (Article 5); No one shall be subjected to arbitrary interference with his privacy, family, home or correspondence, nor to attacks upon his honour and reputation. Everyone has the right to the protection of the law against such interference or attacks (Article 12); Everyone has the right to freedom of thought, conscience and religion; this right includes freedom to change his religion or belief, and freedom, either alone or in community with others and in public or private, to manifest his religion or belief in teaching, practice, worship and observance (Article 18); Everyone has the right to freedom of opinion and expression;

this right includes freedom to hold opinions without interference and to seek, receive and impart information and ideas through any media and regardless of frontiers (Article 19).

The capacity and willingness to promote and protect the abovementioned human rights is a fundamental function of the government (Englehart 2009). As Neil Englehart (2009, p. 163) notes, "it is widely agreed that states ought to ensure that the rights of their citizens are respected by both abstaining from abuse and preventing private parties from committing abuses." Understanding that this obligation is a core governmental product, it follows that nations failing or on the brink thereof may have a lessened capacity (or will) to honor it.

In the six decades since the Declaration of Human Rights was adopted, William Sweet (2003, p. 2) observes, "once-stable societies have collapsed into bloody civil war, totalitarian and single-party states abound, and colonialism has often been replaced only by more subtle forms of imperialism, and the gap between the rich and poor has never been greater." While each of these problems contributes to the deterioration of human rights across the globe, we focus our examination on the particularly dire state of human rights in fragile and failing nations. We give special attention to issues of abuse, as well as attempts by corrupt regimes to circumvent transparency and exact their own, often horrifying, code of draconian justice.

A typical state-sponsored criminal justice system, which is composed of law enforcement, the judiciary, and corrections,* serves as the coercive arm of the government and is responsible for maintaining the safety and security of its citizens. Broadly speaking, law enforcement officers are expected to prevent and control crime (Maguire and Radosh 1996) and they are accorded an enormous set of powers with which to accomplish these goals (Fich 2014). These powers include "the power to search and seize personal property, to detain and make arrests, and to apply varying levels of coercive force, up to and including deadly force" (Fich 2014, p. xvii). With these broad powers comes the expectation that the police will conduct themselves in an ethical manner when working in their capacity as law enforcement officers, as well as in their personal lives (Fich 2014). However, a brief review of the history of policing reveals an uneasy relationship between law enforcement officers and the public they serve.

Policing scholar Egon Bittner (1985, p. 23) characterizes the police role thusly, "The role of the police is best understood as a mechanism for the distribution of non-negotiable coercive force employed in accordance

---

* Corrections will be explored in detail in Chapter 3.

with the dictates of an intuitive grasp of situational emergencies." This description may sufficiently circumscribe the police role in more stable and transparent societies, but in fragile and failing states, the mandate wanders well outside these lines. As Bittner (1970) asserts, the policing profession is tainted; a view that dates back to medieval times and, to varying degrees, still exists. During the time of absolute monarchies, he notes that the police were associated with tyranny and repression, thus creating fear and mistrust of law enforcement (Bittner 1970). While these images may have faded over the centuries, Bittner (1970, p. 7) contends that police officers are still viewed by the public with mixed feelings. Though citizens in stable nations may admire the heroic nature of police work, "no amount of public relations work can entirely abolish the sense that there is something of the dragon in the dragon-slayer." As we will discuss later in the chapter, police power as a tool of repression is commonplace in many fragile nations.

In an ideal world, judicial systems would function independently, render impartial decisions free of political interference, and afford citizens due process. In reality, courts are powerful politicized institutions; and when they break down, the judiciary experiences many of the same problems associated with the collapse of other governmental entities. When examining the effects of fragility on the judiciary, two broad themes emerge: corruption and public mistrust/fear. Judicial corruption includes bribery, as well as any action committed by any member of the court system that unduly influences the outcome of cases (Søreide and Williams 2014). The consequences of a corrupt judiciary have a profound effect on individuals and society. Because one of the main functions of the judiciary is to determine guilt or innocence in criminal matters (Maguire and Radosh 1996), corruption and bias truncate the likelihood of fair and just decisions. Further, this corruption often "leaves ordinary people without effective recourse to justice when the state is the offending party, and with scant protection when the state presses charges" (Søreide and Williams 2014, p. 71).

In stable nations, the roles of each part of the criminal justice system are clearly articulated. Moreover, a wide range of laws govern the actions of the criminal justice system actors to ensure that the rights of citizens are not violated. However, as states become increasingly fragile (whether due to governmental ineptitude, internal conflict, or increasing levels of authoritarianism regime), the system of justice bends to the will of those who control it. A fractured criminal justice system is a dangerous one, as it can become a tool to silence dissent or dispose of enemies. The consequences of this adaptation can "tear at the social fabric, undermine legitimacy of the state,... and endanger public security" (Patrick 2011, p. 141).

Such fissures also breed mistrust and fear of the government, both of which are likely warranted. In short, the misuse and abuse of the state's criminal justice apparatus constitute a violation of basic human rights. Sadly, access to justice is often the first casualty in the departure from stability.

Andrew Goldsmith (2002) argues that when states fail to provide necessary services and protections for their citizens, other groups can step in to fill the void. He notes that private security (or nonstate policing organizations) may offer to replace security services typically provided by the government, or other irregular armed groups may threaten to take over these services (Goldsmith 2002). We see ample evidence of this pattern in several of the brief case studies included in this chapter.

Nonstate policing can take a multitude of forms including, but not limited to, ethnic/clan militias, political party militias, and civil defense forces (Baker 2007). In some cases, the citizens in unstable nations will turn to nonstate police forces for help rather than go to the police, who are often perceived to be ineffective and corrupt (Khan 2007; Baker 2007). Ultimately, when governments fail, citizen safety becomes imperiled and the risk of extrajudicial killings, political imprisonment, and enforced disappearances greatly increases. Nevertheless, the relationship between human rights abuses and a government's capacity to function is both complicated and not well understood.

Noam Chomsky (2007, p. 2) argues that the government in many failed states expresses an unwillingness or inability to protect citizens from violence and may exhibit a tendency "to regard themselves as beyond the reach of domestic or international law, and hence free to carry out aggression and violence." This said, the relationship between state failure and human rights abuse has not received much attention within the criminological literature.

In a 1950 special message to Congress, U.S. President Harry Truman (1950) told the nation, "Once a government is committed to the principle of silencing the voice of opposition, it has only one way to go, and that is down the path of increasingly repressive measures, until it becomes a source of terror to all its citizens and creates a country where everyone lives in fear." As we explore the various modalities of oppression, we see the ongoing truth and relevance of Truman's observation. Additionally, the Cingranelli and Richards (2014) (CIRI) Human Rights Dataset provides quantitative measures for a variety of human rights violations, including extrajudicial killings, enforced disappearances, and torture. Throughout this chapter, we will refer to this dataset in an effort to provide the reader with an objective measure of police abuse and governmental attempts to bypass the formal justice system.

Extrajudicial Killings*

The frequency of extrajudicial killings presents a grave threat to basic human rights the world over. Amnesty International (n.d., para. 16), defines extrajudicial killings as those that are "unlawful (without legal process) and deliberate killings carried out by a government (or with their complicity), or by a state official acting without orders." The United Nations Special Rapporteur on extrajudicial, summary, or arbitrary executions provides a slightly more specific definition, adding that extrajudicial killings include "unlawful killings by the police, deaths in military or civilian custody, and patterns of killings by private individuals which are not adequately investigated and prosecuted by the authorities" (United Nations 2011, p. 6).

Extrajudicial killings can take a variety of forms including those that "occur due to excessive force in police operations, attempts to arrest suspected criminals, crowd or riot control, and purported shoot-outs with alleged armed criminals (sometimes called 'encounter killings')" (Jamal 2012, p. 14). It should be noted that extrajudicial killings are not always intentional and can occur as a result of poor law enforcement training (Jamal 2012), but our focus here is on those killings that represent a systematic effort to silence or marginalize or both, certain segments of society. We begin our examination of extrajudicial killings with a discussion of Uganda, a country with a notorious reputation for disregarding human rights.

Uganda

Extrajudicial killings have reached a crisis point in Uganda, as the nation dangerously nears collapse. With a composite score of 96.5 on the Fragile States Index, Uganda ranks 20th out of 177 nation-states. Like much of the rest of Africa, Uganda only recently emerged from colonial rule, having

---

* A note regarding targeted killings: Extrajudicial killings are not limited to developing nations, as the United States has come under fire for the practice of "targeted killings" of terrorists as part of the global war on terror (Žilinskas and Declerck 2014). Radsan and Murphy (2009, p. 406) define targeted killing "as extra-judicial, premeditated killing by a state of a specifically identified person not in its custody." As it pertains to the war on terror, international humanitarian law is murky at best. It is necessary to first determine whether these killings take place in the realm of armed conflict, rather than sporadic violence (Radsan and Murphy 2009). In the case of the latter, "law of international armed conflicts grants states broad authority to kill opposing 'combatants' but sharply limits their authority to kill 'civilians'" (Radsan and Murphy 2009, p. 416). Clearly, these types of killings present profound legal issues in the area of due process and their use is extremely problematic, especially as it pertains to the potential for human rights abuses. While targeted killings are certainly fraught with the potential for abuse and error (Radsan and Murphy 2009), our focus in this chapter is limited to the use of extrajudicial killings by governments against their own citizens.

gained independence from the United Kingdom in 1962. Unfortunately, colonial independence was followed by a series of dictatorships. The incumbent internal strife has claimed hundreds of thousands of lives (Central Intelligence Agency 2012a).

Much of the violence stems from the Berlin Conference in 1885 (Olayemi 2002). The purpose of the conference, which primarily involved countries with an economic interest in the continent (e.g., the United Kingdom, France, Germany, the United States, the Netherlands, and others), was to divide the continent among them, or in the words of Saleh-Hanna (2008, p. 22) "savagely carve up Africa" in a way that would best benefit foreign interests. Border lines for countries were arbitrarily drawn with little to no consideration of existing tribal and social divisions that were already well established (Human Rights Watch 1999; Saleh-Hanna 2008). As a consequence, there were so many ethnic, cultural, and political differences in Uganda that the development of a sustainable government was virtually impossible following its 1962 independence (Central Intelligence Agency 2012a).

Milton Obote, the first prime minister of Uganda, ruled from 1962 to 1971, when he was overthrown by Idi Amin (Onwumechili 1998). In an effort to quell the ethnic conflicts that plagued the nation, Obote "suspended the constitution, giving more powers to the president, and removing the king. A year later, Obote drafted a new constitution that granted greater powers to his office and abolished the traditional kingdoms" (Onwumechili 1998, p. 54). In 1971, Obote had planned to remove Idi Amin, his chief of army, for embezzlement, but Amin worked quickly to overthrow and exile Obote (Onwumechili 1998).

Amin's dictatorship, which lasted from 1971 to 1979, would be the first of two dictatorial regimes under which the population paid the ultimate price. Initially, many Ugandans were optimistic about Amin's leadership. Phares Mutibwa (1992, p. 78) notes that there was "great jubilation" among many Ugandans. This hope was short-lived. On taking power, Amin created the Public Safety Unit and the State Research Bureau, both of which directly reported to him. These organizations, along with the military police, killed approximately 10,000 people during Amin's first year of leadership (Human Rights Watch 2003).

In 1972, Amin ordered the expulsion of nearly 70,000 Ugandan citizens who were of Asian descent and expropriated "5,655 firms, factories, and farms and U.S.$400 million in personal goods" (Human Rights Watch 1999, p. 2). Predictably, Amin's unchecked megalomania proved to be his ultimate downfall (Onwumechili 1998). In 1978, Amin attempted to annex nearly 1800 square miles of Tanzanian territory (Human Rights Watch 1999). The Tanzanian military and members of the Uganda National Liberation Army (made up of many Ugandans who either fled or were forced to leave Uganda) defeated the Ugandan incursion, prompting Amin's flight from the country

(Onwumechili 1998). Initially, he sought refuge in Iraq, but eventually moved to Saudi Arabia where he lived until his death in 2003. During his rule, it is estimated that he killed 300,000 political dissidents (Central Intelligence Agency 2012a), though some estimates place the number as high as 500,000. Enemies of the state (both real and imagined) as well as Christians were among those most frequently targeted (Ball 2011).

After the defeat of Amin, Milton Obote returned to power and numerous human rights abuses continued to take place. Because Obote was elected in a disputed election, internal strife broke out almost immediately following his rise to power. Yoweri Museveni of the Uganda Patriotic Movement (UPM), who ran against Obote in the 1980 election, was so enraged by the rigged election that he formed the National Resistance Army (NRA) and waged a guerrilla war, with the intention of deposing Obote and changing the Ugandan system of government (Human Rights Watch 1999). Human Rights Watch (1999, p. 5) characterizes the civil war that followed the election "by a wanton disregard for human rights by government troops and a massive loss of human lives, especially in the Buganda 'Luwero triangle,' the area of central Uganda near the capital Kampala." Again, civilians bore the brunt of the civil unrest, as an estimated 100,000–200,000 civilians were killed by Obote's regime (Human Rights Watch 1999; Central Intelligence Agency 2012a). Obote was eventually deposed via a coup and he fled to Zambia, where he lived until his death in 2005 (BBC News 2005).

In the years following the atrocities committed by Amin and Obote, the situation in Uganda has not improved appreciably. Human Rights Watch (2011, p. 189) reports that the Ugandan People's Defense Force kill civilians "with impunity." An estimated 48–55 civilians, including women and children, were killed by members of the Ugandan People's Defense Force during a four-month period in 2010. The Rapid Response Unit (previously named Operation Wembley and then rebranded as the Violent Crime Crack Unit) is perhaps even more problematic than the People's Defense Force insofar as extrajudicial killings are concerned (Human Rights Watch 2011).

Operation Wembley was created in 2002 by President Yoweri Museveni in part to address the growing violent crime problem (Commonwealth Human Rights Initiative 2006), but also as a means to circumvent the inefficient justice system (Human Rights Watch 2011). This ad hoc crime unit was initially staffed by a variety of people, some with dubious backgrounds. Officially, the unit was staffed by "the Chieftaincy of Military Intelligence (CMI), the Criminal Investigation Department (CID) of police, the External Security Organisation (ESO), the Internal Security Organisation (ISO), as well as people who had worked informally as informants for military intelligence and the president's office" (Human Rights Watch 2011, p. 13). Basing their findings on information from several different credible sources, Human Rights Watch (2011) reports that much of the unit was actually staffed by "repentant criminals" and former child soldiers who had fought in the National Resistance Army, a rebel group that President Museveni led before he took power in 1986.

Despite poor training, the rate of violent robberies was reduced. However, human rights violations drastically increased. Within two months of its inception, Operation Wembley arrested and detained 430 individuals and killed an estimated 83 suspects (Human Rights Watch 2011). Some contend that Operation Wembley was actually a terrorist organization because they lacked both the rule of law and formal procedure (Francis 2005). Operation Wembley was officially disbanded in August of 2002 and replaced with the Violent Crime Crack Unit (VCCU; Commonwealth Human Rights Initiative 2006). The VCCU was simply Operation Wembley with a new name, as the tactics remained the same and few changes were made to personnel (Commonwealth Human Rights Initiative 2006; Human Rights Watch 2011). By 2007, the name was once again changed to the Rapid Response Unit (RRU). Rather than just a change in name only, the crime control mission of the RRU was broadened to include the targeting of armed robbers and responding to general crimes (Human Rights Watch 2011).*

An estimate of the number of victims of extrajudicial killings committed by the RRU is understandably difficult to obtain, but the CIRI dataset places Uganda in the top tier for extrajudicial killings. In addition to the quantitative measure, there are several anecdotal accounts of killings committed by members of the RRU that provide some insight into the frequency of such killings. In one case, a robbery suspect, Frank Ssekanjako, was allegedly beaten to death by RRU officers (Human Rights Watch 2011). Witnesses to the beating describe in vivid detail the brutality of the killing. According to witnesses interviewed by Human Rights Watch (2011, p. 27), Ssekanjako and his co-suspects

> were brought back to the scene of the alleged robbery by the two RRU officers and their driver and beaten severely for over an hour with plastic pipes and a large wooden club, known locally as an entolima. At one point, when Ssekanjako was hit repeatedly on the head and blood flowed from wounds on his ankles, knees and flanks, he said, "Why don't you shoot me, so I die?" This angered the officers, who responded by separating Ssekanjako from the others by some distance, saying, "You want to die with a bullet? No, you will die of beatings." The beatings continued.

Ssekanjako died shortly after the incident, and while no cause of death was indicated in the autopsy report, the beatings likely caused his death.

---

* Torture figures prominently in the interrogation methods used by the RRU and this aspect of human rights violations in Uganda will be explored later in the chapter.

Three RRU officers were arrested by the police for their participation in the beating, but it remains unclear whether they will receive any sanctions, as the police have been very slow to collect evidence in the case (Human Rights Watch 2011). Apart from the Ssekanjako case, there are numerous eyewitness reports of RRU forces killing suspects in custody or during the course of routine patrols. It appears that the controversial "shoot to kill" policy enacted during Operation Wembley (Commonwealth Human Rights Initiative 2006) persisted in the RRU. In December 2011, the RRU was officially disbanded and renamed the Special Investigations Unit (SIU) (Human Rights Watch 2013). The SIU appears to be just the next iteration of the RRU, as there has been almost no effort to investigate abuses committed by RRU officers and many of the same RRU ad hoc operatives continue to work with the SIU (Human Rights Watch 2013).

Pakistan

Extrajudicial killings appear to be a regular occurrence in Pakistan, as the CIRI dataset places Pakistan in the top tier for extrajudicial killings, with more than 50 occurring each year. There are a variety of internal threats to both security and democracy in Pakistan, but the struggle between security forces, the civilian government, and radical Islamists is largely responsible for the current discord (Waseem 2011). Government control in many areas has been usurped by military forces who continue to wield great control over political policies and responses (Waseem 2011). The power of the military in Pakistan to use coercive force represents a threat to internal stability because effective control hinges on three factors: power, authority, and legitimacy (Misra and Clarke 2012). While the military has the power and authority to use coercive force, it lacks the critical component of legitimacy, especially in the eyes of the populace (Misra and Clarke 2012).

In an effort to gain popular legitimacy, the military has often aligned itself with either Islamists or democratic forces to capitalize on the existing legitimacy of both groups, but such alliances are subject to shift depending on the political climate (Misra and Clarke 2012). While the prime minister once had constitutional power to dissolve the National Assembly and governors, that power was taken away in 2010 with the modification of the 18th amendment of the constitution (The Commonwealth 2014). The role of the prime minister in contemporary Pakistan has been described as being largely ceremonial (The Commonwealth 2014).

In terms of extrajudicial killings, in 2010, the Human Rights Commission of Pakistan noted 338 executions that occurred during police encounters, a 50% increase from the previous year (Jamal 2012). Police investigated a mere 25 of the 338 cases at the request of (and after much protest by) the victims' families (Jamal 2012). More recent statistics appear to indicate that extrajudicial killings are on the rise, especially in the Balochistan Province. The nongovernmental organization (NGO) International Voice for Baloch Missing Persons (IVBMP 2014) reports that 490 bodies were recovered in the Baloch region between 2009 and 2013 (IVBMP 2014). Of those, 117 were unidentifiable because the bodies were so badly decomposed, but the rest have been identified and their names, pictures, date of arrest, estimated date of death, and primary occupation have been compiled and made publicly available (IVBMP 2014). In one recent case recorded by IVBMP (2014), Qadir Bashk was abducted from the Baloch region on September 13, 2013, by the Pakistani Army and held for an unknown amount of time. His body was found on January 15, 2014, along with 100 other decomposed bodies in a mass grave (IVBMP 2014). Those targeted for execution include journalists, teachers, political activists, students, and human rights activists (Asian Human Rights Commission 2011; IVBMP 2014). The Asian Legal Resource Centre (2012, para. 4) notes that these killings are related to other human rights abuses in the country, which include "arbitrary arrests or abductions, forced disappearances and torture, following which victims are surfaced dead, often by having their mutilated bodies dumped by the roadside."

Extrajudicial killings are especially pervasive in Swat Valley, an area located about 100 miles outside Pakistan's capital city, Islamabad. The area, which was previously under Taliban control, has been subjected to rather heavy-handed rule by the Pakistani military. The army denies allegations that they are behind the killings and instead contend that the killings are a result of citizens attempting to settle old scores (Perlez and Shah 2009). Given that there are remarkable similarities between almost all of the documented killings, it is more likely that the military is responsible (Human Rights Watch 2010).

Enforced or Involuntary Disappearances of Persons

In his oft quoted passage, "It is dangerous to be right in matters on which the established authorities are wrong," Voltaire (1901, xlviii) provides a perfect frame for a discussion of enforced disappearances. As true now as it was in the eighteenth century, there is often a heavy price attached to dissent in autocracies. As the sands of control slip through the fingers of failing regimes, those who are thought to pose a challenge frequently pay with their life.

Amnesty International defines enforced disappearances as a disappearance that takes place when the government or regime in power arrests or detains an individual and then takes measures to either deny that the person is in custody or refuse to notify family members of the victim's location (Amnesty International 2012a). Kolb and Gaggioli (2013, p. 320), note "in practice, the phenomenon of disappearances consists most often in the abduction, by a State or 'political organization', of persons considered to be 'a security threat', their torture and killing, and finally the hiding of their bodies so that the guilty go unpunished." The refusal of the government to notify the victim's families of his or her fate is what differentiates enforced disappearances from other acts that might be committed by a government (e.g., political imprisonment or murder) (Courtney 2010).

The practice of enforced disappearances is certainly not new (Vitkauskaite-Meurice and Zilinskas 2010). Hitler's "Nacht und Nebel Erlass" (the Night and Fog Decree), which resulted in the seizing and disappearance of countless people in Nazi-occupied territories, represented the first time that the issue received widespread attention (Vitkauskaite-Meurice and Zilinskas 2010). In the 1960s, enforced disappearances became common throughout South America, but they were most widely used in Guatemala amid their three-decade-long internal conflict (Scovazzi and Citroni 2007). Since that time, repressive governments throughout South America, Iraq, and the former Yugoslavia have engaged in this human rights violation (Vitkauskaite-Meurice and Zilinskas 2010). In many countries, enforced disappearances are used as a tool by the government to suppress or punish or both, political dis sent or opposition that they perceive as threatening (Haugaard and Nichols 2010; Sarkin 2011). Furthermore, enforced disappearances are intended to serve as a powerful deterrent or suppressant to others who may oppose the ruling regime (Sarkin 2011).

Enforced disappearances represent the gravest of threats to human rights because the victim is most often killed (Akande and Shah 2010). In addition to the profound violation of the right to one's own life, enforced disappearances also encompass a variety of other rights violations including "the right not to be tortured, the right to dignity, the right to a fair trial, and the right of access to justice" (Sarkin 2011, p. 132). Moreover, these violations cause many victims to be denied freedom of thought and expression, as well as religious freedom (Scovazzi and Citroni 2007). While determining the extent of enforced disappearances is by its nature difficult to calculate, various governmental and nongovernmental entities estimate that worldwide 300,000–500,000 people disappeared between 1970 and 2000, with 100,000 of those cases occurring in South America alone (Scovazzi and Citroni 2007).

In December 1992, the United Nations General Assembly adopted the Declaration on the Protection of All Persons from Enforced Disappearance. In this declaration, the United Nations (1992) noted, "enforced disappearance undermines the deepest values of any society committed to respect for the rule of law, human rights and fundamental freedoms, and that the systematic practice of such acts is of the nature of a crime against humanity."

Article 2 of the Declaration on the Protection of All Persons from Enforced Disappearance explains in no uncertain terms that:

1. No State shall practice, permit or tolerate enforced disappearances.
2. States shall act at the national and regional levels and in cooperation with the United Nations to contribute by all means to the prevention and eradication of enforced disappearance (United Nations 1992).

It is important to note that despite its strong language, this declaration does not criminalize enforced disappearances. In an effort to create a legally binding instrument to combat enforced disappearance, the United Nations (UN) passed the International Convention for the Protection of All Persons from Enforced Disappearances in 2006 (Vitkauskaite-Meurice and Zilinskas 2010). The convention sets forth detailed obligations for countries (e.g., countries must bring perpetrators to justice), establishes remedies for victims (e.g., restitution, restoration of reputation, and guarantee of nonrepetition), and establishes monitoring and tracing procedures, which can include requests to the government that the missing person be located (Vitkauskaite-Meurice and Zilinskas 2010). Iraq became the 20th nation to sign the convention (United Nations 2012) and the convention officially came into force one month after their signing date on December 23, 2010.

Because enforced disappearances are an issue in many places, the UN established a working group to examine instances of enforced disappearance in 1980. The primary purpose of the group is to assist families of victims by determining what happened to their family member (United Nations 2010). From 1980 to 2010, the working group examined 53,387 disappearance cases in over 83 countries (United Nations 2010). Of these, 42,633 cases have not been resolved (United Nations 2010). In their annual report, the UN notes a wide variation in the number of disappearance cases, with countries ranging from zero cases (e.g., Albania, Bahrain, and Bosnia Herzegovina) to cases numbering in the thousands (United Nations 2010). The Countries with the most cases of enforced disappearances include Algeria (2,912 cases), Argentina (3,290 cases), El Salvador (2,270 cases), Guatemala (2,899 cases), Iran (16,409 cases), Peru (2,371 cases), and Sri Lanka (5,651 cases) (United Nations 2010).

Columbia

Columbia has the dubious distinction of being among the world leaders in enforced disappearances. Additionally, Columbia is the only Latin American nation where enforced disappearances still occur with a high frequency (Courtney 2010; Haugaard and Nichols 2010). Not surprisingly, the CIRI dataset places Columbia near the top of its rankings with regard to enforced disappearances. Victims of enforced disappearances in Columbia include human rights activists; indigenous persons; young people from rural conflict areas; lesbian, gay, bisexual, transgender, queer (LGBTQ) persons; and anyone else who might be labeled "undesirable" (Haugaard and Nichols 2010). The perpetrators of enforced disappearances tend to be military, police, or other armed groups (e.g., left-wing and right-wing insurgent groups) (Haugaard and Nichols 2010). Persons who disappear at the hands of the military or other armed groups often face a terrible fate. Haugaard and Nichols (2010, p. 5) detail a Columbian news series, entitled In Search of Columbia's 10,000 Dead, which reported that paramilitary groups were teaching their members how to cut up bodies for disposal. The group is said to have forcibly brought people (mostly elderly) to the training camp so members could practice the technique on live individuals. One paramilitary combatant explained, "The instructions were to cut off their arms and heads, to quarter them alive. They started crying and asking us not to hurt them, they had families."

This method of disposal complicates efforts to locate the remains of victims and contributes to the difficulty of making an accurate estimate of disappearance cases. The UN estimates that at least 30,000 people have disappeared in Columbia since the military junta in the 1970s and 1980s (Enforced Disappearance Information Exchange Network 2008), although some victims' groups report that the number may be well over 100,000 (International Commission on Missing Persons 2008). The U.S. Department of State (2011) reports that the Latin America Working Group and the U.S. Office on Colombia have documented 51,000 cases of enforced disappearances. Of these, the reports list "7,197 found alive, 1,366 found dead, and 460 listed as 'annulled'" (U.S. Department of State 2011). With regard to current cases of disappearances, between 2007 and 2010, more than 1100 new cases have been registered (Haugaard and Nichols 2010).

Progress on the part of the government to curb and prevent disappearances has been slow, but there have been some attempts to locate missing persons and bring the perpetrators to justice. In 1991, the Columbian constitution expressly prohibited enforced disappearances, but almost a decade passed before a law was passed that criminalized the act (International Commission on Missing Persons 2008; Haugaard and Nichols 2010). Colombia is a signatory to the Inter-American Convention on Forced Disappearance of Persons, the Rome Statute, and the International Convention for the Protection of All Persons from Enforced Disappearance (International Commission on Missing Persons 2008). In accordance with these treaties, "Colombia agreed not to practice, allow or tolerate the enforced disappearance of individuals and to sanction, within its jurisdiction, the perpetrators, accomplices and those who conceal such crimes" (International Commission on Missing Persons 2008, p. 6). In 2008, the Columbia Chamber of Representatives introduced the Victims law, which would provide protections for citizens against armed conflict and provide restitution for the families of disappeared persons (United Nations 2010). Unfortunately, the bill was shelved, in part because it would not have been financially possible to provide compensation to the tens of thousands of families who would have been eligible for restitution (United Nations 2010).

In terms of prosecution of these cases, formal action has been slow. In July 2010, retired colonel Alfonso Plazas Vega received a 30-year prison sentence for his role in the disappearance of 11 people during the Palace of Justice siege (U.S. Department of State 2011). During the 1985 incident, the Palace of Justice had been taken over by M-19 guerrillas and later reclaimed by the military. As a consequence, Assistant Judge Carlos Horacio Uran, several cafeteria workers, and one guerrilla were never seen again (United Press International 2012). Plazas Vega appealed the 30-year sentence, but the Superior Tribunal of Bogota upheld the lower court's sentence (United Press International 2012).

Investigations of retired generals Juan Salcedo Lora and Alfonso Vaca Perilla also took place concerning the Rochela massacre (U.S. Department of State 2011). The Rochela massacre occurred in January of 1989 "when a paramilitary group kidnapped a 15-person commission of judicial officials who were investigating the civic and military responsibilities involved in various massacres committed in the Magdalena Medio zone" (Center for Justice and International Law 2012). Of the 15 officials, 12 were shot and killed, and three were injured (Center for Justice and International Law 2012). The case was brought before the Inter-American Court of Human Rights 2007 (*Rochela Massacre v. Colombia*). The court declared that the Columbian government was ultimately responsible for the massacre and that they had violated numerous human rights contained within the American Convention on Human Rights. Additionally, the court ordered the government to conduct a criminal investigation to determine who participated in the massacre (*Rochela Massacre v. Colombia* 2007). As a result, Juan Salcedo Lora and Alfonso Vaca Perilla were implicated in the investigations, but at the time of this writing, their case is still pending (U.S. Department of State 2011).

Sri Lanka

Sri Lanka, an island located in the Indian Ocean, is a fragmented country, meaning that it displays symptoms of state failure, but has not yet failed (Jenne 2003). Sri Lanka can neither be considered successful nor failed because there is a relatively stable government in place that holds free and open elections. That said, during the decades-long conflict with the Liberation Tigers of Tamil Eelam (LTTE), the government has lost control over large sections of its country and no longer has a monopoly on the use of coercive force (Jenne 2003). One of the more problematic issues in the Sri Lankan turmoil is the enforced disappearance of persons. Many human rights problems in Sri Lanka can be traced to the civil war between the Sinhalese majority and the minority Tamil (BBC News 2012). While the civil war appears to be at an end, the 25 years of fighting has taken a heavy toll on the island nation.

Necessarily, the events leading up to the 1983 civil war are complicated, but William Clarance (2002) contends that disagreements over whether the Sinhalese or the Tamil people first settled in the region helped fuel the bitterness that ultimately led to war. The point should be largely moot as archeological evidence suggests that the region had been "discovered" and settled long before either group arrived (Clarance 2002). However, the "Sinhala people claim that even if they were not the first inhabitants of the island, a status they allow to the 'primitive' Veddas, they were at least the first 'civilized' settlers of Lanka" (Nissan 1990, p. 20). Historical accounts of how the Tamil settled in the region tend to differ. In one account, the Tamils do not dispute that the Sinhala people settled the area first, but assert that the Tamils have lived in Sri Lanka for a thousand years and have a history of political autonomy (Nissan 1990).

In another (arguably more controversial) version put forth by the Tamil Justice, Satchi Ponnambalam, the Tamil people settled the region first. Initially, there were no differences between the Tamil and the Sinhala; rather "the Sinhala were originally Tamils who converted to Buddhism and adopted Sinhala, a language based on Pali, the language of the Buddhist texts; and that much of what Sinhala people now uphold as monuments of their past greatness was actually produced by Tamil artistry" (Nissan 1990, p. 20). Historical disagreements aside, the relationship between both groups has been extremely contentious since Sri Lanka gained independence from Great Britain in 1948 (Clarance 2002). From that time onward, there have been countless examples of the majority Sinhalese excluding the minority Tamil from the political process and passing laws that favor the majority population.

Following the election of a coalition of Sinhala-dominated parties in 1956, "the Sinhala-Buddhist majority ... [demanded that it] should receive its 'rightful' share of official employment" (Spencer 2007, p. 2).* Shortly thereafter, the "Sinahala Only" Act was passed, which declared that Sinhala was the only official language of Sri Lanka (Spencer 2007; Clarance 2001). During the parliamentary debate over the act, the Tamil Federal Party staged a demonstration that ended in violence (Clarance 2001). Additionally, rioting between both groups broke out in the east (Spencer 2007), especially in Tamil settlements (Clarance 2001). The contentious relationship between the Sinhalese and the Tamil led to the formation of the LTTE.

---

* From 1950 onward, the availability of government work in Sri Lanka was extremely limited (Spencer 2007). By demanding government employment, the Sinahala effectively excluded the Tamil people from state work.

Under the leadership of Velupillai Prabhakaran, the LTTE "began to campaign for a Tamil homeland in northern and eastern Sri Lanka, where most of the island's Tamils reside" (Bajoria 2009). Part of the LTTE strategy involved the utilization of terrorist tactics against the Sinahala government, but this did little to resolve the conflict, as the government launched its own terrorist campaign (Spencer 2007). Tension between the two groups continued to escalate and riots broke out in "1958, 1961, 1974, 1977, 1979, and 1981, culminating in the devastating events of July 1983" (Clarance 2002, p. 45).

In July 1983, the LTTE "ambushed an army convoy, killing thirteen soldiers and triggering riots in which 2,500 Tamils died" (Bajoria 2009, para. 2). Shortly after these tragic events, "militant groups started to operate in the Tamil areas of the east, and attacks on state personnel were replaced by massacres and counter-massacres of civilians in border areas between the two ethnic blocks" (Spencer 2007, p. 2). While the roots of the conflict lay in the oppression of the minority Tamil, the LTTE ultimately became one of the most dangerous terrorist organizations in the world. Their terrorist tactics included "suicide bombings, recruitment of child soldiers, and the ability to challenge Sri Lankan forces from the Jaffna Peninsula in the north down through the eastern side of the island" (Bajoria 2009, para. 3). The LTTE funds its operations through drugs and weapons trafficking, as well as through kidnappings for extortion (Jenne 2003).

This brief overview of the history and conflict in Sri Lanka helps set the stage for a discussion on the issue of enforced disappearances. Enforced disappearances have been used by the government both to suppress political dissent and as a means to deal with the conflict stemming from the civil war (Asian Human Rights Commission 2012). The Sri Lankan government has targeted Sinhala youth who supported the Janatha Vimukthi Peramuna (JVP), also known as the People's Liberation Front, as well as Tamil militants. According to the Asian Human Rights Commission (2012):

[H]undreds were burnt to death or killed and bodies disposed of without any inquest proceedings. Again between 1988 to 1989 thousands of Sinhala youth were kidnapped on suspicion and summarily executed. That was during the height of what is called the "period of terror" (the beeshana samaya).

The government also targeted the Tamil throughout the civil war and enforced disappearance of Tamil youth was a major strategy of the government (Asian Human Rights Commission 2012). This tactic should come as no surprise given the LTTE's recruitment and use of child soldiers.

The events after the civil war ended are just as problematic as the atrocities committed by both sides during the conflict. Beginning in 1992, the government granted the military the authority to use secret detention camps (Scovazzi and Citroni 2007). It is estimated that thousands of Tamil militants and civilians (some of whom surrendered) were taken into custody by security forces and never heard from again (Asian Human Rights Commission 2012). According to Human Rights Watch (2012a), during the last stages of the conflict, thousands of civilians tried to escape the fighting. As they did so, government forces screened each person and attempted to separate out civilians from LTTE members (Human Rights Watch 2012a). Some family members have been successful in locating those taken to "prisons or in so-called rehabilitation centers ... but some are still missing. In spite of public assurances, the government has not published a comprehensive list of detainees and places of detention" (Human Rights Watch 2012a, para. 21).

At present, little has been done to locate those taken into custody or to notify their families as to their whereabouts. When the new government took power in 1994, they bowed to pressure from international groups and NGOs and established three commissions to investigate cases of enforced disappearances (Scovazzi and Citroni 2007). In total, 60,000 cases were reported and the government admitted to just 16,742 kidnappings (Scovazzi and Citroni 2007). While the commissions recommended the prosecution of 500 alleged perpetrators, most were acquitted (Scovazzi and Citroni 2007). The lack of an official response to enforced disappearance cases led Human Rights Watch (2012a, para. 21) to declare, "impunity prevails in relation to the tens of thousands of enforced disappearances that took place in Sri Lanka from the inception of the war in 1983 until the end." In 2012, hundreds of people demonstrated in the capital in an effort to demand answers from the government (Amnesty International 2012b). Similarly, nearly 1300 people have sought information about missing loved ones from the Terrorist Investigation Department, but the majority have found little information (Amnesty International 2012b). Enforced disappearances continue to be problematic, with the Sri Lankan police reporting that nearly 1700 people have been abducted since 2009 (most held for ransom) (Amnesty International 2012b).

Recently, the case of two missing activists garnered international media attention. Lalith Kumar Weeraraj and Kugan Muruganathan both helped organize several demonstrations against the government regarding the issue of enforced disappearances. It now appears that they have become victims themselves (BBC News 2012). The two men disappeared while planning a demonstration in the city of Jaffna. Prior to their abduction, "Weeraraj's father stated that his son had received anonymous phone calls ... telling him that he would be eliminated if he continued his political involvement" (Human Rights Watch 2012c, para. 8). As of 2015, there is no information about their location, despite repeated inquiries by their families and protests held by activists.

Torture

Lastly, and perhaps most importantly, we examine the use of torture by governments in fragile and failing states. In our previous work on corporal punishment (see Pate and Gould 2012), we examined the use of torture in institutional settings (e.g., jails and prisons). Our research found that torture is a mainstay in many correctional institutions throughout the world. In Egypt, for example, prisoners (both those who have been adjudicated guilty and those in pretrial detention) routinely experience torture inside institutions. In an interview with Middle East Watch (1993), one prisoner held without charge for almost a year described brutal beatings from Central Security Forces soldiers. In addition to beatings, the prisoner stated that soldiers would spray liquid into detainees' eyes, which caused swelling so severe that the prisoners could not see. Detainees and convicted offenders have been victims of other forms of "torture including: electric shocks, beatings, whippings, death threats, and sexual victimization" (Pate and Gould 2012, p. 98).

People's Republic of Bangladesh

Bangladesh, a small country roughly the size of Iowa (Central Intelligence Agency 2012b), has been plagued by bloodshed and violence since its inception. Because it was once part of British India, the typical problems of post-colonial legacy are in evidence. Additional problems stem from the secession of West Pakistan and East Bengal from India, which became East Pakistan in 1947 (Central Intelligence Agency 2012b). In 1955, "East Bengal became East Pakistan... but the awkward arrangement of a two-part country with its territorial units separated by 1,600 km left the Bengalis marginalized and dissatisfied" (Central Intelligence Agency 2012b, p. 307). On March 26, 1971, while still part of Pakistan, Bangladesh declared its independence (Ahmed 2004). One of the bloodiest civil wars in contemporary history followed (Ahmed 2004), with an estimated death toll of one million Bengalis (Heitzman and Worden 1988). With the help of the Indian army, the war came to an end on December 16, 1971, and the independent state of Bangladesh emerged (Ahmed 2004; Heitzman and Worden 1988).

While the process to gain national independence is often violent, in Bangladesh the bloodshed and human rights violations have persisted as a defining feature of the nation. The Bangladeshi constitution does state, "No person shall be subjected to torture or to cruel, inhuman, or degrading punishment or treatment." That said, public servants are typically protected from prosecution if they torture persons in custody (Asian Human Rights Commission 2013). Further, Bangladesh has ratified the United Nations Convention Against Torture and Other Cruel, Inhuman or Degrading

Treatment or Punishment (United Nations 1984). This convention defines torture as:

[A]ny act by which severe pain or suffering, whether physical or mental, is intentionally inflicted on a person for such purposes as obtaining from him or a third person information or a confession, punishing him for an act he committed, or intimidating or coercing him or a third person, or for any reason based on discrimination of any kind, when such pain or suffering is inflicted by or at the instigation of or with the consent or acquiescence of a public official or other person acting in an official capacity.

The convention is explicit in its requirements that

Each State Party shall take effective legislative, administrative, judicial or other measures to prevent acts of torture in any territory under its jurisdiction.

No exceptional circumstances whatsoever, whether a state of war or a threat of war, internal political instability or any other public emergency, may be invoked as a justification of torture.

An order from a superior officer or a public authority may not be invoked as a justification of torture.

Despite the constitutional mandate against torture and the ratification of the United Nations Convention Against Torture and Other Cruel, Inhuman or Degrading Treatment or Punishment, torture appears to persist as a regular feature of governance. In addition to the convention, there is an optional protocol to the Convention Against Torture that provides for regular inspection visits to countries for the purposes of examining individuals in custody to ensure that they are not being tortured or physically harmed. Bangladesh has taken no steps to ratify the Optional Protocol to the Convention Against Torture (OPCAT) and there was no law explicitly criminalizing torture until 2013 (Asian Human Rights Commission 2013). Saber Hossain Chowdhury, a member of Parliament and a former torture victim, has been pushing for legislation against torture for nearly a decade (Chowdhury 2013). During an interview with Amnesty International, Chowdhury indicated that one of the principle barriers to reform was a sense of resignation among Bangladeshi citizens that torture was just a part of life (Chowdhury 2013). He noted that citizens "did not feel much could be done about it given that whichever party was in government would find torture an indispensable tool to use against its political opponents" (Chowdhury 2013, para. 9).

The 2009 mutiny by several members of the Bangladesh Rifles (BDR) is but one example of how torture has manifested in Bangladesh. The BDR's main function is to secure the national borders, though they also assist law enforcement in smuggling and cross-border crimes (Human Rights Watch 2012b). While the BDR is a uniformed security force, they are a separate entity from the army. BDR soldiers had long been disgruntled about lower pay and benefits and limitations placed on upward advancement compared with the army. Tensions between the army and the BDR reached boiling point during an event attended by many high-ranking military officials for the annual three-day celebration known as "BDR week" (Human Rights Watch 2012b). During one of the ceremonial events, a BDR member raised his weapon and pointed it at senior army officials, signaling the beginning of the planned mutiny (Human Rights Watch 2012b). An unknown number of shots were fired and rank-and-file members of the BDR began either holding army officers hostage or killing them (Human Rights Watch 2012b).

By the time the violence was quelled, 74 people (including 57 army officers) were dead. In the aftermath, 6000 BDR soldiers were detained and mass trials were conducted under the BDR's mutiny laws (for which the maximum penalty is seven years imprisonment) and the criminal code (for which the maximum penalty is death) (Human Rights Watch 2012b). The majority of those charged had or will have hearings before military tribunals, where the sentences will be lighter. Approximately 850 BDR soldiers are facing criminal charges, where the death penalty is a possibility.

Not surprisingly, widespread reports of the torture of detainees by the police have emerged. Interviews conducted by Human Rights Watch paint a terrifying picture of the harsh treatment visited on BDR soldiers. Detainees were often hung upside down for hours, electric shocks were administered to their genitals, and their fingernails and toenails were ripped out. With an equal lack of surprise, the widespread torture led to most detainees admitting participation in the mutiny. According to the chief prosecutor in the mass trials, Anisul Huq, any statements obtained under duress would not be admitted into evidence. In an interview with Human Rights Watch, he stated, "Passions were running very high in the security forces in the immediate aftermath of the mutiny" (Human Rights Watch 2012b, p. 43). While this is a positive sign, Human Rights Watch maintains that it is unclear as to whether those instructions are being followed.

The psychological effects of torture are profound and can last for decades after the physical torture has ended (Jaranson and Popkin 1998). In studying prisoners of war during World War II, Lance Rintamaki et al. (2009) found that many former solders still had vivid flashbacks of the war and 16.6% met the *Diagnostic and Statistical Manual of Mental Disorders, 4th edition* (DSM-IV) clinical requirements for posttraumatic stress disorder. Ellen Gerrity et al. (2001, p. 115) note that common symptoms among torture survivors include "hyperarousal, reexperiencing the event, avoidance behavior, amnesic episodes, difficulty concentrating, and poor memory." Research from Anne Goldfeld et al. (1988) note myriad psychological effects of torture including anxiety, depression, irritability, aggression, social withdrawal, cognitive impairments, sexual dysfunction, and nightmares. One BDR torture victim (a student), who did not take part in the mutiny, told Human Rights Watch interviewers, "The fear never leaves me. I didn't used to be like this, now I am constantly nervous, I can't sleep, can't be normal. The fear just holds me down all the time" (Human Rights Watch 2012b).

References

Ahmed, S. 2004. *Bangladesh: Past and Present.* New Delhi: A.P.H. Publishing.

Akande, D. and S. Shah. 2010. Immunities of state officials, international crimes, and foreign domestic courts. *European Journal of International Law* 21(4): 816.

Amnesty International. 2012a. Enforced disappearances. http://www.amnesty.org/en/enforced-disappearances (Accessed May 17, 2012).

Amnesty International. 2012b. Sri Lanka, annual report 2012. http://www.amnesty.org/en/region/sri-lanka/report-2012#section-7-5 (Accessed November 12, 2012).

Amnesty International. n.d. International justice. https://www.amnesty.org/en/what-we-do/international-justice/ (Accessed May 27, 2015).

Asian Human Rights Commission. 2011. Pakistan: Extra-judicial killings ongoing with impunity, notably in balochistan. Asian Human Rights Commission. http://www.human-rights.asia/news/alrc-news/human-rights-council/hrc17/ALRC-CWS-17-04-2011/ (Accessed October 17, 2012).

Asian Human Rights Commission. 2012. Sri Lanka: Enforced disappearances have become a permanent weapon in the arsenal of suppression of dissent. http://www.humanrights.asia/news/forwarded-news/AHRC-FPR-042-2012 (Accessed November 2, 2012).

Asian Human Rights Commission. 2013. The state of human rights in bangladesh. http://odhikar.org/the-state-of-human-rights-in-bangladesh-2013/ (Accessed March 5, 2014).

Asian Legal Resource Center. 2012. Pakistan: Human Rights Council urged to act concerning pattern of extra-judicial killings and violations of freedom of expression in Pakistan. http://alrc.asia/pakistan-human-rights-council-urged-to-act-concerning-pattern-of-extra-judicial-killings-and-violations-of-freedom-of-expression-in-pakistan/ (Accessed November 3, 2013).

Bajoria, J. 2009. The Sri Lankan conflict. http://www.cfr.org/terrorist-organizations-and-networks/sri-lankan-conflict/p11407 (Accessed March 17, 2012).

Baker, B. 2007. *Multi-Choice Policing in Africa.* Uppsala: Nordic Africa Institute.

Ball, H. 2011. *Genocide: A Reference Handbook.* Santa Barbara, CA: ABC CLIO.

BBC News. 2005. Former Ugandan leader Obote dies. http://news.bbc.co.uk/2/hi/africa/4328834.stm (Accessed October 9, 2012).

BBC News. 2012. Sri Lanka country profile—Overview. http://www.bbc.co.uk/news/world-south-asia-11999611 (Accessed November 2, 2012).

Bittner, E. 1970. *The Functions of the Police in Modern Society: A Review of Background Factors, Current Practices, and Possible Role Models.* Baltimore, MD: National Institute of Mental Health.

Bittner, E. 1985. The capacity to use force as the core of the police role. In F. Elliston and M. Feldberg (Eds) *Moral Issues in Police Work*, pp. 15–26, Savage, MD: Rowman & Littlefield.

Center for Justice and International Law. 2012. The Rochela Massacre/Colombia. http://cejil.org/en/cases/la-rochela (Accessed May 21, 2012).

Central Intelligence Agency. 2012a. The world factbook: Uganda. https://www.cia.gov/library/publications/the-world-factbook/geos/ug.html (Accessed March 9, 2012).

Central Intelligence Agency. 2012b. The world factbook: Bangladesh. https://www.cia.gov/library/publications/the-world-factbook/geos/bg.html (Accessed March 16, 2012).

Chomsky, N. 2007. *Failed States: The Abuse of Power and the Assault on Democracy*. New York: Henry Holt.

Chowdhury, S. 2013. Bangladesh's landmark law banning torture. Amnesty International. https://www.amnesty.org/en/articles/blogs/2013/11/bangladeshs-landmark-law-banning-torture/ (Accessed December 5, 2013).

Cingranelli, D. and D. Richards. 2014. CIRI human rights data project. http://ciri.binghamton.edu (Accessed March 17, 2014).

Clarance, W. 2001. Woolf and Bandaranaike: The ironies of federalism in Sri Lanka. *The Political Quarterly* 72(4): 480–486.

Clarance, W. 2002. Conflict and community in Sri Lanka: William Clarance explores the origins and complexities of the Sri Lankan civil war. *History Today*, 52: 480–486.

Commonwealth Human Rights Initiative. 2006. *The Police, the People, the Politics: Police Accountability in Uganda*. New Delhi: Commonwealth Human Rights Initiative.

Courtney, J. 2010. Enforced disappearances in Colombia: A plea for synergy between the courts. *International Criminal Law Review* 10: 679–711.

Enforced Disappearance Information Exchange Network. 2008. Un warns about forced disappearances in colombia: EDIEC. http://www.ediec.org/news/newsitem/article/un-warns-about-forced-disappearances-in-colombia (Accessed May 21, 2012).

Englehart, N. 2009. State capacity, state failure, and human rights. *Journal of Peace Research* 46: 163–180.

Fich, B. 2014. *Law Enforcement Ethics: Classic and Contemporary Issues*. Thousand Oaks, CA: Sage.

Francis, D. 2005. *Civil Militia: Africa's Intractable Security Menace?* Aldershot: Ashgate.

Gerrity, E., T. Keane, and F. Tuma. 2001. *The Mental Health Consequences of Torture*. New York: Springer.

Goldfeld, A. E., R. F. Mollica, B. H. Pesavento, and S. V. Faraone. 1988. The physical and psychological sequelae of torture: Symptomatology and diagnosis. *Journal of the American Medical Association* 259(18): 2725–2729.

Goldsmith, A. 2002. Policing weak states: Citizen safety and state responsibility. *Policing & Society* 13: 3–21.

Haugaard, L. and K. Nichols. 2010. Breaking the silence: In search of Columbia's disappeared. Latin American working group and U.S. Office in Columbia. http://www.lawg.org/action-center/lawg-blog/69-general/810-breaking-the-silence-in-search-of-colombias-disappeared (Accessed March 17, 2014).

Heitzman, J. and R. Worden. 1988. *Bangladesh: A Country Study*. Washington, DC: United States Federal Research Division. Library of Congress.

Human Rights Watch. 1999. *Hostile to Democracy: The Movement System and Political Repression in Uganda*. New York: Human Rights Watch.

Human Rights Watch. 2003. Uganda: Idi Amin dies without facing justice. http://www.hrw.org/news/2003/08/18/uganda-idi-amin-dies-without-facing-justice (Accessed October 9, 2012).

Human Rights Watch. 2010. Pakistan: Extrajudicial executions by army in Swat: Military abuses undermine fight against Taliban. https://www.hrw.org/news/2010/07/16/pakistan-extrajudicial-executions-army-swat.

Human Rights Watch. 2011. *World Report, 2011: Events of 2010*. New York: Human Rights Watch.

Human Rights Watch. 2012a. Sri Lanka: Address rights rollback at review. http://www.hrw.org/news/2012/10/29/sri-lanka-address-rights-rollback-review (Accessed November 2, 2012).

Human Rights Watch. 2012b. The fear never leaves me. http://www.hrw.org/reports/2012/07/05/fear-never-leaves-me (Accessed May 3, 2013).

Human Rights Watch. 2012c. Sri Lanka: No progress on justice: Further repression of media. Civil Society, Minorities. http://www.hrw.org/news/2012/01/23/sri-lanka-no-progress-justice (Accessed December 5, 2013).

Human Rights Watch. 2013. *World Report 2013: The Events of 2012*. New York: Human Rights Watch.

Inter-American Court of Human Rights. 2007. Rochela Massacre v. Colombia. http://www. corteidh.or.cr/docs/casos/articulos/seriec_163_ing.pdf (Accessed December 5, 2013).

International Commission on Missing Persons. 2008. ICMP report: Columbia's response to enforced disappearances, overview and recommendations. http://www.ic-mp.org/ (Accessed April 20, 2010).

IVBMP. 2014. Extra-judicially killed. http://www.bygwaah.com/modules/bygwaah/ (Accessed October 25, 2013).

Jamal, A. 2012. *Extrajudicial Executions in Pakistan: Killing with Impunity*. Lahore: Human Rights Commission of Pakistan.

Jaranson, J. and M. Popkin. 1998. *Caring for Victims of Torture*. Washington, DC: American Psychiatric Press.

Jenne, E. 2003. Sri Lanka: A fragmented state. In R. Rotberg (Ed.) *State Failure and State Weakness in a Time of Terror*, pp. 219–244, Cambridge, MA: World Peace Foundation.

Khan, F. 2007. Corruption and the decline of the state in Pakistan. *Asian Journal of Political Science* 15: 219–247.

Kolb, R. and G. Gaggioli. 2013. *Research Handbook on Human Rights and Humanitarian Law*. Boston, MA: Edward Elgar.

Maguire, B. and P. Radosh (Eds). 1996. *The Past, Present, and Future of American Criminal Justice*. New York: Rowman & Littlefield.

Maritain, J. 1951. *Man and the State*. Chicago, IL: University of Chicago Press.

Middle East Watch. 1993. *Prison Conditions in Egypt: A Filthy System*. New York: Human Rights Watch.

Misra, A. and M. Clarke (Eds). 2012. *Pakistan's Stability Paradox: Domestic, Regional and International Dimensions*. Abingdon: Routledge.

Mutibwa, P. 1992. *Uganda Since Independence: A Story of Unfulfilled Hopes*. Trenton, NJ: Africa World Press.

Nissan, E. 1990. The generation of communal identities. In R. L. Stirrat (Ed.) *Sri Lanka: History and the Roots of Conflict*, pp. 19–44, London: Routledge.

Olayemi, A. 2002. *The Colonial Contest for the Nigerian Region, 1884–1900: A History of the German Participation*. London: LIT Verlag Münster.

Onwumechili, C. 1998. *African Democratization and Military Coups*. Westport, CT: Praeger.

Pate, M. and L. A. Gould, 2012. *Corporal Punishment Around the World*. Santa Barbara, CA: Praeger.

Patrick, S. 2011. *Weak Links: Fragile States, Global Threats, and International Security*. Oxford: Oxford University Press.

Perlez, J. and P. Shah, 2009. Pakistan army said to be linked to Swat killings. http://www. nytimes.com/2009/09/15/world/asia/15swat.html

Radsan, A. and R. Murphy. 2009. Due process and targeted killing of terrorists. *Cardozo Law Review* 31: 405.

Rintamaki, L., F. Weaver, P. Elbaum, E. Klama, and S. Miskevics. 2009. Persistence of traumatic memories in World War II prisoners of war. *Journal of the American Geriatrics Society* 57: 2257–262.

Saleh-Hanna, V. 2008. Nigerian penal interactions. In V. Saleh-Hanna and C. Affor (Eds) *Colonial Systems of Control: Criminal Justice in Nigeria*, pp. 173–222, Ottawa: University of Ottowa Press.

Sarkin, J. 2011. The role of the International Criminal Court (ICC) in reducing massive human rights violations such as enforced disappearances in Africa: Towards developing transitional justice strategies. *Studies in Ethnicity and Nationalism* 11: 130–142.

Scovazzi, T. and G. Citroni. 2007. *The Struggle Against Enforced Disappearance and the 2007 United Nations Convention*. Leiden: Martinus Nijhoff.

State Fragility Around the World
Søreide, T. and A. Williams (Eds). 2014. *Corruption, Grabbing and Development*. Cheltenham: Edward Elgar.
Spencer, J. 2007. Introduction: The power of the past. In J. Spencer (Ed.) *Sri Lanka: History and the Roots of Conflict*, pp. 1–18, London: Routledge.
Sweet, W. 2003. *Philosophical Theory and the Universal Declaration of Human Rights*. Ontario: University of Ottawa Press.
The Commonwealth. 2014. Pakistan: Constitution and politics. http://thecommonwealth.org/our-member-countries/pakistan/constitution-politics (Accessed October 20, 2013).
Truman, H. 1950. Special message to the Congress on the internal security of the United States. In G. Peters and J. Woolley (Eds) *The American Presidency Project*. http://www.presidency.ucsb.edu/ws/?pid=13576 (Accessed April 25, 2010).
United Nations. 1984. *United Nations Convention Against Torture and Other Cruel, Inhuman or Degrading Treatment or Punishment*. New York: United Nations.
United Nations. 1992. *Declaration on the Protection of All Persons from Enforced Disappearance*. Draft Resolution. New York: United Nations.
United Nations. 2010. Report of the working group on enforced or involuntary disappearance. Working Group on Enforced or Involuntary Disappearances. http://www.ohchr.org/EN/Issues/Disappearances/Pages/DisappearancesIndex.aspx (Accessed May 18, 2012).
United Nations. 2011. Report on alleged killings by Haitian national police and the response of state authorities. Office of the High Commissioner for Human Rights—Haiti Human Rights Section Minustah. http://www.ohchr.org/EN/Countries/LACRegion/Pages/HTReports.aspx (Accessed December 5, 2013).
United Nations. 2012. Treaty collections. http://treaties.un.org/pages/ViewDetails.aspx?src=TREATY&mtdsg_no=IV-16&chapter=4&lang=en (Accessed May 18, 2012).
United Press International. 2012. Plazas Vega sentence upheld in Colombia. http://www.upi.com/Top_News/World-News/2012/01/31/Plazas-Vega-sentence-upheld-in-Colombia/UPI-63711328035935/ (Accessed May 21, 2012).
U.S. Department of State. 2011. 2010 Human rights reports: Colombia. http://www.state.gov/j/drl/rls/hrrpt/2010/wha/154499.htm (Accessed May 21, 2012).
Vitkauskaite-Meurice, D. and J. Zilinskas. 2010. The concept of enforced disappearances in international law. *Jurisprudencija* 2: 197–214.
Voltaire. 1901. *The Works of Voltaire. A Contemporary Version. A Critique and Biography by John Morley, Notes by Tobias Smollett*. (W. F. Fleming, Trans.) New York: E.R. DuMont. http://oll.libertyfund.org/titles/2132 (Accessed April 24, 2010).
Waseem, M. 2011. *Patterns of Conflict in Pakistan: Implications for Policy*. Working Paper. Washington, DC: Brookings Institution.
Žilinskas, J. and W. Declerck. 2014. Targeted killing under international humanitarian law. *Jurisprudencija* 5: 8–18.

Punishment in
Fragile States

3

We who live in prison, and in whose lives there is no event but sorrow, have to measure time by throbs of pain, and the record of bitter moments.
—Oscar Wilde

While imprisonment is the dominant modality of formal corrections in most Western countries, even a quick global survey reveals that many different methods are used to punish law violators (Tonry 2009). As established in the first and second chapters of this volume, the variations can be partly explained by the relative stability of the government. Much like law enforcement and the judiciary, correctional systems are not immune from governmental abuse. Imprisonment, corporal punishment, and the death penalty are used in many fragile nations for reasons that have very little to do with "justice" (Smith 2004). As Rick Ruddell and Martin Urbina (2007, p. 87) aptly point out, "political leaders may use incarceration as a method of controlling protests, opposition to the regime, or persons who would not ordinarily fit under the definition of a criminal in a nation with a justice system that had high levels of legitimacy and was politically independent." This is especially the case with the imprisonment of political activists in countries such as the People's Republic of China, Myanmar (Burma), and Saudi Arabia.

It should also be noted that the weak economic structure of many fragile nations may influence the type of punishment imposed. As modern correctional facilities and technologies related to offender monitoring are typically expensive to fund and operate, it follows that fragile states adopt methods of punishment to reflect both the resources available and the sensibilities of those in power.

Loïc Wacquant (2009, p. xvii) characterizes prison not simply as an instrument of the criminal justice system designed to punish law violators, but instead as a "core political institution." We concur with this characterization and assert that the intersection of polity and punishment would be difficult to overstate. Dario Melossi (2008, p. 5) likewise agrees, "because one of the main powers of the State is the power to punish, penality is particularly apt to be used to define the powers and boundaries of sovereignty."

While the empirical literature in this area is somewhat limited, many studies have examined correlations between incarceration rates, death penalty retention, corporal punishment, and various measures of political power and repression (see e.g., Gould and Pate 2011, 2012; Jacobs and Kleban 2003;

Killias 1986; Miethe et al. 2005; Neapolitan 2001; Ruddell and Urbina 2007). As above, the weight of evidence suggests that punishment can, and many times is, used for purposes well beyond the simple punishment of law violators. In particular, we find that fragile governments are more likely to use both incarceration and acute physical punishments (i.e., capital punishment and corporal punishment) and at much higher rates compared with their more stable counterparts.

Emphasizing this point, David Jacobs and Richard Kleban (2003, p. 748) caution, "researchers should not overlook political arrangements when they attempt to explain punishments." This is a particularly apt admonishment when considering countries in the midst of internal turmoil. Research such as that performed by Sabine Carey (2010) suggests that human rights are more likely to be violated when internal conflict is high and in times of extreme political unrest (e.g., civil war). During these periods, governments tend to increase their use of torture and political imprisonment.

The dominant theoretical explanation for the relationship between polity and punishment draws heavily from the work of conflict theorists. The perspective put forth by scholars such as William Chambliss (1999), Chambliss and Milton Mankoff (1979), and Richard Quinney (2000) holds that punishment is used as "a tool of oppression by those in power who seek to control segments of the population that challenge existing social, economic and "power arrangements." Not surprisingly, power and conflict are two concepts that are deeply entwined. As Ralf Dahrendorf (1969, p. 165) states, "In every social organization some positions are entrusted with a right to exercise control over other positions in order to ensure effective coercion; it means, in other words, that there is a differential distribution of power and authority." Commenting on Dahrendorf's notion of differential power and authority, Quinney (2000, p. 73) observes, "the differential distribution of power produces conflict between competing groups, and conflict, in turn, is rooted in the competition for power. Wherever human beings live together, conflict and a struggle for power will be found."

Issues of power are also central to understanding how punishment manifests in society. While issues of economic control have received the greatest attention in the scholarly literature (see, e.g., Box and Hale 1986; Greenberg 1977; Hale 1989; Jankovic 1977), the work of Michel Foucault (1977) helps us move beyond solely economic explanations of social control and instead frames the central question as one of cultural context. In an oft-cited quote, Foucault (1977, p. 82) states that punishment reform was prompted largely by a desire "not to punish less, but to punish better; to punish with an attenuated severity perhaps, but in order to punish with more universality and necessity; to insert the power to punish more deeply into the social body."

Extending this line of thought, it is reasonable to assume as we do, that governments may select particular modalities of punishment to fit their localized power requirements. Drawing from Foucauldian thought, "particular modalities" exist as a "technology" of control. As Foucault (1977, p. 215) states, "'Discipline' may be identified neither with an institution nor with an apparatus; it is a type of power, a modality for its exercise, comprising a whole set of instruments, techniques, procedures, levels of application, targets; it is a 'physics' or an 'anatomy' of power, a 'technology.'"

This framing permits Foucault (1977, p. 221) to comment on power relations as an aspect of governance, "Power is exercised only over free subjects, and only insofar as they are free." Foucault (1977, p. 221) continues, "Slavery is not a power relationship when man is in chains (In this case it is a question of a physical relationship of constraint)."

In this, he focuses the discussion around certain intractable social forces. As he states, "At the very heart of the power relationship, and constantly provoking it, are the recalcitrance of the will and the intransigence of freedom" (Foucault 1977, pp. 221–222). In so doing, he gives the reader a very useful lens through which to assail the problem of oppression: "The analysis, elaboration, and bringing into question of power relations and the 'agonism' between power relations and the intransitivity of freedom is a permanent political task inherent in all social existence" (Foucault 1977, p. 223).

When taken together, these assumptions about the nature of power, government, and technologies of control provide a strong theoretical foundation from which to explore punishment in fragile nations.

By nesting these concepts within a complex adaptive systems framework, we can better understand the ebb and flow of power relations. We see how tensions within and perturbations to the established order are managed by the ruling power interests. In some cases, this manifests as oppression and the broadening of acts that are defined as "criminal." In others, we see the normalization of an economic caste structure. In yet others, we see the extant order toppled as society shifts into a new phase of power distribution. In each instance, the governing principle is management of threats to order. Nowhere do we see this laid more bare than in the modalities of punishment that a society chooses.

Incarceration

Previous cross-national research on the relationship between political repression and modalities of punishment can be divided into three general categories: studies of incarceration; studies of capital punishment; and studies of corporal punishment. This research provides a number of important findings. In one of the earliest examinations of the use of incarceration, Killias (1986) analyses the relationship between penal severity, unemployment, and power concentration. He finds that resource considerations largely drive the use of incarceration, with poorer countries being less likely to rely on secure confinement when compared with richer nations. Economics are not the only force behind the reliance on incarceration, however, as countries with dictatorships and greater levels of economic disparity also tend to use more severe sanctions. His findings partially support Durkheim's (1900) hypothesis that development influences penal severity, but Killias (1986, p. 113) cautions, "high income concentration and non-democratic forms of government do not cause under-development, but rather that these forms of power concentration are likely to occur at certain stages of development."

In their cross-national examination of incarceration rates in 13 democracies, Jacobs and Kleban (2003, p. 725) ask, "why does the proportion of the population that is incarcerated differ across societies, and why do these rates fluctuate over time within the same society?" Part of the answer, they contend, can be found in the political arrangements of a given society. Ultimately, they find that corporatism and federalism are highly correlated with incarceration rates among the sample of nations included in their analysis. Specifically, they find "imprisonment rates are most substantial in nations where the public has the greatest political influence, whereas centralized, more hierarchical political arrangements contribute to an integrative penal system that stresses restitutive rather than harsh exclusionary reactions to crime" (Jacobs and Kleban 2003, p. 746). In something of a surprise, the findings did not support the idea that more conservative governments rely on incarceration.

In his study of punitiveness, Jerome Neapolitan (2001) questions why some countries differ in their propensity to use incarceration.* He asserts that there is a relationship between the level of development, unemployment, wealth disparity, and high levels of incarceration. Specifically, he posits that less developed countries, with higher unemployment and greater inequality in the distribution of economic resources, would be more likely to use incarceration compared with nations with higher levels of development, lower unemployment, and more equality of economic resources. Ultimately, findings did not support the idea that less developed nations tend to rely on carceral punishments more than their highly developed counterparts, but consistent with Killias' (1986) findings, more restrictive countries were found to be more punitive.

The Death Penalty

In order to determine salient factors that may be related to death penalty retention, Terrance Miethe et al. (2005, p. 122) examine economic development,

---

* While Neapolitan also examined the death penalty and prison conditions, his findings relating to the use of incarceration are most relevant for present concerns.

primary religion, political conditions (e.g., civil liberties, political rights, and stability), and extrajudicial executions. They observe that retention-ist countries tend to have the following characteristics: "Middle East, Asia, or Caribbean regions; dominant religions other than Christianity; lower economic development; lower political 'voice'; lower political stability; and recent histories of extrajudicial killings." Further, countries with more politi-cal instability have substantially increased odds (about 2.3 times higher) of retaining the death penalty compared with more stable countries. This sug-gests a country's political condition strongly influences how punishment manifests in its criminal justice system.

David Greenberg and Valerie West (2008) present what is perhaps the most extensive analysis of international trends in the retention of capital punishment. They examine a number of economic, political, cultural, and social variables to determine which variables predict the retention of capi-tal punishment. Using indicators of political rights, ethnic fractionaliza-tion, literacy, life expectancy, the structure of a country's legal system, and a country's dominant religious faith, they produced a model that can correctly predict a given state's use of capital punishment 85.33% of the time.

Their findings also reflect that measures of economic activity are not significantly related to the death penalty, especially the gross domestic product (GDP) (a finding somewhat similar to Miethe et al. 2005). In their models, measures of political rights had the most robust predictive power, followed closely by the legal system and religion. These findings suggest that countries where citizens have relatively fewer rights are more likely to employ capital punishment. Similarly, countries with a common law legal system are more likely to retain the death penalty. Furthermore, countries with a larger proportion of Catholics in their population are less likely to retain capital punishment. Much like Miethe et al. (2005), Greenberg and West (2008) find Islamic countries are no more or less likely to retain the death penalty com-pared with any other group. Finally, Greenberg and West do note that coun-tries that imprison more convicted offenders are also more likely to have the death penalty as a possible sanction. Thus, the overall level of punitiveness is clearly related to the use of capital punishment.

Rick Ruddell and Martin Urbina have made many notable contributions to the cross-national punishment literature. In their 2004 study, Ruddell and Urbina examine the minority threat hypothesis and punishment (specifically incarceration rates and the abolition of the death penalty) across 140 nations, controlling for modernization, political repression, violent crime, and eco-nomic stress. Regarding political repression, they note, "it is plausible that imprisonment is used by fledgling governments to control for increases in political, economic, or social uncertainty associated with state formation" (Ruddell and Urbina 2007, p. 917). In the alternative, they state that impris-onment could be "used as a mechanism to maintain or enhance government legitimacy" (Ruddell and Urbina 2007, p. 917). Their findings indicate that punitiveness in the punishment system is related to population heterogeneity; however, political arrangements are also important. Specifically, they observe that more autocratic nations rely heavily on incarceration and democratic nations are more likely to have abolished the death penalty.

More recent research from Ruddell and Urbina (2007) explores the relationship between political repression and punishment. Their analysis reveals that repressive governments tend to limit freedom of the press and punishments tend to be harsher under repressive regimes. They conclude, "nations where the government cannot provide economic security, control ethnic or religious strife, guarantee basic rights or liberties, or is otherwise fragile, are at higher risk of using criminal justice systems for coercion, control, and repression of dissent" (Ruddell and Urbina 2007, p. 101).

This brief review of the political repression literature documents that punishment is strongly shaped by a nation's political structure. However, research in this area has tended to focus only on incarceration and the death penalty. While an exploration of those sanctions is important and has yielded insight into punishment structures, an examination of the relationship between political repression and other common forms of formal sanction, namely, corporal punishment, is still needed. Though they did not focus on political repression, two previous comparative examinations of contemporary corporal punishment practices form the basis for the literature in this area. As such, they will be discussed in detail in the following sections.

Corporal Punishment

In our examinations of global corporal punishment practices, we have evaluated various measures of social inequality to determine which factors best predict the use of corporal punishment against criminal offenders (Gould and Pate 2010, 2011; Pate and Gould 2012). Our findings indicate that the predominance of Islam is an important determinant of corporal punishment, but that effect is strongly conditioned by the amount of economic inequality in a given country (Pate and Gould 2010). Specifically, predominantly Muslim countries are more likely to include corporal punishment as an available sanction compared with other countries where other religions are more prevalent; however, in cases where wealth is more equally distributed (as measured by the Gini coefficient), the likelihood of corporal punishment is markedly decreased. As a stand-alone construct, the Gini coefficient is the best predictor of corporal punishment availability. Notably, there is no statistically significant relationship between corporal punishment and GDP or the incarceration rate per 100,000 people. Thus, it is not simply a lack of economic resources that drives the use of corporal punishment.

In a further study of corporal punishment practices, we (Pate and Gould 2012) examined the minority threat hypothesis and its possible relationship to the use of corporal punishment by the international community. We found that countries with higher levels of ethnolinguistic fractionalization are more likely to employ corporal punishment. This led us to conclude that "the degree to which the population of a given nation is fractionalized has a demonstrable bearing on whether that nation will employ corporal punishment against criminal offenders" (Pate and Gould 2012, p. 223). Of most importance to our present consideration is the finding that countries that extend fewer political rights and civil liberties to their citizens are more likely to use corporal punishment.

A consistent theme in each of the aforementioned studies is the relationship between power and modalities of punishment. Power that manifests in the political or economic system of a given society extends into the realm of punishment. To make sense of this observed relationship with specific regard to corporal punishment, it is helpful to recall the words of Foucault (1977, pp. 121–122), "At the very heart of the power relationship, and constantly provoking it, are the recalcitrance of the will and the intransigence of freedom." In this framing, Foucault implies that the modalities of power assertion are linked and reactive to the will and freedom of the individual. Often, the body of the corporally punished individual is permanently marked as one who has received official sanction. With this marking, the power structure is visibly reiterated in the body of the offender. Of course, the offender need not be obviously scarred for the power relationship to be reasserted.

The positioning and visibility of the power structure are crucial for Foucault. Following his reasoning, more sustainable states are able to instill a "…surveillance [that] is permanent in its effects, even if it is discontinuous in its action; that the perfection of power should tend to render its actual exercise unnecessary…" (Foucault 1977, p. 195). Accordingly, in those places where such continuity is undermined by governmental failure, more visible technologies of punishment would be necessary to reinforce the state's power to circumscribe formal social boundaries.

This said, Foucault's perspective suffers as Poulantzas (2000, p. 77) states, "…[from an underestimation] of the role of law in the exercise of power within modern societies… also… the role of the State itself and [he] fails to understand the function of repressive apparatuses (army, police, judicial system, etc.) as a means of exercising physical violence… located at the heart of the modern state."

Acknowledging this "underestimation," one of the goals of this chapter is to demonstrate the determinative role that state character, openness, fragility, and function each have on the delivery of punishment. To that end, we note that countries with more repressive regimes tend to rely on high levels of incarceration (Neapolitan 2001) and retain the death penalty (Ruddell and

Urbina 2004; Miethe et al. 2005; Greenberg and West 2008). Moreover, in those countries where power rests in the hands of the very few, corporal punishment is more likely to persist (Gould and Pate 2010). As we have repeatedly discussed, a key aspect of punishment is control (i.e., suppression) of dissent. A common way that this manifests is the state's direct co-optation of the criminal justice system by using political imprisonment as a means of individualized suppression.

Political Imprisonment

Bo Kyi and Hannah Scott (2010, p. 4) note, "nothing is more revealing about the situation of human rights in a country than the existence of political prisoners." Despite a long global history of governments unlawfully detaining citizens for beliefs that run contrary to the regime in power, there is little consensus regarding the definition of political imprisonment (Martin 2012). Kyi and Scott (2010, p. 4) go on to say, "anyone imprisoned for peacefully speaking out against their government, for practicing their religion, or for their culture, race or gender can be considered a political prisoner, a term often used interchangeably with prisoner of conscience, which is a designation used by Amnesty International and sometimes the United Nations." The U.S. State Department, Bureau of Democracy, Human Rights, and Labor provides a more detailed definition. A person can be labeled a political prisoner if

1. The person is incarcerated in accordance with a law that is, on its face, illegitimate; the law may be illegitimate if the defined offense either impermissibly restricts the exercise of a human right; or is based on race, religion, nationality, political opinion, or membership in a particular group;
2. The person is incarcerated pursuant to a law that is on its face legitimate, where the incarceration is based on false charges where the underlying motivation is based on race, religion, nationality, political opinion, or membership in a particular group; or
3. The person is incarcerated for politically motivated acts, pursuant to a law that is on its face legitimate, but who receives unduly harsh and disproportionate treatment or punishment because of race, religion, nationality, political opinion, or membership in a particular group; this definition generally does not include those who, regardless of their motivation, have gone beyond advocacy and dissent to commit acts of violence. (Martin 2012, p. 3)

While the United States has provided a very detailed definition of political prisoner criteria, international bodies have been very slow at setting forth similar bright-line criteria. On October 3, 2012, the Council of Europe

Parliamentary Assembly (PACE) became the first major intergovernmental organization to define political imprisonment with Resolution 1900. Article 3 of the resolution states that a person is a political prisoner

   a. If the detention has been imposed in violation of one of the funda-
      mental guarantees set out in the European Convention on Human
      Rights (ECHR) and its Protocols, in particular freedom of thought,
      conscience and religion, freedom of expression and information,
      freedom of assembly and association;
   b. If the detention has been imposed for purely political reasons with-
      out connection to any offence;
   c. If, for political motives, the length of the detention or its conditions
      are clearly out of proportion to the offence the person has been found
      guilty of or is suspected of;
   d. If, for political motives, he or she is detained in a discriminatory
      manner as compared to other persons; or,
   e. If the detention is the result of proceedings which were clearly unfair
      and this appears to be connected with political motives of the author-
      ities." (Martin 2012, p. 34, para. 10)

Article 4 of Resolution 1900 further clarifies:

Those deprived of their personal liberty for terrorist crimes shall not be considered political prisoners if they have been prosecuted and sentenced for such
crimes according to national legislation and the European Convention on
Human Rights. (Martin 2012, ETS No. 5)

There is a significant overlap between the United States' definition and the European Council's definition; however, it is interesting to note that Article 4 of the resolution places terrorists in a separate category. It is necessary to make this distinction, given that much of the world is in some way impacted by the global war on terror. The president of Freedomhouse (an independent monitoring agency for civil liberties and human rights), David J. Kramer, praised Resolution 1900 for its unequivocal criteria, which he believes will thwart "attempts by authoritarian states to deny the existence of politically motivated cases and allows the Council to hold all of its member nations accountable for their human rights record" (Freedomhouse 2012).

The United Nations has yet to outline specific criteria for political impris-
onment, but it is likely that will change in the coming years. While the issue of political imprisonment affects many people worldwide, Myanmar (Burma) and China provide perhaps the best examples of its use and consequences.

Myanmar (Burma)

While definitive numbers on the rates of political imprisonment worldwide are difficult to obtain, estimates for some countries are available.

In Myanmar, for example, some scholars believe that the current number could be as low as 840 (Martin 2012). In reality, there may be as many as 2000 political prisoners behind bars (Kyi and Scott 2010). Amnesty International (2007) documents a host of human rights abuses in Myanmar, including the detention of 700 political prisoners, with some receiving prison sentences as long as 9.5 years. Additionally, there is an official policy in place whereby family or friends or both of accused political prisoners can be held hostage until the accused turns himself or herself in to the authorities (Amnesty International 2007). Other significant issues include an increase in "enforced disappearances since the crackdown, including at least 72 individuals whose whereabouts the authorities have failed to account for ... [and] failure by the Myanmar authorities to account for the number of people killed during the crackdown" (Amnesty International 2007, para. 5).

The problem of political imprisonment in Myanmar can be traced directly to the military junta that ruled the nation for more than 50 years. Prior to the military takeover, Myanmar was largely ruled by a number of rebel groups for whom fighting was a part of daily life (Reid and Grosberg 2005). The national government eventually regained control of the country; however, by 1958 Myanmar was in economic ruin due to a number of failed development projects (Reid and Grosberg 2005). The then prime minister, U Nu, voluntarily handed control of the country over to the military in 1958, a move which some contend paved the way for complete military control of the country (Lwin 2011). Because economic upheaval and violence defined the country for so many years, the citizenry initially welcomed military rule (Reid and Grosberg 2005). However, the situation for most of Myanmar's citizens did not improve under the military junta.

Military rule continued until elections were held in 1960, at which point U Nu was reelected—a turn that brought political turmoil back to the forefront. Just two years later, a new leader, Ne Win, took control of the government (Reid and Grosberg 2005). However, U Nu did not voluntarily cede governmental control to Ne Win as he did with the military. Rather, Ne Win rose to power via a coup d'état initiated by the National Military Council (OECD 2013). Following the coup, Ne Win abolished the Burmese Parliament, established a 17-member revolutionary council, and imprisoned U Nu along with several of his ministers (Reid and Grosberg 2005). After seizing control of the government, Ne Win began to isolate Myanmar from the rest of the international community (Taylor 2015). His stated ultimate goal was the creation of a socialist state (Reid and Grosberg 2005). The Revolutionary Council established the Burmese Way to Socialism, which combined various elements of Marxism, Buddhism, and Mysticism to help guide the nation through the transition to a socialist state (OECD 2013). In addition to recommending a transition to socialism, the 28-point manifesto recommended, "the nationalization of all major industries, rejected parliamentary democracy, increased the role of the military, and reduced foreign influence. In the phase that followed 1962, Burma transformed from being one of Asia's most prosperous countries into one of the world's poorest" (OECD 2013, p. 59). It should be noted that the transition to socialism was not popular among most people in the nation (Reid and Grosberg 2005). It was also during this time that the government began to make extensive use of political imprisonment (Taylor 2015) with other human rights violations also becoming commonplace (OECD 2013).

By the 1980s, the citizenry had grown tired of their largely ineffective government. Protests for democracy ensued (Reid and Grosberg 2005). Initially, the protests were largely composed of students in Yangon, but the prodemocracy sentiment began to spread throughout the country, drawing support from a wide cross section of society (e.g., farmers, lawyers, and civil servants) (OECD 2013). The demonstrations culminated in the 8888 uprising, a nationwide protest that occurred on August 8, 1988 (OECD 2013). Not surprisingly, the government reacted violently, killing an estimated 3000 people during a six-week period in late 1988 (Reid and Gosberg 2005). Some estimate the death toll to be as high as 10,000 (Lwin 2011). Although Ne Win was forced to resign in response, the military remained in power (OECD 2013) and implemented a number of repressive regulations. The new restrictions included a ban on the assembly of more than five people and a law requiring any assembly of persons to receive permission from the government (Lwin 2011). The regime attempted to mollify the people through the creation of the State Law and Order Restoration Council, which abandoned the Burmese Way to Socialism and permitted some private sector expansion (OECD 2013). The repressive military junta changed the name of the country to Myanmar (Green and Mitchell 2007; OECD 2013) and remained in power until 2011.

To better understand Myanmar's path, it is also instructive to retrace the nation's history with regard to national elections. In 1990, the government allowed the first elections in over 30 years. In those elections, the ruling National Unity Party (NUP) lost to the National League for Democracy (NLD) party by a landslide margin, with nearly 80% of the seats in Parliament going to NLP members (Lwin 2011). The ruling NUP party disregarded the election results and reacted brutally by targeting NLP opponents (Reid and Grosberg 2005; Green and Mitchell 2007).

In the months following the election, the government raided the offices of NLP members and arrested key leaders of the party (Reid and Grosberg 2005). During this drive, some NLP members were able to flee the country and seek refuge elsewhere (Human Rights Watch 2010). All told, 100 parliamentary members were disqualified, imprisoned, exiled, or killed (Reid and Grosberg 2005). Throughout the tenure of military rule in Myanmar, innumerable political dissidents were imprisoned. Saw Naing Naing, a member of Parliament who was arrested by the government following the sham election, was imprisoned for nearly a decade (Hague 2007). He was released in 1999, but imprisoned again just one year later when he signed a statement denouncing the repressive government (Hague 2007). Naing "received a 21-year sentence for violating laws which ordain the junta's official approval of anything written and which allow the regime to punish all threats to internal stability" (Hague 2007).

Aung San Suu Kyi, leader of the NLP and the daughter of the much beloved leader General Aung San, who helped free Myanmar from British and Japanese control, was placed under house arrest on July 20, 1989 (Green and Mitchell 2007). Kyi was kept under house arrest for six years without being charged with any crime. She spent 14 of the next 21 years under house arrest (Lwin 2011). Kyi was awarded the Nobel Peace Prize in 1991, making her the most famous political prisoner in Myanmar. When she received the honor, students celebrated by demonstrating at Rangoon University, a move that resulted in the imprisonment of nearly 200 demonstrators (Lwin 2011).

International reaction to the repressive regime was mixed at best, with some countries advocating for punitive sanctions and others promoting ways to actively engage the government to effect change (Green and Mitchell 2007). The resulting disjointed approach to nation-building proved largely unsuccessful until 2010, when, for the first time in two decades, Myanmar held governmental elections. In total, 49 political parties took part in the elections, with the largest ethnic minority party being the Shan Nationalities Democratic Party (Lwin 2011). Interestingly, the NLD did not take part in the election process because they felt that the military was once again controlling rigged elections (Lwin 2011). Much of the international community concurred, with the United States going so far as to declare them as "neither free nor fair, [having] failed to meet any of the internationally accepted standards associated with legitimate elections" (Lwin 2011, p. 533). While the 2010 elections were neither free nor open, they did present a path to potential change. Kyi was released from house arrest just after the November 2010 elections (Lwin 2011). In 2012, the NLD won 45 seats in Parliament, marking a dramatic shift in the country.

Myanmar has released a significant number of political prisoners, many of whom were dissidents (Martin 2012). Most recently, 651 inmates were released, and of those over 300 were political prisoners (Martin 2012). Many of the releases had conditions attached; conditions that prohibit political prisoners from reengaging in the political process, thus continuing to deny them basic rights of expression and free association (Amnesty International 2012). While this release does represent a small step for human rights, there are still many political prisoners in Myanmar (Martin 2012). Again though, it is difficult to obtain accurate estimates of just how many remain captive. As Martin (2012, p. 4) notes, "President Thein Sein told reporters in Bali,

Indonesia, on November 20, 2011, that there were no political prisoners in Myanmar and that all prisoners have broken the law." Part of the difficulty in obtaining accurate estimates stems from the opaque nature of Myanmar's political and judicial systems (Martin 2012). Adding to these difficulties is the fact that individuals are still arrested without the benefit of formal judicial proceedings.

The Assistance Association for Political Prisoners (Myanmar) estimates that hundreds of people have been arrested for political reasons by the current government (Martin 2012). Among those detained without charges include those who "have generally either been engaging in public protests (purportedly legalized by Myanmar's new Peaceful Demonstration and Gathering Law, passed in December 2011) or were suspected of having ties to ethnic resistance groups, particularly the Kachin Independence Army (KIA)" (Martin 2012, p. 5). Myanmar remains a country in flux, with elements of the old repressive regime still clearly evident. While the release of political prisoners does represent a positive step in the troubled nation, more time is needed to assess whether recent changes will lead to a freer and more democratic society.

The People's Republic of China

Political imprisonment in China is a serious issue that persists even as it has increased its presence and prominence in the global economy. China ranks among the category of states that display the warning signs of failure (they rank number 76 on the Fragile States Index, with the most problematic areas identified as "mounting demographic pressures" and "uneven economic development"). One of the most common methods used by the Chinese government to arrest political dissidents is the *xinfang* system, or petitioning system. This was not always the case, however, as petitioning was the primary method used by the government to mediate government/citizen issues (Li and O'Brien 2008).

The petitioning system, which dates back to imperial China, "allows Chinese citizens to seek official redress for alleged abuse by local officials ... [Additionally, petitioning allows citizens who are] unsatisfied with decisions handed down by such officials or local courts to complain in writing or in person at special petition bureaus throughout the country" (Human Rights Watch 2008, p. 52). Human Rights Watch (2005) reports that over 10 million petitions were filed in 2004, most of which (40%) were filed against the police. Petitions against the government constituted 33% of all complaints, followed by corruption (13%) and injustice (11%) (Human Rights Watch 2005). Citizens have the right to file a petition, but it is very common for petitioners to be targeted by the government, intimidated, beaten, kidnapped, and imprisoned in retaliation (Human Rights Watch 2005).

One widespread method of political imprisonment is the use of an administrative sanction, called Re-education Through Labor (RTL). With RTL, the government can hold people for up to four years without a trial (Chinese Human Rights Defenders 2009). First introduced by the newly formed Chinese Communist Party in the 1950s, this sanction was aimed at imprisoning political dissidents (Chinese Human Rights Defenders 2009). Little has changed since the 1950s, as RTL is still used as a tool to oppress a host of different constituencies including people who suffer from drug addiction and those who engage in prostitution, as well as those "petitioning, advocating for human rights, or being a member of an illegal religion such as a Christian house church or Falun Gong" (Chinese Human Rights Defenders 2009, p. 3). According to figures released by the Chinese government, 190,000 people are being held in RTL camps. This number must be considered with some caution, as China is one of the more opaque governments with regard to "official" statistics. The true number is likely much higher (Amnesty International 2010). Interviews with former prisoners paint a particularly bleak picture of prison conditions and the treatment of detainees. According to the Chinese Human Rights Defenders (2009, p. 3), prisoners held in labor camps are subjected to

> frequent beatings and torture inflicted by fellow detainees as instructed by camp staff; heavy, coerced and unpaid labor in hazardous working conditions; poor diet and unsanitary living conditions; extortion by camp administration; little to no exercise; being barred from family visits; and extremely limited medical care. The conditions are so poor that they constitute a gross violation of the right not to be tortured or subjected to other cruel, inhuman and degrading treatment.

RTL is one form of political imprisonment among many that are routinely used in China. There are countless examples of political dissidents being prosecuted in the Chinese judicial system. In 1989, Qisheng Jiang was arrested and imprisoned for 17 months for his participation in a protest against the Tiananmen Square massacre (Popescu and Seymour-Jones 2007). A decade later, Jiang was "charged with propagating and instigating subversion for writing and distributing an open letter to commemorate the tenth anniversary of the 4 June crackdown in Tiananmen Square" (Popescu and Seymour-Jones 2007, p. 10).

Following his second arrest, Jiang wrote a memoir recounting his experience at a detention center (before he was transferred to prison). According to Jiang (2012), political prisoners tend to be more closely monitored by prison officials to ensure that they are not communicating with the outside world. However, Jiang (2012, p. 6) also states, "political prisoners are generally treated with more respect than ordinary prisoners. ... [He was] able to resist certain humiliations, like having to stand with his hands on his head ... because many in the prison, guards and fellow inmates alike, respect him for what he stands for." Despite having more respect inside prisons, in his memoir (and in various open letters) Jiang (2012) describes the five prison facilities in which he was housed as "dismal."

Liu Xiaobo is one of the more famous political prisoners in China. In 2010, Xiaobo, an ardent opponent of the Communist Party, as well as a literary critic, professor, and human rights activist was found guilty of "inciting subversion of state power." He was subsequently sentenced to 11 years' imprisonment and 2 years deprivation of his political rights (*The Guardian* 2011). The charges were brought because Xiaobo had written a series of six papers critical of the Communist Party, and demanded that China respect human rights and the rule of law (Béja 2011).

This was not the first time that Xiaobo was labeled a political subversive. In 1989, during the Tiananmen Square massacre, Xiaobo and three others attempted to negotiate the safe evacuation of the student demonstrators (Béja 2011). When that proved unsuccessful and the massacre occurred, he was apprehended by the police while attempting to locate his partners (Béja 2011). The government labeled him as one of the "black hands" behind the prodemocracy movement. For his involvement in the demonstration, he spent 26 months in detention, his release coming only after authoring a self-criticism (Béja 2011).

Jiang and Xiaobo are just two political prisoners among thousands. All but a few suffer in anonymity or as Xiaobo (2012) describes them, they are "nameless heroes." Following the Tiananmen Square massacre, a number of students received especially severe sentences as a result of their participation. Xiaobo (2012, p. 9) helps give names to the nameless and describes the plight of students such as Wang Yi who was "sentenced to eleven years for blocking a military vehicle ... and Chen Lantao, a youngster from Qingdao, [who] got eighteen years merely for making a protest speech in public once the massacre had begun." He goes on to say, "there are uncountable others all across the country, and many remain behind bars today" (Xiaobo 2012, p. 9).

Xiaobo was awarded the Nobel Peace Prize in 2010 for his human rights work in China. This was an enormous accomplishment, as the Nobel Prize committee had never before awarded the prize to a Chinese citizen (Béja 2011). He was not permitted to have a representative there on his behalf and the government barred hundreds of people who were on his guest list (drafted by his wife, Liu Xia) from attending. His wife was placed under house arrest (and still remains under house arrest), making her attendance impossible. Xiaobo's absence was acknowledged with an empty chair.

Former Prisoners as Agents of Terror

As a kind of coda to our examination of corrections in fragile states, there is one more nexus that needs brief consideration. It is well established that failing regimes often use imprisonment to secure their hold on society. While this is the primary way in which illegitimate imprisonment is used, there is another utility for prisons in fragile states that is far more grim and cynical. In short, if the machinations of your regime require the service of people with a penchant for violence, there is one place in society where a great concentration may be found.

John Mueller (2000) writes about genocide in the former Yugoslavia and Rwanda during the 1990s. In his research, Mueller offers a novel perspective on both conflicts by asserting that ethnic rivalries ultimately played less of a role in the violence than did the excesses of unleashed criminal gangs. Regarding Serbia, Mueller (2000, p. 8) reports that fighters loyal to Slobodan Milosevic "were composed... not of committed nationalists or ideologues, nor of locals out to get their neighbors, nor of ordinary people whipped into a frenzy by demagogues and the media, but of common criminals and hoodlums recruited for the task." As he goes on to clarify, "[P]oliticians urged underworld and hooligan groups to get into the action... thousands of prison inmates, promised shortened sentences and enticed by the prospect that they could 'take whatever booty you can,' were released for the war effort" (Mueller 2000, p. 8). Tim Judah (1997, p. 233) offers something very similar in his account of violence in the region. As he states, "[R]eal psychopaths were rampaging across the countryside indulging in cruel, bizarre, and sadistic killings" (Judah 1997, p. 233).

The situation was eerily similar in Rwanda, according to both Mueller (2000) and Gourevitch (1998). As violence began to unfold, Hutu-trained militia (interahamwe) began forming. According to Gerard Prunier (1995, pp. 231–232), there was a "dark carnival" atmosphere fueled by drunkenness where "militias crumbled into armed banditry."

In his concluding observations, Mueller (2000, p. 25) makes a point that has a direct bearing on our theme of complex adaptive systems. Recalling his primary thesis that ethnic conflict was in many regards a mere backstop to more carnal predilections, he states, "Ethnicity, then, was important as an ordering, organizational or predictive device" (Mueller 2000, p. 25). He holds that "the crucial dynamic was not in the risings of neighbor against neighbor" but in the violence visited on communities by "comparatively small groups of violent thugs" (Mueller 2000, p. 25).

What these small-band violent incursions represent in a more mechanistic sense are perturbations to a fragile stasis. Often fanned by extremists, hordes of ultraviolent criminals and opportunists provided just enough momentum to push society into a chaotic tailspin beyond the system's ability to correct.

References

Amnesty International. 2007. Myanmar needs a comprehensive international arms embargo. https://www.amnesty.org/en/documents/ASA16/014/2007/en/ (Accessed March 4, 2014).

Amnesty International. 2010. Annual report: Myanmar (Burma). http://www.amnestyusa. org/research/reports/annual-report-myanmar-burma-2010 (Accessed March 5, 2014).

Amnesty International. 2012. Myanmar: Political prisoner release 'major step' but gates must open 'even wider'. https://www.amnesty.org/en/latest/news/2012/01/myanmar-political-prisoner-release/ (Accessed March 3, 2014).

Beja, J. (Ed.) 2011. *The Impact of China's 1989 Tiananmen Massacre.* London: Routledge.

Box, S. and C. Hale. 1986. Unemployment, crime and imprisonment, and the enduring problem of prison overcrowding. In R. Matthews and J. Young (Eds) *Confronting Crime*, pp. 72–99, London: Sage.

Carey, S. 2010. The use of repression as a response to domestic dissent. *Political Studies* 58: 167–186.

Chambliss, W. J. 1999. *Power, Politics, and Crime.* Boulder, CO: Westview.

Chambliss, W. J. and M. Mankoff. 1979. *Whose Law? What Order?: Conflict Approach to Criminology.* Hoboken, NJ: Wiley.

Chinese Human Rights Defenders. 2009. Report on re-education through labor camps. http://docs.law.gwu.edu/facweb/dclarke/public/CHRD_RTL_Report.pdf

Dahrendorf, R. 1969. *Class and Class Conflict in Industrial Society.* London: Routledge.

Durkheim, E. 1900. *The Evolution of Punishment.* In S. Lukes and A. Scull (Eds) *Durkheim and the Law*, pp. 25–77, New York: St. Martin's Press.

Foucault, M. 1977. *Discipline and Punish: The Birth of the Prison.* (A. Sheridan Trans.) London: Peregrine Books.

Freedomhouse. 2012. New Council of Europe criteria will help define "political prisoners." https://www.ifex.org/europe_central_asia/2012/10/05/political_prisoners (Accessed November 22, 2012).

Gould, L. and M. Pate. 2010. Discipline, docility and disparity: A study of inequality and corporal punishment. *British Journal of Criminology* 50(2): 185–205.

Gould, L. and M. Pate. 2011. Penality, power and polity: Exploring the relationship between political repression and modalities of punishment. *International Criminal Justice Review* 21(4): 443–461.

Gourevitch, P. 1998. *We Wish to Inform You That Tomorrow We will be Killed with Our Families.* New York: Farrar, Straus & Giroux.

Green, M. and D. Mitchell. 2007. Asia's forgotten crisis. *Foreign Affairs* 86(6): 147–158.

Greenberg, D. 1977. The dynamics of oscillatory punishment processes. *The Journal of Criminal Law and Criminology* 68: 643–651.

Greenberg, D. and V. West. 2008. Siting the death penalty internationally. *Law & Social Inquiry* 33(2): 295–343.

Hague, W. 2007. It could have been me. *New Statesman.* http://www.newstatesman.com/ human-rights/2007/05/naing-burma-democracy-regime.

Hale, C. 1989. Unemployment, imprisonment, and the stability of punishment hypothesis: Some results using cointegration and error corrections models. *Journal of Quantitative Criminology* 5: 169–186.

Human Rights Watch. 2005. China: We could disappear at any time. http://hrw.org/ reports/2005/china1205 (Accessed December 11, 2015).

Human Rights Watch. 2008. China's forbidden zones: Shutting the media out of Tibet and other "sensitive" stories. https://www.hrw.org/report/2008/07/06/chinas-forbidden-zones/shutting-media-out-tibet-and-other-sensitive-stories (Accessed December 11, 2015).

Human Rights Watch. 2010. Burma: Eyewitness accounts of abuses in Eastern fighting—Thai authorities should ensure protection of refugees fleeing conflict. https://www.hrw.org/news/2010/12/04/burma-eyewitness-accounts-abuses-eastern-fighting (Accessed December 10, 2015).

Jacobs, D. and R. Kleban. 2003. Political institutions, minorities, and punishment: A pooled cross-national analysis of imprisonment rates. *Social Forces* 80: 725–755.

Jankovic, I. 1977. Labour market and imprisonment. *Crime and Social Justice* 8: 17–31.

Jiang, Q. 2012. *My Life in Prison: Memoirs of a Chinese Political Dissident.* Lanham, MD: Rowman & Littlefield.

Judah, T. 1997. *The Serbs: History, Myth and the Deconstruction of Yugoslavia.* New Haven, CT: Yale University Press.

Killias, M. 1986. Power concentration, legitimation crisis and penal severity: A comparative perspective. In W. B. Groves and G. Newman (Eds) *Punishment and Privilege,* pp. 95–117, New York: Harrow and Heston.

Kyi, B. and H. Scott. 2010. Torture, political prisoners and the UN rule of law: Challenges to peace, security, and human rights in Burma. First International Conference on Human Rights in South East Asia. http://aappb.org/wp/Torture_political_prisoners_and_the_un-rule_of_law.pdf (Accessed December 30, 2010).

Li, L. and K. O'Brien, K. 2008. Protest leadership in rural China. *China Quarterly* 193: 1–23.

Lwin, S. 2011. Forgotten securities market eying revival. *The Myanmar Times.* www.mmtimes.com/2011/news/590/news59021.html (Accessed April 30, 2010).

Martin, M. 2012. Burma's political prisoners and U.S. sanctions. Congressional Research Service, Washington, DC. https://www.fas.org/sgp/crs/row/R42363.pdf (Accessed May 3, 2014).

Melossi, D. 2008. *Controlling Crime, Controlling Society: Thinking About Crime in Europe and America.* Cambridge, MA: Polity Press.

Miethe, T., H. Lu, and G. Deibert. 2005. Cross-national variability in capital punishment: Exploring the sociopolitical sources of its differential legal status. *International Criminal Justice Review* 15: 115–130.

Mueller, J. 2000. The Banality of "Ethnic War": Yugoslavia and Rwanda. Paper presented to the annual meeting of the American Political Science Association. Washington, DC. http://politicalscience.osu.edu/faculty/jmueller/apsa2000.pdf (Accessed March 25, 2010).

Neapolitan, J. 2001. An examination of cross-national variation in punitiveness. *International Journal of Offender Rehabilitation and Comparative Criminology* 45: 691–710.

OECD. 2013. *Myanmar Multidimensional Study.* Paris: OECD.

Pate, M. and L. Gould. 2010. Discipline, docility and disparity: A study of inequality and corporal punishment. *British Journal of Criminology* 50: 185–205.

Pate, M. and L. Gould. 2012. The discipline of difference: Ethnolinguistic heterogeneity and corporal punishment. *International Journal of Comparative and Applied Criminal Justice* 36(3): 211–228.

Popescu, L. and C. Seymour-Jones. 2007. *Writers Under Siege: Voices of Freedom from Around the World: A PEN Anthology.* New York: New York University Press.

Poulantzas, N. 2000. *State, Power Socialism.* (P. Camiller Trans.) London: Verso.

Prunier, G. 1995. *The Rwanda Crisis: History of Genocide.* New York: Columbia University Press.

Quinney, R. 2000. *Bearing Witness to Crime and Social Justice.* Albany, NY: State University of New York Press.

Reid, R. and M. Grosberg. 2005. *Myanmar (Burma).* Footscray, Melbourne: Lonely Planet.

Ruddell, R. and M. Urbina. 2004. Minority threat and punishment: A cross-national analysis. *Justice Quarterly* 21: 903–931.

Ruddell, R. and M. Urbina. 2007. Weak nations, political repression, and punishment. *International Criminal Justice Review* 17: 84–107.

Smith, K. 2004. The politics of punishment: Evaluating political explanations of incarceration rates. *The Journal of Politics* 66: 925–938.

Taylor, R. 2015. *General Ne Win: A Political Biography*. Singapore: Institute of Southeast Asian Studies.

The Guardian. 2011. Chinese dissident jailed for 10 years: Democracy activist Liu Xianbin has already served 10 years in prison for subversion. http://www.theguardian.com/world/2011/mar/25/chinese-dissident-jailed-10-years (Accessed June 3, 2013).

Tonry, M. 2009. Explanations of American punishment policies: A national history. *Punishment & Society* 11: 377–394.

Wacquant, L. 2009. *Punishing the Poor: The Neoliberal Government of Social Insecurity*. Durham, NC: Duke University Press.

Xiaobo, L. 2012. *June Fourth Elegies*. New York: Random House.

Terrorism in Fragile States

4

Violence occurs when the social geometry of a conflict—the conflict structure—is violent. Every form of violence has its own structure, whether a beating structure, dueling structure, lynching structure, feuding structure, genocide structure—or terrorist structure. Structures kill and maim, not individuals or collectivities.

—Donald Black

Fragile and failing states have a notorious link to terrorism and terrorist group activities. This ignominious connection owes largely to the fact that terrorist groups tend to flourish in countries with governments that are ineffective or illegitimate or both. In this chapter, we explore how fragile states support terrorism by serving as safe havens for terrorist groups. In particular, we examine how political weakness, institutionalized corruption, and the inability to provide core political goods and services, as well as popular support for militant groups among the citizenry help create hospitable environments for terrorist organizations in fragile and failing states.

Theoretical Perspectives

Before we examine terrorism specifically, it is instructive to revisit some of the theoretical underpinnings of this volume. In so doing, we can better explore the complicated relationship between state sovereignty, power, and violence. From a Weberian perspective, power is a fundamental aspect of the modern nation-state. As Andreas Anter and Keith Tribe (2014, p. 124) note, Weber "sees power as a universal element of political, social, and economic life, and he considers 'the inevitable eternal struggle of man with man' to be a fundamental fact." Heinrich von Treitschke offers something similar, "the nature of the state is firstly power, secondly power, and again thirdly power" (Anter and Tribe 2014, p. 126). Weber goes on to argue that the possession of power results in domination, which he holds to be the most salient element of collective action. This said, he also notes "as a specific form of social power, domination must be legitimized to be politically effective" (Nelson 2006, p. 115). Thus, power and domination provide the foundation for a Weberian view of the modern nation-state as an entity which has a monopoly on the legitimate deployment of power in the form of violence or the use of force. When states fail, the legitimacy of the government to exercise power is lost; the government can no longer effectively enforce laws, nor can it control escalating violence within its own borders.

To this point, Durkheim's previously cited observations about the devaluation of the individual and his or her subordination bear recalling. Regarding war (and other forms of state violence), Durkheim (1964, p. 117) states that this process pushes "into the background all feelings of sympathy for the individual" and that "a rigid authoritarian discipline is imposed on all violations." Similarly, Ruggiero's (2006, p. 53) thoughts on the underlying mechanism also warrant recollection, "If we follow Durkheim's logic, we may link... political violence, to contingent social morality, connecting it to the social structure, rather than to universal moral codes." Therefore, failed states often exhibit civil war and violent internal struggles for power (e.g., Rotberg 2004). Indeed, the Stockholm International Peace Research Institute considers state failure to be one of the most critical factors leading to armed conflicts (Lemay-Hébert 2010).

As above, the concept of anomie is particularly useful in any examination of state failure. First introduced in Durkheim's influential work, *Division of Labor* (1897), the contemporary interpretation of anomie is best described as a state of deregulation where once clear social rules either become difficult to discern or lose their erstwhile attachments. The sweeping changes that occurred during the Industrial Revolution, along with a lack of societal forces in place to control it, are largely credited with increasing levels of anomie, but any strong social change can trigger anomie (Adler and Laufer 2000). At the macro level, rules and norms in anomic societies either cease functioning or are in a state of flux. Durkheim argues that this normatively fluid state produces an increase in deviant behavior because "the rules of society are less clear and ambiguous resulting in the weakened regulation of human conduct" (Franzese 2009, p. 34). Anomic societies also put the population in a perilous position by exacerbating existing group tensions and through conflict or war or both (Tiryakian 2009). At the micro level, anomie leads to widespread mistrust between groups because the lack of societal rules makes it impossible to predict the behavior of others (Marc et al. 2013). Alexandre Marc et al. (2013, p. 50) go on to note that anomie serves to further destabilize the precarious relationship between the government and its citizens and ultimately leads "individuals to perceive unmanageable dangers, doubts, and fears in virtually every aspect of ordinary life." In addition to providing a strong theoretical foundation for explaining the mechanisms that promote failure, anomie has also been especially instructive for understanding how to rebuild nations that have experienced extended periods of unrest (see e.g., Braithwaite et al. 2010).

The framing of terrorism employed by Black's (2004) quote at the heading of this chapter speaks to more than a traditional structural-functionalist approach. It also leads us toward a much more modern understanding of social phenomena as outputs of a complex adaptive system. As we argue in the introduction, a theoretical vocabulary that is more adept at capturing evolving social structures and the forces that compel that evolution is clearly needed. Additionally, said vocabulary must follow the principle of scalability (i.e., it must work both at micro and macro levels of analysis).

Monty Marshall and Benjamin Cole (2009, p. 2) make this point in their characterization of the state as a complex system. Through their work, we begin to see how fragility and failure can become hospitable environments for religious extremism. From the structuralist perspective, we see a history of irrelevant national borders, postcolonial legacies, economic distress, marginalization of large subpopulations, and a paucity of governmental or other social stabilizers. This creates a vacuum where there is no broadly shared dominant social narrative or focalization. The social process side of the equation involves human suffering, disenfranchisement, and anomic chaos.

In this sea of uncertainty, an ordering principle is needed; and religion is a ready provider of such. Religion works particularly well because it emanates from a nonrational* place. Often, the acceptance of religious ordering is predicated on the acceptance of a higher power (i.e., supernaturalism) and a similar acceptance that this will might require full submersion of the individual and the performance of difficult tasks. Because this will is a nonnegotiable, unidirectional and nonrational force, we may not be capable of understanding it—we only need obey it.

Submersion is further facilitated by the emotive connection between religion and the individual. As Robert Marett (1914, p. x) states, "[T] the most deep seated and persistent springs of behavior are furnished less by our ideas than by our emotions, taken together with the impulses that are therein manifested." Marett goes on to explain the importance of "awe" in this process:

> [A]we may therefore expect, will [have] a marked effect on social behavior....
> It will suffice to prove that supernaturalism, the attitude of the mind dictated
> by awe of the mysterious... provides religion with its raw material... objects
> towards which awe is felt may be termed powers. (Marett 1914, p. 1)

This then also explains some of the attachment to terrorism that more radicalized religious groups clearly espouse. Acts of terrorism tend to have an articulable "awe" component. Explosions, mass executions, computer hacking, and other media-attracting atrocities often spark a visceral emotive reaction in both the adherent and his or her foe. These acts serve to reconfirm

---

* This should not be taken to imply that religion is irrational. Rather, that religious beliefs may arise from valid, but nonrational or nonempirically derived sources.

the respective beliefs about and social actions toward the other party. They bind the moral consensus and justify future behavior. As above, these acts also solidify the natural adaptive feedback process by positioning acts of the individual as an agent of the greater societal will.

Terrorism Defined

At first blush, defining terrorism might seem to be an easy task; however, this is an errant notion, because an examination of the extant literature on terrorism reveals that there is no universally agreed-on definition of the phenomenon (Patrick 2011; United Nations 2014). The term *terrorism* has its origins in the Latin word, *terrere*, which means "to frighten." As has been well documented in the historical literature, the modern understanding of the term *terror* comes from the French Revolution's Reign of Terror, which claimed the lives of tens of thousands of citizens (Tilly 2004; Hoffman 2006). Based on this definition, terrorism has (at least historically) been used to describe state-sponsored violence and political repression (Tilly 2004). However, as we have seen with the global war on terror, this definition fails to capture a variety of actions that now fall under the umbrella of terrorism. The U.S. government relies on two definitions of terrorism derived from the Federal Bureau of Investigation (FBI) and the U.S. Code. The FBI defines terrorism as "the unlawful use of force or violence against persons or property to intimidate or coerce a government, the civilian population, or any segment thereof, in furtherance of political or social objectives." This traditional law enforcement definition fails to differentiate between sovereign nations and nonstate actors that employ terrorism; however, Title 22 of the U.S. Code, Section 2656f(d) does offer some clarification regarding the role of nonstate actors in terrorist conflict. In this context, terrorism is defined as "premeditated, politically motivated violence perpetrated against noncombatant targets by subnational groups or clandestine agents, usually intended to influence an audience." Insofar as the general public is concerned, the media tends to generate confusion because virtually any form of violence directed toward a society can be (and often is) placed within the general context of terrorism (Hoffman 2006). Media representations of terrorism run the gambit from deliberately poisoning foodstuffs at grocery stores to assassinations and bombings (Hoffman 2006, p. 1).

While a universally accepted definition of terrorism remains elusive, the United Nations (2014, para. 1) asserts that terrorist activities attack "the values that lie at the heart of the Charter of the United Nations: respect for human rights; the rule of law; rules of war that protect civilians; tolerance among peoples and nations; and the peaceful resolution of conflict."

Additionally, an examination of representative definitions reveals four major themes: (1) violence that is directed toward people; (2) the utilization of fear to intimidate citizens and government actors in an effort to effect change; (3) the terrorists' motive, whether religious, political, or ideological, are generally not referenced; and (4) most definitions generally refrain from making references to group size or collective action (Walter 2003). For the purposes of this chapter, we rely on the broad definition provided by Patrick (2011, p. 63) and define terrorism as "the deliberate use or threat of violence against noncombatants by a non-state actor for the achievement of political ends, typically with the intent of creating a wider psychological impact."

The Intersection of Anomie and Terrorism

While there are myriad theories that address how governments can either promote or foster terrorist activity, anomie is perhaps the most instructive. As noted in Chapter 1, any crisis can trigger anomie. Without shared norms and the ability to regulate human behavior, anomic societies lose the capacity to manage sociopolitical and economic forces. Additionally, conflict over physical space or resources or both becomes more likely and cultural divisions are intensified due to increasing levels of mistrust. Ervin Staub (2007, p. 334) helps illustrate this point by noting, "violence, especially terrorism, can be the result of social conditions and culture at a particular place at a particular time," and can emanate from "difficult life conditions" such as economic distress and social and political upheavals. In other words, as societies become increasingly anomic, violence in the form of terrorism becomes increasingly likely. Following our complex adaptive systems metaphor, acts of terrorism represent perturbations designed to shift a system from one state to another (i.e., chaos to order or order to chaos).

In addition to difficult social conditions, the control of physical space and resources also plays a critical role in creating environments conducive to terrorist groups. French philosopher and sociologist Henri Lefebvre suggests "that space is the ultimate locus and medium of struggle and is therefore a crucial political issue ... space is not just the place of conflict, but an object of struggle itself" (Elden 2009, p. xviii). Following this perspective, terrorism can emanate from a loss of governmental control in some regions, as well as a fight for control of contested physical space.

With regard to the control of physical space, fully functional governments are able to control their territorial boundaries, provide social order for their citizens, and have a monopoly on the legitimate use of coercive force. In contrast, fragile nations typically have a region or perhaps large swaths of territory over which they have lost control and are either unable or unwilling to provide governance. These regions, referred to as ungoverned spaces or "differentially governed" spaces, help promote violence and terrorism due to a lack of governmental control and the enforcement of norms. As Anne Clunan and Harold Trinkunas (2010, p. 17) explain, "ungoverned spaces are viewed as social, political, and economic arenas where states do not exercise 'effective sovereignty' or where state control is absent, weak, or contested." When a government loses the ability to govern effectively in some locations, the ability to enforce the law becomes impossible, borders can become porous, and criminals are free to act with impunity (Patrick 2011). Examples of *complete* governmental collapse are exceedingly rare and are generally not advantageous to terrorist groups because the chaotic environment that accompanies a fully collapsed state increases the chances of international intervention in the region (Patrick 2011). Moreover, excessive chaos and violence may hinder the groups' activities (Patrick 2011). Consequently, terrorist organizations find fragile states with differentially governed spaces more hospitable, partially due to the presence of an existing infrastructure that can help facilitate the groups' activities (e.g., roads, communication lines) (Piazza 2008; Patrick 2011). When selecting a host country, Patrick (2011) describes additional conditions that often attract terrorist groups, including overcrowding in urban areas, the availability of weapons, existing extremist jihadist ideology, and a local population that may have jihadist leanings. In short, terrorist groups in differently governed spaces are able to recruit new members, amass resources, and plan and execute attacks, all with very little risk of being caught (Piazza 2008).

In a related strain of research, scholars who study civil wars have examined the role that grievances and greed play in the escalation of violence in countries experiencing internal conflict. As Sagheer Khan (2011) notes, the civil war research is largely divided into two groups, grievance theorists and greed theorists. Grievance-based conflict is thought to result from extreme relative deprivation, while greed-based conflict relies on the assumption that people are rational actors capable of weighing the costs and benefits of their actions.

Useful as both these paradigms may be, we attenuate one of the postulate assumptions of the greed/grievance hypotheses. We assert that humans are not rational in the sense that they apply a Bayesian probability scheme to all decisions, but rather that they are boundedly rational. They factor in localized inputs within their space of action (be it a neighborhood, a region, or a state); and they calculate for their own maximum utility (however defined), but they are boundedly rational because no human has perfect global information. Their appraisals of potential utility are typically based only on their spatially and temporally localized neighborhood of information. That information may be strongly conditioned on many factors with deprivation and religious ardor among them. While many terrorist groups increasingly employ outwardly focused appliances of technology, most are far more provincial and inwardly focused as agents of their own order. As such, understanding the roles of civil conflict, group grievances, and greed are all essential criteria in the study of fragile states (whether they experience civil war or not); thus, linkages can be made between civil war research and state failure research.

There is a demonstrable relationship between group grievance and terrorism. Scholars such as Samuel Huntington have argued that culture clashes or high levels of ethnolinguistic heterogeneity strongly contribute to terrorism; however, there is some question as to whether the mere presence of sociocultural divisions leads directly to terrorism. Posed differently, is there a causal relationship between heterogeneity and terrorism, or is there an intervening variable at work?

Dan Cox et al. (2009) argue that cultural or ethnic cleavages are often exploited by governments and used as tools to foster or further entrench hatred against groups that are marginalized or oppressed or both. In the absence of this, or other external factors, Cox et al. (2009, p. 4) assert that there is no direct causal link between culture clashes and terrorism. We concur with Cox et al. (2009) and contend that some sort of catalyst is required to promote terrorism in fractionalized countries and in many countries the catalyst emanates from postcolonial legacy.

An examination of the historical development of many of today's fragile nations reveals that postcolonial legacy has greatly contributed to the volatile nature of governance today. Many fragile states were once colonized territories whose borders were arbitrarily drawn, without consideration of existing relationships between different cultural or ethnic groups. As a consequence, disparate groups, some with a long history of hostilities toward one another, were often thrust together into one colonial territory. As colonial powers withdrew and former territories gained independence, colonial borders remained intact, along with many deep ethnic and cultural divides. Depending on how the colonial powers managed their territories, existing hostilities between groups may have been exploited; however, even if the colonial powers did not actively exploit cultural divides to further their own agenda, often little care was taken to address group hostilities. Accordingly, many former colonies have found themselves without a shared dominant social narrative or even a national identity (e.g., Syria).

The ethnic and cultural cleavages that help drive instability in fragile states can be partially attributed to postcolonial legacy. Also, governments in the twenty-first century have continued to exploit group grievances in much the same way that the governments depicted in Alexis de Tocqueville (1966/1866) and Michel Foucault's (1977) *Ancien Régime* use social power to control and oppress "undesirable" behaviors and people. Contemporary governments can and do use their power to exacerbate group tensions in an effort to further their own goals. This is clearly problematic for a variety of reasons, but the most salient problem insofar as state fragility is concerned regards the lack of effective governance that results from culture conflict. Within the cultural studies literature, two distinct forms of state power have been identified, coercive power and directive power (Oswell 2006). Antonio Gramsci argues:

> [T]he supremacy of a social group manifests itself in two ways, as "domination" and as "intellectual and moral leadership". A social group dominates antagonistic groups, which it tends to "liquidate", or to subjugate perhaps even by armed force; it leads kindred and allied groups. A social group can, and indeed must, already exercise "leadership" before winning governmental power (this indeed is one of the principal conditions for the winning of such power); it subsequently becomes dominant when it exercises power, but even if it holds it firmly in its grasp, it must continue to "lead" as well. (Gramsci 1971, pp. 57–58, as cited in Oswell 2006, p. 45)

In this view, the ability to effectively govern rests on the ability to wield directive power as well as coercive power. Additionally, administrative functioning (i.e., the ability to deliver core political goods and services) and the retention of the monopoly on coercive force have been linked to the ability to raise revenues from society (Andersen et al. 2007). Andersen et al. (2007, p. 8) describe the complex interplay of all of these factors:

> The state's administrative capacity as well as its ability to uphold a monopoly of violence are thus closely linked to its capacity to raise revenues from society, which in turn is linked to its legitimacy in the eyes of the population, which in turn is linked to the state's capacity to provide services for which it needs both administrative capacity and a monopoly of violence.

Ungoverned Spaces in the Middle East

The Middle East has been especially vulnerable to differentially governed spaces, in part because the rugged mountain terrain and desert conditions that comprise much of the land area were not conducive to the early development of large cities (Kamrava 2014). As a consequence, large portions of the population resided in small desert villages, with tribal affiliation providing the central social structural system. In many countries, this is still the case, as current statistics indicate that the population distribution in some Middle Eastern nations is still heavily concentrated in rural areas. For example, the percentage of the population residing in rural areas in Syria is 43.9%, 74% in Afghanistan, 47% in Georgia, 62% in Pakistan, and 67% in Yemen (CIA World Factbook 2014). Mehran Kamrava (2014, p. 13) contends that this pattern of the "dispersion of populations outside the walls of the city and in remote and mostly inaccessible areas has often resulted in the state's inability to effectively establish its authority over the areas it has claimed to control." Terrorist groups can thrive in tribal regions, provided they are able to make arrangements with local leaders that permit them to develop an infrastructure, as well as provide protection for the "official" government, should that become necessary (Patrick 2011).

There are myriad examples of violence brought on by conflicts over the control of physical space; however, the rise of the Islamic State provides perhaps the best contemporary example of how differentially governed spaces and the fight over territory contributes to terrorism.

Syria in Historical Context

As Daniel Pipes (1992) rightly points out, historically, Syria has received little attention, especially compared with other nations in the Middle East. This is problematic for a variety of reasons, many of which are becoming increasingly evident as the civil war and the conflict with the Islamic State continues. The current violence in Syria is best understood in its proper historical context. Syria was once part of the Ottoman Empire and until about 1920, "Greater Syria" encompassed numerous countries, including present-day Syria, Lebanon, Israel, Jordan, the Gaza Strip, and parts of Turkey (Pipes 1992). The once powerful Ottoman Empire was already in steep decline when World War I broke out. Despite this, the empire joined the war and fought alongside Germany (Kamrava 2014).

Their involvement in the war prompted the Allied forces to capture numerous Ottoman provinces (Kamrava 2014), and provided fertile ground for revolt. As World War I was coming to an end, residents of Hijaz revolted against the Ottoman Empire and captured the major city, Damascus, thus bringing an end to the Ottoman rule (Provence 2005; BBC News 2014). The revolt, led by Amîr Fayal,* took place largely because Fayal was led to believe that Britain would create an Arab kingdom spanning from Iran to the Mediterranean, once the war reached its conclusion (Provence 2005). However, throughout the war, both France and Britain made a series of contradictory promises about how the Ottoman Empire would be divided (Provence 2005). Ultimately, Britain, France, and Russia had established their own secret plans for the division of the Ottoman Empire through a series of negotiations that culminated with the Sykes–Picot Agreement in May 1916. The agreement involved redrawing country borders in ways that would maximize the benefits to Britain and France, as well as increase the influence of colonial powers in the region (Rogan 2009; Krämer 2008).

---

* Fayal was the son of a former Ottoman religious governor.

In accordance with the agreement, France was given control of the majority of the land area now known as Syria (Krämer 2008; Provence 2005; CIA World Factbook 2014). Specifically, France was given direct control over the Syrian coastline and indirect control over the rest of Syria (Wagner 2004). As Wagner (2004, p. 34) notes, "long before the Ottoman Empire had signed an armistices, its lands had been divided up by its enemies. Through agreements, treaties, and letters, that fate of the Middle East had been decided by men who, in many cases, had never been there. Borders and boundaries—many overlapping and contradictory—had been sketched out by men who did not understand what they were dividing."

When the war ended, France sought to establish a sufficient buffer zone bordering Germany; however, in order to gain control over Alsace-Lorraine and Saar, France was forced to cede much of its Syrian territory to Britain at the Paris Peace Conference (Wagner 2004). As a result, Syria would effectively be divided into two regions, a French-controlled region in the north and a British-controlled region containing oil fields (Wagner 2004). While France and Britain were able to reach some conciliatory agreements, total consensus regarding control of the Middle East remained elusive. Accordingly, the signing of the treaty was postponed and another meeting of the Allied forces was held to cement plans for the division of the Middle East (Wagner 2004). In 1920, the Allied powers met in San Remo to decide the fate of the Middle East and "the outcome was the concept of mandatory rule, a polite disguise for what a couple of decades earlier had been unabashedly called colonialism" (Kamrava 2014). The division of the Middle East was cemented in the Treaty of Sevres, a slightly modified version of the Sykes–Picot Agreement that gave France control over Greater Syria (Kamrava 2014). However, mandatory rule (or a mandate) under the League of Nations required France to prepare Syria for eventual independence, which France failed to accomplish (Polk 2013).

While the Allied forces bickered over how to divide the spoils of war, Syria declared sovereignty (Rogan 2009). In 1919, national congressional elections were held and Fayal was named King of Syria* (Rogan 2009; BBC News 2014). Sovereignty proved to be short-lived and ended in 1920 when France invaded Damascus and removed King Fayal (Polk 2013; Kamrava 2014). Once in control of the territory, France experimented with a number of unsuccessful tactics designed to restructure Syrian society (Polk 2013). France annexed land from Syria to establish the "Greater Lebanon State," a controversial move that Syria never fully accepted[†] (Olmert 1985). It quickly

---

* The territory of Fayal's Syria included land in Turkey and Egypt.
[†] During a public speech in 1976, President Assad stated, "Syria and Lebanon have always been one state and one people. History teaches us, that Syria and Lebanon constitute one people and therefore they have common interests... and common security interests... thousands of families in Syria have relatives in Lebanon and vice versa..." (Olmert 1985, p. 308).

became clear that the redrawing of regional borders in an effort to divide and conquer was ineffective, so attempts were made to reunify the nation. This too proved to be unsuccessful because France's version of a unified state involved sweeping cultural changes in the region including a mandate that French be the common language and attempts to bolster the Catholic faith among the populace, both of which were designed to weaken the influence of Islam. Perhaps the most damaging policy, in terms of deepening cultural divides, involved marginalizing the Muslim population by favoring minority groups (Polk 2013). Polk (2013, p. 9) argues that the French did not create these cultural divides, but their policies "certainly magnified it and while they did not create hostility to foreigners, they gave the native population a target that fostered the growth of nationalism."

Syria officially gained sovereignty in 1946, but the country had limited infrastructure, almost no governmental oversight, high levels of group conflict, and extensive political divisions (Lawson 2006). In short, Syria was an extremely fragile nation from the start. The fragile nature of this nascent country should come as no surprise given that Syria had never been a sovereign entity; rather, it had always been a province or a colony of another kingdom (Pipes 1992; Polk 2013). Because of this, a cohesive national Syrian identity failed to emerge and Syrian citizens did not consider themselves to belong to the Syrian nation (Pipes 1992). Further, the deep social divisions in place at the time of independence (Sunni Muslims, Christians, Alawites, Druze, Kurds, Turkomans, and Isma'ili) "blocked the acceptance of the Syrian state in the public mind and accounted for the failure to develop a widespread sense of loyalty to and identification with it. Rather, many Syrians tended to seek focuses of identity beyond Syria's territorial limits" (Zisser 2006, p. 7). Pan-Syrianism has provided one unifying ideology. In contrast to Pan-Arabism, which takes the view that Muslims should form one nation and current country borders should be eliminated in the Middle East and North Africa to form an Arab State, Pan-Syrianism reflects the desire to return to the old borders that comprised Greater Syria.*

Pan-Syrianism has driven politics in the Middle East and has helped fuel violence and conflict. Pipes (1992, p. 3) asserts that Pan-Syrianism is partially responsible for "the volatility of public life in Jordan and Syria; and it partially accounts for the Lebanese civil war and the Arab-Israeli conflict. The goal of piecing Syria's parts together drove Jordanian foreign policy for over two decades, and it had nearly as great a role in Iraq." While Pipes asserts that Syrian leader Hafez-al-Assad promoted Pan-Syrianism as a way to dilute the Sunni Muslim population, Sadowski (2002, p. 151) points to

---

* Greater Syria would include the land that Syria currently controls, as well as Jordan, Lebanon, Israel, and Palestinian territories, and some regions in Turkey (Sadowski 2002).

the volatility of Syria during the 1950s and 1960s as one driving force. As he explains:

> In the 1950s Syrian politics were so internally divisive that (as later happened in Lebanon) virtually all of the country's neighbors were able to finance local proxies. Turkey, Iraq, and Egypt took turns sponsoring military coups in Damascus. Anyone who wished to stabilize the situation in Syria, whether Ba'thist or Islamist, was going to have to undercut these networks of foreign penetration—perhaps by counterattacking and fostering surrogates for Syrian power in the surrounding states.

Hafez-al-Assad's approach to foreign relations with neighboring countries accomplished this goal. Using a variety of means, some economic and some violent, Assad was able to exert control and somewhat stabilize Lebanon, while also forming an alliance with Iran (Cordesman and Khazai 2014). Following the Iranian revolution in 1979, Syria was the first Islamic country to formally recognize the new Iranian government and by 1982 the Iran/Syria alliance was cemented with a series of trade and military agreements (Goodarzi n.d.). Further, during the Iran/Iraq war in the 1980s, Assad allied with Iran due to his deep opposition to Saddam Hussein's Ba'thist regime (Cordesman and Khazai 2014). At first blush, the alliance between Syria and Iran may seem odd, given their vast differences in religious and political ideology. As Goodarzi (n.d.) notes, the Syrian Ba'thist regime is largely secular and socialist, while the Iranian regime follows a strict religious code and is opposed to atheism and any form of communism. Both countries were able to put these differences aside and were brought together by their "mutual contempt for Saddam Hussein's Iraq ... and mutual fear and loathing of the United States and Israel has helped sustain them" (Sadjadpour 2014, para. 2). Their continued alliance is also driven by a mutual need for survival coupled with the fact that "together they ... stand a better chance of achieving their long-term goals. Syria wants to regain the strategic Golan Heights, lost to Israel in the 1967 War, and keep its veto power over Lebanese politics. Iran wants to be the preeminent regional player in the Persian Gulf and ensure its allies rule in Iraq. Both also want to protect Arab interests (in the case of Damascus) and Islamic interests (in the case of Iran) throughout the region" (Goodarzi n.d., para. 6).

Modern Syria

Modern Syria is only one-and-a-half times the size of the U.S. state of Pennsylvania and borders Iraq, Israel, Jordan, Lebanon, and Turkey (CIA World Factbook 2014). In 2002, President George W. Bush included Syria as a member state of the "axis of evil" in the global war on terror. Bashir

Assad, the current leader and son of former president Hafez-al-Assad, is an authoritarian leader and by all appearances, is a tyrant (Polk 2013). Under Assad's leadership, the Syrian government has allegedly supported Lebanon's Hezbollah, attempted to build nuclear reactors, and used chemical weapons against its citizens (BBC News 2014).

Since 2011, Syria has been in the midst of a civil war, with the Islamic State assuming control of large regions in both Syria and Iraq. At the time of this writing, two wars are being fought on multiple fronts in three countries: Syria, Iraq, and Turkey. Postcolonial legacy and Pan-Syrianism are largely responsible for the present conflicts; however, on a more pragmatic level, drought conditions ultimately proved to be the tipping point that led to war.

Due to Syria's rough terrain, only about 25% of the land is suitable for agriculture, with the rest composed of desert terrain (Polk 2013). Because most of Syria's land is inhospitable, population density and overcrowding are problematic. Frequent droughts, which have become more common and more extreme due to global warming, have devastated the region and contributed to growing tension in the area (Gleick 2014). Between 1900 and 2005, Syria experienced six major droughts that were relatively short in duration; however, the 2006 drought lasted nearly five years (Gleick 2014). The long-lasting drought devastated the agricultural industry and left 800,000 farmers without a livelihood (Sohl 2010; Polk 2013). The persistent drought conditions displaced more than 1.5 million people, most of whom moved to cities and surrounding areas within Syria (The Pacific Institute 2014). In some cases, city populations rose from roughly 2,000 people to nearly 400,000 people in less than a decade (Gleick 2014). The Syrian government failed to respond to the increasing numbers of internally displaced persons, despite being warned by U.S. diplomats "that the influx of rural people to cities could act as a multiplier on social and economic pressures already at play and undermine stability in Syria" (Gleick 2014, p. 5). Four years into the drought, an estimated 200,000 farmers had abandoned their farmlands; crop failures reached nearly 75% in some regions; and a staggering 85% of livestock died (Polk 2013). There simply was not enough food or water to sustain the Syrian population and the large influx of displaced farmers increased competition over scarce resources (Sohl 2010; Polk 2013). By 2011, Syria was a tinderbox. The persistent drought had widespread social and health ramifications,* caused resource depletion, and triggered dust storms that eroded the topsoil. More importantly, as Polk (2013) states, "they triggered a civil war."

---

* Sohl (2010) reports that the drought resulted in malnourished young children. Additionally, many parents withdrew their children from school and sent them to work.

The tipping point was reached when security forces reportedly shot and killed prodemocracy protesters who were demanding the release of political prisoners during a peaceful demonstration. The deaths triggered violent anti-government uprisings throughout the country, and the violence quickly escalated into civil war (BBC News 2014). The nature of the conflict and the sheer volume of the armed groups involved have created a very confusing political situation in the country. It is often difficult to discern between groups that comprise the anti-Assad opposition and armed militants with jihadist goals. Syrian society has quickly descended into an anomic morass, providing terrorist groups with an opportunity to exploit the tenuous situation.

One such group is the Islamic State, initially referred to as the Islamic State of Syria and Levant and the Islamic State in Syria and Iraq. Virtually all of the conditions that promote terrorism—a history of conflict, the availability of weapons, a large pool of potential recruits, minimal border control, and a dearth of government-provided social services such as medical care, education, and employment (Patrick 2011)—were in place once the civil war broke out.

The Development of the Islamic State

The Islamic State, which has seemingly appeared out of nowhere, is not a new organization, as it has existed in various forms under a variety of names since the 1990s. Jordanian terrorist Abu Musab al-Zarqawi* was the first leader of the Islamic State, as well as several early iterations of the group (Teslik 2006; Weaver 2006; Ghosh 2014). Al-Zarqawi's former neighbor, Ibrahim Izzat, described him as "of a modest social class, isolated and hardly socialized" (Brisard and Martinez 2005, p. 13). Peter Chambers (2012, p. 35) characterizes al-Zarqawi's life as one of "poverty, early exposure to the traumas of a neighboring conflict, a life of petty crime on the margins of a dilapidated, poor, disenfranchised urban landscape; arrests and imprisonment, torture, radicalization, release, commitment to a movement intended, in its own words to redress the cumulative pain and humiliation these conditions had imposed on his existence through the infliction of an even greater counterterror." After the death of his father, al-Zarqawi dropped out of high school (Kirdar 2011) and by age 20 he had completed his two years of mandatory military service (Brisard and Martinez 2005). Following his tour in the military, al-Zarqawi returned to Jordan, and with little direction in his life, he quickly turned to crime (Brisard and Martinez 2005). He reportedly drank heavily and earned the nickname "the green man" because his body

---

* His given name was Ahmad Fadhil Nazzal al-Khalaylah, but he later changed it to Abu Musab al-Zarqawi.

was covered in tattoos (Brisard and Martinez 2005). Zarqawi was arrested numerous times for assault, drug dealing, and shoplifting, and he eventually served two years in prison on charges of drug possession and sexual assault (Teslik 2006; Kirdar 2011).

According to fellow inmates, al-Zarqawi's stay in prison planted the seeds of his extremist ideology. While incarcerated, he gave up drinking and became a practicing Muslim. Ultimately, he came to believe that fighting the jihad in Afghanistan offered him a way to fulfill his destiny (Brisard and Martinez 2005). After his release from prison, al-Zarqawi traveled to Afghanistan to fight the jihad, but the war was nearing its end and his contributions were minimal (Kirdar 2011; Brisard and Martinez 2005). While his trip to Afghanistan did not fulfill his destiny, it did open the door to further radicalization of al-Zarqawi's belief system. During a visit to Peshawar, Zarqawi met fellow radical, mentor, and cofounder of Bayat al-Imam (a very early forerunner to the Islamic State), Sheikh Abu Muhammad al-Maqdisi (Kirdar 2011). In 1992, both men returned to Jordan and began planning terrorist attacks; however, the following year, al-Zarqawi and Maqdisi were arrested and sentenced to 15 years in prison for planning a suicide bombing at a movie theater (Kirdar 2011). Incarceration only fueled the fire of his extremism and motivated him and Maqdisi to expand their nascent terrorist organization (Kirdar 2011).

Following his release from prison a second time, al-Zarqawi attended numerous terrorist training camps and eventually established his own during the latter part of the 1990s. Though Osama bin Laden reportedly asked al-Zarqawi to join Al-Qaeda, he refused and instead formed the Jama'at al-Tawhid w'al-Jihad (the Party of Monotheism and Jihad), another early forerunner to the Islamic State (Ghosh 2014). In October 2004, al-Zarqawi formally joined Al-Qaeda and changed his group's name to Al-Qaeda in Iraq (AQI). Though AQI was affiliated with Al-Qaeda (at least nominally), under al-Zarqawi's leadership AQI quickly began targeting Shia Muslims, which drew the ire of the Al-Qaeda leadership (Teslik 2006; Mapping Militant Organizations 2014).

In something of a fateful ironic twist, al-Zarqawi, who at the time was relatively unknown outside of Jordan, gained international notoriety by virtue of a mistake. According to Weaver (2006), on February 5, 2003, Secretary of State Colin Powell errantly taught the world al-Zarqawi's name. In an address to the United Nations where Powell hoped to make the case for war in Iraq, he identified al-Zarqawi "…mistakenly, as it turned out—as the crucial link between Al-Qaeda and Saddam Hussein's regime. Subsequently, al-Zarqawi became a leading figure in the insurgency in Iraq." This misattribution emboldened the enigmatic figure to commit greater and greater acts of terror. By most accounts, al-Zarqawi's radicalized thought began with a trip to Afghanistan where he met Sheikh Abu Muhammad al-Maqdisi (whose real name is Isam Muhammad Tahir al-Barqawi), a revered and militant Salafist cleric (Weaver 2006).

The Salafiya are a late-nineteenth-century reform movement of the Sunni, with a particularly intense animosity toward Shia Muslims. They can be described as anti-Western, puritanical, and adhering to a "literal" interpretation of the Qur'an. As sectarian violence propels so much of the current conflict in Syria and Iraq, it is instructive to understand some of the differences between the Sunni and Shia.

There is a deep sectarian divide within Islam that stems from a disagreement over the line of succession following the Prophet Muhammad's death. At the time, the majority of Muslims believed that Muhammad's close friend, Abu Bakr, should be named Caliph. A smaller group of Muslims disagreed and contended that Muhammad's son-in-law and cousin, Ali, should be Caliph. As we note in a previous work (Pate and Gould 2012, p. 45), their "claim rested on the contention that Muhammad had appointed Ali as the rightful heir to his legacy, in both political and spiritual terms." In the end, Bakr was named Caliph and the religious division was cemented. Bakr's supporters would go on to become the larger Sunni sect, while Ali supporters would become the much smaller Shia (or Shiite) sect. In the 14 centuries that have passed since the schism, both groups have evolved culturally, developed different customs, and now consider themselves distinct from one another. The Sunni and the Shia separately compiled different collections of hadith and while each provided roughly the same historical account of events, the two groups differed in their interpretation. As Lesley Hazleton (2009, p. 207) explains:

> They told different versions of the same stories, disagreeing not on what had taken place in the 7th century, but on what it meant. Where Sunnis would see Muhammed's choice of Abu Bakr as his companion on the *hija*—emigration to Medina—as proof that he intended Abu Bakr to be his successor, for instance, the Shia would see his declaration at Ghadir Khuum as proof of his designation of Ali. The Sunnis, in effect, would honor history as it had taken shape; the Shia would honor it as they believe it should have taken shape, and as they maintain it did in a realm other than the worldly one.

Sunni Muslims comprise about 85% of modern Islamic adherents. Shia Muslims are a minority group in most Islamic nations; however, Iran, Yemen, and Azerbaijan are predominantly Shia (Amin 2010). Like the Islamic State, Sunni terrorist group Al-Qaeda and its leader, Osama bin Laden, viewed Shia Muslims as heretics (Ghosh 2014). Despite this, by the 1990s, Al-Qaeda urged cooperation, not violence, between the two sects (Ghosh 2014). Al-Zarqawi, on the other hand, directly targeted and killed Shiite Muslims almost immediately on gaining power (Ghosh 2014).

In 2005, Ayman al-Zawahiri* sent a letter to al-Zarqawi wherein he outlined the necessary steps to achieve their ultimate goal of establishing a caliphate. Additionally, al-Zawahiri expressed concern about the attacks on fellow Muslims. Though he did appear to share al-Zarqawi's opinion of Shiite Muslims, al-Zawahiri explicitly warned against further attacks. Specifically, al-Zawahiri stated:

> The collision between any state based on the model of prophecy with the Shia is a matter that will happen sooner or later. This is the judgment of history, and these are the fruits to be expected from the rejectionist Shia sect and their opinion of the Sunnis. These are clear, well-known matters to anyone with a knowledge of history, the ideologies, and the politics of states.
>
> We must repeat what we mentioned previously, that the majority of Muslims don't comprehend this and possibly could not even imagine it. For that reason, *many of your Muslim admirers amongst the common folk are wondering about your attacks on the Shia.* The sharpness of this questioning increases when the attacks are on one of their mosques, and it increases more when the attacks are on the mausoleum of Imam Ali Bin Abi Talib, may God honor him. My opinion is that *this matter won't be acceptable to the Muslim populace however much you have tried to explain it, and aversion to this will continue.* (emphasis added) (Al-Zawahiri 2005)

Zawahiri also expressed alarm due to the public nature of killing hostages or "scenes of slaughter." He writes

> *Among the things which the feelings of the Muslim populace who love and support you will never find palatable—also- are the scenes of slaughtering the hostages.* You shouldn't be deceived by the praise of some of the zealous young men and their description of you as the shaykh of the slaughterers, etc. They do not express the general view of the admirer and the supporter of the resistance in Iraq, and of you in particular by the favor and blessing of God. (emphasis added) (Al-Zawahiri 2005)

Al-Zarqawi did not heed these warnings and continued his militant campaign by targeting Shiite Muslims, Shiite symbols of identity, non-Islamic Westerners, and those perceived as being sympathetic to Western ideals (Hafez 2011). In one particularly shocking attack, explosives were set off during Shiite Ashura† processionals, killing 181 people. Al-Zarqawi was eventually killed by an air strike launched by U.S. forces on June 7, 2006 (Teslik 2006), but his

---

* When al-Zawahiri penned the letter to al-Zarqawi, he was second in command of Al-Qaeda; currently, he is the group's top leader.
† Ashura is a highly significant day for Shiite Muslims, as it commemorates the martyrdom of Muhammad's grandson, Hussein. Hussein's death was a critical event in the Islamic world and ultimately led to the divide between the Sunni and Shiite Muslims (BBC News 2011).

successor, the Egyptian-born Abu Ayyub al-Masri (also known as Abu Hamza al-Muhajir), was named within a week of al-Zarqawi's death (Kaplan 2006). It had been widely anticipated that Abu Abdelrahman al-Iraqi, al-Zarqawi's deputy, would lead the organization. As such, al-Masri's appointment was largely unexpected. When he assumed leadership, al-Masri was virtually unknown, he was not on any U.S. or Iraqi wanted lists, and he never appeared in any of al-Zarqawi's propaganda (Kaplan 2006). Though al-Masri lacked name recognition, he had a fairly extensive terrorist background, beginning with his involvement in the Muslim Brotherhood (Garamone 2006). He attended an Al-Qaeda training camp in Afghanistan where he received training in explosive devices. He also played an integral role in helping Zarqawi establish an Al-Qaeda cell in Iraq (Garamone 2006; BBC News 2010).

As the AQI leader, al-Masri continued to employ al-Zarqawi's tactics, including the targeting of Shiite Muslims and security forces (Boon et al. 2010). In October 2006, al-Masri announced the formation of the Islamic State of Iraq (Cordesman and Khazai 2014) and established a nine-person cabinet led by al-Masri (minister of war) and Abu Umar al-Baghdadi (head of the cabinet) (Boon et al. 2010). By 2007, it appeared as though the death of al-Zarqawi, combined with a surge in U.S. forces in Iraq and a violent backlash from Sunni Muslim groups (referred to as the "awakening" movement against AQI), had weakened the Islamic State of Iraq (Boon et al. 2010; Cordesman and Khazai 2014).* While attacks did lessen for a time, the steady withdrawal of coalition forces from Iraqi cities resulted in a tenuous security situation to be readily exploited by the Islamic State in Iraq (Cordesman and Khazai 2014). In addition to steady troop withdrawals, the actions of Iraqi Prime Minister Nouri Al-Maliki contributed a great deal to instability because he "arranged his power structure around a Shi'ite dominated state with close ties to Iran ... [which further] alienated Sunnis and exacerbated tensions" (Cordesman and Khazai 2014, p. 1). AQI carried out a series of attacks in 2009 and 2010, but both leaders, al-Masri and Abu Umar al-Baghdadi, were killed in an Iraqi/U.S. coordinated attack (BBC News 2010). The group once again proved to be resilient with a new leader, Abu Bakr al-Baghdadi, being named shortly after the deaths of al-Masri and Abu Umar al-Baghdadi (Zelin 2014).

Abu Bakr al-Baghdadi: Current Leader of the Islamic State (Caliph)

The goal of the Islamic State is to create a single nation that is based on Shari'ah law, ruled by one Muslim leader known as a caliphate (BBC News 2014). By all

---

* At this time, the Islamic State of Iraq purportedly served as an umbrella group for AQI and other terrorist organizations.

accounts, Abu Bakr al-Baghdadi has been a very "successful" leader, with some observing that he has surpassed al-Zarqawi's accomplishments by amassing more resources and developing more sophisticated mechanisms of governance (Zelin 2014).* It is unknown exactly how many resources the Islamic State has amassed, but some estimate that their war chest grows between $850,000 and $1.6 million per day (Financial Action Task Force 2015).[†] Additionally, the group has amassed (through illegal smuggling or theft) a large stockpile of weapons that include assault rifles, missiles, rockets, and tanks, just to name a few (Financial Action Task Force 2015). The exact size of the Islamic States' fighting forces is unknown, but *The Economist* (2012) estimates the group's size to be approximately 11,000, with 6,000 fighters coming from Syria and 3,000–5,000 fighters in Syria. Richard Barrett (2014) of the Soufan Group[‡] estimates the group to be much larger, with at least 12,000 fighters, 3,000 of whom are believed to be Westerners. With its current level of resources, the Islamic State can fight for up to two years, meaning that the struggle to destroy the Islamic State will not be a short one.

The Islamic State has quickly gained a reputation for being one of the most brutal militant Islamic extremist groups in history. The group has committed a number of atrocities and human rights violations in Syria and Iraq. Shia Muslims, non-Muslims, and coalition forces are the main targets of the Islamic State with numerous reports indicating that the group commonly commits mass executions, beheadings,[§] forced marriages, and human trafficking (primarily for the purposes of sex).

Mass Executions

During the fight for Mosul in Iraq, Islamic State fighters reportedly took control of Badoush Prison and killed an estimated 600 inmates, mostly Shia Muslims (Human Rights Watch 2014a–c). Just 15 inmates survived the attack. Survivors recounted the details to Human Rights Watch interviewers. The survivors indicated that Islamic State fighters drove the inmates to an isolated area where they separated Sunni Muslims and Christians from the rest of the inmates (Human Rights Watch 2014a–c). The remaining inmates (the vast majority of which were Shia) were marched to the edge of a ravine

---

* Governance by the Islamic State is sophisticated only when compared with other extremist groups. Their version of governance, and especially their criminal justice system, is primitive and rudimentary at best.
[†] The bulk of this money is obtained through sales of oil taken from reserves located just outside Mosul. However, other sources of revenue stem from extortion, the sale of stolen antiquities, and ransom payments (Financial Action Task Force. 2015. 2014).
[‡] The Soufan Group is a private company that offers intelligence and security services to governments, as well as the private sector.
[§] Since beheadings have a direct bearing on the Islamic States criminal justice system, this practice will be discussed later in the chapter.

and told to kneel down (Human Rights Watch 2014a, para. 7). According to one survivor:

> They started by saying, "Each person raise his hand and say his number." I was number 43. I heard them say "615," and then one ISIS guy said, "We're going to eat well tonight." A man behind us asked, "Are you ready?" Another person answered "Yes," and began shooting at us with a machine-gun. Then they all started to shoot us from behind, going down the row.

Once out of ammunition, the fighters set fire to the ravine that contained most of the corpses, and left the area (Human Rights Watch 2014a–c). The next day, Islamic State militants in Tikrit carried out another mass execution of Iraqi soldiers (Human Rights Watch 2014a–c). Figures from Islamic State propaganda indicate that 1700 Iraqi soldiers were killed in the incident, but Human Rights Watch estimates that between 560 and 770 soldiers were summarily executed, though they did not rule out a higher death toll (Human Rights Watch 2014a–c).

Treatment of Women: Forced Marriages and Human Trafficking

The treatment of women under the Islamic State is very disconcerting because the group is instituting a "pure" form of Sharia, based on a literal interpretation of the Qur'an. Shia, Christian, Yazidi, and other minority women are subjected to some of the most brutal forms of sexual violence imaginable. In an interview with PBS, Manal Omar, acting vice president for the Middle East and Africa Center at the United States Institute of Peace, noted that sexual violence has been used as a tool of war for quite some time, but the Islamic State has increased the level of brutality and begun targeting women in earnest (PBS 2014). As Omar explains, "it's not something that's new, but ISIS has taken it to a very brutal level. And what we have seen is that they're not only using it as a way of targeting communities, but they're also using it as a way of creating a reward system with soldiers, as well as then income-generating in terms of selling and human trafficking" (PBS 2014, para. 21). Women captured by the Islamic State are typically forced to marry jihadists, sold at auction as sex slaves, or trafficked out of the country for sex work in other areas.

During the latter part of 2014, the Research and Fatwa Department of the Islamic State issued a pamphlet containing answers to 27 frequently asked questions about how sex slaves should be treated. The following are just a few of the questions and answers detailed in a pamphlet obtained from the Middle East Media Research Institute (2014):

Question 3: Can all unbelieving women be taken captive?
There is no dispute among the scholars that it is permissible to capture
  unbelieving women [who are characterized by] original unbelief

[kufr asli], such as the kitabiyat [women from among the People of the Book, i.e. Jews and Christians] and polytheists. However, [the scholars] are disputed over [the issue of] capturing apostate women. The consensus leans towards forbidding it, though some people of knowledge think it permissible. We [ISIS] lean towards accepting the consensus...

Question 5: Is it permissible to have intercourse with a female captive immediately after taking possession [of her]?

If she is a virgin, he [her master] can have intercourse with her immediately after taking possession of her. However, if she isn't, her uterus must be purified [first]...

Question 6: Is it permissible to sell a female captive?

It is permissible to buy, sell, or give as a gift female captives and slaves, for they are merely property, which can be disposed of [as long as that doesn't cause [the Muslim ummah] any harm or damage.

Question 13: Is it permissible to have intercourse with a female slave who has not reached puberty?

It is permissible to have intercourse with the female slave who hasn't reached puberty if she is fit for intercourse; however if she is not fit for intercourse, then it is enough to enjoy her without intercourse.

Question 19: Is it permissible to beat a female slave?

It is permissible to beat the female slave as a [form of] darb ta'deeb [disciplinary beating], [but] it is forbidden to [use] darb al-takseer [literally, breaking beating], [darb] al-tashaffi [beating for the purpose of achieving gratification], or [darb] al-ta'dheeb [torture beating]. Further, it is forbidden to hit the face.

Question 20: What is the ruling regarding a female slave who runs away from her master?

A male or female slave's running away [from their master] is among the gravest of sins...

Question 21: What is the earthly punishment of a female slave who runs away from her master?

She [i.e. the female slave who runs away from her master] has no punishment according to the shari'a of Allah; however, she is [to be] reprimanded [in such a way that] deters others like her from escaping.

The release of documents, such as the pamphlet previously detailed, are part of a broader media campaign designed to recruit potential fighters, as well as reinforce the group's brutal image. As Farwell (2014) notes, the Islamic State has employed a very sophisticated media/public relations campaign using social networking sites such as Facebook and Twitter, as well as other digital communication online services such as Flicker and Tumblr. In addition to establishing a prominent web presence, two mobile applications, Ask.fm and Kik, have been developed to help facilitate communication between jihadists, as well as recruit potential new members. As Jarret Brachman

(2014) explains, Ask.fm allows users to ask jihadists for advice about a host of activities, which run the gamut from questions related to grooming to logistical advice about travel to Syria. These questions are publicly viewable to anyone following a particular jihadist's newsfeed, thereby reaching a much larger audience. The mobile application Kik is a somewhat secure messaging environment for more personal one-on-one communication between jihadists, supporters, and potential recruits (Brachman 2014). As Brachman (2014, p. 2) notes, "these social media channels feed into one another, where an individual inspired by visual propaganda he sees on Instagram may follow a foreign fighter on Twitter until he decides to ask that fighter a question on Ask.fm, which may result in a direct messaging session on Kik until they move to an encrypted direct message conversation on Surespot." The technical savvy of the Islamic State is something of a paradox because the group's tactics "seem to come from a different century, [but] its use of media is up to the moment" (Shane and Hubbard 2014).

The United Nations (2014) reports that the violent images of beheadings and mass executions widely available on the Internet have served as valuable recruitment tools for attracting jihadists within the region, as well as the West. The success of the Islamic State's propaganda campaign is owed in large part to the central message that all Muslims have a duty to restore a caliphate (Farwell 2014). As Farwell (2014, p. 49) observes, "the narrative portrays ISIS as an agent of change, the true apostle of a sovereign faith, a champion of its own perverse notions of social justice, and a collection of avengers bent on settling accounts for the perceived sufferings of others."

Earlier in this chapter, we discussed the complex adaptive systems paradigm and the role that awe plays in supernaturalism. The adoption of modern technological appliances by the Islamic State represents an interesting nexus of these concepts. On the one hand, the Islamic State represents a stridently reactionary worldview that one might otherwise assume to be very Luddite. On the other, they very effectively use the digital realm to both consolidate commitment within their ranks and recruit from the outside world. This technological savvy also helps the Islamic State to impart the "awe" response that Robert Marett (1914) argues is the core of religious emotion. As Jeremy Stolow (2012, p. 222) states, "Awe brings humans into a personal emotional relationship with 'superior powers'... Awe... is something 'not so much thought out as danced out': only when it is moralized can it become religion's essence." In the case of the Islamic State, the "awesome" spectacles of hyperviolence (i.e., terrorist attacks and beheadings) are positioned as acts of religious devotion. They are also used to show the individual actor as a microcosm of the greater truth—a single terrorist actualizing and reconfirming the fullness of the faith.

Echoing a Weberian position,* Jon Elster (1989) provides a useful explanation of the adaptive feedback mechanism, "The elementary unit of social life is the individual human action. To explain social institutions and social change is to show how they arise as the result of the actions and inter-action of individuals." Undergirded by awe, the secular act is transformed into the sacred and the individual into the whole. The process is recursive in that the whole then transmits normative standards and expectations back to individuals. As the Islamic State's embrace of technology demonstrates, their socio-organizational structure is capable of adaptive responses unparalleled in modern Islamic militancy.

Governance

While it is easy to focus on the brutal tactics employed by the group, we must be cognizant that the ultimate goal of the Islamic State is purportedly state-building (Shane and Hubbard 2014). In order to establish the caliphate, the Islamic State has had to gain, as well as maintain, control over Syrian and Iraqi territories. This two-pronged approach has necessitated military force, followed by the establishment and provision of political goods and services that were previously the exclusive domain of the existing govern-ments of both nations (Caris and Reynolds 2014, p. 5). Recent reports indi-cate the Islamic State has established a caliphate that stretches from Aleppo in Syria to Diyala in Iraq (BBC News 2014). Other cities currently under the control of the Islamic State include Mosul, Falluja, and portions of the Iraqi city Ramadi; however, heavy fighting continues in Kobani, which borders Syria (BBC News 2014). In total, the Islamic State controls nine provinces in Syria and seven provinces in Iraq; however, the group has made it clear that it has ambitions that extend well beyond the Syrian and Iraqi borders and into Jordan and Lebanon (BBC News 2014). These ambitions are certainly attain-able given the level of ideological and tactical support the Islamic State has received from foreigners, some of whom are disaffected youth from Western industrialized nations (i.e., France, England, and the United States). As Haim Malka (2014, p. 57) notes:

> While U.S. rhetoric describes ISIS in polemical terms, the reality is that ISIS has two powerful drivers of support: it is a utopian social and political entity that appeals to disaffected young people, and it is a powerful protector of sec-tarian interests for millions of Sunni Arabs in Syria and Iraq who feel system-atically disenfranchised.

---

* Which in this instance is to say, a position informed by the assumptions of methodological individualism.

Malka (2014) further contends that the Islamic State will continue to attract foreigners, provided they keep the goal of establishing a caliphate at the forefront (at least for appearances) and as long as a caliphate is still viewed by supporters as being a viable alternative to other forms of government in the region.

The Islamic State has established quasi-governmental institutions in the areas under its control, and in some areas the groups have instituted holistic systems of governance (Caris and Reynolds 2014). Ar-Raqqa, the first province captured by the Islamic State and its self-proclaimed capital, has developed the most expansive system of governance that includes education, criminal justice, security, and infrastructural development (Caris and Reynolds 2014). As Charles Caris and Samuel Reynolds (2014) report, the Islamic State has a bifurcated system consisting of administration and Muslim services. The administrative side of the government is responsible for the educational system (al-Ta'lim), the criminal justice system, the office of recruitment, and a bureau of public and tribal relations, while the Muslim services half of the government provides goods and services such as water and electricity, humanitarian aid, and bakeries (Caris and Reynolds 2014).

The organizational structure of the Islamic State includes one leader, the caliph (Al-Baghdadi*), and four councils (Sharia, Shura, Military, and Security) (BBC News 2014; United Nations 2014). At the province and local levels, the structure is the same with one leader (governor) and four councils. The usurping of governmental functions by the Islamic State is certainly not a unique phenomenon, given that extremist and terrorist groups in chaotic fragile states often step in to fill voids in the delivery of political goods and services. For example, in Pakistan, a country that rates high among many indices of state failure, the government is widely mistrusted and viewed as corrupt by a considerable portion of its citizens (Khan 2011). Because citizens doubt the government's capacity or willingness to offer needed services, militant Islamic groups flourish in many regions of the country. During the 2005 earthquake in northern Pakistan, relief efforts were largely spearheaded by militant Islamic groups. As such, many citizens preferred to make charitable donations to militants (instead of the government) because there were reasonable assurances that the money would be used to help earthquake victims (Khan 2011). While this is a far less extreme example than what we currently see with the Islamic State, it does help to illustrate the point that fragile governments provide ample opportunities for nonstate actors to engage in functions typically reserved for legitimate governments.

Once in control of regions in Syria and Iraq, the Islamic State engaged in a well-planned, systematic process designed to maintain control over the

---

* Muslims wishing to join the Islamic State are expected to swear allegiance to al-Baghdadi (BBC News 2014).

populace and institute its own mechanisms of governance. The Islamic State seized control of the Syrian city Ar-Raqqa in March 2013, but the implementation of government institutions and the provision of services did not begin until January 2014, after the last of the Islamic States' rivals were driven out of the city (Caris and Reynolds 2014). The need to have sole control over cities is driven by the desire to establish a caliphate, which necessitates a system of governance.

The delivery of public goods is often well publicized and used as a propaganda tool. For example, in November 2014, the Islamic State released photos of children (all male) returning to school in Kirkuk, Iraq, to demonstrate the normality of life under the rule of the Islamic State (Fields 2014). While the Islamic State has not banned education for girls yet, new rules have been implemented that require girls to wear a niqab and to be segregated from male students and teachers (Fields 2014). Reports coming out of the region highlight some notable changes to the Islamic States' educational system. According to Ali Mamouri (2014, para. 9), "labels such as the Republic of Iraq and the Syrian Republic were both changed to become the Islamic State. All topics related to the values of citizenship, patriotism and the like have been omitted, in addition to chants and anthems that might be in contradiction with the religious views of the caliphate state." Other changes include the cancellation of classes in art, music, philosophy, sociology, and psychology, and a ban on teaching the history and religious ideology of religious minorities (Mamouri 2014).

These acts are all part of a larger process of cultural cleansing perpetrated by the Islamic State. The Islamic State seeks to eradicate all history and heritage that it views as "non-Islamic" (i.e., *shirk* or "idolatry"). As Elliott Frieland reported in March 2015, "The group's fighters in Mosul destroyed ancient artifacts from the Mosul museum, including many irreplaceable pieces from the Assyrian period, some 3000 old. They also torched the library, which contained many antique and rare books." Friedland (2015) went on to state that "8,000 books" and "112,709 manuscripts and books, some of which were registered on a UNESCO rarities list were destroyed."

Even with a zealous drive to redact all but a narrow band of history and culture, the Islamic State still faces core nation-building hurdles. While Raqqa has seen a quasi-formalized system of governance led by the Islamic State, other regions under the Islamic States' control do not appear to be as well organized and the provision of goods and services is limited or nonexistent. During an interview with National Public Radio (NPR), an Iraqi government worker living in Mosul (known by the name Sermat) revealed that the electricity is barely functional, garbage collectors are not working because they have not been paid, and food is scarce due to a lack of refrigeration (Kenyon 2014).

Criminal Justice Under the Islamic State

The Islamic State has instituted their own criminal justice system in many of the regions under its control. Their system is based on a strict interpretation of Shari'ah law where justice is often dispensed in a swift and brutal manner. *Shari'ah* is a term that many Westerners may have heard, but lack an understanding of its intricacies. They may associate it with beheadings, corporal punishments, and other "Islamic" things that gain media attention, but such superficial portrayals betray the deeper cultural embeddedness of Shari'ah.

The Arabic word Shari'ah (meaning "the right path") refers to traditional Islamic law, which is primarily derived from the Qur'an and the Sunnah (Anyanwu 2011). There are 6241 verses in the Qur'an and of those, just 200 directly apply to matters of law. As a consequence, other sources of law are needed to form a functional legal system that addresses social expectations/obligations and the penalties associated with violations of these expectations. The other sources of Shari'ah law include the *Hadith*, a collection of Muhammad's sayings; *Ijma* ("to determine" or "consensus"); analogies or *Qiyas*; *Ijtihad* ("independent judgments); *Istislah* ("public good"); sayings of Imams or *Ravayat*; and local customs or *Urf* (Lippman et al. 1998).

Within Shari'ah law, there are three broad classes of sanctions that comprise the majority of punishments rendered by courts—*Hudud, Qisas/Diya*, and *Ta'zir* (Human Rights Watch 2004). Ta'zir punishments have not received international criticism because they are typically meted out for very minor crimes and judges in these cases have discretion when determining appropriate punishments. The same cannot be said of Hudud and Qisas cases, as they have been the subject of intense criticism from human rights groups and the international community.

Hudud punishments are specifically addressed in the sacred text of the Qur'an; therefore, they represent acts against Allah, the gravest of sins in the Islamic religion. The perceived severity of these crimes, coupled with the specific punishments mandated by the Qur'an, leaves no room for judicial discretion to determine the penalty. Hadd (singular) punishments are justified on the basis of "retribution against the wrongdoer for contravening the laws of society, expiation for the culprit after the punishment has been inflicted, and as a general and specific deterrent" (Hakeem et al. 2012, p. 13). Some of the more commonly committed Hadd offenses include falsely accusing someone of having an extramarital affair and the consumption of alcohol, both of which are punishable by flogging. Theft carries a punishment of amputation. First-time offenders face having their right hand cut off at the wrist and a subsequent conviction for theft is punishable by amputation of the left hand at the wrist.* Armed robbery can also carry a sentence of amputation, though the death penalty is possible depending on the circumstances. Adultery is punishable by death, most commonly in the form of death by stoning. The process varies depending on the country in question, but typically the condemned are buried in the ground up to their necks and then stones are thrown at their heads until they succumb to death. Because the stones that are used to carry out this punishment are large enough to be painful, but not so large that the condemned could die from a single stone, it takes an excruciatingly long time to die. Lastly, Muslims who renounce their faith, otherwise known as apostasy, face the death penalty. The justification for this sentence stems from a hadith in which Mohammed proclaimed, "Whoever changes his religion kill him." However, some have noted that the hadith directly contradicts verses in the Qur'an, such as "There is no compulsion in religion" (2:256), and "Whoever so wills may believe and whoever so wills may deny" (18:29) (Ghlian 2014, para. 6).

Qisas punishments are reserved for murder or injury and generally involve a very literal application of retribution. The justification for retaliatory punishments is found in the Qur'an (2:178), which reads:

O ye who believe! Retaliation is prescribed for you in the matter of the murdered; the freeman for the freeman, and the slave for the slave, and the female for the female. And for him who is forgiven somewhat by his (injured) brother, prosecution according to usage and payment unto him in kindness. This is an alleviation and a mercy from your Lord. He who transgresseth after this will have a painful doom.

There are three basic requirements that must be fulfilled before Qisas can be applied in injury cases. The first requirement that must be met addresses the issue of intent. Specifically, those who accidently injure another are not subjected to Qisas (Hakeem et al. 2012). Secondly, the part of the accused's body to be injured must correspond to the location of the victim's injury (Hakeem et al. 2012). In a very recent case, Iranian authorities gouged out the left eye of an unnamed man convicted of blinding another man with acid (Dehghan 2015). The attacker was initially sentenced to have both eyes gouged out; however, the victim in this case has delayed the scheduled injury of his attacker's right eye for six months (Dehghan 2015). Because victims have the right to change their mind about sentencing, it is unknown at this time if the attacker will be rendered fully blind in six months. The last requirement that must be met centers on the ability of the court to inflict the

* Amputation penalties vary from country to country. Some nations such as Saudi Arabia opt for cross-amputation or the amputation of both the right hand and the left foot.

punishment (Hakeem et al. 2012). This provision has, at times, prevented authorities from meting out the punishment, even in cases where the victim insists on retaliation. Victims in injury cases do have the right to accept *Dyia* (blood money) in lieu of retaliatory punishments.

While the foregoing discussion of Shari'ah law is by no means comprehensive, it does provide a basis from which to discuss the Islamic State's application of Shari'ah law. Though they proclaim to implement a pure form of Shari'ah law, it is clear that the system of justice implemented by the Islamic State represents a perversion of the religion. Initially, many Sunni Arabs welcomed the Islamic State, with some describing their arrival as a joyous moment (Cockburn 2015). During an interview with a reporter from the UK newspaper, *The Independent*, a Sunni farmer in Fallujah described the transformation of the Islamic State from victorious liberators championing the Islamic cause to a brutal authoritarian regime that uses fear and terror to render their populace docile. As he describes:

> Everything was going well until Isis also took Mosul. Then restrictions on our people increased. At the mosques, local imams started to be replaced by people from other Arab states or Afghanistan. During the first six months of Isis rule, the movement had encouraged people to go to the mosque, but after the capture of Mosul it became obligatory and anybody who violated the rule received 40 lashes. (Cockburn 2015, para. 15)

Limited accounts from people currently living in areas controlled by the Islamic State report that communities are under near constant surveillance by the morality police (United Nations 2014). Moreover, it is believed that the Islamic State has conscripted children to monitor their parents' behavior and inform the authorities of any rule violations (United Nations 2014). Rule violators face flogging, limb amputation, and various forms of death (e.g., beheading and crucifixion) depending on the infraction. Even small rule infractions can carry a stiff penalty.

Beheadings

The beheading of hostages (in particular, Western hostages being held for ransom) has received perhaps the most sustained attention in the media, largely because of the sheer brutality involved. The beheadings of U.S. journalists James Foley and Steven Sotloff and British aid workers David Haines and Alan Henning were videotaped and circulated via YouTube and other websites. The executions captured international attention, thereby reinforcing the group's image as a brutal fighting force, and also serving as a valuable propaganda and recruitment tool. In addition to hostages, Islamic State authorities use beheading as a method of execution for some crimes.

While certainly shocking and abhorrent, beheadings are hardly a new tactic. According to Timothy Furnish (2005), beheadings have a long history in Islam, but they have become increasingly common because the shock value of other forms of violence has significantly diminished. Since one of the primary purposes of terrorism is to spread fear, Furnish (2005) asserts that decapitations have simply become the latest "fashion" for terrorist groups. The justification for beheading can be found in a verse from the Qu'ran (47:3): "When you encounter the unbelievers on the battlefield, strike off their heads until you have crushed them completely; then bind the prisoners tightly." Furnish (2005) points to another, slightly more obscure passage in the Qu'ran that addresses beheading. Chapter 8, verse 12 reads, "I will cast dread into the hearts of the unbelievers. Strike off their heads, then, and strike off all of their fingertips." Both verses can be viewed as "justification" for the beheading of non-Muslims; however, the more modern interpretation holds that these verses are simply pragmatic. As Furnish (2005, p. 4) explains, "Yusuf 'Ali is one of the few modern commentators who addresses this passage, interpreting it as utilitarian: the neck is among the only areas not protected by armor, and mutilating an opponent's hands prevents him from again wielding his sword or spear." Setting aside differing interpretations of these verses, it is clear that the Islamic State utilizes decapitation to strike fear into those that oppose their ideology. Here again, we see the presence of awe as a modality of social consolidation.

The Islamic State has taken a harsh stance against music, smoking cigarettes, being late to prayer, and most recently, skinny jeans. With the exception of smoking, the penalty for violating the rules in these matters is typically 10 days in prison, coupled with a mandatory course on Islam (Joshi 2015). After 10 days, "offenders" are required to take a test that they must pass if they are to be released from prison (Joshi 2015). Those caught smoking cigarettes face a far harsher punishment, finger amputation* (United Nations 2014). Punishments are typically carried out in public view to serve as a deterrent to others (United Nations 2014). A witness to an amputation recounted the following details to the United Nations (2014, p. 6):

> ISIS declared through mosques that "Al-Hadd", an Islamic punishment, in this case for looting, would be implemented against someone in [a public square]. At the designated time on the following day, a man was brought to the square, blindfolded. A member of ISIS read the group's judgment. Two people held the victim tightly while a third man stretched his arm over a large wooden board. A fourth man cut off the victim's hand. It took a long time. One of the people who was standing next to me vomited and passed out due to the horrific scene.

---

* There have been some limited accounts of the Islamic State beheading cigarette smokers, but the veracity of these reports cannot be confirmed.

Despite the brutality of their legal system, it appears that the Islamic State does have limits. Though difficult to confirm, reports on Salafi Jihadi online forums indicate that a number of Shari'ah judges have been taken into custody and executed by the Islamic State. One judge, Sheikh Abu Jaafar Al-Hattab, was accused of being overly aggressive in Takfir cases. Takfir is defined as "the act of passing the verdict of kufr on anyone whose utterances or deeds openly manifest disbelief" (Skelly 2010, p. 149). In simpler terms, Takfir is the process of labeling someone who professes to follow the Islamic faith as an infidel, in response to an action that calls the legitimacy of Islam into question. Takfir does have an exemption for those who unknowingly violate the law, as "takfir would be legitimate only when a Muslim intentionally violated the prescriptions of the faith and defended these practices in public" (Loimeier 2013, p. 118). This exemption applies even to those under the jurisdiction of the Islamic State. However, Judge Al-Hattab had publicly stated that ignorance is not a valid excuse in these cases (Middle East Monitor 2015). Al-Hattab's belief is not supported in the Qu'ran or the Sunnah and, since the punishment for being labeled an infidel is typically death, his over-zealous stance could be considered one of the gravest of offenses against Islam. Hadith 40:2 explicitly states:

> The blood of a Muslim man who testifies that there is no god but Allah and that I am the Messenger of Allah is not lawful to shed unless he be one of three: a married adulterer, someone killed in retaliation for killing another, or someone who abandons his religion and the Muslim community. (Sekulow 2014, p. 32)

Al-Hattab was executed by the Islamic State in September 2014 and with more judges still in custody, there are likely others that will share the same fate.

Scholarly Backlash

The Islamic State has gained support from large numbers of Muslims, but moderate Muslims and Islamic scholars alike have made it clear that the Islamic State does not reflect their views. Over 100 Islamic scholars from across the globe wrote an open letter to al-Baghdadi challenging his actions and declaring that the Islamic States' interpretation of the Qu'ran is both "illegitimate and perverse" (Oakford 2014). In the letter, scholars noted that the Islamic States' brutal tactics, such as torture, killing, the oppression of women, and slavery, are forbidden in the Islamic religion (Oakford 2014). The scholars went on ask:

> Who gave you authority over the ummah [Muslim people]? ... Was it your group? If this is the case, then a group of no more than several thousand has appointed itself the ruler of over a billion and a half Muslims. This attitude is

based upon a corrupt circular logic that says: Only we are Muslims, and we decide who the caliph is, we have chosen one and so whoever does not accept our caliph is not a Muslim. (Oakford 2014)

With regard to the killing of innocent non-Muslims or Shiite Muslims, scholars noted:

You have killed many innocents who were neither combatants nor armed, just because they disagree with your opinion. ... there is no such thing as offensive, aggressive jihad just because people have different religions or opinions. (Oakford 2014)

In short, there is widespread agreement among religious scholars that the Islamic State does not represent the views of Muslims worldwide and they find the brutal tactics employed by the Islamic State to be morally repugnant.

Boko Haram: The Other Caliphate

To this point, our examination has focused on terrorism in the Middle East. Any complete telling requires an express acknowledgment that terrorism is flourishing in many other regions of the globe. The conflict between Nigerian security forces and the terror group, Boko Haram, provides a ready example of the proliferation of extremist ideology outside the Middle East. Understanding the tactics that Boko Haram uses to create their own caliphate in Northern Nigeria provides an interesting counterpoint to those of the Islamic State. Moreover, the Nigerian government's response to the violence perpetrated by Boko Haram yields a similarly instructive contrast to the situation in Syria. Different as the groups may be, Boko Haram has stated its allegiance to the Islamic State. What this allegiance may portend for the future of both groups also merits some consideration.

Nigeria has long been a state on the verge of failure. Like many other states in Africa, the turbulent nature of Nigeria can be attributed to the early slave trade and a postcolonial legacy (Ifedi and Anyu 2011). While a complete review of the history leading up to the creation of modern-day Nigeria is beyond the scope of this chapter, a brief discussion of England's colonization of Nigeria is needed to understand the relationship between postcolonial legacy and the proliferation of terrorism in Nigeria.*

The colonization of the Niger Delta region began shortly after negotiations at the 1885 Berlin Conference. While there were many reasons cited for

---

* See Falola and Heaton (2008) and Metz (1991) for a more extensive historical examination of Nigeria.

the need to develop and occupy the African continent, economic influence and control of natural resources were the primary motivating factors. Since economic interests reigned supreme, the African continent was divided between colonial powers (England, France, Germany, and others) in ways which best suited their economic and political ambitions. As Viviane Saleh-Hanna and Affor (2008, p. 22) plainly state it, European powers "savagely carved up Africa" with little regard for tribal, cultural, or social divisions that were already in place. England sought and eventually gained control over much of the Niger Delta region because the area was rich in palm oil, a highly sought after ingredient used in making soap, lubricants, and candles (Ifedi and Anyu 2011).

In 1886, England officially took control of the Colony and Protectorate of Lagos (Anyanwu 2011). Other regions soon fell under England's control including the Niger Coast Protectorate in 1893 and the Northern Protectorate in 1900 (Anyanwu 2011). To facilitate the palm oil trade, England granted George Dashwood Taubman Goldie control over the Royal Niger Company (RNC), later known as the United African Company (Metz 1991; Ifedi and Anyu 2011). In accordance with the charter, Goldie was effectively given control over all of the lower Niger territory; however, the charter also stipulated that there would be free trade in the region and local customs were to be respected (Metz 1991).

In practice, little was done to respect free trade or the local culture. Ngozi Okonjo-Iweala (2012, p. 2) notes, "British colonialists and Nigerian politicians regularly exploited ethnic, religious (Christian, Muslim), and regional differences to divide the country rather than to build a nation. As a result, tensions abounded in the early days of the country." Additionally, the RNC implemented a system of high taxes and strict licensure regulations, which ensured that native traders were unable to legally trade (Ifedi and Anyu 2011). To protect the company's interests and strengthen their monopoly, the RNC functioned as a quasi-government entity, complete with a secret service agency, police, customs courts, and prisons (Ifedi and Anyu Hakeem 2011). Those who attempted to illegally smuggle palm oil were often shot and attempts by tribal leaders to establish trading monopolies of their own were met with violence (Ifedi and Anyu 2011). The native population reacted violently to the actions of the RNC by attacking company officials. This, in turn, prompted a series of retaliatory attacks from the RNC, including the 1888 Asaba attack and the 1889 attack on Obosi (Falola and Heaton 2008). By the mid-1890s, the RNC began preemptive attacks in the north to prevent other colonial powers from gaining a foothold in the region (Falola and Heaton 2008). Eventually, England launched an investigation into the company's trading practices, which resulted in a change of ownership, a merger with another company, and a name change (Ifedi and Anyu 2011).

The turbulent nature of life in the Niger Delta did not abate in the absence of the RNC; nor did the economic deprivation experienced by the native populace. Due to the RNC's restrictive trading practices, many native Nigerian traders had lost their livelihoods. Additionally, economic problems were compounded because colonial authorities required that all taxes be paid in cash (Heilbrunn 2014). This policy forced many people who were already marginalized and poor into wage labor (Heilbrunn 2014). Also during this time, borders continued to shift. In 1906, the Niger Coast Protectorate and the Colony and Protectorate of Lagos were merged to create the Southern Protectorate (Anyanwu 2011). The last merging of territory occurred in 1914, when the southern and northern protectorates were thrust together to form modern Nigeria (Anyanwu 2011). To say that the north and south were vastly different regions would be a gross understatement. The creation of Nigeria failed to take existing ethnic and religious divisions between the north and south into consideration. Instead, more than 250 ethnic groups without a shared language, religion, or identity were forced together to form Nigeria (Anyanwu 2011). As Hill (2012, p. 1) explains:

> The flimsiness of the cultural, linguistic, and religious links between these communities stood in stark contrast to the strength of those they shared with the inhabitants of neighboring countries. Hausa in the north were bound more tightly to their kin in Niger and Cameroon than they were to the Ijaw in the south-south. And Yoruba in the southwest looked to Benin and Ghana before Kano and Sokoto.

Nigeria remains the most ethnically diverse nation in Africa. There are 19 major ethnic divisions that make up the majority of the population, and several hundred smaller groups within them. In addition to ethnic cleavages, religious divisions between the northern and southern states have been a catalyst for violence, both historically and currently. With the exception of some small pockets of traditional religions, the north is predominantly Islamic and the south is predominately Christian.

As Helen Metz (1991) explains, the influence of Islam accounts for "the dichotomy between north and south and for the divisions within the north that have been so strong during the colonial and postcolonial eras." There is evidence that Islam may have been brought to the region as early as the seventh or eighth century; however, Islam's presence in the region was cemented with a jihad in 1804, led by the Uthman Dan Fodio, that united northern Nigeria and some parts of Niger and Camaroon into one Islamic state (Smith and Lewis 1966). When comparing the sociopolitical conditions in colonial Nigeria with colonial Syria, several broad themes emerge—artificially drawn borders imposed by an outside power, a lack of shared identity among the populace, and the previous existence of (and a desire to return to) one Islamic

State. A century later, the effects of postcolonial legacy in both Syria and Nigeria are readily apparent.

When Nigeria gained independence from England in 1960, the nation was politically unstable. The first elected government was overthrown by a military coup in less than five years. Unfortunately, military rule proved no more efficacious and no less corrupt than the civilian government. Deeply embedded corruption has come to be a defining feature of modern Nigeria. Some scholars even contend that corruption is woven into the very fabric of Nigeria (Smith 2009). Indeed, corruption is so pervasive that most citizens view government as synonymous with corruption (Smith 2009). Smith (2009) also points out that citizens are forced to navigate through (and sometimes participate in) government corruption in order to satisfy basic needs.

In sum, that Nigeria is a fragile state should come as no surprise to any informed onlooker. The chaos and corruption that fuel instability have been instrumental in both creating and perpetuating an environment conducive to terrorist activities.

The Rise of Boko Haram

The northern Nigerian terror group, Boko Haram, was created in 2002 by Mohammed Yusuf, a Muslim cleric (Council on Foreign Relations 2015). Boko Haram has been responsible for a great deal of violence throughout Nigeria. Though its goals have shifted slightly since inception, the stated ultimate goal of Boko Haram is to overthrow the Nigerian government (Council on Foreign Relations 2015). Recently, the group has increased the number, size, and scope of its attacks in an effort to implement Shari'ah law and establish a caliphate (Council on Foreign Relations 2015; Human Rights Watch 2013; IntelCenter 2014).

Southern Nigeria is home to the nation's oil reserves and compared with the north, the region has a robust economy (Vice News 2015). The Muslim-dominated north, however, has seen increasing unemployment rates and is in dire economic circumstances (Okoro and Oteze 2015). The difference between the two regions is stark; Nigeria's poorest states are all located in the north, where approximately 75% of the population lives in poverty (Steven et al. 2014; Okoro and Oteze 2015), compared with 27% in the south. As a consequence, "the north has the lowest school attendance rates, the lowest vaccination rates, the highest infant and child mortality rates, and the highest maternal mortality rate in the country" (Steven et al. 2014, p. 105). In some northern regions, the infant mortality rate is double that of the south and children in some southern regions are vaccinated on average about seven times the rate of children in the north (Steven et al. 2014). These circumstances, along with an absence of governance in the north, have helped fuel the group's growth (Vice News 2015).

The group's name, Boko Haram,* roughly translates to *Western education is sin* or *Western education is forbidden*, depending on the colloquial translation (Council on Foreign Relations 2015; IntelCenter 2015). As the name implies, the group maintains that public schools brainwash children with Western ideals. As such, public schools, along with other secular government institutions, are viewed as significant targets in the fight to control Nigeria (IntelCenter 2015). A review of the group's attacks reveals that during the period July 2014 to March 2015, Boko Haram had carried out 147 attacks against cities, towns, and villages, compared with 32 attacks directed toward military forces (IntelCenter 2015). While Boko Haram directs much of its ire toward the Nigerian government, it appears that civilians ultimately bear the brunt of the violence.

Though accurate figures are difficult to obtain, an estimated 10,000 people have been killed and nearly 1.5 million have been displaced due to violence associated with Boko Haram (Council on Foreign Relations 2015). "In Borno... the military went on a rampage after a bombing injured two soldiers, killing at least thirty civilians. Meanwhile, in Benue... communal conflict resulted in the deaths of at least thirty people and the destruction of homes and farmland... at least six hundred people were killed in October 2012" (Council on Foreign Relations 2012).

During the first half of 2014, Boko Haram carried out at least 95 attacks, killing over 2000 people (Human Rights Watch 2014a–c), nearly double the death toll in 2011 and 2012 (Steven et al. 2014). The April 2014 kidnapping of almost 300 schoolgirls from Chibok has received perhaps the most media coverage, but there have been other school attacks perpetrated by the group (Human Rights Watch 2014a–c). Just two months before the abduction of the Chibok girls, Boko Haram fighters purportedly locked the doors and then set fire to a male dormitory at the Federal College of Buni Yadi, killing almost 60 people (Human Rights Watch 2014a–c). To date, Boko Haram has destroyed approximately 211 schools in the Borno state alone; figures for the other Nigerian states are either unavailable or unreliable, but it is safe to estimate that the total number of schools destroyed nationwide is devastatingly large. Including the Chibok incident, more than 500 women and girls were kidnapped in 2014 and of those, at least 400 are still in captivity (Human Rights Watch 2014a–c). The number of hostages in the group's custody nearly doubled in March 2015 when Boko Haram kidnapped at least 400 people a day

---

* Okoro and Oteze (2015, p. 108) note that Boko Haram strongly rejects the name and prefers to be referred to by its more official name, "Jama 'atu Ahlis Sunna awati wal-jihad" ("People committed to the propagation of the Prophet's teachings and Jihad" or, more literally translated "Association of Sunnas for the Propagation of Islam and for Holy War").

prior to the siege by Nigerian security forces that liberated the northeastern town of Damask (Oakford 2015). Just 50 residents of Damask remained in the town (Oakford 2015), making it a somewhat hollow victory for the government. Reports from those who have escaped or been released indicate that women captured by Boko Haram face much the same fate as those kidnapped by the Islamic State (e.g., sexual violence and forced marriages) (Human Rights Watch 2014a–c). Apart from the media coverage surrounding the kidnapping of the Chibok girls, international attention and media coverage has largely focused on the Islamic State. This is troubling because Boko Haram has proved to be deadlier than the Islamic State. During 2014, the Islamic State was responsible for 1070 deaths and 1018 injuries, compared with Boko Haram with 2457 deaths and 127 injuries (IntelCenter 2015).

Boko Haram primarily engages in guerrilla warfare, though they have also been responsible for kidnappings, suicide bombing, and the use of improvised explosive devices (IntelCenter 2015). The majority of fatalities have occurred in the northeast regions, though pockets of violence have erupted throughout the nation, with some reported attacks occurring in Chad and Niger.

Both Boko Haram and the Islamic State have perpetrated countless human rights violations to achieve their goals, but key differences remain in the realm of establishing governance. As Julia Payne (2015, para. 4) notes, "while it [Boko Haram] has matched Islamic State in Syria and Iraq in its brutality—it beheads its enemies on camera—it has seriously lagged in the more mundane business of state building." Unlike the Islamic State, which provides much-needed services to win the hearts and minds of the communities they occupy, Boko Haram relies almost exclusively on violence to maintain control of the populace (Keating 2015; Payne 2015). Though a stable and consistent form of governance has yet to emerge in Boko Haram–controlled areas, some reports indicate that Shari'ah law was implemented in Gwoza, the former headquarters for the group (Moore 2014).

In response to Boko Haram's violence, Nigerian security forces have opted to use a very heavy-handed approach. Unfortunately, this decision has led Nigerian security forces to perpetrate innumerable human rights violations. According to Human Rights Watch (2014a–c), once in the custody of security forces, suspected terrorists or those presumed to have ties to Boko Haram are tortured and held in secure confinement, without charge or access to an attorney. During the first half of 2013, Amnesty International (2013) reports that at least 950 people with suspected connections to Boko Haram have died while in military detention. Further, Human Rights Watch (2014a–c) reports that only 50 of the 500 suspects recommended for trial have actually been tried.

In conclusion, the failure of the Nigerian government to protect its citizens, along with the exclusion of northerners from the political process, has only served to bolster Boko Haram (Solomon 2014). Recently, Nigerian security forces have successfully reclaimed some of Boko Haram's territory, thus weakening the group somewhat. While certainly a positive step, ultimately this does little to solve the underlying problems that sparked the development and growth of Boko Haram in the first place.

The newly elected Nigerian president, Muhammadu Buhari (2015), who defeated incumbent Goodluck Jonathon, aims to set Nigeria on a more stable footing. Buhari is a former military general with a reputation for deep resolve. As John Campbell (2015) writes for *Foreign Policy*, "[Buhari] as military chief of state from 1983 to 1985, is remembered as a strongman with an iron will. During his reign, he cracked down on corrupt politicians and led the 'war against indiscipline,' which sought to bring a culture of patriotism and order to society."

In an April 2015 op-ed to the *New York Times*, Buhari demonstrated an awareness that the ills of his nation will require more than military force to cure:

> But as our military pushes Boko Haram back, as it will, we must be ready to focus on what else must be done to counter the terrorists. We must address why it is that young people join Boko Haram.... My government will first act to defeat it militarily and then ensure that we provide the very education it despises to help our people help themselves. Boko Haram will soon learn that, as Nelson Mandela said, "Education is the most powerful weapon which you can use to change the world." (Buhari, 2015)

Until corruption, instability, and systemic gaps in core governmental resources are effectively addressed, Nigeria will likely continue to act as host to extremist groups such as Boko Haram. Of course, troubles for Nigeria may not be exclusively of domestic origin.

During the first half of 2015, videos published by Boko Haram have begun to depict a convergence of sorts between Nigerian militants and the Islamic State. The similarities can be seen in terms of the symbolism used by both groups, the religious and political ideologies, and, most alarmingly, their insurgency doctrines. The first evidence of this nexus came during the summer of 2014 when Boko Haram leader Abubakar Shekau publically expressed support for the Islamic State caliph, Abu Bakr al-Baghdadi. Around the same time, Boko Haram added the jihadist black banner to its logo (Pham 2015).

References

Adler, F. and W. Laufer. 2000. *The Legacy of Anomie Theory*, 2nd edn, New Brunswick, NJ: Transaction.
Al-Zawahiri, A. 2005. Letter from Al-Zawahiri to Al-Zarqawi. *Homeland Security*. http://www.globalsecurity.org/security/library/report/2005/zawahiri-zarqawi-letter_9jul2005.htm (Accessed December 5, 2014).

108State Fragility Around the World

Amin, H. 2010. The origins of the Sunni/Shia split in Islam. *Islam for Today.* http://www. islamfortoday.com (Accessed April 5, 2011).Amnesty International. 2013. Nigeria: Deaths of hundreds of Boko Haram suspects in custody requires investigation. https://www.amnesty.org/en/articles/news/2013/10/nigeria-deaths-hundreds-boko-haram-suspects-custody-requires-investigation/ (Accessed April 6, 2015).
Andersen, L., B. Møller, and F. Stepputat. 2007. *Fragile States and Insecure People? Violence, Security, and Statehood in the Twenty-First Century.* New York: Palgrave MacMillan.
Anter, A. and K. Tribe. 2014. *Max Weber's Theory of the Modern State: Origins, Structure and Significance.* New York: Palgrave Macmillan.
Anyanwu, J. 2011. Towards reducing poverty in Nigeria: The case of Igboland. *Journal of Economics and International Finance* 3(9): 513–528.
Anyanwu, O. 2011. *The Politics of Access: University Education and Nation-Building in Nigeria, 1948–2000.* Ontario: University of Calgary Press.
Barrett, R. 2014. Foreign fighters in Syria. The Soufan Group. http://soufangroup.com (Accessed June 23, 2014).
BBC News. 2010. Senior Iraqi Al-Qaeda leaders "killed". http://news.bbc.co.uk/2/hi/middle_east/8630213.stm (Accessed December 5, 2014).
BBC News. 2011. What is Ashura? http://www.bbc.com/news/world-middle-east-16047713 (Accessed December 5, 2014).
BBC News. 2014. What is Islamic State? http://www.bbc.com/news/world-middle-east-29052144 (Accessed January 14, 2015).
Black, D. 2004. The geometry of terrorism. *Sociological Theory* 22: 14–25.
Boon, K., A. Huq, and D. Lovelace. 2010. *Assessing the GWOT.* New York: Oxford University Press.
Brachman, J. 2014. Transcending organization: Individuals and "the Islamic State". START Analytical Brief. Maryland, MD: College Park. http://www.start.umd.edu/pubs/START_TranscendingOrganizationIndividualsandtheIslamicState_AnalyticalBrief_June2014.pdf (Accessed July 4, 2015).
Braithwaite, J., V. Braithwaite, M. Cookson, and L. Dunn. 2010. *Anomie and Violence: Non-Truth and Reconciliation in Indonesian Peacebuilding.* Acton, ACT: ANU Press.
Brisard, J. and D. Martinez. 2005. *Zarqawi: The New Face of Al-Qaeda.* New York: Other Press.
Buhari, M. 2015. Muhammadu Buhari: We will stop Boko Haram. *New York Times.* http://www.nytimes.com/2015/04/15/opinion/muhammadu-buhari-we-will-stop-boko-haram.html?_r=0 (Accessed April 23, 2015).
Campbell, J. 2015. Buhari is the man to defeat Boko Haram. *Foreign Policy.* http://foreign-policy.com/2015/04/10/buhari-is-the-man-to-defeat-boko-haram-nigeria/ (Accessed May 2, 2015).
Caris, C. and S. Reynolds. 2014. ISIS governance in Syria. Institute for the Study of War. http://www.understandingwar.org/report/isis-governance-syria (Accessed January 16, 2015).
Chambers, P. 2012. Abu Musab Al Zarqawi: The making and unmaking of an American monster (in Baghdad). *Alternatives: Global, Local, Political* 3: 30–51.
CIA World Factbook. 2014. https://www.cia.gov/library/publications/the-world-factbook/ (Accessed March 26, 2010).
Clunan, A. and H. Trinkunas. 2010. *Ungoverned Spaces: Alternatives to State Authority in An Era of Softened Sovereignty.* Stanford, CA: Stanford Security Studies.
Cockburn, P. 2015. Life under Isis: The everyday reality of living in the Islamic 'Caliphate' with its 7th century laws, very modern methods and merciless violence. *The Independent.* http://www.independent.co.uk/news/world/middle-east/life-under-isis-the-everyday-reality-of-living-in-the-islamic-caliphate-with-its-7th-century-laws-very-modern-methods-and-merciless-violence-10109655.html (Accessed April 4, 2015).

Cordesman, A. and S. Khazai. 2014. *Iraq in Crisis.* Center for Strategic and International Studies. http://csis.org/publication/iraq-crisis-1 (Accessed June 5, 2014).

Council on Foreign Relations. 2012. Boko Haram and Nigeria's pervasive violence. http://www.cfr.org/nigeria/boko-haram-nigerias-pervasive-violence/p29706 (Accessed December 11, 2015).

Council on Foreign Relations. 2015. Backgrounders: Boko Haram. http://www.cfr.org/nigeria/boko-haram/p25739 (Accessed March 6, 2015).

Cox, D., J. Falconer, and B. Stackhouse. 2009. *Terrorism, Instability, and Democracy in Asia and Africa.* Boston, MA: Northeastern University Press.

Dehghan, S. 2015. Eye for an eye: Iran blinds acid attacker. *The Guardian.* http://www.theguardian.com/world/2015/mar/05/eye-for-an-eye-iran-blinds-man-who-carried-out-acid-attack (Accessed June 2, 2015).

Durkheim, É. 1964. *The Division of Labor in Society.* New York: Free Press of Glencoe.

Elden, S. 2009. *Terror and Territory: The Spatial Extent of Sovereignty.* Minneapolis, MN: University of Minnesota Press.

Elster, J. 1989. *Nuts and Bolts for the Social Sciences.* Cambridge. Cambridge University Press.

Falola, T. and M. Heaton, 2008. *The History of Nigeria.* Cambridge: Cambridge University Press.

Farwell, J. 2014. The media strategy of ISIS. *Survival* 56: 49–55.

Fields, L. 2014. In photos: Kids go to school in Islamic State-held territory in Iraq. Vice News. https://news.vice.com/article/in-photos-kids-go-to-school-in-islamic-state-held-territory-in-iraq (Accessed December 10, 2014).

Financial Action Task Force. 2015. Financing of the terrorist organisation Islamic State in Iraq and the Levant (ISIL). www.fatf-gafi.org/topics/methodsandtrends/documents/financing-of-terrorist-organisation-isil.html (Accessed June 10, 2015).

Foucault, M. 1977. *Discipline and Punish: The Birth of the Prison.* (A. Sheridan Trans.) London: Peregrine Books.

Franzese, R. 2009. *The Sociology of Deviance: Differences, Tradition, and Stigma.* Springfield, IL: Charles C. Thomas.

Friedland, E. 2015. Islamic State destroying ancient cultural treasures. *The Clarion Project.* http://www.clarionproject.org/analysis/islamisms-totalitarian-vision-control-or-destroy-all-culture (Accessed March 30, 2015).

Furnish, T. 2005. Does Islam condone beheadings? *George Mason University History News Network.* http://historynewsnetwork.org/article/12071 (Accessed July 4, 2015).

Garamone, J. 2006. United States Department of Defense. Defense.gov News Article: Masri Now Leads Iraq Al Qaeda, Coalition Officials Say. http://www.defense.gov/news/newsarticle.aspx?id=16029 (Accessed December 5, 2014).

Ghlian, M. 2014. Islam, Saudi and apostasy: Does Islamic law really proscribe the death penalty for apostasy? *Al Jazeera English News.* http://www.aljazeera.com/indepth/opinion/2014/05/islam-saudi-apostasy-201458142128717473.html (Accessed April 4, 2015).

Ghosh, B. 2014. ISIS: A short history. *The Atlantic.* http://www.theatlantic.com/international/archive/2014/08/isis-a-short-history/376030/ (Accessed December 5, 2014).

Gleick, P. 2014. Water, drought, climate change, and conflict in Syria. *Weather, Climate, and Society* 6: 331–340.

Goodarzi, J. n.d. *The Iran Primer. Iran and Syria.* http://iranprimer.usip.org/resource/iran-and-syria (Accessed November 3, 2014).

Hafez, M. 2011. Al Qaeda in Iraq. In G. Martin and H. W. Kushner (Eds) *The Sage Encyclopedia of Terrorism,* 2nd edn, pp. 34–35, Thousand Oaks, CA: Sage.

Hakeem, F., M. Haberfeld, and A. Verma. 2012. *Policing Muslim Communities: Comparative International Context.* New York: Springer.

Hazleton, L. 2009. *After the Prophet: The Epic Story of the Shia-Sunni Split in Islam.* New York: Anchor Books.

Heilbrunn, J. 2014. *Oil, Democracy, and Development in Africa*. West Nyack, NY: Cambridge University Press.

Hill, J. 2012. *Nigeria Since Independence: Forever Fragile?* New York: Palgrave MacMillian.

Hoffman, B. 2006. *Inside Terrorism*, 2nd edn, New York: Columbia University Press.

Human Rights Watch. 2004. Political Shari'a? Human Rights and Islamic Law in Northern Nigeria. http://www.hrw.org/reports/2004/nigeria0904/3.htm (Accessed June 3, 2013).

Human Rights Watch. 2013. *World Report 2013: Nigeria*. https://www.hrw.org/world-report/2013/country-chapters/nigeria (Accessed April 23, 2014).

Human Rights Watch. 2014a. Iraq: ISIS executed hundreds of prison inmates. http://www.hrw.org/news/2014/10/30/iraq-isis-executed-hundreds-prison-inmates (Accessed January 16, 2015).

Human Rights Watch. 2014b. Nigeria: Boko Haram kills 2,053 civilians in 6 months: apparent crimes against humanity. http://www.hrw.org/news/2014/07/15/nigeria-boko-haram-kills-2053-civilians-6-months (Accessed August 1, 2014).

Human Rights Watch. 2014c. *World Report 2015: Events of 2014*. New York: Human Rights Watch.

Ifedi, J. and J. Anyu. 2011. Blood oil, ethnicity, and conflict in the Niger Delta Region of Nigeria. *Mediterranean Quarterly* 22: 74–92.

IntelCenter 2014. Total killed in terrorist and rebel incidents by group in 2014. https://www.intelcenter.com/reports/charts/killed-group-2014/index.html (Accessed April 23, 2014).

Joshi, P. 2015. Isis: Skinny jeans for men outlawed under new sharia laws. *International Business Times*. http://www.ibtimes.co.uk/isis-skinny-jeans-men-outlawed-under-new-laws-1494912 (Accessed April 4, 2015).

Kamrava, M. 2014. *The Modern Middle East: A Political History Since the First World War*, 3rd edn, Berkeley, CA: University of California Press.

Kaplan, E. 2006. *Abu Hamza Al-Muhajir, Zarqawi's Mysterious Successor* (aka Abu Ayub Al-Masri). Council on Foreign Relations. http://www.cfr.org/iraq/abu-hamza-al-muhajir-zarqawis-mysterious-successor-aka-abu-ayub-al-masri/p10894 (Accessed December 05, 2014).

Keating, J. 2015. The war against Boko Haram is going international. *Slate News*. http://www.slate.com/blogs/the_slatest/2015/01/20/boko_haram_massacre_the_insurgency_in_northern_nigeria_is_going_international.html (Accessed April 17, 2015).

Kenyon, P. 2014. Life under the Islamic State: Sharia law and few services. *National Public Radio*. http://www.npr.org/blogs/parallels/2014/08/29/343986937/life-under-the-islamic-state-sharia-law-and-few-services (Accessed April 3, 2015).

Khan, S. 2011. Civil war research and international development discourse: Evolving centrality of state and nature of its institutions. *Journal of Alternative Perspectives in the Social Sciences* 3: 656–673.

Kirdar, M. 2011. *Al Qaeda in Iraq*. Washington, DC: Center for Strategic and International Studies. http://csis.org/files/publication/110614_Kirdar_AlQaedaIraq_Web.pdf (Accessed July 5, 2011).

Krämer, G. 2008. *A History of Palestine: From the Ottoman Conquest to the Founding of the State of Israel*. Princeton, NJ: Princeton University Press.

Lawson, F. 2006. *Constructing International Relations in the Arab World*. Stanford, CA: Stanford University Press.

Lemay-Hébert, N. 2010. *Trying to Make Sense of the Contemporary Debate on State-Building: The Legitimacy and the Institutional Approaches on State, State Collapse and State-Building*. Edinburgh: Proceedings of Political Studies Association.

Lippman, M., S. McConville, and M. Yerushalmi. 1988. *Islamic Criminal Law and Procedure: An Introduction*. Westport, CT: Praeger.

Loimeier, R. 2013. *Muslim Societies in Africa a Historical Anthropology*. Bloomington, IN: Indiana University Press.

Malka, H. 2014. The challenge of non-state actors. http://csis.org/publication/challenge-non-state-actors-0 (Accessed January 16, 2015).

Mamouri, A. 2014. IS imposes new rules on education in Syria, *Iraq. Al-Monitor.* http://www. al-monitor.com/pulse/originals/2014/10/islamic-state-impose-education-program-iraq-syria.html##ixzz3LbndRZct (Accessed January 16, 2015).

Mapping Militant Organizations. 2014. http://web.stanford.edu/group/mappingmilitants/ cgi-bin/ (Accessed February 1, 2014).

Marc, A., A. Willman, and G. Aslam. 2013. *Societal Dynamics and Fragility: Engaging Societies in Responding to Fragile Situations.* Washington, DC: World Bank.

Marett, R. 1914. *The Threshold of Religion.* New York: MacMillan.

Metz, H. (Ed.). 1991. *Nigeria: A Country Study.* Washington, DC: GPO for the Library of Congress.

Middle East Media Research Institute. 2014. Islamic state (ISIS) releases pamphlet on female slaves. http://www.memrijttm.org/islamic-state-isis-releases-pamphlet-on-female-slaves. html#_edn1 (Accessed January 16, 2015).

Middle East Monitor. 2015. ISIS Executes one of its sharia judges. *Middle East Monitor.* https://www.middleeastmonitor.com/news/middle-east/17435-isis-executes-one-of-its-sharia-judges (Accessed April 3, 2015).

Moore, J. 2014. Boko Haram Nigeria insurgency: 'Dozens' killed in slaughter in northeastern town of Gwoza. *International Business Times.* http://www.ibtimes.co.uk/boko-haram-nigeria-insurgency-dozens-killed-slaughter-northeastern-town-gwoza-1460132 (Accessed February 10, 2015).

Nelson, B. 2006. *The Making of the Modern State: A Theoretical Evolution.* New York: Palgrave Macmillan.

Oakford, S. 2014. Foreign fighters are flooding into Iraq and Syria to join the Islamic State. https://news.vice.com/article/foreign-fighters-are-flooding-into-iraq-and-syria-to-join-the-islamic-state (Accessed November 1, 2014).

Oakford, S. 2015. Alleged mass abduction could undermine Nigeria's campaign against Boko Haram. Vice News. https://news.vice.com/article/alleged-mass-abduction-could-undermine-nigerias-campaign-against-boko-haram (Accessed April 3, 2015).

Okonjo-Iweala, N. 2012. *Reforming the Unreformable Lessons from Nigeria.* Cambridge, MA: MIT Press.

Okoro, C. and Oteze, A. 2015. *Life is a Dance.* San Francisco, CA: Blurb Publishing.

Olmert, Y. 1985. Basic data on six key Arab states: Egypt, Syria, Iraq, Saudi Arabia, Jordan, and Lebanon. In I. Stockman-Shomron (Ed.) *Israel, the Middle East, and the Great Powers*, pp. 303–318, Piscataway, NJ: Transaction Publishers.

Oswell, D. 2006. *Culture and Society: An Introduction to Cultural Studies.* London: Sage.

Pate, M. and L. Gould, 2012. *Corporal Punishment Around the World.* Santa Barbara, CA: Praeger.

Patrick, S. 2011. *Weak Links: Fragile States, Global Threats, and International Security.* Oxford: Oxford University Press.

Payne, J. 2015. Nigerians face killings, hunger in Boko Haram's 'state'. Reuters. http://www.reuters.com/article/2015/01/20/us-nigeria-boko-haram-insight-idUSK-BN0KS1S120150120 (Accessed April 17, 2015).

PBS. 2014. How Islamic State uses systematic sexual violence against women. http://www.pbs.org/newshour/bb/islamic-state-uses-systematic-sexual-violence-women/ (Accessed January 16, 2015).

Pham, J. 2015. March for Paris, but don't overlook Boko Haram horror. CNN News. http://www.cnn.com/2015/01/12/opinion/pham-boko-haram-threat/index.html (Accessed April 29, 2015).

Piazza, J. 2008. Incubators of terror: Do failed and failing states promote transnational terrorism? *International Studies Quarterly* 52: 469–488.

Pipes, D. 1992. *Greater Syria: The History of an Ambition.* Cary, NC: Oxford University Press.

Polk, W. 2013. Understanding Syria: From pre-civil war to post-Assad: How drought, foreign meddling, and long-festering religious tensions created the tragically splintered Syria we know today. *The Atlantic.* http://www.theatlantic.com/international/archive/2013/12/understanding-syria-from-pre-civil-war-to-post-assad/281989/ (Accessed June 10, 2015).

Provence, M. 2005. *The Great Syrian Revolt and the Rise of Arab Nationalism.* Austin, TX: University of Texas Press.

Rogan, E. 2009. *The Arabs: A History.* New York: Basic Books.

Rotberg, R. 2004. *When States Fail: Causes and Consequences.* Princeton, NJ: Princeton University Press.

Ruggiero, V. 2006. *Understanding Political Violence: A Criminological Approach.* Maidenhead: Open University Press.

Sadjadpour, K. 2014. Examining what a nuclear Iran deal means for global security, testimony before the house foreign affairs subcommittee on the Middle East and North Africa. http://docs.house.gov/meetings/FA/FA13/20141120/102758/HHRG-113-FA13-Wstate-SadjadpourK-20141120.pdf (Accessed January 20, 2015).

Sadowski, Y. 2002. The evolution of political identity in Syria. In S. Telhami and M. Barnett (Eds) *Identity and Foreign Policy in the Middle East,* pp. 137–154, Ithaca, NY: Cornell University Press.

Saleh-Hanna, V. and C. Affor, 2008. *Colonial Systems of Control: Criminal Justice in Nigeria.* Ottawa: University of Ottawa Press.

Sekulow, J. 2014. *Rise of ISIS: A Threat We Can't Ignore.* Brentwood, TN: Howard Books.

Shane, S. and B. Hubbard. 2014. ISIS displaying a deft command of varied media. *The New York Times.* http://www.nytimes.com/2014/08/31/world/middleeast/isis-displaying-a-deft-command-of-varied-media.html (Accessed January 14, 2015).

Skelly, J. 2010. *Political Islam from Muhammad to Ahmadinejad: Defenders, Detractors, and Definitions.* Santa Barbara, CA: Praeger Security International.

Smith, D. 2009. Population participation in corruption in Nigeria. In R. Rotberg (Ed.) *Corruption, Global Security, and World Order,* pp. 283–309, Cambridge, MA: World Peace Foundation.

Smith, M. G. and M. Lewis. 1966. In Islam in tropical Africa. In I. M. Lewis (Ed.) *The Jihad of Shehu Dan Fodio: Some Problems,* pp. 408–424, London: Oxford University Press.

Sohl, M. 2010. Tackling the drought in Syria. *Nature Middle East.* http://www.natureasia.com/en/nmiddleeast/article/10.1038/nmiddleeast.2010.206 (Accessed January 15, 2015).

Solomon, D. 2014. Boko Haram's predatory state within a predatory state. *Al Jazeera America.* http://america.aljazeera.com/opinions/2014/9/boko-haram-nigeriacorruptionislamicgovernance.html (Accessed April 17, 2015).

Staub, E. 2007. Preventing violence and terrorism and promoting positive relations between Dutch and Muslim communities in Amsterdam. *Peace and Conflict: Journal of Peace Psychology* 13: 333–360.

Steven, D., E. O'Brien, and B. Jones. 2014. *The New Politics of Strategic Resources: Energy and Food Security Challenges in the 21st Century.* Washington, DC: Brookings Institution Press.

Stolow, J. 2012. *Deus in Machina: Religion, Technology, and the Things in Between.* New York: Fordham University Press.

Teslik, L. 2006. Profile: Abu Musab Al-Zarqawi. Council on Foreign Relations. http://www.cfr.org/iraq/profile-abu-musab-al-zarqawi/p9866 (Accessed December 5, 2014).

The Economist. 2012. The Islamic State of Iraq and greater Syria: Two Arab countries fall apart. http://www.economist.com/news/middle-east-and-africa/21604230-extreme-islamist-group-seeks-create-caliphate-and-spread-jihad-across (Accessed January 16, 2015).

The Pacific Institute. 2014. Water and conflict in Syria: Drought, water and agricultural management, and climatic conditions are factors in the Syrian conflict. http://pacinst.org/news/water-drought-climate-change-conflict-in-syria/ (Accessed December 11, 2015).

Tilly, C. 2004. Terror, terrorism, terrorists. *Sociological Theory* 22: 5–13.

Tiryakian, E. 2009. *For Durkheim: Essays in Historical and Cultural Sociology.* Burlington, VT: Ashgate.

de Tocqueville, A. 1966/1866. *The Ancien Regime and the French Revolution.* New York: Collins.

United Nations. 2014. United Nations action to counter terrorism, counter-terrorism, global counter-terrorism strategy, general assembly and counter-terrorism, secretary-general and counter terrorism, SG, UN, SC, terrorism, GA, general assembly. http://www.un.org/en/terrorism/highlevelpanel.shtml (Accessed November 5, 2014).

Vice News. 2015. The war against Boko Haram. https://news.vice.com/video/the-war-against-boko-haram-part-1 (Accessed April 30, 2015).

Wagner, H. 2004. *The Division of the Middle East: The Treaty of Sèvres.* Philadelphia, PA: Chelsea House Publishers.

Walter, B. 2003. Re-conceptualizing conflict resolution as a three-stage process. *International Negotiation* 7: 299–311.

Weaver, M. 2006. The short, violent life of Abu Musab al-Zarawi. *The Atlantic.* http://www.theatlantic.com/magazine/archive/2006/07/the-short-violent-life-of-abu-musab-al-zarqawi/304983/ (Accessed March 25, 2015).

Zelin, A. 2014. Abu Bakr Al Baghdadi: Islamic State's driving force. BBC News. http://www.bbc.com/news/world-middle-east-28560449 (Accessed December 3, 2014).

Zisser, E. 2006. *Commanding Syria: Bashar Al-Asad and the First Years in Power.* London: IB Tauris.

The Relationship between Transnational Crime and State Fragility

5

Opiate—an unlocked door in the prison of identity. It leads into the jail yard.

—**Ambrose Bierce, The Devils Dictionary**

The issue of transnational crime is unique when compared with other criminological issues. Historically, researchers have focused on examinations of domestic crime problems, but a new interest in the broader issue of transnational crime represents an emerging focus within the discipline (Friedrichs 2007). Albanese (2010, p. 3) defines transnational crimes as "violations of the law that involve more than one country in their planning, execution, or impact." The United Nations coined the phrase *transnational crime* over 25 years ago, "but it was a catchall term that incorporated some eighteen categories of activity, including terrorism and hijacking, alongside organized crime activities" (Shelley et al. 2003, p. 145). The range of crimes has since expanded and now there are approximately 52 activities that fall under the transnational crime classification (Council on Foreign Relations 2013). Examples include counterfeit products such as pharmaceutical drugs and electronics, drug trafficking, organ trafficking, software piracy, and international adoptions (Havocscope 2012). Of the 52 activities now under the transnational crime umbrella, most involve the transfer of illicit property. According to the Transnational Organized Crime, property is defined as "assets of every kind, whether corporeal or incorporeal, movable or immovable, tangible or intangible, and legal documents or instruments evidencing title to, or interest in, such assets" (United Nations 2004, p. 5).

Transnational crimes occur across the globe and represent a grave threat to governmental stability, economic development, and peace (Andreas 2011). Because transnational crimes permeate borders, they present unique problems, both in determining their origin and in efforts to combat them (Albanese 2010; Council on Foreign Relations 2013).

Transnational crime is generally, though not exclusively, perpetrated by complex organized criminal networks. Definitions of organized criminal networks can vary considerably. In the United States, the Federal Bureau of Investigation uses a somewhat broad definition of an organized criminal group, with no specific mention of how large the organization must be. It is simply defined as any group with a formalized structure "whose primary objective is to obtain money through illegal activities. Such groups maintain their position through the use of actual or threatened violence, corrupt public officials, graft, or extortion, and generally have a significant impact on the people in their locales, region, or the country as a whole" (Federal Bureau of Investigation 2013). Russia uses a somewhat similar definition,* but at least 50 people are required before the group can be classified as an organized criminal group in their framing.

The United Nations has perhaps the most comprehensive definition of transnational criminal organizations. According to the United Nations (2004) Convention Against Transnational Organized Crime, a structured group[†] consists of at least three people working together to commit serious crimes[‡] in exchange for some material benefit (financial or other) (United Nations 2004). In accordance with the convention, offenses are transnational if they meet one of the following criteria:

> (a) It is committed in more than one state; (b) It is committed in one state but a substantial part of its preparation, planning, direction or control takes place in another state; (c) It is committed in one state but involves an organized criminal group that engages in criminal activities in more than one state; or (d) It is committed in one state but has substantial effects in another state. (United Nations 2004, p. 6)

In a sense, criminal networks and legitimate businesses have overlapping goals, as both entities exist to generate money (U.S. House of Representatives 2012). However, the "return of these profits to the legitimate corporation or illicit organization is one point at which the common goal deviates. The illicit organization undertakes the launderant's profits and avoid detection by law enforcement, including the payment of taxes" (U.S. House of Representatives 2012, p. 2). In addition to the steps taken to conceal profits from governments or law enforcement agencies, other key differences lie in the illegal nature of transnational criminal organizations. Organized criminal groups "now engage in a web of overlapping illegal activities, from cybercrime to

---

* Russian law defines an organized criminal group as one that engages in criminal activities while simultaneously protecting itself from law enforcement through the use of corruption (Politi 2001).
† In this context, a "structured group shall mean a group that is not randomly formed for the immediate commission of an offence and that does not need to have formally defined roles for its members, continuity of its membership or a developed structure" (United Nations 2004, p. 5).
‡ Serious crimes are defined as "conduct constituting an offence punishable by a maximum deprivation of liberty of at least four years or a more serious penalty" (United Nations 2004, p. 5).

trafficking in persons, money laundering, and distribution of materials for weapons of mass destruction" (Wechsler and Barnabo 2013, p. 233).

Shelley (2005) contends that the end of the Cold War and the increase in globalization have led to the proliferation of transnational criminal networks. She goes on to note that some Cold War–era countries (or post-fall constituent areas thereof), such as the former Yugoslavia, Sri Lanka, Afghanistan, and many other Soviet bloc states, are home to groups that now sell a variety of illicit goods such as drugs, people, and arms on the global market.

Globalization is "a process (or set of processes), which embodies a transformation in the spatial organization of social relations and transactions generating transcontinental or interregional flows and networks of activity, interaction, and the exercise of power" (Held et al. 1999, p. 16). Through the process of globalization, the world has in effect become smaller and much more interconnected (Passas 2001). Globalization and state instability are intrinsically linked because weak states have been unable to meet the challenges associated with globalization, especially in the realm of economic development (Kostovicicova and Bojicic-Dzelilovic 2009).* Because of globalization, illicit goods now easily cross borders and permeate the actions or events in countries far from their originating point—often with a significant (and potentially devastating) impact (Passas 2001). Because of this, "local events and destinies can hardly be interpreted and understood without looking beyond national boundaries. The world is being reconstituted as 'one place' with global communications and media, transnational corporations, supra-national institutions, integrated markets and a financial system that trades 24 hours a day" (Passas 2001, p. 405).

Globalization has obvious benefits for many nations and their law-abiding citizens, but there is a dark side to the ever-shrinking world. According to Nikos Passas (2001), the process of globalization can undermine state autonomy. Even in the most benign circumstances, governments can lose their ability to regulate cross-national business transactions (Passas 2001). One sees this manifest even in the most powerful, fully modernized and economically diverse nations. Legitimate economic interests appear to attenuate the force of political ideologies. Nowhere does one see this more clearly than in the complex web of economic and diplomatic relationships between the United States and the People's Republic of China.

Of course, transnational criminal networks (as well as terrorist groups) are typically less involved in legitimate economic activities. As a latent consequence, a culture of violence often arises. As Alison Jamieson (2001, p. 378) observes, these bad actors can keep a nation in "a state of permanent low intensity conflict. In the process, the most vulnerable sectors of the

---

* For a detailed discussion of the intersection between international economic norms and weak states, see Carment (2003).

population become impoverished while the unscrupulous make their fortunes. Among the unscrupulous are of course transnational organized crime groups."

This said, not all political science and international relations scholars share this view. Sonny Lo (2009) asserts that states are not entirely powerless, as they can adapt to the global economy. Similarly, Andreas (2011, p. 405) argues, "that popular claims of loss of state control are overly alarmist and misleading and suffer from historical amnesia."

In a competing view, Louise Shelley (1999) contends that organized criminal networks can thrive in all states, including democratic nations and global superpowers. She notes, "in all of the countries where they are based, they infiltrate government, assume governmental functions, and neutralize law enforcement. They undermine democratic institutions and the transition to a free market economy" (Shelley 1999, p. 33).

Just as there exists no universal scholarly agreement on the operationalization of state failure as a theoretical construct, so too does the relationship between globalization, transnational crime, and global instability provide a complex sphere of analytical dissensus. As with the concept of state failure, the most profitable path requires a willingness to synthesize and amend the more informative elements of disparate theories.

Regarding the debate surrounding the relationship between globalization and the loss of state control, we concur with Passas' (2001) assessment. While Shelley (1999) holds that any state can be infiltrated by organized criminal groups, and thus fall victim to the effects of transnational crime, we contend that fragile states are more vulnerable to the effects of transnational crime, when compared with stable nations. When countries lack the proper infrastructure to combat crime or a political system capable of setting and enforcing policies, organized criminal groups can and do flourish.

Andreas (2011), an ardent opponent of the globalization/state autonomy link, appears to (at least partially) support this view. In the case of migrant smuggling, he notes that criminal groups avoid "or pay off state authorities rather than to violently challenge them.... Here, corruption—purchasing the non-enforcement of laws through bribes and payoffs—can have a pacifying effect, since it reflects informal accommodation" (Andreas 2011, p. 420).

While we concur that bribes can have a pacifying effect (thereby avoiding violent conflict), we assert that such acts undermine legitimate government functioning and have the potential to create violent conflict if organized criminal groups or state officials view themselves as beyond the reach of the law. Moreover, this gambit is especially perilous for officials with respect to its overall effect on system functions and stability.

The mechanism undergirding this risk can best be understood in terms of the aforementioned state monopoly on coercion. As discussed in the introduction to this volume, Gary King and Langche Zeng (2001, p. 623) frame state failure with respect to "the collapse of the authority of the central government to impose order, as in civil wars, revolutionary wars, genocides, politicides, and adverse or disruptive regime transitions." The pacification effect of bribing officials creates a kind of paradox. Officials who become permissive of illegal activity may ensure a minimized risk of direct violent conflict with the criminal or terrorist organization, but by so doing, officials weaken their claim of a state monopoly over coercion. This in turn lessens the need for criminal or terrorist groups to obtain their tolerance.

As this dynamic matures, allegiances may shift with officials becoming more entwined if not wholly absorbed by the criminal organizations. In the long term, the apparatus of state and the operation of the criminal enterprise may become indistinct or nonexistent. More broadly, it bears keeping in mind that corruption and an inability (or unwillingness) to enforce the rule of law are hallmarks of a fragile or failed state.

Krista Hendry (2013, para. 2) notes that no country is an island and the effects of state failure are often not contained within the borders of the failing country: "issues such as slavery, genocide, child labor, and poverty spill over borders in the form of people, weapons, and conflict." For this reason, a coordinated international response to transnational crime is badly needed. However, combating transnational crime is inherently difficult because criminal activities involve more than one country, thus making them problematic to trace and difficult to establish jurisdiction. Even when criminals are captured, meaningful interdiction is further challenged due to issues of extradition.

The United Nations Convention Against Transnational Organized Crime (CTOC) represents the main legal instrument for combating transnational crime (Council on Foreign Relations 2013). This convention is further supplemented by three protocols that address specific types of organized crime: the Protocol to Prevent, Suppress and Punish Trafficking in Persons, Especially Women and Children; the Protocol Against the Smuggling of Migrants by Land, Sea and Air; and the Protocol Against the Illicit Manufacturing of and Trafficking in Firearms, their Parts and Components and Ammunition (United Nations 2004, p. 2). The overarching purpose of the CTOC "is to promote cooperation to prevent and combat transnational organized crime more effectively" (United Nations 2004, p. 5).

In an effort to achieve this goal, the convention calls on member states to criminalize activities associated with or facilitating transnational crimes. Typical examples include laundering proceeds from criminal acts, participating in an organized criminal group, and corruption. Additionally, the convention requires member states to ensure that transnational crimes are prosecuted effectively by maximizing "discretionary legal powers" and providing an adequate statute of limitations. Article 16 of the United Nations CTOC, which deals specifically with extradition, states:

> Extradition from another state party may be sought for the four specific offences established by the Convention, or for any "serious crime", where an "organized criminal group" is involved, the person whose extradition is sought is in the requested State Party, and the offence itself is punishable by the domestic laws of both states. Offences established by the protocols will only be extraditable where they meet these conditions, or where the protocol in question so specifies" (13).

Regarding the coordinated international effort to combat transnational crime, former secretary general of the United Nations, Kofi Annan, notes that criminal groups have been quick to take advantage of globalization and new technologies, but law enforcement agencies have been unsuccessful in fighting transnational crime, due to a lack of a coordinated response and ineffective weapons or strategies or both (United Nations 2004). In essence, traditional low tech and reactive policing methods do little to suppress transnational crime. The CTOC was designed with this in mind and provides the international community with the necessary tools to address the global nature of crime (United Nations 2004). Regarding the convention, Kofi Annan stated, "with enhanced international cooperation, we can have a real impact on the ability of international criminals to operate successfully and can help citizens everywhere in their often bitter struggle for safety and dignity in their homes and communities" (United Nations 2004, p. iv).

While the CTOC represents a step in the right direction, not all countries are signatories of the convention and many fragile nations may not have the infrastructure in place to identify, capture, prosecute, extradite, and punish perpetrators of transnational crimes. Even with the United Nations convention in place, combating transnational crime is still a difficult task. A lack of coordinated efforts between nations has resulted in a world that is "fraudster-friendlier" (Passas 2001).

Given the critical nature of transnational crime, more research in this area is clearly warranted. As such, the purpose of this chapter is twofold. First, we take the position that the overall effectiveness of the state in delivering core goods and services plays an integral role in the cause and proliferation of transnational crime. Secondly, we hold that the types of transnational crimes more likely to manifest in a given country will be linked to that nation's placement along the continuum of failure. Before interrogating these suppositions, it is important to recall a few foundational concepts from the introduction to this volume.

Transnational Crimes

As previously stated, the concept of transnational crime encompasses a broad set of illicit activities. Technically, any crime that involves two or more countries is transnational in nature, though this is not necessarily the case with all types of crimes. Human trafficking, for example, need not necessarily involve the transportation of a person from one location to another (U.S. Department of State 2011), though typically that is the case.

A more daunting problem in transnational crime research concerns the acquisition of sufficient information from which to draw valid, generalizable conclusions. To this point, data availability and reliability, which present difficulties in most types of cross-national research, are even more pronounced where transnational crime is concerned. To overcome these issues, a process of data triangulation often takes places. Even so, we recognize the hurdles endemic to this enterprise.

Given this, it is the more prudent course to examine a small subset of criminal activities about which more data are commonly gathered. To that end, this chapter will consider the following types of illicit activities: drug trafficking, cybercrime, and money laundering.* These categories were selected because data tend to be more reliable in these areas and the types of crimes/activities are sufficiently broad to allow for a proper examination of the relationship between state failure and transnational crime.

Drug Trafficking

Worldwide, there is great demand for illicit drugs, such as opium, cocaine, heroin, and cannabis, and this demand is largely met by the cultivation, manufacturing, and distribution of these substances by organized criminal networks. The drug trade is quite lucrative and some estimates place the economic impact of illegal drug sales to be as much as $500 billion each year, which equates to roughly 1% of the total global economy[†] (Jenner 2011). The United States is the world's largest drug market, with users spending an estimated $150 billion per year on illicit drugs (Bagley 2012).

The process of trafficking drugs generally takes place across three geographical areas: (1) the nation producing the drug; (2) the county or countries that transport the drug; and (3) the country in which the population will consume the drug (Jenner 2011). In terms of cocaine, the European Union receives much of its supply from Colombia (Caunic et al. 2011). There are two major trafficking hubs in Europe, a southwest hub in the Iberian Peninsula,

---

* Human trafficking, another type of transnational crime, will be explored in Chapter 7, as it has broad implications for women.
† Drug trafficking is second only to arms trafficking in terms of revenue (Jenner 2011).

whose groups use France as a primary transit country and a "Northwest organized crime hub, with groups located in and around Netherlands and Belgium, which have a major transport infrastructure, generating a significant volume of commercial traffic through connections with the illegal markets around the world" (Caunic et al. 2011, p. 150). It is estimated that Europeans consume approximately 29% of the world's cocaine supply, compared with the Americas' consumption of 63% (Bagley 2012).

The networks that engage in each phase of the process may involve large organized networks or small closely linked connections. In their empirical study of small trafficking networks, Boris Salazar and Lina Restrepo (2011, p. 201) found "any pair of its members is linked through a finite and bounded path of steps or contacts. Moreover, they are pretty close to each other: only four steps separate, on average, any pair of its members." In contrast, large-scale social networks generally have at least six or seven steps between members.

Opium Production

The consumption of illicit drugs is an enduring practice that is nearly as old as civilization itself (Buxton 2006). Evidence of cultivated poppy seeds and pods (*Papaver somniferum*) has been discovered that dates back as far as 4000 BC, making opium the first drug to be discovered (Booth 1999). Opium, in particular, was regarded as having high medicinal value and was used to treat a large number of illnesses (Buxton 2006).

In ancient Greece, opium was used to numb pain, though not everyone supported its medicinal use (Booth 1999). In 300 BC, Greek philosopher Diagoras of Melos stated, "it was better to suffer pain than to become dependent on opium," a view shared earlier in the fifth century by Erasistratus who advocated complete eschewal of opium (Booth 1999, p. 17). In ancient Egypt, opium was used to treat battle wounds (Belenko and Spohn 2015).

In the 1500s, European healers concocted a strong soporific when they mixed a tincture of opium with alcohol, creating a substance now known as laudanum. As with other prior uses of opioids, laudanum was also used to treat wounds and for recreational purposes (Belenko and Spohn 2015).

In the nineteenth century, other derivatives were developed, chief among these morphine. Morphine was commonly found in a variety of patent medicines used to treat every ill from menstrual cramps to colicky babies (Belenko and Spohn 2015; Musto 1997). By the middle of the nineteenth century, governments also began to recognize the high potential for the abuse and misuse of these drugs. It is around this time that bans on opiates started to appear, thus spawning an underground economy of illegal narcotics.

From the 1950s until the 1990s, opium production was concentrated in the Golden Triangle, a region comprising Myanmar, Laos, and Thailand

(Chouvy 2009). The difficult terrain of the region made the cultivation of poppies almost ideal, as mountains, heavy rains, and little or no infrastructure made it nearly impossible for governments to access and eradicate poppy fields (Chouvy 2009). Opium production in the Golden Triangle decreased significantly during the 1970s and 1980s, owing in part to increased efforts on the part of the U.S. Drug Enforcement Agency (1993a, 1993b) to eliminate opium production (Booth 1999). However, a major drought in the Golden Triangle during 1978 probably had more to do with the decline in opium production (Booth 1999). The combination of these two factors opened the door for a new "Golden Crescent" to emerge, consisting of Iran, Pakistan, and Afghanistan (Chouvy 2009; Chossudovsky 2011). Of these, Afghanistan has emerged as the world's largest producer of opium, producing an estimated 5800 tons in 2011, representing nearly 63% of global production (United Nations Office on Drugs and Crime [UNODC] 2012).

Opium plays a critical role in the Afghan economy, comprising roughly 27% of the country's GDP. As William Byrd and Doris Buddenberg (2006, p. 1) note, "the sheer size and illicit nature of the opium economy mean that not surprisingly, it infiltrates and seriously affects Afghanistan's economy, state, society, and politics." Afghanistan is by no means the only country involved in opium production, as large quantities are produced in Lao People's Democratic Republic and Myanmar (United Nations Office on Drugs and Crime 2012). While the cultivation of poppies for opium has decreased in recent years, 2011 data suggest a resurgence of production in many areas. For example, Afghanistan produced 3700 tons of opium in 2010, but the next year production increased by an additional 2200 tons (United Nations Office on Drugs and Crime 2012).

Michel Chossudovsky (2011) of the Centre for Research on Globalization proffers a different analysis, "There is reason to believe that this figure of 3700 tons is grossly underestimated. Moreover, it contradicts the UNOCD's own predictions of record harvests over an extended area of cultivation."

Chossudovsky's argument is somewhat radical in that he goes on to accuse the UNODC of outright manipulation of opium cultivation data. Interrogating the motives for such manipulation, he states that the U.S. Central Intelligence Agency (CIA) had a central role in developing the Afghan opium industry. Moreover, Chossudovsky (2011) argues, "[T]he dividing line between 'businesspeople' and criminals is blurred. In turn, the relationship among criminals, politicians and members of the intelligence establishment has tainted the structures of the state and the role of its institutions."

Whether one is prepared to endorse the more polemical aspects of Chossudovsky's thesis, the scenario he lays out represents a perfect mechanism for generating vast sums of money, funneling said money into Western financial institutions and then using that wealth to buttress whatever political or economic agendas are desired. Fragile and failing states (such as Afghanistan) provide an extremely lax regulatory environment in which external forces might gain a substantial foothold.

Of course, Afghanistan is but one of many burgeoning opium producers. For example, opium production in Myanmar increased by 30 tons between 2010 and 2011 (from 580 to 610 tons). To this point, Michael Steinberg and Kent Mathewson (2004, p. 248) state directly, "[T]he Myanmar government [has] relied almost exclusively on opium production to fuel their military efforts."

On the other hand, the Lao People's Democratic Republic (Laos) saw more incremental increases, expanding by just 7 tons between 2010 and 2011 (18–25 tons, respectively) (United Nations Office on Drugs and Crime 2012). Here again, some argue that American intelligence assets had a strong role in the distribution process. A familiar trope among some circles stems from a *Christian Science Monitor* (May 29, 1970, p. 14) article in which the reporter states, "Clearly the CIA is cognizant of if not party to the extensive movement of opium out of Laos."

The seizure of opiates has not kept pace with the level of production. Globally, authorities seized 81 tons of heroin in 2010 and 76 tons in 2009 (United Nations Office on Drugs and Crime 2012), numbers which fall vastly short in comparison to opiate production. However, certain trafficking routes have seen slight increases in heroin seizures in recent years (e.g., East Asia and some Central and South American countries) (United Nations Office on Drugs and Crime 2012). In Afghanistan, poppy eradication efforts and seizures have been thwarted by several factors, not the least of which is the fragile and unstable nature of the government. In some cases, farmers must pay corrupt government officials in order to save their poppy crops from eradication (Byrd and Buddenberg 2006). Because many farmers are too poor to pay bribes, eradication efforts tend to disproportionately affect the most disadvantaged populations (Byrd and Buddenberg 2006).

Cocaine Production

Many of the same political and economic mechanisms that facilitate opium production in the Golden Crescent also fuel the South American cocaine market, but with a notable difference regarding production control. The primary country to note here is Colombia. Simply put, Colombia controls the world cocaine market. Its annual output accounts for approximately 90% of the cocaine supplied for consumption in the United States and 80% worldwide (Chalk 2011).

The production and trafficking of cocaine is dominated by paramilitary groups in Colombia, such as the Revolutionary Armed Forces of Colombia (FARC) (Caunic et al. 2011). FARC is a Marxist-Leninist guerrilla organization that emerged over four decades ago and much of its funding is derived from drug trafficking (Rollins 2010). With at least 50% of its funding directly tied to drug trafficking, some observe that activities relating to the production, transportation, and sale of cocaine have become more important than terrorist activities (Rollins 2010). The increased involvement in drug trafficking may signal that FARC is moving away from terrorism and becoming a purely criminal group (Chalk 2011). Groups such as FARC have a monopoly on the "purchase and sale of coca paste and cocaine base, setting the prices these products can be purchased from the manufacturers and sold for processing" (Caunic et al. 2011, p. 149).

Colombian involvement in cocaine production and trafficking began in the 1970s and peaked in 1989 (Thoumi 1995). Evidence suggests that drug money in Colombia has infiltrated most sectors of the economy (O'Conner 2009). In an attempt to launder drug money, cartels establish narco-firms that engage in pyramid schemes or set up construction projects or both, which provide jobs to the local populace (O'Conner 2009).

In recent years, however, Mexico has increasingly become involved in the production and trafficking of both cocaine and amphetamines into the U.S. market (Brouwer et al. 2006). Since the 1970s, Mexico has been an important transit country for cocaine, but its foray into the production and distribution of illicit drugs is a recent phenomenon (Brouwer et al. 2006). As Kimberly Brouwer et al. (2006) explain, beginning in the 1980s, the United States began to crack down on Colombian cartels with drug interdiction efforts by the Drug Enforcement Administration and the U.S. Coast Guard substantially increasing. In the 1990s, the Colombian government began a series of successful eradication efforts, resulting in the destruction of 900 hectares* of coca in 1990; 992 hectares in 1991; and 941 hectares in 1992 (U.S. Drug Enforcement Agency 1993a, 1993b).

These crackdown efforts did not necessarily lead to a reduction in cocaine trafficking, but instead resulted in Colombian cartels allowing Mexican traffickers to assume a larger role in the cocaine trade (Brouwer et al. 2006). In 1989, Mexico's role in the narcotics trade expanded when the Drug Enforcement Agency seized nearly 21 metric tons of cocaine in Colombia (Brouwer et al. 2006). The large seizure of cocaine fundamentally changed Mexico's relationship with Colombia. As Brouwer et al. (2006) note, Mexican traffickers became increasingly upset over their lack of payment from the Colombian cartels and retaliated by withholding shipments of cocaine. Beginning in the 1990s, Mexican traffickers opted to receive cocaine, instead of (traceable) cash, as payment for services rendered to the drug cartels

---

* Nine hundred hectares is the equivalent of 3.4749 square miles.

(Brouwer et al. 2006). While this meant that Colombian drug cartels essentially ceded control of large portions of the U.S. cocaine market, "it eased logistics and removed some of the vulnerabilities of the Colombian cartels. The result has been that Mexican crime organizations now control much of the wholesale cocaine distribution in the west and midwest of the United States" (Brouwer et al. 2006, p. 710). Currently, Mexico remains largely a transit country, with Colombia supplying approximately 90% of all of the cocaine trafficked into the United States (Chalk 2011).

In addition to the expansion of cocaine production, methamphetamine (i.e., crystal meth) production has also seen widespread increases in Mexico (Brouwer et al. 2006). What was once the domain of small-scale producers in the United States, the crystal meth trade is now dominated by Mexican criminal organizations (Brouwer et al. 2006). Mexico's involvement in this class of drugs is largely isolated to markets in the United States.

Methamphetamine, amphetamine, and ecstasy (3,4-methylenedioxy-methamphetamine [MDMA])—amphetamine-type stimulants—are the second most widely used class of illicit drugs worldwide (United Nations Office on Drugs and Crime 2012). Organized criminal groups in South America, Central America, and East and Southeast Asia are responsible for the profusion of crystalized methamphetamine and MDMA worldwide (United Nations Office on Drugs and Crime 2012).

According to Mark Galeotti (2014, p. 39), "Latin American narcotic traffickers have reacted to increased pressure from law enforcement not only by adopting new structures but also by diversifying." Galeotti (2014) further explains that the high profitability of MDMA has weakened the traditional Russian and Israeli holds on the market. The profit potential has attracted other drug trafficking organizations based especially in Colombia, the Dominican Republic, Mexico, and Asia.

For more than a decade, Dominican drug trafficking organizations working with Colombian cartels have been deeply involved in U.S. cocaine trafficking. In the mid-1990s, this changed as the Dominicans became the first Latin American smugglers to assume a major role in MDMA distribution. Some Colombian and Mexican crime groups have also become involved in recent years (Galeotti 2014).

This said, the groups involved in the production and trafficking of these drugs are typically small. Such small-scale enterprises make the seizure of these drugs by law enforcement agencies quite challenging, particularly in the case of amphetamines (United Nations Office on Drugs and Crime 2012). The inherently difficult nature of drug interdiction, combined with smaller group activities, is reflected in the 42% decline in global seizures of amphetamine-derived drugs, particularly in the Middle East and Southwest Asia (United Nations Office on Drugs and Crime 2012).

The United Nations Office on Drugs and Crimes (2012) notes that recent seizures of amphetamines have reached their lowest level in nearly a decade, with only 5.4 tons being seized by European authorities. Consequently, the availability and use of ecstasy in Europe and the United States has seen marked increases over several years.

Mexico: A Country on the Brink of Failure?

To state the matter simply, Mexico is a country teetering on the edge of disaster. Mexico's ranking on the Failed States Index has been deteriorating rapidly over the past several years. Currently, Mexico ranks 97th out of 177 countries analyzed by the Fragile States Index (FSI). This places it alongside Russia, China, and Turkey in terms of its relative fragility. The FSI identifies Mexico's most problematic areas as "uneven economic development" and the loss of the security apparatus' monopoly on the use of legitimate force. Uneven economic development is characterized by large disparities in wealth distribution, limited access to services in rural areas, and a large percentage of the population living in slums (Fund for Peace 2012).

Issues involving the security apparatus occur when the government loses its monopoly on the use of force and nongovernmental or external groups step in to fill the void. The loss of a monopoly on coercive force is related to a host of factors including internal conflicts, military coups, and imprisonment of political opponents. Clearly, these factors contribute considerably to the proliferation of organized criminal networks, which in turn promote the large amount of violence that currently exists within the country. George Grayson (2011, p. 4) makes a compelling argument for the characterization of Mexico as a failed state. He notes, "a soaring murder rate, a jump in sadistic executions, increased kidnappings, prison escapes, the venality of local, state, and federal police, a failure of policy makers to enforce safety codes, and the disenchantment with institutions occupied by officials who often live like princes even as 35 percent of Mexico's 110 million people eke out a living in hard scrabbled poverty."

Adam Morton (2012) disagrees with this assessment and proffers the argument that the characterization of Mexico as a failed state is little more than a caricature. His argument centers on the idea that "states are not simply fixed and unchanging entities but experience continual structural shifts in the geographical restructuring of space" (Morton 2012, p. 1636). In one such example, he discounts the lack of governmental control over violence-ridden border towns in Mexico as an example of state failure. Morton believes that "the challenge is to better understand the nature of the political economy of the 'borderlands,' reimagining the transformation of state space as less about the collapse and breakdown of social relations leading to power vacuums and more about the transformation of space according to new hierarchies of power" (Morton 2012, p. 1640). This view ultimately discounts the role of the state and runs contrary to notions of state power.

We argue that Nicos Poulantzas' (1978) view of state powers provides a more fecund theoretical basis for an examination of state failure. While Poulantzas (1978, p. 77), much like Foucault, acknowledges that the state is not the only mechanism of power in society, he concludes that "the repressive apparatuses (army, police, judicial system, etc.) as a means of exercising physical violence ... are at the heart of the modern State."

Whether state apparatuses have any tangible monopoly on violence, it has nonetheless become the norm in many parts of Mexico. As Juan Nava (2011, p. 31) notes, "violent deaths in Mexico nearly doubled in 2009 to just over 7000, and the manner of death in some cases was especially gruesome." In addition to the deleterious effects of violence on the people of Mexico, violence is spilling over into the United States. General Michael Hayden, former director of the CIA, has described the violence along the U.S./Mexico border "as greater than Iraq and on par with Iran as the greatest potential threat to U.S. national security in the future" (Nava 2011, p. 31).

Organized Criminal Networks: Mexico

While the smuggling of drugs, arms, and migrants through Mexico was historically limited to family-based groups in the 1960s, increasingly, contraband smuggling has become dominated by larger organized groups with military roots (Dudley 2012). The four largest cartels to emerge from the shift from a predominantly family business–centered model to organized criminal networks are the Sinaloa, Tijuana, Juarez (renamed Nuevo Cartel de Juarez or the New Juarez cartel), and Gulf cartels (Dudley 2012; Hesterman 2013).

Of all the cartels in Mexico, the Gulf cartel is the oldest, with its origins dating back to the 1930s (Hesterman 2013). Initially known as the Matamoros criminal syndicate, the Gulf cartel was responsible for smuggling alcohol into the United States during the prohibition era (Hesterman 2013). By the 1970s, the Gulf cartel had begun trafficking cocaine and their presence in Mexico remained strong, though shifting alliances appear to have diminished their power in recent years. Currently, the Gulf cartel operates in 13 Mexican states, but its primary bases are located in Tamaulipas (which borders Texas) and along the Gulf of Mexico (Cook 2009; Mallory 2012). Their leader, Osiel Cardenas, was arrested in 2003 (Hesterman 2013), but has managed to exert control over the cartel from prison (Mallory 2012). In addition to being the oldest cartel in Mexico, the Gulf cartel was also the first to create its own paramilitary wing, Los Zetas (Cook 2009). There is some debate regarding the current relationship between Los Zetas and the Gulf cartel. Some report that the two groups split in 2010 (Hesterman 2013), but others contend that Los Zetas may still have considerable power over the Gulf cartel (Mallory 2012). Most recently, it appears that the Gulf cartel has formed an alliance with the Sinaloa (Hesterman 2013), Guzman, and the La Familia Michoacan (Mallory 2012). The Gulf cartel is also reportedly expanding its trafficking business and entering the realm of migrant smuggling, possibly due to crack-down efforts by U.S. law enforcement (Cook 2009). On the other hand, the foray into migrant smuggling may also serve as a way to divert the attention of law enforcement away from drug activities (Cook 2009).

The Sinaloa cartel, which emerged in the 1960s, represents a pivotal shift in the move from family-based enterprises to large-scale drug trafficking (Hammond 2011). Their influence and power saw large increases during the 1980s, as Colombian cartels were in need of a way to get cocaine into Mexico (Grayson 2011). Most recently led by Joaquin "El Chapo" Guzman, the Sinaloa are responsible for at least half of the narcotics that enter the United States each year (Keefe 2012). In addition to their stronghold on the drug market, the Sinaloa are also noteworthy because they are linked to terrorist groups in Iraq and Afghanistan (Hammond 2011). While drug trafficking is still a primary activity for the Sinaloa, they have expanded their enterprise to include smuggling terrorists and weapons into the United States (Hammond 2011). Corruption on the part of the Mexican government has allowed the Sinaloa cartel to flourish. The arrest data of drug cartel members show that arrests of the Sinaloa cartel make up just 12%, compared with 44% for Los Zetas (Burrnett et al. 2010). Evidence also suggests that the Sinaloa may have bribed police and military officials in an effort to avoid arrest and protect their business interests (Burrnett et al. 2010). For example, "a Sinaloan faction controlled several airports around the country through a network of corrupt federal agents. The faction even had its own hangar at the international airport in Mexico City" (Burrnett et al. 2010, n.p.). At one point, Guzman allegedly received military protection while en route to his marijuana ranch (Burrnett et al. 2010). Lastly, Jose Gomez Llanos, the top prosecutor in the state of Tamaulipas, purportedly launders money for Guzman (Burrnett et al. 2010). Guzman was once described as the world's most powerful drug trafficker (Keefe 2012); however, his recent arrest will likely change his status. On February 22, 2014, Guzman was arrested by Mexican and U.S. authorities and is facing multiple drug trafficking charges (Agren 2014). It is likely that the Sinaloa cartel's operations have been interrupted, at least in some measure.

The Nuevo Cartel de Juarez (Juárez cartel) reached its height in the 1990s, when it controlled nearly 50% of the cocaine market entering the United States (Hesterman 2013). The profits were enormous, totaling nearly $200 million each week (Hesterman 2013). In recent years, their power has waned substantially following the death of their leader, Vicente Carrillo

Fuentes, the arrest and prosecution of many of the group's members, and conflict with Los Zetas (Cook 2009). Beginning in the 1990s and continuing through 2007, the Juárez cartel was targeted by the "Maxiproceso" effort, which arrested 65 people with suspected ties to the Juárez cartel (Cook 2009). Not all Maxiproceso prosecutions resulted in convictions; notably, Arturo Hernández, suspected leader of the hitmen and spies for the Juárez cartel, was aquitted in 2007 (Cook 2009). Legal setbacks notwithstanding, the Juárez cartel continues to threaten Mexico's national security, as they continue to fight with the Sinaloa and Los Zetas for control of key border areas and have recently formed an alliance with the Gulf cartel (Hesterman 2013). In 2010, they began to escalate the violence by using "vehicle-borne incendiary devices to target federal police" (Hesterman 2013, p. 139).

Having only recently emerged within the last decade (Grayson 2011), Los Zetas is the newest organized criminal network in Mexico. Arturo Guzman Decenas, a former lieutenant with the Mexican Army Airborne Special Forces Group, founded the group with the help of 30 commandos who deserted the army (Nava 2011). All had received special training from the United States, Israel, and some European nations and all had access to high power weapons, missiles, and technologically advanced communications equipment (Nava 2011). Los Zetas engages in drug trafficking, but their criminal enterprise is expansive and includes, "murder for hire, kidnapping, the sale of protection, extortion, human smuggling, loan sharking, and wholesale contraband commerce" (Grayson 2011, p. 89). The manner in which Los Zetas kill their enemies is particularly gruesome. There are reports that they "have burned rivals alive, boiled them in large drums filled with diesel [fuel], and beheaded both police and rivals" (Mallory 2012, p. 72).

Deaths resulting from warring Mexican drug cartels number in the thousands. Between 2006 and 2010, deaths related to violence between cartels totaled 34,611 (Hesterman 2013). The Sinaloa cartel is responsible for a disproportionate amount of this violence, with approximately 19,097 deaths resulting from conflicts with Juarez (8,236 deaths), the Betran Leyva (5,864 deaths), Gulf–Zetas (3,199 deaths), and Tijuana (1,789) (Hesterman 2013). As Hesterman (2013, p. 137) explains, "many murders are premeditated and gruesome, such as beheadings, death by gasoline induced fire, dismemberment, and acid baths." Political leaders and law enforcement officers are especially targeted as a means to send a message to the government and to other cartels (Hesterman 2013).

Criminal Justice Response in Mexico

The criminal justice system in Mexico can best be described as corrupt, ineffectual, and disorganized. Clare Seelke (2013) reports that the criminal justice system has been overwhelmed by the spike in violence, and only about 20% of homicides are successfully prosecuted. Given the close proximity of Mexico to the United States and the spillover violence into many American border towns, the U.S. government has a vested interest in helping Mexico reform its criminal justice system. To that end, the U.S. Congress has allocated nearly $2 billion to assist with reform efforts since 2007 (Seelke 2013).

The absence of an effective criminal justice response to drug violence can be linked to failures in the judicial sector; therefore, much of the reform efforts have been directed toward changes in the judiciary (Seelke 2013). However, corruption among criminal justice officials represents another critical issue. Transparency International (2013) reports that 90% of those surveyed believe that the police are extremely corrupt and 80% believe that the judiciary is extremely corrupt. Further, 55% of respondents reported having to pay a bribe to the judiciary and 61% reported bribing law enforcement officers during the previous 12 months (Transparency International 2013). A number of reforms have been proposed including more involvement of the police in the investigation process (with prosecutorial oversight); limiting the use of pretrial detention to violent crimes; creating new judgeships whereby one judge will preside over the initial hearing, a second will preside over the trial, and a third will be responsible for sentencing; new methods of case resolution (e.g., plea bargaining and victim compensation); the use of public hearings; and public trials and verdicts (Seelke 2013). Of the five states that have enacted these reforms, initial reports appear to be positive— pretrial detention has decreased; case processing time has decreased; the use of alternative dispute mechanisms has increased and they appear to be more efficient; and judges are present at pretrial hearings (Seelke 2013).

The government has also made efforts to address organized crime, though reforms in this area appear to have introduced a bifurcated system whereby defendants in standard criminal cases have rights and those suspected of organized crime do not (Seelke 2013). In particular, suspects believed to be involved in organized crime can be held for up to 80 days without access to counsel (the law provides a 40 day holding period, with an option to extend by another 40 days if necessary [Seelke 2013]). Additionally, the "law also permits prosecutors in organized crime cases to submit evidence gathered from witnesses during the investigatory phase of a criminal process; that evidence does not need to be presented in front of the judge and defense attorney at trial" (Seelke 2013, p. 6).

All told, improvements to the criminal justice mechanisms in Mexico are at best minimal. With the tremendous amount of money at stake, the ensconced culture of organized crime–related violence, and a government seemingly incapable (or unwilling) to make deep, system-level changes, tenuous internal security and transnational crime will likely flourish for many years to come. While U.S. efforts have made some small inroads toward establishing a more effective Mexican government, the broader issue of weakened state monopoly over violence lies at the heart of that nation's bleak situation.

Afghanistan

Organized Criminal Networks

The Taliban are undoubtedly the most powerful organized criminal network/ terrorist group in Afghanistan. This power derives heavy financial support from that organization's involvement in transnational heroin trade. The United Nations Office on Drugs and Crime (2011) estimates that the Taliban earned approximately $155 million in 2009 from heroin-related activities, though their economic benefit is considerably less compared with the $2.2 billion for drug traffickers and $440 million for opium farmers. While the Afghan Taliban benefit from heroin production and trafficking, most members are not directly responsible for the cultivation, manufacturing, or transportation of heroin (United Nations Office on Drugs and Crime 2011). In 2009, the Taliban were paid upward of 10% of the value of their opium shipments by drug traffickers (United Nations Office on Drugs and Crime 2011). Individual heroin laboratory owners also pay the Taliban an estimated $600–$1200 per month and poppy farmers pay the Taliban a 5%–10% tax on their crops. The Taliban "taxes" opium farmers, producers, and traffickers because in some cases fighters will "provide security for processing labs and for shipments of the chemicals needed to make heroin" (Rollins and Wyler 2013, p. 11). In addition to providing protection for heroin shipments, the Taliban has actively helped drug cartels in their fight against government attempts at poppy eradication. Some Taliban members have directly engaged in drug trafficking as a means to generate income (Rollins and Wyler 2013). The bulk of the money collected by the Taliban, as well as weapons and other equipment that drug traffickers provide in lieu of monetary payment, directly funds insurgent groups. Further, terrorist involvement in the drug trade can provide fertile ground for recruitment. As John Rollins and Liana Sue Wyler (2013, p. 10) note, "the narcotics trade has the potential to provide terrorist groups with an added bonus: recruits and sympathizers among impoverished, neglected, and isolated farmers who can not only cultivate drug crops but also popularize and reinforce anti-government movements." The line between organized crime and terrorism is becoming increasingly blurred and complicated.

The U.S. government has acknowledged the complex link between transnational crime and terrorism and notes several patterns in these relationships (Rollins and Wyler 2013). Criminal networks and terrorist groups may collaborate with one another, which can serve to enhance the power of both groups; criminal networks and terrorist groups often use similar tactics (such as violence and money laundering); lastly, some criminal groups may become terrorist groups (if they desire to promote a certain ideological perspective) and some terrorist groups may become criminal groups (if they become increasingly motivated by greed) (Rollins and Wyler 2013). Organized criminal networks, terrorist groups, and others have exploited the weaknesses in the government "and engage in illegal activities, impeding the establishment of democratic norms and principles" (Byrd and Buddenberg 2006, p. 191). The relationship between state failure and transnational crime then becomes self-reinforcing. State failure helps perpetuate transnational crime, and as transnational crime grows, government instability increases.

While the Taliban are certainly influential in the Afghanistan heroin trade, they are but one group among many. Another group has emerged in the post-Taliban Afghanistan, the Haqqani network (Rollins and Wyler 2013). The Haqqani network, formed by Mawlawi Jalaluddin Haqqani, a former anti-Soviet mujahedeen leader, has become influential in the Afghan drug trade (Council on Foreign Relations 2011). During the Soviet invasion of Afghanistan in the 1980s, Haqqani received extensive support from the United States and Pakistan, which afforded him the opportunity to build a formidable militia (Council on Foreign Relations 2011). In the 1990s, the Haqqani network aligned with the Taliban and they maintain strong relationships with Al-Qaeda and other terrorist groups (Rollins and Wyler 2013). In addition to drug trafficking, the Haqqani network is involved in a number of illicit activities including "extortion and protection rackets, robbery schemes, kidnapping for ransom, and contraband smuggling" (Rollins and Wyler 2013, p. 19). According to the United Nations Office on Drugs and Crime (2011), there are organized criminal networks in the Caucasus, Africa, Pakistan, the Balkans, Turkey, Russia, Tajikistan, Uzbekistan, and throughout Europe, all of which are involved with the Afghanistan heroin trade.

A notable terrorist organization of more recent vintage, the Islamic State in Iraq and Syria (e.g., ISIS, ISL, and the Islamic State), is in many ways distinct from any antecedent extremist organization. Speaking about the general evolution of terrorist groups, Michel Chossudovsky (2010, pp. 195–196) states, "Legal and illegal undertakings are increasingly intertwined, the dividing line between 'businesspeople' and criminals is blurred... the relationship among criminals, politicians and members of the intelligence establishment has tainted the structures of the state and the role of its institutions." Nowhere is this truer than ISIS. This group is in many ways a large, well-diversified corporate interest with multiple streams of revenue. To be certain, the bulk of ISIS's income is derived from sales of oil from captured Syrian oil fields, but this is hardly their sole source. Louise Shelley (2014) observes that ISIS receives funding from typical terrorist activities, such as "smuggling, kidnapping, extortion, and robberies" as well as the less common ventures. As she goes on to note, "cigarette smuggling has increased, fuel smuggling is estimated to have tripled, and cell phone smuggling has risen fivefold. ISIS is also taxing black market antiquities at 20–50 percent, depending on the region and type of antiquity."

Interestingly, there is some dissensus on ISIS's involvement in narco-trafficking. One report from Russia's Federal Drug Control Service (FSKN) characterizes ISIS's illicit drug income as "fabulous" (Paraszczuk 2014). Joanna Paraszczuk (2014) further cites a November 2014 announcement from Viktor Ivanov, head of the FSKN, declaring, "large-scale transit of Afghan heroin acts as a renewable financial base for the functioning of the Islamic State group, which obtains fabulous profits by providing half of the total heroin supply to Europe via destabilized Iraq and some African countries."

Some sources have even gone so far as to claim an intricately entwined relationship between ISIS and Mexican drug cartels, but this assertion largely has been limited to members of the American political far right and media outlets amenable thereto. Of these claims, perhaps the most unlikely is one alleging that U.S. Border Patrol agents arrested 10 members of ISIS attempting to cross into Texas via the Mexican border.

As U.S. House member Rep. Duncan Hunter told reporters, "At least 10 ISIS fighters have been caught coming across the Mexican border in Texas [and there are] dozens more that did not get caught by the Border Patrol" (Fox News 2014).

Daveed Gartenstein-Ross, director of the Center for the Study of Terrorist Radicalization at the Foundation for Defense of Democracies Disputes, responded to Hunter's dramatic claim by stating that he knows of "no reporting coming through [the Department of Homeland Security] suggesting … ISIS fighters have been intercepted at the border. I've talked to a large number of people within the department, and the department has unequivocally denied it. There's not one shred of evidence this is the case" (Baddour and Gardner 2014).

Whatever the truth of this matter, the fact that such scenarios are being offered for mass consumption says something important about the nexus of terrorist groups in the post-September 11 world. It speaks to a level of transnationality, a loosening of state monopolies on both the economy and violence, and an unprecedented global connectedness. One of the most critical ways that these dynamics find purchase is by exploiting deficits in local power structures, principally the apparatuses of criminal justice. Here again, the chaos of Afghanistan provides an instructive example.

Policing in Afghanistan

The fragile nature of the Afghan government and corruption among law enforcement officers has helped facilitate the opium trade. During the period following Taliban rule, it became clear that political reform in Afghanistan was badly needed. On November 6, 2001, the Agreement on Provisional Arrangements in Afghanistan Pending Re-establishment of Permanent Institutions, more commonly known as the Bonn Agreement, was signed into force (Guttieri and Piombo 2007). The purpose of the agreement was to form a political roadmap for the Afghan people (Guttieri and Piombo 2007), as well as to establish "an Afghan Interim Authority to run the country and provided the basis for an interim system of law and governance" (Perito 2009, p. 2). The future of armed groups in Afghanistan was addressed in section six of the agreement, which states, "upon official transfer of power, all mujahedeen, Afghan armed forces, and armed groups shall come under the command and control of the Interim Authority, and be recognized according to the requirements of the new Afghan security and armed forces" (Guttieri and Piombo 2007, p. 290). To affect this change, the security apparatus was divided into four areas, with the United States, Italy, Germany, and Great Britain each taking responsibility for different sectors (Perito 2009). Germany was responsible for overseeing the reestablishment of the Afghan National Police (ANP; Perito 2009) and five areas were given top priority: (1) advise reforms for structure and organization; (2) reform the police academy in Kabul; (3) rebuild police buildings; (4) provide necessary equipment; and (5) organize police donor activity (Kelly et al. 2011). The reforms were intended to address the many problems associated with policing in Afghanistan, which include a lack of training and equipment, illiteracy, and allegiances between police and warlords (Perito 2009).

Reform efforts began with the rebuilding of the Kabul Police Academy using a training model common in European policing (Kelly et al. 2011). The academy would provide a university education to police leadership (officers) and less intensive training for lower-level officers (Perito 2009). The first class of cadets to begin the new program in 2002 comprised 1500 officers (Kelly et al. 2011), who would complete a five-year training period, and 500 noncommissioned officers who would receive three months of academy training (Perito 2009). The Germans elected to first focus on training police leadership in the hope that the development of professional leaders would "trickle down" and spark an increased professionalism among lower-level officers (Kelly et al. 2011).

In 2003, the United States became nominally involved in police training when they helped establish the National Police Training Center (Ellison and Pino 2012). Since the Kabul Police Academy focused largely on training police leadership, the National Police Training Center focused on rank-and-file officers (Ellison and Pino 2012). Over the course of eight weeks, police recruits received training in ethics, human rights, democratic principles, and international policing standards (Ellison and Pino 2012). The hopes for a "trickle down" effect of professionalism from police leadership to rank-and-file officers ultimately did not manifest. Police leadership remained corrupt and lower-level officers were uneducated, had little police experience, and followed a military model, which did little to improve police/citizen relations (Kelly et al. 2011). Additionally, officers were paid extremely low wages, had few necessary resources, and virtually no infrastructure (Ellison and Pino 2012).

By 2005, nearly $6 billion had been invested in the ANP, but officers were still largely incapable of performing their duties (Johnson 2008). The inability of the police to function properly at this juncture was attributed to numerous factors, including a lack of mentors for most ANP officers, which effectively meant that nearly two out of three of the ANP did not receive proper field training (Johnson 2008). Additionally, the police had a very low supply of necessary equipment such as trucks, radios, and body armor (Johnson 2008). Lastly, the weak judiciary hindered police services/operations "and [there were] problems with police pay, corruption, and attacks, including by insurgents" (Johnson 2008, para. 5).

By 2009, the ANP had grown from 68,000 in 2002 to 86,000 (Perito 2009). The addition of personnel and the considerable foreign investment for training and equipment (approximately $10 billion in total; $6.2 billion from the United States alone) failed to address the core problems of the ANP (Perito 2009). In addition to the problems noted by the U.S. Government Accountability Office, the ineffectiveness of the ANP is directly attributed to the opium trade (Perito 2009).

The opium trade is linked to unprecedented levels of corruption at all levels of government, including the Interior Ministry (the agency responsible for overseeing the police) (Perito 2009). Most Afghan citizens believed that Interior Ministry officials, police chiefs, and law enforcement officers were participating in the illicit drug trade. This view was not without merit as there were reports of Interior Ministry officials "accepting large bribes for protecting drug traffickers and for 'selling' senior provincial and district police positions to persons engaged in drug trafficking. A combination of local loyalties, links to criminal networks, low or no pay, and a residual culture of impunity contributed to endemic corruption in the ANP" (Perito 2009, p. 7). The U.S. Department of State (2013, para. 16) supports these claims, as "many central, provincial, and district level government officials are believed to directly engage in and benefit from the drug trade. Corrupt practices range from facilitating drug activities to benefiting from drug trade revenue streams."

Afghan police have been described by citizens as "predatory" and in some cases even worse than the Taliban (Perito 2009, p. 7). There have been reports of Afghan police demanding bribes, illegally taxing citizens, and engaging in various human rights abuses (Perito 2009). The police also reportedly use house searches as a ruse to extort money or steal from citizens (Perito 2009). Unfortunately, "corrupt police practices were felt most directly by the poorest members of society: taxi and truck drivers, traders, small businessmen, and farmers. High levels of corruption and a culture of impunity severely undermined the legitimacy of the Afghan government and further eroded public support for the police" (Perito 2009, p. 7).

The situation was further complicated by the fact that the government did not control the use of force by outside armed groups, an important marker of state failure. As Karen Guttieri and Jessica Piombo (2007, p. 297) explain, "warlordism was not merely pervasive, it was seemingly permitted: The U.S. and its coalition partners ... failed to back immediate efforts to centralize military authority. ... The external powers that had pledged to support Karzai thus undermined his authority. ... Instead, Karzai continued to fight with them [warlords] for authority, money, and legitimacy." In short, the lack of a capable law enforcement system, coupled with competing interests from warlords, outside military forces, and the government, has made it extremely difficult to combat the organized criminal networks that grow, cultivate, and export heroin to the rest of the world.

Judicial System in Afghanistan

In addition to setting parameters for policing reforms, the Bonn Agreement also helped establish a new constitution for the Afghan people. The constitution, ratified on January 26, 2004, contains 20 articles that specifically deal with the judicial system (Afghanistan Constitution 2004). Chapter 7 (Article 116) states that the judicial system will operate as an independent entity. Further, "the judiciary shall be comprised of one Supreme Court, Courts of Appeal as well as Primary Courts whose organization and authority shall be regulated by law. The Supreme Court shall be the highest judicial organ, heading the judicial power of the Islamic Republic of Afghanistan" (Afghanistan Constitution 2004, p. 33). The right to an open trial is safeguarded by the constitution, but secret trials are not necessarily prohibited. Specifically, Chapter 7 (Article 128) states, "In the courts in Afghanistan, trials shall be held openly and every individual shall have the right to attend in accordance with the law. In situations clarified by law, the court shall hold secret trials when it considers necessary, but pronouncement of its decision shall be open in all cases" (Afghanistan Constitution 2004, p. 35).

Despite corruption among some governmental officials, Afghanistan has had some success combating drug trafficking. In 2005, Afghanistan established the Criminal Justice Task Force (CJTF), which operates independently and is composed of prosecutors, investigators, and members of the judiciary (U.S. Department of State 2013). The CJTF is responsible for the prosecution of all drug cases that involve a substantial amount of narcotics (a minimum of 2 kg of heroin, 10 kg of opium, or 50 kg of hashish or chemicals involved in the early stages of drug production) (U.S. Department of State 2013). By all accounts, the CJTF appears to be successful, both in prosecuting drug traffickers and corrupt officials. The U.S. Department of State (2013, para. 10) reports, "between April 2011 and March 2012, the CNJC primary court heard 468 cases and tried 788 suspects, involving more than 185 metric tons of illegal drugs"; 97% of the cases resulted in a conviction. As stated previously, Afghanistan produced 5800 tons of heroin in 2011. While the seizure of 185 metric tons (equivalent to almost 204 tons) is positive, it falls vastly short of what is needed to result in any appreciable decline in heroin trafficking.

With regard to corrupt officials, "The CJTF actively investigates and prosecutes public officials who facilitate drug trafficking. ... The CJTF has successfully prosecuted high-ranking government officials, including members of the CNPA. Between April 2011 and March 2012, 44 public officials were prosecuted in the CJTF primary court" (U.S. Department of State 2013, para. 10). While the successful prosecution and conviction of traffickers and corrupt political officials is certainly a positive step, a tremendous amount of work, reform, and reeducation remains to be done. Even now, Afghanistan is the world leader in opium production and complete eradication will need a coordinated response from the international community, as well as vast resources (both money and personnel).

Common Drug Trafficking Routes

East Africa is increasingly being used as a transit country for illicit goods, narcotics chief among them. Weak governments in the region are partially responsible—border controls are lacking and the criminal justice systems in many East African nations are ill-equipped to handle problems associated with drug trafficking (United Nations Office on Drugs and Crime 2012). Countries that produce heroin and cannabis resin tend to prefer ports in East African nations, such as Djibouti, Eritrea, Kenya, and Tanzania (United Nations Office on Drugs and Crime 2012).

Somalia, which has long been described as the exemplar of state failure, is increasingly involved in both drug and arms trafficking (United Nations Office on Drugs and Crime 2012). Major international airports in Ethiopia and Kenya provide ideal transit hubs, as they "have connections between West Africa and the heroin-producing countries in South West and South East Asia. There is also an increasing use of postal and courier services for cocaine, heroin and hashish" (United Nations Office on Drugs and Crime 2012). West African drug organizations have extensive ties to Latin American cartels and are increasingly being used as transit countries for cocaine and methamphetamine (United Nations Office on Drugs and Crime 2012).

As discussed above, the majority of the world's heroin originates in Afghanistan, Myanmar, and the Lao People's Democratic Republic. From these origin countries, heroin is then transported through the Iranian or Northern routes. The Iranian route is the primary trafficking route for heroin, given its geographic proximity to Pakistan and Afghanistan (Chouvy 2009). Additionally, Iran has a 2440 km coastline, which makes it an ideal location for maritime drug trafficking (Chouvy 2009). Heroin transported through the Northern route is generally moved through Tajikistan and Kyrgyzstan (or sometimes Uzbekistan or Turkmenistan) and then to Kazakhstan and the Russian Federation (United Nations Office on Drugs and Crime 2012).

Much of the cocaine that is destined for the United States and Canada originates in Colombia, and then moves through Mexico and Central America before it reaches the North American market (United Nations Office on Drugs and Crime 2008). Colombia is a major producer of cocaine for the European market, but Peru and Bolivia are also suppliers (United Nations Office on Drugs and Crime 2008). Typically, cocaine is trafficked to Europe in container shipments by sea (United Nations Office on Drugs and Crime 2008), though West Africa is often used as a transit country.

One of the most interesting and complex manifestations of transnational drug production and trafficking directly involved Syria, Lebanon, Afghanistan, Liechtenstein, Turkey, Bolivia, Colombia, and France. During the 1980s, General Mustafa Tlass, the Syrian minister of defense and M. Roland Dumas, the French foreign minister, entered into an agreement whereby Syria exerted control of Lebanese politics through a systematic program of smuggling, extortion, money laundering, and financial support of multiple terrorist organizations (Albani 2001). According to the Lebanese-Canadian Coordinating Council, "Western investigators have learned that the Syrian control over Lebanon by means of drugs is carried out on the institutional level. This is a structured network whose head belongs to the circles closest to [Syrian] President Hafez Assad" (Albani 2001). In something of a grotesque irony, Mustafa Tlass organized a charity foundation based in Liechtenstein—the Tlass Foundation. The foundation was a primary conduit organization for the laundering of proceeds from various illicit activities. The Lebanese-Canadian Coordinating Council reported that the president of this foundation, who resided in Paris, Nahed Ojjeh (the daughter of Tlass and widow of Saudi Arabian arms dealer, Akkram Ojjeh), "...offered M. Roland Dumas, when he was Foreign Minister, hi-tech electronic equipment... for a bargain sum of 8.2 million francs...This asset is one among many that enables Mustafa Tlass to protect his drug traffic in France" (Albani 2001).

By creating a series of small cocaine and heroin refineries in the Druze region of Lebanon, Syrian military and government officials orchestrated the importation of raw materials from places such as Colombia, Bolivia, and Afghanistan. The huge influx of money created a situation in which Lebanese regional officials became dependent on and deeply beholden to Syrian wishes. By further exploiting the Druze's political, military, and financial situations, a connection was forged between the Druze party and the pro-Iranian fundamentalist party, Hezbollah. Hezbollah cultivated opium poppies in the region where it was also refined before being shipped either to Turkey or France before spreading across the whole of Europe.

As Jihad Albani (2001) observes, this is how Syrian intelligence officials became "intermediaries" in transnational drug trade while at the same time exerting control over important Lebanese political factions. As he states, "In Lebanon, war between ideologies stops at the edge of cannabis and poppy fields... [the drug trade] creates a bridge between [political] ideologies."

The Effects of the Drug Trade

The harmful effects of the drug trade include health-related issues for consumers of illicit substances, as well as violence that stems directly from the drug trade. Worldwide, it is estimated that between 153 million and 300 million people aged 15–64 have used some type of illicit drug in the past year (United Nations Office on Drugs and Crime 2012). Of these, approximately 15.5–38.6 million (or 12% of illicit drug users) are classified as problem drug users (United Nations Office on Drugs and Crime 2012). Globally, between 99,000 and 253,000 deaths are linked to drug use annually (United Nations Office on Drugs and Crime 2012).

Though difficult to estimate because of a lack of reliable data (Institute of Medicine 2007), it is estimated that approximately 11–21 million people worldwide may be injectable drug users (IDU) (Stathdee and Stockman 2010). International HIV/AIDS rates among this population are alarmingly high, with an estimated one to three million IDUs having contracted the disease (Stathdee and Stockman 2010), or about 10% of the IDU population (Institute of Medicine 2007). HIV infection rates of IDUs are estimated to be as high as 20%–40% in some countries: 37.2% of IDUs in Russia have HIV, 39.7% in Spain, and 33.9% in Vietnam (Stathdee and Stockman 2010). In nine countries, the rate of HIV among IDUs is greater than 40%: Estonia (72.1%), Ukraine (41.8%), Burma (42.6%), Indonesia (42.5%), Thailand (42.5%), Nepal (41.4%), Argentina (49.7%), Brazil (48.0%), and Kenya (42.9%) (Stathdee and Stockman 2010, p. 100). The Institute of Medicine (2007) notes that rates of HIV have increased nearly twentyfold in a matter of 10 years, mainly because of increases in IDUs.

There is a demonstrable link between drug trafficking transit countries and an increase in HIV rates due to dirty needles. As Steffanie Stathdee and Jamilia Stockman (2010, p. 100) contend, "the burgeoning number of drug injectors is believed to be linked to the role that many African countries now play as trans-shipment routes in the global trafficking networks for heroin, cocaine, and other drugs."

An examination of drug-related deaths (excluding deaths from HIV/AIDS from the use of dirty needles) reveals that mortality rates are higher in destination countries compared with originating or transit countries. For example, drug-related deaths in the United States and Canada totaled 181.1 and 104.5 per million aged 15–64, respectively, compared with just 13.2 per million aged 15–64 in Argentina* (United Nations Office on Drugs and Crime 2012). In many Western and Central European nations, opioids are responsible for the majority of drug deaths. Death rates per million of the population aged 15–64 range from a low of zero in Liechtenstein and Monaco to a high of 220.7 in Iceland (United Nations Office on Drugs and Crime 2012). North American and European countries have the highest drug mortality rates in the world, with the exception of El Salvador (161.1 per million aged 15–64), Kazakhstan (115.8 per million aged 15–64), and Australia (123 per million aged 15–64) (United Nations Office on Drugs and Crime 2012). Drug-related deaths are one indicator of the devastating toll of the drug trade, but drug trafficking is also fraught with violence. The U.S. Bureau of Justice Statistics, Office of Justice Programs (1994, p. 3) sums the situation succinctly, "Drug trafficking generates violent crime." While the Office of Justice Programs (OJP) observation speaks directly to trafficking in the United States, the sentiment is fully applicable in all corners of the world. As to the modality of this violence, the Office of Justice Programs (1994, p. 3) lists several contributory scenarios: competition for drug markets and customers; disputes (and subterfuge) among individuals involved; proclivities toward violence among traffickers; the fact that locations where street drug markets proliferate tend to be disadvantaged economically and socially; and legal and social controls against violence in such areas tend to be ineffective.

The last two situations on the OJP list bear special consideration when considering global drug trafficking in failed or fragile states. Rather than framing the question in terms of street markets, one substitutes global markets, and these are exactly the conditions one sees in most failed states—widespread poverty, vulnerable and socially marginalized populations coupled with a lax or nonexistent culture of effective formal social controls.

A solitary example ably demonstrates the grave consequences. During 2008, there were an estimated 6290 drug trafficking–related murders in Mexico alone (Jenner 2011). From 2006 until 2009, the combined death toll from drug trafficking in Mexico was 13,000 people, 800 of whom were law enforcement officers (Jenner 2011).

---

* In the wake of the Mexican drug war, Argentina has emerged as a large producer of cocaine.

Recent law enforcement efforts to address drug trafficking have been met with mixed success. One way to understand the magnitude of the problem is to examine interdiction strategies such as is done by the UNODC. In their studies of drug lab seizures, the UNODC report highlights efforts in Colombia, a major global source of cocaine. During 2009–2010, Colombian law enforcement officers seized 5,511 cocaine labs and 852,778.57 kg of coca leaf, 253,447.1 kg of cocaine (base, paste, and salts), and 20,885.96 kg of "other" cocaine-related contraband (United Nations Office on Drugs and Crime 2010).

Cybercrime and Cyberwarfare

In late 2014, the government of North Korea was widely suspected of initiating a cyberattack on Sony Pictures Corporation as a reproach for the film company's release of *The Interview*, a comedy premised on the assassination of that nation's leader, Kim Jong Un. This attack served to raise public consciousness of threats to information security and digital communications infrastructures. Attacks based in the digital and informational realms are hardly new. With rising technological savvy among the world's more maleficent actors, this topic has increasing relevance to the study of failed and fragile states.

Before delving into specific manifestations of this burgeoning area of conflict, it is important to note that terms such as *cybercrime*, *cyberterrorism*, and *cyberwarfare* are not easily defined concepts. As Victoria Baranetsky (2009) argues, even experts in the field do not agree on a consensus as to specific constitutional criteria, "The FBI alone has published three distinct definitions of Cyberterrorism: 'Terrorism that initiates ... attack[s] on information' in 1999, to 'the use of Cyber tools' in 2000 and 'a criminal act perpetrated by the use of computers' in 2004."

Speaking to the highly varied, context-specific, and often "emotionally-loaded" aspects of these acts, Kostas Mavropalias (2011) contends, "Cyberterrorism usually has a stronger meaning than Cybercrime, describing acts that have similar characteristics to real-world terrorism attacks, but not always. On the other hand, Cybercrime is often used as a catch-all term to describe illegal, harmful and/or hostile activity on the Internet (including Cyberterrorism)."

Adding to this discussion, the United Nations Interregional Crime and Justice Research Institute (2014, para. 1) provides the following definition of cyberwarfare: "cyberwarfare refers to any action by a nation-state to penetrate another nation's computer networks for the purpose of causing some sort of damage. However, broader definitions claim that cyberwarfare also includes acts of 'cyberhooliganism', cybervandalism or cyberterrorism." While the nature of the attacks may be very similar (e.g., destroy data or interrupt service), a fundamental difference lies in who initiates the act (Gercke 2012). For example, "a denial of service attack can be a regular cybercrime if it is carried out by a student against his university. It can also be a terrorist act if it is carried out by a terrorist organization and directed against critical national infrastructure" (Gercke 2012, p. 20). As the old aphorism holds, "one person's terrorist is another person's freedom fighter."

Even using a concrete example, the question of how to classify such acts (cybercrime vs. cyberwarfare) is inherently difficult. Take, for instance, the 2008 cyberattacks that occurred during the Russia-Georgia conflict. While troops were fighting on the ground, several cyberattacks targeted government websites and businesses (Gercke 2012). These types of attacks could be considered cyberwarfare (rather than cybercrime), but in many cases this is made difficult due to the "inability to determine the origin of the attacks, as well as the fact that the discovered acts significantly differ from traditional warfare, makes it difficult to characterize them as cyberwarfare" (Gercke 2012, p. 20).

With all this as a backdrop, digital technology is inarguably assuming a larger and more important role in international affairs as organized criminal networks are increasingly involved in cybercrime and cyberwarfare. As Louise Shelley et al. (2003, p. 151) note, "just as pirates are now focusing on high technology cargo, criminals are realizing high profits from pursuing the hardware of technology, and their Internet schemes reveal their capacity to engage in cybercrime." According to the United Nations Office on Drugs and Crime (2013, p. xvii), "upwards of 80% of cybercrime acts are estimated to originate in some form of organized activity, with cybercrime black markets established on a cycle of malware creation, computer infection, botnet management, harvesting of personal and financial data, data sale, and 'cashing out' of financial information."

Victimization surveys reveal that between 1% and 17% of the online population in 21 countries have been victims of some type of cybercrime (United Nations Office on Drugs and Crime 2013). While that figure may not seem large when compared with the less than 5% rates of burglary, robbery, and car theft in the same countries surveyed (United Nations Office on Drugs and Crime 2013), it is clear that cybercrime is a pressing issue in many parts of the world. Rob McCusker (2006, p. 257) considers cybercrime an "integral part of the transnational threat landscape and conjures up pressing images of nefarious and increasingly complex online activity."

Fear of becoming a victim of a cyberattack is widespread, but it is especially common in Western countries. As Warwick Ashford (2007) observes, "Cybertheft is the UK's most feared crime... according to a study of more than 1,400 regular internet users... research, commissioned by security software makers AVG, reveals that 43 percent of Britons feel most vulnerable to cybertheft compared with burglary (29 percent), assault (18 percent) and robbery (11 percent)."

Similarly, in a 2003 study conducted by *Federal Computer Week* magazine and the Pew Internet & American Life Project, researchers concluded that, "Half of Americans [49 percent] fear that terrorists might cripple American utilities such as electric, transportation and water systems, or its banks and major corporations through cyber-attacks" (Raines 2003).

While these studies are a bit dated, they nonetheless demonstrate the presence of cybersecurity fears in the popular imagination. As Stuart Sutherland (2007, p. 89) notes, lack of control over a situation perceived as threatening or dangerous gives rise to feelings of emotional distress, fear, and insecurity. Such strong emotions can inhibit flexible thinking and lead to irrational behavior. Because cyber threats exist in a largely "invisible" world, they may hold a particularly tight rein on members of more developed, technologically advanced societies. Global terrorists, criminals, and other malefactors know and exploit this dimension of the tactic.

Compared with other transnational crimes, cybercrime is a relatively new phenomenon. The first instances of cybercrime occurred in the 1960s, when computer technology was still in its infancy (Gercke 2012). Early computer attacks generally took the form of inflicting physical damage on computers, as evidenced by a 1969 student riot in Canada, during which students set a fire and destroyed university-held data (Gercke 2012). As technology has become more sophisticated, the nature of cyberattacks has become more complex and organized. What once began as a largely disorganized group of young hackers, cybercrime has emerged as an integral part of many organized criminal networks. Much like drug trafficking, cybercrime tends to thrive in fragile and failing states.

According to Misha Glenny, the proliferation of cybercrime in Russia and the Ukraine is a direct result of the legal and economic collapse in the two regions. Glenny (2012, p. 147) goes on to note, "the legal structures regulating markets largely collapsed, and, in order for people to make a living, they had to engage in corruption and criminal structures to a greater degree."

Governmental corruption is a pressing issue in many fragile and failing nations. Corruption among governmental officials often leads to the disenfranchisement of the populace and a lack of respect for governmental institutions. This lack of respect negatively affects the ability of justice officials to effectively enforce laws (Etges and Sutcliffe 2008). In the case of weak and unstable governments, other groups will attempt to step in and fill the power vacuum. Organized criminal networks will "employ tactics like intimidation, fear, financial incentives and propaganda to secure its bases and permeate society as much as possible" (Etges and Sutcliffe 2008, p. 89). In the case of armed groups or terrorist groups, they may use computer technology to spread propaganda (cybercrime) or they may direct an attack against critical infrastructure (cyberwarfare).

Cybercrime threatens stability across the globe, as it endangers "vital infrastructure and state security, steals identities and commits fraud" (United Nations 2010, p. ii). Just as the Internet has expanded legitimate opportunities for people, it has also allowed for the expansion of transnational crimes (United Nations 2010). Identity theft and the proliferation of child pornography have vastly increased due to the ubiquity of the Internet (United Nations 2010). In the realm of state failure, cybercrime has the potential to further destabilize governments in countries already on the brink of failure, "including both in countries where insurgencies and illegal armed groups are funded through trafficking (in the Andean region, South and Central Asia and Central Africa), and in countries where violence and corruption pose a serious challenge to the rule of law (West Africa and Mesoamerica)" (United Nations 2010, p. vi).

Organized Criminal Groups Involved in Cybercrime

A variety of existing criminal networks have turned to cybercrime to enhance their existing criminal enterprises or to enter new fields (Choo 2008). The Japanese crime syndicate, the Yakuza, are one such criminal group. The roots of the modern-day Yakuza date back to at least the eighteenth century, though the exact timing of the group's formation is a point of debate among scholars (Kaplan and Dubro 2012). The Yakuza adapted the structure of the Italian mafia (a central authority figure—the Godfather and the rest of the clan), but added an element that was distinctly their own (Kaplan and Dubro 2012). They used the *oyabun–kobun* (father–child) structure, whereby the oyabun "provides advice, protection, and help, and in return receives the unswerving loyalty and service of his kobun whenever needed" (Kaplan and Dubro 2012, p. 8). This structure is still largely in place today and has led to a level of trust and loyalty that is generally not found in organized crime groups in the United States (Kaplan and Dubro 2012). The Yakuza provide an interesting example of an organized criminal network because, until recently, they were able to operate in the open and membership was not clandestine (Scherrer 2009). This has begun to change, however, as in recent years they have lost popular support and law enforcement has stopped turning a blind eye to their criminal activities (Kingston 2011). Additionally, the Japanese government has passed legislation to crack down on organized criminal activity.

Despite this, the Yakuza have remained involved in an array of traditional crimes (e.g., gambling, debt collection, rape, and extortion), as well as transnational crimes including arms trafficking, human trafficking, smuggling, and cybercrime (Broadhurst et al. 2012). However, the Yakuza are reportedly moving away from traditional criminal activities and are increasingly focused on cybercrime, either by directly committing cybercrimes or by sponsoring cybercriminals in other countries (Kshetri 2010). The shift into cybercrime is partly attributed to the recession, which reduced the revenue stream coming from more traditional criminal activities (Kingston 2011). Aging membership and a lack of well-educated recruits are increasingly becoming problematic for the Yakuza, especially given their shift toward more technologically sophisticated criminal activities (Kingston 2011). To combat this growing problem, the Yakuza have begun outsourcing their work to other criminal organizations and allowing foreigners to join the organization (Kingston 2011). Outsourcing and foreign recruiting may not provide a long-term solution for the Yakuza and there is evidence that overall membership is waning. For the first time in the organization's history, membership recently fell below 60,000 (*The Guardian* 2014). This could either signal the beginning of the end for the Yakuza or it could indicate that the organization is beginning to decentralize, a move that would impede law enforcement efforts to combat the group's criminal activities.

Fighting transnational cybercrime presents obvious difficulties for law enforcement agencies. Susan Brenner (2012, p. 178) notes that "transnational crimes—including transnational cybercrimes—create two kinds of challenges for law enforcement officers: collecting evidence from abroad and obtaining custody of a suspect who is abroad." Typically, the fastest way to obtain evidence in a transnational cybercrime case is to make a request under the Mutual Legal Assistance Treaty (MLAT), an instrument that calls for legal assistance in cases involving the United States and another country (Brenner 2012).* The type of assistance required can include a variety of requests depending on the nature of the crime and the country involved. The 1994 MLAT between the United Kingdom and the United States illustrates the type of assistance that may be requested: "taking the testimony or statements of persons; providing documents, records, and evidence; serving documents; locating or identifying persons; transferring persons in custody for testimony (or for other purposes); executing requests for searches and seizures; identifying, tracing, freezing, seizing, and forfeiting the proceeds and instrumentalities of crime and assistance in related proceedings; and such other assistance as may be agreed between Central Authorities" (U.S. Department of State 1994, p. 2). Also included in the treaty are provisions for the denial of a request for assistance. For instance, the United Kingdom can refuse to grant assistance under the following circumstances:

1. The Requested Party is of the opinion that the request, if granted, would impair its sovereignty, security, or other essential interests of would be contrary to important public policy.

---

* As of 2009, the United States had MLAT agreements with 53 nations (Brenner, 2012).

2. The request relates to an offender who, if proceeded against in the Requested Party for the offence for which assistance is requested, would be entitled to be discharged on the grounds of a previous acquittal or conviction; or

3. The request relates to an offence that is regarded by the Requested Party as:

   a. An offence of a political character; or
   b. An offence under military law of the Requested Party which is not also an offence under the ordinary criminal law of the Requested Party. (U.S. Department of State 1994, p. 4)

MLATs are designed to provide a quicker turnaround time compared with other legal avenues (i.e., a letter of rogatory), but the process can take months or sometimes years to produce demonstrable evidence that legal assistance is warranted (Brenner 2012). This is problematic because as Brenner (2012, p. 181) notes, "while delays can be aggravating or problematic in traditional criminal investigations, they are likely to be devastating in cybercrime investigations."

Once law enforcement officers have identified a suspect or suspects, obtaining custody of the individual(s) is the next hurdle. In order to get a suspect into custody, the person must first be extradited. Extradition is only possible if there is an extradition treaty in place* and even then, countries can refuse extradition. Though not a transnational cybercrime case, Edward Snowden (the National Security Agency [NSA] information leaker) provides an interesting example of the difficulties associated with extradition. When Snowden first left the United States, Hong Kong was his destination country. The United States and Hong Kong have had an extradition treaty in place since 1998 (Neuman 2013), but the request was rejected on a technicality and Snowden was permitted to leave Hong Kong on a plane bound for Russia. As of late 2015, Snowden remains in Russia (having been granted temporary asylum) and extradition will be difficult, if not impossible, because the United States and Russia do not have an extradition treaty in place. When countries do not have treaties in place, extradition is not viewed as a binding obligation (Brenner 2012).

Money Laundering

The origin of the term *money laundering* dates back to the 1920s (Lilley 2006). In an effort to conceal the origin of their profits, criminal groups in the United States would assume control of businesses that generated large

---

* The United States has approximately 100 extradition treaties in place with countries throughout the world, leaving significant gaps in many parts of the world (Brenner, 2012).

quantities of cash, such as car washes or laundries (Lilley 2006). Once in control of these businesses, criminal groups "mingled their dirty cash with genuine clean cash receipts. Thus, whilst 'laundering' today is associated with the washing of criminal funds, the original use of the phrase related to the very real business of washing clothes" (Lilley 2006, p. xii).

As already indicated, money laundering represents a substantial aspect of transnational criminal facilitation. David Jordan (1999), a former U.S. diplomat, makes an important distinction with respect to the role of financial institutions in illicit money processing. In his study of narcotics trafficking, Jordan observes that there are two paradigms from which to view banking practices in the underground economy of transnational crime.

One perspective asserts that financial institutions are "merely victims and not part of the problem." Further, he argues that a given state's financial system, "is essentially victimized... [by criminals]. In this view, banks and the financial systems... are essentially opposed to allowing criminals to launder their profits and invest them in legitimate businesses but find that, under the globalizing financial system, it is too difficult for them to staunch such activity" (Jordan 1999).

An opposing view posits that major components of the national and international financial system are not victims, but active participants in the money laundering operations of the narcotics trade (Jordan 1999). He further notes that the first official U.S. subscription to this position took place in 1998 when a federal grand jury in Los Angeles charged 3 Mexican banks and 26 Mexican bankers with laundering millions of dollars in drug profits.

While money laundering is certainly not a new activity for organized criminal groups, it is interesting to note that until 1986 there were no laws against money laundering in any country (Sharman 2008). Much has changed in the past two decades with 170 countries having enacted criminal laws that directly address money laundering (Sharman 2008). Guy Stessens (2000) notes that because money laundering did not involve the direct harm of a victim, the only legal mechanism available in most countries to address criminal profits was forfeiture, but this was only applicable to the instruments of the crime or the subject of the crime. Noticeably absent was the availability of any legal instrument to seize the profits of a crime (Stessens 2000). Stessens (2000, p. 4) goes on to note, "this gap in law often became painfully clear in the course of criminal proceedings against drug traffickers, for example in the English case of *R v. Cuthbertson* (1981), where criminal courts had to acknowledge their lack of competence to take away the profits from crime." Indeed, the shift in the legal status of money laundering can be partly attributed to the increase in the profitability of drug trafficking. In 1992, the U.S. Department of the Treasury (2010) estimated that drug traffickers laundered over $100 billion per year in the United States alone (Webster and Campbell 1992). Other reasons cited for the shift include "the rise of both cross-border crime and the growth in legitimate international finance and trade," both of which have led to globalization of money laundering (Sharman 2008, p. 11). Worldwide, it is estimated that money laundering exceeds $2 trillion every year (Lilley 2006).

The United States passed its first money laundering law with the Money Laundering Control Act of 1986 (Lynden 2003). The 1986 act criminalized money laundering by rendering criminally culpable "anyone involved in a financial transaction who knows or has reason to know that the funds involved were obtained illicitly" (Lynden 2003, p. 209). The act also stipulated harsh punishments for those found guilty of engaging in money laundering: 20 years in prison and a fine of up to $500,000, double the amount of the laundered money, or both (Lynden 2003). Under the act, each count of money laundering can carry a separate charge; thus, when launderers divide their illicit proceeds up into smaller deposits, they can be charged for each deposit made (Lynden, 2003). The Money Laundering Control Act of 1986 only addressed domestic money laundering, leaving international money laundering virtually untouched.

International involvement in anti-money laundering efforts began in 1989 with the creation of the Financial Action Task Force (FATF) (U.S. Department of the Treasury 2010). FATF is an international policy making body which "1) Sets international standards to combat money laundering and terrorist financing; 2) Assesses and monitors compliance with the FATF standards; 3) Conducts typologies studies of money laundering and terrorist financing methods, trends and techniques; and 4) Responds to new and emerging threats, such as proliferation financing" (Financial Action Task Force 2010, p. 2).

Money laundering is an essential enterprise for organized criminal networks, because money generated through illicit activities is essentially useless to the organization unless the source of the funds can be concealed (Lilley 2006). Virtually every transnational crime, such as drug trafficking, human trafficking, and theft of cultural property, produces dirty money (Lilley 2006). Money laundering has become a global problem because often the proceeds of illicit activities are reinvested back into the criminal enterprise, allowing organized criminal networks to increase their size, scope, and reach (Lynden 2003; Lilley 2006). The techniques used to launder money have stayed relatively consistent since the 1920s, as they still involve "comingling dirty money with clean funds and trying to pass it off together as legitimate business receipts" (Lilley 2006, p. xiii). However, the process has become much more complex than seizing control of legitimate laundromats. The process of money laundering involves three stages: placement, layering, and integration (Lynden 2003). The first stage, placement, presents the biggest risk of detection for criminal organizations because the proceeds from an illicit activity can either be deposited into a legitimate bank account or business or converted to other monetary instruments, such as traveler's checks or money orders (Lynden 2003). To mitigate risk, some criminal organizations will also use a technique called "smurfing, whereby the placement stage is accomplished by distributing illicit funds to numerous couriers who make large numbers of deposits that avoid bank reporting requirements" (Lynden 2003, p. 206). The next phase, layering, involves transferring the money into offshore shell corporations, which conceal the identities of the criminals involved (Lynden 2003). If successful, the final stage, integration, will yield nearly untraceable money because the funds have usually traveled through enough banks and shell corporations that the source of the money can no longer be determined (Lynden 2003). It is at this point that the criminal networks are able to access the money and invest it back into the criminal enterprise (Lynden 2003).*

Just six weeks after the terrorist attacks in the United States on September 11, 2001, the U.S. Congress passed the Patriot Act. The act, which provided sweeping changes in privacy, surveillance, and detention, also contained the "International Money Laundering Abatement and Anti-Terrorist Financing Act (IMLAFA) of 2001" (Lynden 2003). The IMLAFA provided sweeping changes to foreign and domestic financial institutions' policies and practices (Soloman and Saret 2009). In accordance with IMLAFA, all financial institutions (banks, securities firms, insurance companies, and any other entity engaged in large-scale financial transactions) must use due diligence before allowing non-U.S. financial institutions to open correspondent accounts†; all financial institutions must implement anti-money laundering programs; and all banks and security firms are barred from opening accounts for shell corporations (Thompkins 2012). In addition to these provisions, the IMLAFA gives the United States broad jurisdictional authority as it allows the secretary of the treasury the power to "designate non-U.S. jurisdictions, classes of transactions, financial institutions, or types of accounts as of 'of primary money laundering concern.' Under these rules, the Secretary may also require domestic financial institutions and domestic financial agencies to take any of five types of special measures designed to detect and prevent money laundering" (Soloman and Saret 2009, p. 568). The special measures specifically outlined in IMLAFA require banks to keep records of account ownership, as well as identity information for banking customers and persons who transfer money through banking institutions (Soloman and Saret 2009). The IMLAFA gives the United States unprecedented jurisdiction

---

* An example of how specific groups engage in money laundering will be presented in Chapter 8, as Somali pirates regularly launder the proceeds from successful attacks.

† "A correspondent account is an account established by a bank for a foreign bank to receive deposits from, or to make payments or other disbursements on behalf of the foreign bank, or to handle other financial transactions related to the foreign bank" (FFIEC Bank Secrecy Act/Anti-Money Laundering InfoBase, n.d.).

over foreign banking practices, including the right to seize funds believed to be the result of a criminal activity (provided there is a correspondent account in the United States) and the right to subpoena banking records (again provided there is a correspondent account in the United States) (Lynden 2003).

The United States is primarily concerned with money laundering proceeds that fund terrorist groups and activities. By freezing and seizing the assets of terrorist groups, the FATF and the U.S. Department of the Treasury hope "to create a hostile environment for terrorism, constraining overall capabilities of terrorists and helping frustrate their ability to execute attacks" (Financial Action Task Force 2008, p. 4). Terrorist groups rely on money both to maintain their organization and to execute attacks (Financial Action Task Force 2008), with the latter requiring the smallest expenditure because many terrorist acts can be carried out for relatively small sums of money. For example, the Madrid train bombing in 2004 cost approximately $10,000 to carry out, as did the bombing of the U.S.S. *Cole* in 2000 (Financial Action Task Force 2008). The September 11th attacks on the World Trade Center and the Pentagon are estimated to have cost between $400,000 and $500,000* (Levy 2003), quite a low sum considering the amount of damage done and the small number of terrorists involved. Operational costs for individual cells, training, travel, and salaries can require large expenditures, necessitating the need for terrorist groups to raise funds. There are myriad examples of terrorist groups raising funds through illicit means, such as the Taliban's involvement with the drug trade. The Financial Action Task Force (2008) notes that illegal moneymaking activities among terrorist groups have increased as state sponsorship of terrorism has decreased. Additionally, the nature of terrorist groups' organizational structure has changed wherein "newer decentralized, independent cells often do not have the same level of access to foreign funding as traditional terrorist groups. As a result, terrorist groups have turned to alternative sources of financing, including criminal activities such as arms trafficking, kidnap-for-ransom, extortion, racketeering and drug trafficking" (Financial Action Task Force 2008, p. 15). The aim of the international community is to cut off the flow of money to terrorist groups in an effort to "degrade the capability of terrorist groups over time, limiting their ability to launch attacks, increasing their operational costs and injecting risk and uncertainty into their operations" (Financial Action Task Force 2008, p. 27). This goal can be accomplished if terrorist groups use financial institutions or other mainstream methods to hold their funds. However, terrorist groups are increasingly turning to less formal (and hence almost untraceable) means to move their assets. One such method is the ancient practice known as *hawala*,

---

* Costs for individual terrorist attacks include all direct costs associated with the attack (surveillance, materials, transportation, bomb components, etc.) (Financial Action Task Force 2008).

which means "transfer" in Arabic (also referred to as *hundi* in India and *havala* in Iran) (International Monetary Fund 2005).

Hawala is based on a system of trust (International Monetary Fund 2005) and involves the transfer of money without actually moving it (Jost and Harjit 2000). Hawala is generally considered an illegal practice, though laws against it are extremely difficult to enforce (Jost and Harjit 2000). While the practice is illegal, it is used legitimately by individuals who do not have bank accounts or by poor migrant workers who need to send money home and cannot afford the extensive fees that are often associated with bank transfers or mail (International Monetary Fund 2005). Indeed, hawala is an "informal and efficient funds transfer method used by millions of expatriates to send remittances to their families around the world" (International Monetary Fund 2005, p. 7).

The typical hawala scenario involves the following: (1) a person who needs to send money to another person (usually in another country); (2) a hawala dealer in the originating country (referred to as a hawaladar); (3) a hawaladar in the receiving country; and (4) the recipient of the funds. When a person uses hawala, he or she first contacts a hawaladar in his or her country of current residence and specifies the amount of money that he or she would like to send (International Monetary Fund 2005). The hawaladar will then contact a hawaladar in the receiving country with whom he or she has a good relationship and request that funds be made available for delivery to the specified person (International Monetary Fund 2005). The relationship between hawaladars is critical because hawala is a system based on trust and not actual currency. The hawaladar dealer in the receiving country will distribute funds to the designated person or family without receiving funds from the hawaladar in the originating country (International Monetary Fund 2005). There is generally no receipt or record keeping of individual transactions because hawala transactions are agreements between hawaladars (Jost and Harjit 2000). When a request for money is sent between hawaladars, the transaction will be recorded as a debit for the originating hawaladar and a credit balance for the destination hawaladar. Typically, accounts will be settled by a hawaladar at the end of each month, with those in debt either mailing a check or transferring money to the hawalader they owe (Levy 2003). Additionally, debts can be cleared "by adjusting invoices in connection with their other business dealings" (Levy 2003, p. 2–22.2). There are several possible relationships that hawaladars can have with one another: they could be business partners and the hawala transaction is part of their regular business dealing; one hawaladar might owe another hawaladar money and the hawala transactions are part of paying off the debt; lastly, a hawala dealer may have excess money in need of disposal (Jost and Harjit 2000).

The benefits of hawala for individuals who legitimately need to send money to friends or relatives in other countries are myriad and include: faster delivery times compared with more traditional means of money transfers (money can often be delivered the same day); fewer fees and better rates for money transfers compared with legal monetary transfers; and greater availability in rural areas that may not have many banking options (International Monetary Fund 2005). While many hawala transactions are initiated by law-abiding people who wish to transfer funds in the most expedient and inexpensive way possible, hawala can also be used to launder the proceeds from illicit activities (Jost and Harjit 2000). Hawala can be used in any phase of the money laundering process; placement, layering, or integration. Because individual transactions are not recorded and there is little to no regulation involved, hawala provides an ideal mechanism for money laundering by organized criminal networks. In the case of terrorist groups, "the September 11 commission found that before the terrorist acts on the United States, al Qaeda relied mainly on hawala to move money used for training camps and other operations in Afghanistan" (Levy 2003, p. 2–22.2).

Liechtenstein: Europe's Most Successful "Laundry"

By turning a blind eye toward their investors' source of income, many smaller states have become centers of secret banking for the world's criminal and terrorist organizations. While the Cayman Islands have become somewhat synonymous with dubious banking practices, arguably the tiny European principality of Liechtenstein has posed a greater threat as a nexus of illicit financial traffic (Pate 2009). According to Matthew Pate (2009, p. 337), a long-dominant and widely shared view holds Liechtenstein as an excellent place to process the gains of illicit activities. With a low tax rate, accommodating laws of incorporation and corporate governance, and legendarily secret banking practices, the principality represents an idyllic climate for money laundering.

The U.S. Department of State (2006) contends that this amenability to anonymous banking, "Contribute[s] significantly to the ability of financial intermediaries to attract funds from abroad… these same factors have historically made this country attractive to money launderers."

In a concurring view, *The Independent* newspaper of London characterizes banking secrecy and money as, "the core of its economy. They account for 14.3 percent of the workforce and contribute to 30 percent of a gross domestic product of €2.7bn (£2bn)" (Patterson 2008). The report goes on to state that the Liechtenstein royal house, owners of the nation's largest bank, "wields more power than any other monarchy in Europe."

According to the U.S. Department of State, the Liechtenstein Global Trust (LGT) royal bank is in good company. In this nation of roughly 33,000 people, there are 15 other banks, 3 nonbank financial companies, 16 public investment companies, numerous insurance and reinsurance companies, 230 licensed fiduciary companies, and more than 60 lawyers.

Again, as *The Independent* describes, "Overlooked by its medieval mountain-top castle, glistening bank facades jostle for space with investment firms and dubious 'letter-box' holding companies of which the country boasts an estimated 73,700." The U.S. Department of State (2006) estimates that the number is closer to 75,000. A report by the International Monetary Fund observes, "Non-resident business constitutes more than 90% of the private banking activities conducted in Liechtenstein."

An *International Herald Tribune* (Kroon 2000) interview with Liechtenstein's monarch, Prince Hans-Adam II, states, "a German intelligence report described [Liechtenstein as] a financial haven for Colombian drug barons, the Mafia and the Russian underworld." The report further quotes the Organization for Economic Co-operation and Development (OECD) in their listing "Liechtenstein as a 'harmful' tax shelter" and criticizes "its lack of cooperation in the fight against money laundering."

A report in *The Guardian* explores similar themes, "Millions of dollars of South American drug money were allegedly laundered here; Saddam Hussein's government even registered a jet. In 2000… the [Organization for Economic Co-operation and Development] named the country as the only money-laundering nation in Europe and put it on its blacklist" (MacDonald 2004).

Cooperative Research History Commons (2007), an international watchdog organization, reveals a stark detail about Liechtenstein's role in global terrorist funding, "Leaders of the Muslim Brotherhood found[ed] the Al Taqwa Bank. This bank will later be accused of being the largest financial supporter of al Qaeda, Hamas, the GIA in Algeria, and other organizations officially designated by the U.S. as groups that sponsor terrorism." As the Cooperative Research History Commons (2007) goes on to explain, the U.S. Department of the Treasury will later allege that $60 million in financial support for Hamas was processed through Al Taqwa in 1997.

In 2001, the White House Press Office described the Al Taqwa bank as "…a network of companies in Switzerland, Liechtenstein, the Bahamas, and Milan. It is controlled by Youssef Nada, a naturalized Italian citizen. Al Taqwa provides investment advice and cash transfer mechanisms for al-Qaida and other radical Islamic groups."

Motivated by the events of September 11, 2001, disquieting revelations such as these demanded an international response. By the end of September 2001, the U.S. government enacted Executive Order 13,224 effectively halting Al Taqwa financial activities domestically and in 39 countries. Shortly thereafter, the United Nations Security Council passed the U.S.-sponsored Resolution 1373 on September 28. This resolution provides for the freezing, suppression, and monitoring of all funds and financial activities related to terrorist organizations.

While Liechtenstein is perhaps the leading example of a European money laundering haven, as Lucy Komisar (2002, p. 32) observes, the principality is only one of many states that "offered state-of-the-art financial services for crooks." What the case of Liechtenstein perhaps does best is to illustrate how a very stable, fully modernized, and financially successful regime can play a pivotal role in the dealings of wholly chaotic, dysfunctional, and fragile nations a seeming world away.

State Fragility and Transnational Organized Crime

It should be evident at this point in the unfolding discussion that fragile or failing states are of great import to the global community. Former Secretary of State Condalezza Rice noted "the US faced an unparalleled threat from 'weak and failing states that serve as global pathways that facilitate the spread of pandemics, the movement of criminals and terrorists, and the proliferation of the world's most dangerous weapons'" (Rice 2005, as cited in Huria 2008). However, issues associated with failed states have the capacity to affect all nations, not just the United States; therefore, dealing effectively with state failure ultimately requires a coordinated response from the global community. Interestingly though, this line of thinking is not without controversy. Stewart Patrick (2011) argues that state failure plays only a minimal role in transnational crime. He notes, "far greater dangers emerge from stronger developing countries that may suffer from corruption and lack of government accountability but come nowhere near qualifying as failed states" (Patrick 2011).

We both concur and disagree with Patrick's central assessment. Patrick tends to dismiss the idea that failing states influence other nations and instead suggests that failed states have the most negative impact on the citizenry of these countries. We do not dispute the idea that inhabitants of failed states are often imperiled by their governments' inability to function, but we are not so quick to dismiss the idea that state failure has profound effects on the global community.

Transnational crime occurs in all parts of the globe and can proliferate in sustainable as well as fragile nations. We hold that the type and nature of transnational crime will be largely dependent on the relative strength of the state. Shelley (2005, p. 102) observes that transnational crime groups "have become ever-more important actors in the global illicit economy centered in weak states, whereas state intervention in countries with strong governments has slowed the growth of the mafia in Italy and the United States, the *boryokudan* in Japan, and contributed to the collapse of the Medellin cartel in Colombia." In essence, no state, whether fragile or sustainable, is immune to the effects of transnational crime. More sustainable countries may have the resources to intervene and lessen the effects of some types of transnational crime, but they will still nonetheless be affected.

The motivations behind transnational crimes may well be different in fragile states versus sustainable nations. While transnational crimes in sustainable nations may arise for strictly monetary reasons, in fragile nations, mere survival is likely a stronger motivational factor. In fragile nations, transnational crimes may be the result of a poor economy and limited chances for employment. As Shelley (2005, p. 103) notes, "globalization has marginalized and impoverished many communities in the developing world, forcing them to engage in illicit activities to survive. With the collapse of prices for raw commodities in the globalized economy, many farmers, mentored by drug traffickers, have turned to drug cultivation to survive economically."

The United Nations (2010) provides the clearest explanation of the link between transnational organized crime and state failure. In particular, they note that while governmental destabilization is often not the primary goal of transnational organized groups:

> they can provoke a reaction that can also threaten long-term peace prospects. A clear sign that crime has become a national security threat comes when exceptional legal and security measures are taken, including calling on the military to help re-establish the government's authority. While sometimes necessary to reacquire lost territory, the long-term use of regular military forces to police civilian populations presents risks for the rule of law and civil liberties. Military and police officials may become frustrated with a corrupt or ineffective criminal justice system and begin to engage in extrajudicial executions. The public may form civilian vigilante groups as well. Over time, these paramilitary vigilantes can become as big a security challenge as the criminals they were formed to combat. (United Nations 2010, p. 223)

Transnational crime of all types threatens the stability of governments. However, we have primarily focused on the deleterious effects of the drug trade, money laundering, and cybercrime on governmental stability. As discussed earlier in the chapter, the cocaine trade in Mexico has had drastic negative consequences for the government and the populace. Murder rates of governmental officials and citizens caught in the crossfire have been increasing dramatically in recent years. Colombia, a country which is improving in many dimensions of failure, has experienced many of the same issues with drug cartels since the 1960s. Fuerzas Armadas Revolucionarias de Colombia (FARC) and the Ejercito de Liberacion Nacional (ELN) were the two main guerrilla groups responsible for Colombian drug violence in the 1960s (United Nations 2010). In the 1980s, right-wing guerrilla groups consolidated under the umbrella of the Autodefensas Unidas de Colombia (AUC), initially to protect local farmers, but later to provide protections for organized criminal groups (United Nations 2010). As FARC, the ELN, and the AUC became more powerful, their influence spread throughout Colombia and they began to seize control of parts of the country (United Nations 2010). Not surprisingly, as the government lost control, murder rates increased from approximately 5,000 in the 1970s to a high of 30,000 in the 1990s (United Nations 2010).

When examining the link between state failure and money laundering, we find an inverse relationship between banking practices that are complicit in money laundering enterprises and stability. That is to say, more stable nations (such as Switzerland, Liechtenstein, and others) often have loose banking laws that make money laundering easier for criminal networks. Donato Masciandaro and Alessandro Portolano (2002) and Peter Reuter and Edwin Truman (2004) note the lack of a relationship between state failure and money laundering and explain that the primary goal of organized criminal networks is to keep the money safe throughout the laundering process, something that cannot be attained in a politically unstable region. The informal practice of hawala often takes place in regions that are unstable (e.g., Pakistan). However, because hawala leaves no paper trail and provides almost complete anonymity for its users, it is almost impossible to obtain the data necessary to examine the link between hawala and state failure.

References

Afghanistan Constitution. 2004. The Constitution of the Islamic Republic of Afghanistan. http://www.afghanembassy.com.pl/cms/uploads/images/Constitution/The%20 Constitution.pdf (Accessed October 5, 2014).

Agren, D. 2014. Notorious Mexican drug cartel leader arrested. USA Today. http://www.usatoday.com/story/news/world/2014/02/22/drug-cartel-arrested/5725169/ (Accessed December 5, 2014).

Albanese, J. 2010. Organized Crime: Oxford Bibliographies Online Research Guide. New York: Oxford University Press.

Albani, J. 2001. History of the drug traffic in Lebanon and Syria. http://www.gotc-se.org/statements/Albani/Drug_trafficking.html (Accessed June 10, 2011).

Andreas, P. 2011. Illicit globalization: Myths, misconceptions, and historical lessons. Political Science Quarterly 126(3): 403–425.

Ashford, W. 2007. Cybercrime is biggest UK fear. Computer Weekly.com. http://www.computer-weekly.com/news/2240083689/Cybercrime-is-biggest-UK-fear (Accessed January 4, 2015).

Baddour, D. and S. Gardner. 2014. Pants on fire: Duncan Hunter makes unconfirmed claim border patrol caught at least 10 ISIS fighters. http://www.politifact.com/texas/statements/2014/oct/10/duncan-hunter-2/duncan-hunter-makes-unconfirmed-claim-border-patro/ (Accessed April 4, 2015).

Bagley, B. 2012. *Drug Trafficking and Organized Crime in the Americas: Major Trends in the Twenty-First Century.* Washington, DC: Woodrow Wilson International Center for Scholars.

Baranetsky, V. 2009. What is cyberterrorism? Even experts can't agree. *Harvard Law Record.* http://hlrecord.org/what-is-cyberterrorism-even-experts-cant-agree/ (Accessed April 4, 2015).

Belenko, S. and C. Spohn. 2015. *Drugs, Crime and Justice.* Thousand Oaks, CA: Sage.

Booth, M. 1999. *Opium: A History.* New York: St. Martin's Griffin.

Brenner, S. 2012. *Cybercrime and the Law: Challenges, Issues, and Outcomes.* Lebanon, NH: Northeastern University Press.

Broadhurst, R., S. Gordon, and J. McFarlane. 2012. Transnational and organized crime in the Indo-Asia Pacific. In F. Allum and S. Gilmour (Eds) *Routledge Handbook of Transnational Organized Crime,* pp. 143–156, New York: Routledge.

Brouwer, K. C., P. Case, R. Ramos, R. C. Magis-Rodríguez, J. Bucardo, T. Patterson, and S. Strathdee. 2006. Trends in production, trafficking and consumption of methamphetamine and cocaine in Mexico. *Substance Use & Misuse* 41(5): 707–727.

Burrnett, J., M. Penaloza, and R. Benincasa. 2010. Mexico seems to favor Sinaloa cartel in drug war. *National Public Radio.* http://www.npr.org/2010/05/19/126906809/mexico-seems-to-favor-sinaloa-cartel-in-drug-war (Accessed March 18, 2014).

Buxton, J. 2006. *The Political Economy of Narcotics: Production, Consumption, and Global Markets.* Nova Scotia, CA: Fernwood Publishing.

Byrd, W. and D. Buddenberg. 2006. Afghanistan's drug industry: Structure, functioning, dynamics, and implications for counter-narcotics policy. *United Nations Office of Drugs and Crime and The World Bank.* http://www.unodc.org/pdf/Afgh_drugindustry_Nov06.pdf (Accessed July 25, 2014).

Carment, D. 2003. Assessing state failure: Implications for theory and policy. *Third World Quarterly* 24: 407–417.

Caunic, I., F. Suciu, and I. Muntele. 2011. European Union: Destination and transit area for cocaine trafficking. *Romanian Review on Political Geography* 13: 149–156.

Chalk, P. 2011. *The Latin American Drug Trade: Scope, Dimensions, Impact, and Response.* Santa Monica, CA: Rand Corporation.

Choo, K. R. 2008. Organized crime groups in cyberspace: A typology. *Trends in Organized Crime* 11: 270–295.

Chossudovsky, M. 2010. War and economic crisis. In M. Chossudovsky and A. M. Montreal (Eds) *The Global Economic Crisis: The Great Depression of the XXI Century,* pp. 181–211, Montreal, Quebec: Global Research.

Chossudovsky, M. 2011. *The Spoils of War: Afghanistan's Multibillion Dollar Heroin Trade. Washington's Hidden Agenda: Restore the Drug Trade.* Ottawa: The Centre for Research on Globalization/University of Ottawa. http://www.globalresearch.ca/the-spoils-of-war-afghanistan-s-multibillion-dollar-heroin-trade/91 (Accessed November 26, 2011).

Chouvy, P. 2009. *Opium: Uncovering the Politics of the Poppy.* Cambridge, MA: Harvard University Press.

Christian Science Monitor. May 29, 1970. Quoted in Scott, P. 2003. *Drugs, Oil, and War: The United States in Afghanistan, Colombia, and Indochina.* Lanham, MD: Rowman and Littlefield.

Cook, C. 2009. Mexico's drug cartels. In B. Rosen (Ed.) *Drug Transit and Distribution, Interception and Control Co-operation With Drug Transit Countries of Illegal Drugs,* pp. 39–59, New York: Nova Science.

Cooperative Research History Commons. 2007. Context of 1997-september 11, 2001: US knows Swiss bank funds Hamas and top Al-Qaeda leaders, yet considers bank 'low priority'. http://www.cooperativeresearch.org/context.jsp?item=a97lowpriority (Accessed October 25, 2013).

Council on Foreign Relations. 2011. Institute for the study of war: Haqqani network. http://www.cfr.org/afghanistan/institute-study-war-haqqani-network/p26126 (Accessed October 25, 2013).

Council on Foreign Relations. 2013. The global regime for transnational crime: Issue brief. http://www.cfr.org/transnational-crime/global-regime-transnational-crime/p28656 (Accessed January 7, 2014).

Dudley, S. 2012. Transnational Crime in Mexico and Central America: Its Evolution and Role in International Migration. Woodrow Wilson Center for Scholars. https://www.google.com/url?sa=t&rct=j&q=&esrc=s&source=web&cd=1&ved=0CB4QFjAAahUK EwjTidDy4O_IAhWJWSYKHfG2CR4&url=http%3A%2F%2Fwww.migrationpolicy.org%2Fpubs%2FRMSG-TransnationalCrime.pdf&usg=AFQjCNGZZIwZAUo4goSJB JI.oggImRe3hyA&sig2=lS6Unefq0gq_jcSlLcG4KA (Accessed June 6, 2013).

Ellison, G. and N. Pino. 2012. Globalization, Police Reform, and Development: Doing It the Western Way? New York: Palgrave MacMillan.

Etges, R. and E. Sutcliffe. 2008. An overview of transnational organized cyber crime. Information Security Journal: A Global Perspective 17: 87–94.

Federal Bureau of Investigation. 2013. Organized crime. http://www.fbi.gov/about-us/investigate/organizedcrime/glossary (Accessed October 18, 2013).

FFIEC Bank Secrecy Act/Anti-Money Laundering InfoBase (n.d.). Foreign correspondent account recordkeeping and due diligence—Overview. Bank Secrecy Act/Anti-Money Laundering Examination Manual. http://www.ffiec.gov/bsa_aml_infobase/pages_manual/OLM_027.htm (Accessed October 15, 2013).

Financial Action Task Force. 2008. Terrorist Financing. Financial Action Task Force. http://www.treasury.gov/resource-center/terrorist-illicit-finance/Documents/terrorist-financing_022008.pdf (Accessed March 16, 2014).

Financial Action Task Force. 2010. An introduction to the FATF and its work. http://www.fatf-gafi.org/trash/aboutfatf/whatisfatf/aboutthefatf.html (Accessed March 16, 2014).

Fox News. 2014. ISIS pushes toward Turkey. [Video file]. http://video.foxnews.com/v/3826440735001 (Accessed January 15, 2014).

Friedrichs, D. 2007. Towards a criminology of international crimes: Producing a conceptual and contextual framework. In R. Havenman and A. Smeulers (Eds) Towards a Criminology of International Crimes, Chapter 2, Anterwerp: Intersentia.

Fund for Peace. 2012. Failed states index 2012. http://fsi.fundforpeace.org/rankings-2012-sortable (Accessed December 10, 2015).

Galeotti, M. 2014. Global Crime Today: The Changing Face of Organised Crime. New York: Routledge.

Gercke, M. 2012. Cybercrime, terrorist use of the internet and cyberwarfare: The importance of a clear distinction. In D. R. Voica (Ed.) Trends and Developments in Contemporary Terrorism, pp. 17–31, Amsterdam: IOS Press.

Glenny, M. 2012. Organized crime in a network society. Journal of International Affairs 66: 145–149.

Grayson, G. 2011. Mexico: Narco-Violence and a Failed State? New Brunswick, NJ: Transaction.

Guttieri, K. and J. Piombo. 2007. Interim Governments: Institutional Bridges to Peace and Democracy? Washington, DC: U.S. Institute of Peace.

Hammond, J. April 9, 2011. The Afghan drug trade and the elephant in the room. Foreign Policy Journal. http://www.foreignpolicyjournal.com/2011/04/09/the-afghan-drug-trade-and-the-elephant-in-the-room/ (Accessed May 5, 2013).

Havocscope. 2012. Transnational crime. http://www.havocscope.com/category/transnational-crime/ (Accessed June 6, 2013).

Held, D. M., A. D. Goldblatt, and J. Perraton. 1999. *Global Transformations*. Stanford, CA: Stanford University Press.

Hendry, K. 2013. No state is an island: The importance of a multisectoral approach. Fund for Peace. http://library.fundforpeace.org/fsi13-multisector (Accessed July 10, 2013).

Hesterman, J. 2013. *The Terrorist–Criminal Nexus: An Alliance of International Drug Cartels, Organized Crime, and Terror Groups*. Boca Raton, FL: CRC Press.

Institute of Medicine. 2007. *Preventing HIV Infection Among Injecting Drug Users in High-Risk Countries*. Washington, DC: The National Academies Press.

International Monetary Fund. 2005. *Regulatory Frameworks for Hawala and Other Remittance Systems*. Washington, DC: International Monetary Fund.

Jamieson, A. 2001. Transnational organized crime: A European perspective. *Studies in Conflict and Terrorism* 24: 377–387.

Jenner, M. 2011. International drug trafficking: A global problem with a domestic solution. *Indiana Journal of Global Legal Studies* 18: 901–927.

Johnson, C. 2008. *Afghanistan Security: Further Congressional Action May Be Needed to Ensure Completion of a Detailed Plan to Develop and Sustain Capable Afghan National Security Forces*. Washington, DC: U.S. Government Accountability Office.

Jordan, D. C. 1999. *Drug Politics: Dirty Money and Democracies*. Norman, OK: University of Oklahoma Press. http://www.jahrbuch2001.studien-von-zeitfragen.net/Global/DRUGPO_1/drugpo_12.HTM#Jordan%20English (Accessed March 21, 2014).

Jost, P. and S. Harjit. 2000. The hawala alternative remittance system and its role in money laundering. INTERPOL. http://www.interpol.int/Public/FinancialCrime/MoneyLaundering/hawala/default.asp (Accessed June 16, 2014).

Kaplan, D. and A. Dubro. 2012. *Yakuza: Japan's Criminal Underworld*. Berkley, CA: University of California Press.

Keefe, P. 2012. Cocaine Incorporated. *The New York Times*. http://www.nytimes.com/2012/06/17/magazine/how-a-mexican-drug-cartel-makes-its-billions.html?pagewanted=all&_r=0 (Accessed August 11, 2015).

Kelly, T., N. Bensahel. and O. Oliker. 2011. *Security Force Assistance in Afghanistan: Identifying Lessons for the Future*. Santa Monica, CA: The Rand Corporation.

King, G. and L. Zeng. 2001. Improving forecasts of state failure. *World Politics* 534: 623–658.

Kingston, J. 2011. *Contemporary Japan: History, Politics, and Social Change Since the 1980s*. Chichester: Wiley.

Komisar, L. 2002. Dirty money and global banking secrecy. In R. Kick (Ed.) *Everything You Know Is Wrong: The Disinformation Guide to Secrets and Lies*, pp. 30–34, New York: The Disinformation.

Kostovicicova, D. and V. Bojicic-Dzelilovic. 2009. *Persistent State Weakness in the Global Age*. Aldershot: Ashgate.

Kroon, R. October 30, 2000. "Q&A/Prince Hans-Adam II : Liechtenstein's Future As a 'Clean Tax Haven" *International Herald Tribune*. http://www.iht.com/articles/2000/08/31/prince.2.t.php?page=1 (Retrieved October 19, 2007).

Kshetri, N. 2010. *The Global Cybercrime Industry: Economic, Institutional and Strategic Perspectives*. Greensboro, NC: Springer.

Levy, S. 2003. *Federal Money Laundering Regulation: Banking, Corporate and Securities Compliance*. Waltham, MA: Aspen.

Lilley, P. 2006. *Dirty Dealing: The Untold Truth About Global Money Laundering, International Crime, and Terrorism*, 3rd edn. London: Kogan Page.

Lo, S. 2009. Globalization, state autonomy and the fight against cross-border crime: Greater China's cooperation with the world. *Asian Journal of Political Science* 17: 299–322.

Lynden, G. 2003. International money laundering abatement and anti-terrorist financing act of 2001: Congress wears a blindfold while giving money laundering legislation a face-lift. *Fordham Journal of Corporate & Financial Law* 8: 200–243.

MacDonald, L. 2004. The future is aubergine for former shady haven. *Guardian Newspapers.* http://www.theguardian.com/world/2004/jul/03/lukeharding (Accessed March 25, 2014).

Mallory, S. 2012. *Understanding Organized Crime*, 2nd edn. Sudbury, MA: Jones & Bartlett.

Mavropalias, K. 2011. Cybercrime & cyberterrorism: Inducing anxiety & fear on individuals. *Cyberpsychology.* http://iconof.com/blog/cybercrime-cyberterrorism-inducing-anxi-ety-fear-on-individuals/ (Accessed March 5, 2011).

Masciandaro, D. and A. Portolano. 2002. *Inside the Black (List) Box: Money Laundering, Lax Financial Regulations, Non-Cooperative Countries: A Law and Economic Approach.* Paulo Baffi Center, Bocconi University and Bank of Italy.

McCusker, R. 2006. Transnational organised cyber crime—Distinguishing threat from reality. *Crime Law and Social Change* 46: 257–273.

Morton, A. 2012. The war on drugs in Mexico; a failed state? *Third World Quarterly* 33: 1631–1645.

Musto, D. 1997. Opium, cocaine and marijuana in American history. In L. K. Gaines and P. B. Kraska (Eds) *Drugs, Crime and Justice: Contemporary Perspectives*, pp. 32–49, Long Grove, IL: Waveland Press.

Nava, J. 2011. Mexico: Failing state or emerging democracy. *Military Review* March–April: 31–40.

Neuman, S. 2013. White House official: U.S. has asked for Snowden's extradition. National Public Radio. http://www.npr.org/blogs/thetwo-way/2013/06/22/194528758/snowden-extradition-could-get-snarled-in-hong-kong-courts (Accessed March 3, 2014).

O'Conner, D. 2009. The political economy of Columbia's cocaine industry. *Columbia* 14: 81–106.

Office of Justice Programs. 1994. *Drugs & Crime Data.* Fact Sheet: Drug-Related Crime. Washington, DC: Bureau of Justice Statistics, U.S. Department of Justice. http://www.bjs.gov/content/pub/pdf/DRRC.PDF (Accessed March 25, 2014).

Paraszczuk, J. 2014. Russia claims IS supplying half of all Afghan heroin coming to Europe. Radio Free Europe Radio Liberty. http://www.rferl.org/content/islamic-state-drug-smuggling-heroin/26711721.html (Accessed January 5, 2015).

Passas, N. 2001. Globalization and transnational crime: Effects of crimiogenic asymmetries. In P. Williams and D. Vlassis (Eds) *Combating Transnational Crime: Concepts, Activities, and Responses*, pp. 22–56, Abingdon: Frank Cass.

Pate, M. 2009. Crime and punishment in Liechtenstein: A country profile. *International Journal of Comparative and Applied Criminal Justice* 33: 325–348.

Patrick, S. 2011. Why failed states shouldn't be our biggest national security fear. http://www.cfr.org/international-peace-and-security/why-failed-states-shouldnt-our-biggest-national-security-fear/p24689 (Accessed June 19, 2012).

Patterson, T. 2008. Liechtenstein: Where the missing billions go. *The Independent.* London. http://www.independent.co.uk/news/world/europe/liechtenstein-where-the-missing-billions-go-787282.html (Accessed March 25, 2014).

Perito, R. 2009. *Afghanistan's Police: The Weak Line in Security Sector Reform*, Volume 31. http://www.usip.org/publications/afghanistan-spolice/.

Politi, A. 2001. The threat of organized crime in the Balkans. *Southeast European and Black Sea Studies* 1: 39–63.

Poulantzas, N. 1978. *State, Power, Socialism.* London: Verso.

Raines, L. 2003. *The Internet and Emergency Preparedness.* Pew Research Center. http://www.pewinternet.org/2003/08/31/the-internet-and-emergency-preparedness/ (Accessed April 3, 2014).

Reuter, P. and E. Truman. 2004. *Chasing Dirty Money: The Fight Against Money Laundering.* Washington, DC: Institute for International Economics.

Rollins, J. 2010. *International Terrorism and Transnational Crime: Security Threats, U.S. Policy, and Considerations for Congress*. Washington, DC: Congressional Research Service.

Rollins, J. and L. Wyler. 2013. *Terrorism and Transnational Crime: Foreign Policy Issues for Congress*. Washington, DC: Congressional Research Service.

Salazar, B. and L. Restrepo. 2011. Lethal closeness: The evolution of a small-world drug trafficking network. *Desafíos* 232: 197–221.

Scherrer, A. 2009. *G8 Against Transnational Organized Crime*. Abingdon: Ashgate.

Seelke, C. 2013. Supporting criminal justice system reform in Mexico: The U.S. role. Washington, DC: Congressional Research Service Report for Congress.

Sharman, J. C. 2008. Power and discourse in policy diffusion: Anti-money laundering in developing states. *International Studies Quarterly* 52: 635–656.

Shelley, L. 1999. Transnational organized crime: The new authoritarianism. In H. Friman and P. Andreas (Eds) *The Illicit Global Economy and State Power*, pp. 25–51, Oxford: Rowman and Littlefield.

Shelley, L. 2005. The unholy trinity: Transnational crime, corruption, and terrorism. *Brown Journal of World Affairs* 11: 101–111.

Shelley, L. 2014. Blood money: How ISIS makes bank. *Foreign Affairs*. http://www.foreignaffairs.com/articles/142403/louise-shelley/blood-money (Accessed January 5, 2015).

Shelley, L., J. Picarelli, and C. Corpora. 2003. Global crime inc. In M. Love (Ed.) *Beyond Sovereignty: Issues for a Global Agenda*, 2nd edn, pp. 143–166, Independence, KY: Thomas Wadsworth.

Steinberg, K. and C. Mathewson. Landscapes of drugs and war: Intersections of political ecology and global conflict. In C. Flint (Ed.) *The Geography of War and Peace: From Death Camps to Diplomats*, pp. 242–258, New York: Oxford University Press.

Soloman, L. and L. Saret. 2009. *Asset Protection Strategies*. Chicago, IL: CCH.

Stathdee, S. and J. Stockman. 2010. HIV among people who use drugs: A global perspective of populations at risk. *Journal of Acquired Immune Deficiency Syndrome* 55(1): S17–S22. http://www.ncbi.nlm.nih.gov/pubmed/21045594 (Accessed June 4, 2014).

Stessens, G. 2000. *Money Laundering: A New International Law Enforcement Model*. Cambridge: Cambridge University Press.

Sutherland, S. 2007. Irrationality: The Enemy Within. London: Pinter & Martin.

The Guardian. March 6, 2014. *Membership of Japan's yakuza crime gangs falls to all-time low*. http://www.theguardian.com/world/2014/mar/06/membership-japan-yakuza-crime-gangs-low (Accessed June 4, 2015).

Thompkins, J. 2012. *The Impact of the USA Patriot Act of 2001 on Non-U.S. Banks*. Washington, DC: Seminar on Current Developments in Monetary and Financial Law.

Thoumi, F. 1995. *Political Economy & Illegal Drugs in Columbia*, Volume 2. Tokyo: United Nations University Press.

Transparency International. 2013. Global corruption barometer: Mexico country report. http://www.transparency.org/gcb2013/country/?country=mexico (Accessed March 15, 2014).

United Nations. 2004. United Nations Convention Against Transnational Organized Crime and the Protocols Thereto. http://www.unodc.org/unodc/treaties/CTOC/index.html (Accessed January 15, 2013).

United Nations. 2010. *Globalization of Crime: A Transnational Organized Crime Threat Assessment*. New York: United Nations Office on Drugs and Crime.

United Nations Interregional Crime and Justice Research Institute. 2014. *Cyberwarfare*. http://www.unicri.it/special_topics/cyber_threats/cyber_crime/explanations/cyberwarfare/ (Accessed March 16, 2014).

United Nations Office on Drugs and Crime. 2008. World drug report 2008. http://www.unodc.org/documents/wdr/WDR_2008/WDR_2008_eng_web.pdf

United Nations Office on Drugs and Crime. 2010. World drug report 2010. http://www.unodc.org/unodc/en/data-and-analysis/WDR-2010.html (Accessed June 4, 2014).

United Nations Office on Drugs and Crime. 2011. The global Afghan opium trade: A threat assessment. http://www.unodc.org/documents/data-and-analysis/Studies/Global_Afghan_Opium_Trade_2011-web.pdf (Accessed March 1, 2014).

United Nations Office on Drugs and Crime. 2012. World drug report. http://www.unodc.org/unodc/en/data-and-analysis/WDR-2012.html (Accessed January 15, 2014).

U.S. Department of State. 1994. Mutual legal assistance treaty between the United States of America and the United Kingdom of Great Britain and Northern Ireland. http://www.state.gov/documents/organization/176269.pdf (Accessed January 15, 2014).

U.S. Department of State. 2006. International narcotics control strategy report, country reports G-M: Liechtenstein. http://www.state.gov/p/inl/rls/nrcrpt/2006/vol2/html/62144.htm (Accessed January 15, 2014).

U.S. Department of State. 2011. Trafficking in persons report 2011. http://www.state.gov/j/tip/rls/tiprpt/2011/ (Accessed June 12, 2013).

U.S. Department of State. 2013. International narcotics control strategy report (INCSR) bureau of international narcotics and law enforcement affairs. http://www.state.gov/j/inl/rls/nrcrpt/2013/vol1/204048.htm (Accessed January 18, 2014).

U.S. Department of the Treasury. 2010. Financial action task force. http://www.treasury.gov/resource-center/terrorist-illicit-finance/Pages/Financial-Action-Task-Force.aspx (Accessed January 20, 2014).

U.S. Drug Enforcement Agency. 1993a. The illicit drug situation in Columbia: Drug intelligence report. Washington, DC: U.S. Department of Justice.

U.S. Drug Enforcement Agency. 1993b. The illicit drug situation in Columbia: Drug intelligence report. Second session, Washington, DC: U.S. Department of Justice.

U.S. House of Representatives. 2012. Hearing Before the Subcommittee on Crime, Terrorism, and Homeland Security. 112th Congress, Second session.

Webster, B. and Campbell, M. 1992. International Money Laundering: Research and Investigation Join Forces. National Institute of Justice Research Brief. U.S. Department of Justice. https://www.ncjrs.gov/pdffiles1/Digitization/135942NCJRS.pdf (Accessed June 4, 2014).

Wechsler, W. and G. Barnabo. 2013. The Department of Defense's role in combating transnational organized crime. In M. Miklaucic and J. Brewer (Eds) *Convergence: Illicit Networks and National Security in the Age of Globalization*, pp. 233–242, Washington, DC: National Defense University Press.

http://www.unodc.org/documents/wdr/WDR_2008/WDR_2008_eng_web.pdf

Gender Violence and Gender-Based Disparities in Fragile States

6

> Society as a whole benefits immeasurably from a climate in which all persons, regardless of race or gender, may have the opportunity to earn respect, responsibility, advancement and remuneration based on ability.
>
> —Sandra Day O'Conner

Having discussed the implications of state failure on the general populace in previous chapters, we now turn to a discussion of how state failure influences women. There is little doubt that all citizens are affected by violence in fragile and failing states; however, women are especially at risk and often doubly victimized, both by society and in the home. In addition to a greater likelihood of violence, women also face significant barriers to full participation in society in the majority of fragile states. In this chapter, we will first explore the issue of gender violence and then turn to a discussion of gender-based disparities in fragile and failing states.

Worldwide, violence against women takes many forms and can include, but is certainly not limited to, domestic violence, sexual and psychological abuse, forced prostitution, and femicide. Article 2 of the United Nations Declaration on the Elimination of Violence Against Women defines violence against women thusly:

> Physical, sexual and psychological violence that occurs in the family, including battering; sexual abuse of female children in the household; dowry-related violence; marital rape; female genital mutilation and other traditional practices harmful to women; non-spousal violence; and violence related to exploitation; Physical, sexual and psychological violence that occurs within the general community, including rape; sexual abuse; sexual harassment and intimidation at work, in educational institutions and elsewhere; trafficking in women; and forced prostitution; Physical, sexual and psychological violence perpetrated or condoned by the State, wherever it occurs. (United Nations 1996)

The aforementioned forms of violence can stem from a variety of factors, but Vincent Fauveau and Therese Blanchet (1989, p. 1127) note, "the underlying causes of violent deaths among women of reproductive age, i.e.

complications of an induced abortion, suicide and homicide, are clearly social. Many of them may be seen as a consequence of the strict control enforced by males over the sexual life of women and reproduction." Societal factors that promote violence against women include cultural (e.g., gender-specific socialization or belief in male superiority), economic (e.g., limited education and employment opportunities), legal (e.g., laws favoring males in matter of divorce or lesser legal status for women), and political factors (e.g., limitations in political participation) (United Nations Children's Fund 2000).

In recognition of the importance of this issue, the United Nations appointed a special rapporteur on violence against women in 1994. Further, the United Nations passed a mandate,

> *Strongly condemning* all acts of violence against women and girls and in this regard *called*, in accordance with the Declaration on the Elimination of Violence against Women, for the elimination of all forms of gender-based violence in the family, within the general community and where perpetrated or condoned by the State, and *emphasized* the duty of Governments to refrain from engaging in violence against women and to exercise due diligence to prevent, investigate and, in accordance with national legislation, punish acts of violence against women and to take appropriate and effective action concerning acts of violence against women, whether those acts are perpetrated by the State, by private persons or by armed groups or warring factions, and to provide access to just and effective remedies and specialized, including medical, assistance to victims. (United Nations Office for the High Commissioner for Human Rights 1996, 2012)

The special rapporteur has several tasks including, but not limited to, information gathering as it pertains to violence against women and making recommendations to help eliminate violence.

As is well-documented within the feminist literature, the underlying causes of gender violence and social disparities stem "[from patriarchal] control by men of most key positions in dominant social structures: government, state bureaucracies, corporations, the military and professional bodies" (Brian 1984). One also sees this manifest in male control over the sexual and reproductive lives of women (Farr 2005; Fauveau and Blanchet 1989; Sanday 1981; Gould and Agnich 2014). While feminist discussions of violence against women and gender inequities are important for the current chapter, the intersection of Foucault's theories of power and feminism produce the most fecund theoretical underpinning, insofar as state failure is concerned. The relationship between Foucault and feminism is complicated, but as Irene Diamond and Lee Quinby (1988, p. x) note

> both identify the body as the site of power, that is, as the locus of domination through which docility is accomplished and subjectivity constituted.

Both point to the local and intimate operations of power rather than focusing exclusively on the supreme power of the state. Both bring to the fore the crucial role of discourse in its capacity to produce and sustain hegemonic power and emphasize challenges contained within marginalized and/or unrecognized discourses. And both criticize the ways in which Western humanism has privileged the experience of the Western masculine elite as it proclaims universals about truth, freedom, and human nature

The intersections previously noted are not meant to imply that feminism and Foucauldian thought represent a perfect theoretical marriage; rather, that each brings differing insights that can help explain how power relations in various spheres impact women (Diamond and Quinby 1988).

Before a discussion of Foucauldian ideas about power can take place, it is necessary to note that the supreme power of the state is not the exclusive source of power. It is reasonable to ask how a study on state failure can be nested in a theory that discounts the power of the government. As Nicos Poulantzas (1978, p. 77) rightly points out, Foucault underestimates "the role of law in the exercise of power within modern society ... he also underestimates the role of the State itself, and fails to understand the function of the repressive apparatuses (army, police, judicial system, etc.) as a means of exercising physical violence that are at the heart of the modern State." Poulantzas' critique of Foucault may at first seem damning as there are countless nation-states in varying stages of failure that have strong authoritarian regimes (e.g., North Korea). In these countries, the central locus of power is most certainly the state and the government doubtlessly affects the treatment of women. However, there are also myriad examples of failed states that have almost no functional or even discernable governmental structure (e.g., Somalia). In these states, power emanates from other sources, which coalesce and ultimately have a detrimental effect on women. The position taken here is that Foucault is partially correct—the government is not the sole source of power in a given society, but we must be careful not to overlook or discount the role of the government where power is concerned.

In *The History of Sexuality*, Michel Foucault (1988, p. 93) analyses the intersection of sex and power, and while he does not examine state power and domination (as these are simply forms that power can take), he does note, "power is omnipresent." While feminists have taken issue with some aspects of his assessment of sexuality, namely, that rape should be treated as a civil offense (Woodhull 1988), his discussion of power bears directly on issues of gender disparities. He states, "power is not something that is acquired, seized or shared, something that one holds on to or allows to slip away, power is exercised from innumerable points, in the interplay of nonegalitarian and mobile relations." Political science and international relations scholars likely disagree with Foucault's assessment that power cannot be seized. There are countless examples of violent and bloodless coups that contradict that point.* However, power does exist everywhere, both in the home, the economy, the government, and countless other spheres. In each realm, women in fragile states are often rendered docile with very little or no agency. Of power, Foucault (1988, p. 93) also states:

> Relations of power are not in a position of exteriority with respect to other types of relationships (economic processes, knowledge relationships, sexual relations), but are immanent in the latter; they are the immediate effects of the division, inequalities, and disequilibriums which occur in the latter, and conversely they are the internal conditions of these differentiations; relations of power are not in superstructual position, with mere a role of prohibition or accompaniment; they have a directly productive role, wherever they come into play.

Finally, in what is perhaps his most widely read work, *Discipline and Punish*, Foucault (1977, p. 25) expounds on the intersection between the political field and the body. He states:

> But the body is also directly involved in a political field; power relations have an immediate hold upon it; they invest it, mark it, train it, torture it, force it to carry out tasks, to perform ceremonies, to emit signs.

The fact that power is ever-present and has a complex relationship with other social forces helps to partially explain why states in differing stages of failure produce different outcomes for women. R.W. Connell (1987, p. 120) notes, "gender relations are present in *all* types of institutions. They may not be the most important structure in a particular case, but they are certainly a major structure of most." Thus, the omnipresence of power and gender relations provides the basis for gender disparities in fragile and failing states.

With regard to the protection of women's rights, Winifred Woodhull (1988, p. 173) argues that when women seek protection from the state, they are forced to rely on men for their safety. Additionally, legal systems, especially those in fragile nations, do not apply the law equally to men and women. Woodhull (1988, p. 173) contends, "the very coherence of the bourgeois state depends upon an illusory legal equality masking not only economic inequality and class domination, but also the general social and sexual subordination of women."

While more sustainable nations provide the illusion of gender equality, in some fragile nations, gender inequality is essentially built into the system.

---

* In particular, the tumultuous political histories in Nepal, Uganda, and Sri Lanka illustrate that governmental power can indeed be seized.

For example, in Afghanistan,* nearly 90% of criminal and civil cases are tried in the ba'ad justice system (a form of tribal justice), and the only way that women can access the courts is through a male family member, even if the male family member is the perpetrator of the act in question (MacKenzie 2012). The head of the Training Human Rights Association for Afghan Women, Roshan Sirran, states that women are often sacrificed in cases before the ba'ad courts (MacKenzie 2012). Sirren explains that "if there is a fight for land, for water, if there is violence, a girl can be given in ba'ad to settle these things" (MacKenzie 2012).

In fragile nations, women can be bartered and in some cases killed with few repercussions. Again, Afghanistan helps to illustrate this point. Jean MacKenzie (2012) cites reports from nongovernmental organizations (NGOs) that "a daughter who disgraces her father by ignoring his wishes can expect little protection from the law. Even the law on Elimination of Violence Against Women (EVAW) cites 'mitigating factors' in certain types of killings; a man who murders an unfaithful wife or her lover, for example, faces a maximum of two years in prison." In this example, and in countless similar situations, state power and family power work in tandem to control and limit the freedoms of women. This is regularly the case in fragile nations with strong authoritarian regimes or fragile nations in which other armed groups have stepped in to fill the power vacuum of a weak or nonexistent government.

Gender Violence Cross-Nationally

A growing body of literature links the treatment of women in society with large-scale issues such as civil violence, state security, and willingness to use military force to resolve disputes (Marshall and Marshall 1999; Caprioli 2000, 2003, 2005; Melander 2005; Hudson et al. 2009). The idea that a relationship exists between micro-level relationships and macro-level state functioning is certainly not a new one, as sociologists have been interested in these linkages for decades (Liska 1990). Even so, Carlo Jaeger et al. (2001) note that social theorists have long debated the micro–macro linkage. The debate essentially stems from a central question, "how can we theoretically integrate the agency of individual social actors with the social and institutional structures that mediate or condition agency?" (Jaeger et al. 2001, p. 28). An additional issue stems from the direction of the causal relationship. Do gender-based disparities cause armed conflict and internal strife or are they merely by-products? Valarie Hudson et al. (2009, p. 8) frame the question thusly, "How could the

---

* Afghanistan ranks number 6 out of 177 nation-states on the Failed State Index, making it among the most failed nations.

treatment of women possibly be linked to matters of high politics, such as war and national security?" While an authoritative exploration of the issue of causality is beyond the scope of this chapter, we can safely rely on an idea presented by international relations researchers, which argues that "states that typically exhibit discrimination and violence in their domestic affairs will, theoretically, rely on the same tools in the international arena" (Caprioli 2000, p. 52). An extensive body of literature has emerged over the last decade which solidifies the link between domestic and international tools and tactics (Caprioli 2003).

As above, the literature examining the relationship between the role of women in society and state behavior in the realm of civil violence, inter-state conflict, and war has been emerging for over a decade. In one of the earliest studies, Monty Marshall and Donna Marshall (1999) examine how gender empowerment (analyzed using the United Nations gender empowerment measure [GEM]) influences a nation's willingness and decision to use military force. The GEM includes several variables that speak to women's participation in society, including the percentage of seats in Parliament held by women, the percentage of female professional and technical workers, the ratio of estimated female-to-male earned income, the year women received the right to vote and to stand for election, and the percentage of women in ministerial positions. These variables are then combined to form a composite GEM for a given nation.

Their analysis reveals a strong association between the level of gender empowerment and a country's willingness to use force. Specifically, the greater the gender empowerment, the less likely it would be that a country would use military force to resolve disputes. Of course, gender empowerment does not exist in a vacuum. As Marshall and Marshall (1999, p. 24) indicate, "gender empowerment itself appears to be a conscious corollary policy to a political development process that is characterized by (i.e., strongly, positively correlated to) economic prosperity, military power, and active gender development policies." They untimely concluded, "there appears to be a very real and robust relationship between the quality of gender empowerment and the unwillingness of states to use force" (Marshall and Marshall 1999, p. 35).

In one of her earliest articles in this area, Mary Caprioli (2000) examined the relationship between gender equality and the amount of military violence used by a country. Three dimensions of gender equality were examined in the study: social (measured by the fertility rate); political (measured by the percentage of female Parliament members and the year that women gained the right to vote); and economic (measured by the percentage of females participating in the paid labor force). Analysis revealed that each dimension significantly contributes to the level of militarization of disputes. Specifically, "higher levels of gender equality correlate with lower levels of military action to settle international dispute" (Caprioli 2000, p. 63). This was the case even when controlling for factors such as wealth and democracy.

In later studies, Caprioli (2003; 2005) examines the relationship between gender equity and internal conflict, as well as the relationship between gender-based disparities and the willingness to use force. She observes that nations with fewer gender-based disparities in society are less likely to use force to resolve conflicts with other nations. Further, states with greater gender-based disparities are more likely to experience high levels of armed conflict. In particular, she notes, "states characterized by gender discrimination and structural hierarchy are permeated with norms of violence that make internal conflict more likely" (Caprioli 2005, p. 172). Other research in this area has also supported the relationship between gender disparity and armed conflict. Building on Caprioli's work, Erik Melander (2005) found that countries with a higher percentage of female members of Parliament and countries with a more equal ratio of males and female in higher education were less likely to engage in armed conflict. Lastly, Hudson et al. (2009) observe a statistically significant relationship between the physical security of women and the security of nation-states. Economic wealth, compliance with international treaties, level of democracy, and the degree of adherence to Islam are also important factors, though much less so than the gender variable.

Gender-Based Violence

There are myriad forms of violence in society, but in order to provide a detailed explication of gender violence only the following forms of violence will be explored: murder, rape, suicide, and domestic violence. In terms of large-scale data, the WomanStats project represents one of the most comprehensive data sources for information about violence against women across the globe and it is from this source that the majority of the information on gender-based violence will be drawn. WomanStats is an ongoing project that has compiled quantitative and qualitative data on 310 indicators for 174 countries.* Accordingly, it provides one of the most comprehensive single-source databases from which to draw a global perspective on violence against women.

Murder

In places where the quality of crime reporting data is good, murder rates may be one of the more accurate measures of violence in society. Therefore, we

---

* The WomanStats project provides both qualitative and quantitative data regarding violence against women. The qualitative measure of various forms of violence provides information about the social perceptions and practices about violence against women.

can then infer that the murder rate of women provides an accurate picture of the aggregate violence against women. According to the United Nations special rapporteur on violence against women, "globally, the prevalence of different manifestations of such killings is increasing, and a lack of accountability for such crimes is the norm. Terms such as femicide, feminicide, honor killings and crimes of passion, among others, have been used to define these killings (United Nations 2012, p. 4)."

In their study of state failure and its consequences for women, Laurie Gould and Laura Agnich (2014) find a link between a given state's ranking in the Fragile States Index and rates of female murder. In specific, states that rank more highly on the Fragile States Index tend to also rank highly in terms of female murder rates as well as cultural beliefs and practices permissive of violence toward women. Gould and Agnich (2014) observe that the Fragile States Index composite score, which contains all 12 indicators of state failure, tends to be highly correlated with attitudes condoning murder and the overall female murder rate. In terms of specific failure indicators, Gould and Agnich (2014) found that mounting demographic pressures, massive movement of refugees, group grievance, human flight, uneven economic development, sharp economic decline, widespread violations of human rights and arbitrary application or suspension of the rule of law, and the intervention of other states to be strongly associated with attitudes condoning murder and the overall female murder rate.

Examinations of specific countries further substantiate the relationship between state failure and female murder. In the most recent ranking of fragile states, the Fund for Peace ranked the following six states among the most fragile: Somalia, Democratic Republic of Congo, Sudan, Chad, Zimbabwe, and Afghanistan. When comparing the qualitative measures of female murder with the Fragile States Index, all of the aforementioned countries either have some cultural practices that condone the murder of women (Somalia and Chad) or substantial evidence thereof (Sudan, Democratic Republic of Congo, and Zimbabwe). In Afghanistan, the WomanStats data provide considerable evidence of attitudes and practices that condone female murder; however, it is difficult to provide an accurate quantitative measure of the rate of female murder, ostensibly due to the unrest in the country related the global war on terror. However, the United Nations special rapporteur on violence against women noted the following situation in Afghanistan,

> women's rights defenders continue to be regularly threatened and intimidated, and high-profile women, mainly political activists, have been assassinated, and their killers have not been brought to justice. The Taliban's interpretation of Shari'ah law is used to justify harsher punishments for women seen to be mixing with men outside their immediate families. A common means of intimidation and control of local communities, mainly women, is the use of night

letters. These are threatening letters, usually hand- delivered, or pasted onto a door or in a mosque, by insurgent groups. The content of these letters varies, but the main message is a threat of harm to women and girls (or their parents) if they go to school or to work, leave their homes, speak to non-family men, or call radio stations with music requests (United Nations Special Rapporteur 2012, p. 14).

This said, completely failed states are not the only nations with high rates of female murder and social attitudes that condone murder. Countries on the verge of failure, such as Guatemala, have historically carried out campaigns of murder against women (with indigenous women being the primary targets) and past practices reflect a social permissiveness of such actions (United Nations 2012). During the colonial era in Guatemala, indigenous Maya women represented 88% of murder and rape victims. These acts, which were carried out by military and paramilitary groups, were never punished, even after the 1996 Peace Accords (United Nations 2012). Further, "article 200 of the Penal Code (repealed in 2006) afforded immunity to perpetrators of sexual violence and kidnapping of women and girls over 12 years old, where the perpetrator subsequently married the victim. Thus a State-endorsed impunity was established, condoning all forms of violence, particularly against indigenous women" (2012, p. 16). At present in Guatemala, WomanStats notes there is some evidence of cultural/social practices that condone the murder and injury of women. In Guatemala, the female murder rate falls between 1.30 and 2.99 per 100,000 of the total female population.

Rape

Sexual violence against women continues to be a problem worldwide. Here again though, reliable statistical reporting and data remain significant challenges. Even so, the WomanStats project provides data about the incidence of rape per 100,000 of the population and the conviction rates for rape. Data pertaining to sexual assault are fraught with problems because underreporting is a seemingly intractable issue in many parts of the world. There is a strong reluctance among women to report such crimes. This is due in part to the cultural stigmatization of rape and sexual assault; a phenomenon that persists in the most developed and advanced parts of the world. While official statistics provide a less than an ideal perspective, there are anecdotal accounts of female rape that suggest that it is a severe problem in failing states.

As mentioned in previous chapters, a large number of internally displaced persons (IDPs) is a key measure of states failure. Internal conflict, as in the case of war, often leads to a large number of IDPs. The Internal Displacement Monitoring Centre (2012, p. 67) notes that in countries such as Colombia, the Democratic Republic of Congo, and Sudan, rape is often used as a tool of war "to punish communities for their political allegiances, as a form of ethnic cleansing, and to forcibly displace civilians.... Armed groups engaged in acts of sexual violence to attack the values of the community, punish or terrorize communities and individuals accused of collaborating with enemy forces, or provide gratification for fighters."

Sexual violence against women has been used extensively in the Darfur region of the Sudan (prior to the division of the country). In this instance, rape is used primarily as a tool of ethnic cleansing and an effort to dishonor the women (Internal Displacement Monitoring Centre 2012). In 2006,

> A group of about 25 armed men in Sudan Liberation Army uniforms threatened, beat and robbed six separate groups of women and girls in Hajar Jalanga, in West Darfur. During the same month, Janjaweed militia attempted to rape women and girls displaced from villages near Kutum, in North Darfur. And in July, approximately 25 armed militias, some in army uniforms, assaulted 20 women outside the Kalma IDP camp in Nyala, South Darfur. Increasing numbers of rapes by displaced men of displaced women were also reported within IDP camps in Darfur. (Internal Displacement Monitoring Centre 2012, p. 67)

The Democratic Republic of Congo provides another example of the relationship between displacement and sexual violence. According to Human Rights Watch, at least 1.8 million people have been displaced in the eastern Congo. While the region has been highly volatile since the early 1990s, the most recent bout of trouble stems from shifting alliances between Rwanda and the Congo. Previously, Rwanda and the Congo had an antagonistic relationship; however, in 2008, both "announced a joint military operation against the Democratic Forces for the Liberation of Rwanda (Les Forces démocratiques de libération du Rwanda, FDLR), a predominantly Rwandan Hutu armed group operating in eastern DRC, and its allies" (Human Rights Watch 2010, p. 6). These military operations also brought both governmental and rebel attacks against civilian populations, which resulted in the internal displacement of countless people. It is estimated that "various armed groups have abducted and kept as sex slaves thousands of women to provide sexual, domestic and agricultural services" (Internal Displacement Monitoring Centre 2012).

In an interview with Human Rights Watch, one displaced person reported

> my older sister was raped in her house that month (September 2008). We fled to the fields, but the FDLR [Democratic Forces for the Liberation of Rwanda] followed us there and so we fled to Kirumba. We went back in November but the same thing happened again and we fled again in January, to Bingi. We tried to go back in March (2009) but then we heard the Congolese army was coming and we were afraid the FDLR would punish us so we fled again, back to Kirumba. (Human Rights Watch 2010a, p. 25).

Suicide

In addition to studying violence against women perpetrated by others, it is also important to consider circumstances where women may be pressured into committing suicide (i.e., "honor suicides"). These types of suicides fall within the broader category of honor-related violence (HRV; Idriss and Abbas 2011). Idriss and Abbas (2011, p. 1), define HRV as "acts of violence predominantly against women who are perceived to have transgressed a religious-cultural divide, particularly in matters relating to sexuality." While this problem may occur more frequently in predominately Islamic countries, HRV is increasingly being found in North America and Europe. Actual rates of female suicide are somewhat difficult to obtain; and the reliability of such data is problematic because honor suicides can easily be misclassified in many countries. Nevertheless, the World Health Organization (WHO) does collect data pertaining to suicide with rates broken down by gender. However, WHO data are incomplete and many fragile states are excluded from the dataset.

If we compare the available suicide data with states that are ranked among the most failed, we see a clear relationship between attitudes that promote or condone honor suicides and state failure. There is some evidence to suggest that Chad, the Democratic Republic of Congo, and Zimbabwe have practices or attitudes that promote female suicide. In Somalia and Afghanistan, there is also substantial evidence of such practices. Since honor suicide rate data are not available for most failed states, we must rely on anecdotal accounts of this practice.

In Afghanistan and Iran, "The Special Rapporteur on violence against women has raised concerns about the phenomenon of self-immolation, ... whereby women and girls attempt suicide by setting themselves on fire because they feel they are—dishonoring the family" (United Nations 2012, p. 13). In Turkey, which ranks number 85 out of 177 on the Fragile States Index (placing it in the "warning" category), honor killings have been supplanted by honor suicides.

Dan Bilefsky, a reporter for the *New York Times* notes, "Women's groups here say the evidence suggests that a growing number of girls considered to be dishonored are being locked in a room for days with rat poison, a pistol or a rope, and told by their families that the only thing resting between their disgrace and redemption is death." Previously, if a daughter disgraced her family (usually by having sexual intercourse outside of marriage), a young male relative would kill the woman in an effort to restore honor to the family name (Bilefsky 2006). In Turkey, sentences for these crimes were typically light, in part because of the young age of the offender. Recently, however, the Turkish government has increased sentence lengths for these crimes, thus leading to increased pressure on women to commit suicide (Bilefsky 2006).

Domestic Violence

The last area of violence to be considered is domestic violence, that is to say, violence committed against a woman by her intimate partner or her family. While this category subsumes some of the violence already discussed, it is worth specific exploration because domestic violence transcends the cultural and social values that appear to undergird previously discussed issues. Domestic violence is by no means a problem relegated to failing states, as women across the globe experience violence at the hands of their intimate partners all too frequently. However, given the lack of legal protection that women typically have in fragile states, domestic violence is an especially serious issue in these countries.

Using the Fragile States Index, Gould and Agnich (2014) found that mounting demographic pressures, group grievance, uneven economic development, sharp economic decline, and the intervention of other states were strongly associated with reported lifetime experience with domestic violence. Their findings were robust even though underreporting of domestic violence is problematic. In addition to Gould and Agnich's findings, there are also myriad anecdotal accounts from the United Nations and many NGOs that indicate domestic violence is a problem in many failed states. The United Nations' independent expert on Somalia, Shamsul Bari, reports:

> Ninety eight percent of Somali women suffer female genital mutilation, domestic violence against women is widespread throughout the country and as victims women have no legal recourse. Rape and other forms of gender-based violence are generally dealt with by the clans and are often solved, according to the report, by the payment of blood money or forced marriage between the victim and the perpetrator. (United Nations 2009, para. 3)

In Kenya, which scores high in each indicator of state failure, domestic violence is increasingly problematic; and not surprisingly, there are disparities between official reports and independent survey reports. Johnathan Chebogut and Godfrey Ngeno (2010) note that the official Kenya Demographic and Health Survey reports that 39% of women were victimized by their intimate partner. However, a "2008 report by the Federation of Women Lawyers of Kenya, or FIDA, says almost 75% of women they surveyed reported being beaten" (Chebogut and Ngeno 2010, p. 6). Given that underreporting of domestic violence to law enforcement agencies is problematic in virtually every country, the latter statistic likely represents the more accurate percentage of domestic violence victims.

Nancy Russo and Angela Pirlott (2006, p. 183) explain, "gender-based entitlements, power, objectification, and status are now recognised as playing critical roles in the dynamics of gender-based violence. Major institutions (including criminal justice) ..., are seen as reinforcing patriarchal values that encourage and maintain those entitlements, foster gender-based violence, and encourage stigmatisation of voices that challenge the status quo." While these institutions may indeed foster gender violence, we find that when these systems are failing or fragile, gender violence is a by-product. While the likelihood of violence is increased for the entire populace in fragile and failing states, women represented an especially vulnerable population.

Gender-Based Disparities

Next, we turn to a discussion of gender-based disparities that prevent women in fragile and failing states from having full participation in social life. For decades, researchers have paid special attention to gender inequalities in legal protection, education, health, employment, and political empowerment. Ricardo Hausmann et al. (2008, p. 3) note, "although gender-based inequalities exist in the majority of the world's cultures, religions, nations, and income groups, there are differences in the way these disparities manifest themselves and how they evolve over time." The degree of governmental stability is a salient issue in how gender-based disparities can manifest. Again, all citizens are doubtlessly affected when states fail, but women are especially marginalized and experience governmental failure in a fundamentally different way compared with their male counterparts.

Gender-Based Gaps in Legal Protection

Access to legal protection and justice are core expectations that all citizens should have of their governments. However, when women are limited in terms of participation in the legal system, the consequences typically manifest in two core realms: little or no legal protection from various types of violence; and virtually no protection of private property for women (Baranyi and Powell 2005). Legal protection from human trafficking is also a salient problem in fragile and failing states. While trafficking in women and girls is by no means a new issue, the scale of trafficking operations has dramatically increased (United Nations Office on Drugs and Crime 2014). Trafficking in persons can affect both men and women, but women and girls represent especially vulnerable populations. As with most gendered violence, there is great difficulty in accurately estimating the total number of persons trafficked each year. While this activity is often highly secretive, the United Nations (2006) estimates that 2.5 million people annually are in forced labor as a result of human trafficking. By far, the most common form of human trafficking is trafficking for the purposes of sexual exploitation. According to the United Nations, "in the 52 countries where the form of exploitation was specified, 79 percent of the victims were subjected to sexual exploitation," and the majority of victims were women and children (United Nations Office on Drugs and Crime 2012, p. 8). Across all types of trafficking, nearly two-thirds of the victims are women and children (United Nations Office on Drugs and Crime 2012). Trafficking in persons is an extremely lucrative enterprise, with criminal networks earning as much as $32 billion annually (United Nations Office on Drugs and Crime 2012).

Human trafficking continues to flourish in many areas principally because of poverty (Truong 2006; Myint 2008). Truong (2006, p. 25) describes the intersection of poverty and trafficking:

> In times of cutbacks in State services and subsidies, women assume the consider-
> able burden of diminished resources as they are subject to the rigid gender-based
> division of labor assigning them the household and men tend not to devote their
> earnings to the household, leaving the women responsible for the survival of
> their families. These women then seek to diversify their sources of income, which
> increases their risk of being trafficked. Furthermore, they are more likely to send
> their children either to live with other family members in wealthier communi-
> ties or to seek employment outside of the family network. This thereby increases
> the risk that those children will be trafficked, as the traditional practice of child
> fostering has been manipulated by traffickers in order to exploit children.

Given the close relationship between poverty and trafficking, efforts to combat the problem are inherently difficult. Nikolas Win Myint (2008) notes that an effective response to human trafficking requires governmental respect for human rights and cooperation among governmental departments and NGOs. Governmental respect for human rights and the rule of law are arguably lacking in fragile and failed states.

The primary tool for combating human trafficking has been the adoption of several international treaties, including the United Nations Convention Against Transnational Organized Crime; the Protocol to Prevent, Suppress and Punish Trafficking in Persons, Especially in Women and Children; and the International Protocol Against Illegal Trafficking in Migrants on Land, Air and Sea (Cochintu et al. 2011).

> Article 3, paragraph (a) of the Protocol to Prevent, Suppress and Punish
> Trafficking in Persons defines Trafficking in Persons as the recruitment, trans-
> portation, transfer, harboring or receipt of persons, by means of the threat or
> use of force or other forms of coercion, of abduction, of fraud, of deception, of
> the abuse of power or of a position of vulnerability or of the giving or receiving
> of payments or benefits to achieve the consent of a person having control over
> another person, for the purpose of exploitation. Exploitation shall include, at
> a minimum, the exploitation of the prostitution of others or other forms of
> sexual exploitation, forced labor or services, slavery or practices similar to
> slavery, servitude or the removal of organs. (United Nations Office on Drugs
> and Crime 2014, p. 42)

While 117 countries have become signatories, full international compliance has yet to be achieved (United Nations Office on Drugs and Crime 1999). Reservations were expressed among many countries that ultimately became signatories to the convention. Countries such as Colombia, China, Malaysia, the Lao People's Democratic Republic, and Saudi Arabia took issue with Article 15, paragraph 2 that deals specifically with the International Court of Justice:

> Any dispute between two or more States Parties concerning the interpretation or application of this Protocol that cannot be settled through negotiation within a reasonable time shall, at the request of one of those States Parties, be submitted to arbitration. If, six months after the date of the request for arbitration, those States Parties are unable to agree on the organization of the arbitration, any one of those States Parties may refer the dispute to the International Court of Justice by request in accordance with the Statute of the Court.

Even though several nations do not feel bound to abide by the International Court of Justice, the aforementioned countries still became signatories to the convention because decisions rendered by the court are not binding. Futher, Keith Shimko (2005, p. 221) notes "nothing compels states to attend trials ... and the Statutes of the International Court of Justice (the treaty creating the ICJ) contains an optional clause allowing states to choose whether to be subject to the compulsory jurisdiction of the ICJ." To date, less than one-third of nation-states have accepted compulsory jurisdiction (Shimko 2005).

In the United States, the Victims of Trafficking and Violence Protection Act (TVPA) of 2000 provides the basis of domestic and international protection against illegal trafficking in persons. The U.S. Department of State compiles an annual list of countries and ranks them into three tiers according to their degree of compliance with the minimum standards set forth in the TVPA. Tier 1 countries include those countries that comply with the act; Tier 2 countries include those that currently do not fully comply with the act; and Tier 3 countries include those that are not in compliance with the act and have made no steps to do so. Countries in Tier 3 include: the Central African Republic, the Democratic Republic of Congo, Cuba, Equatorial Guinea, Eritrea, Guinea-Bissau, Iran, North Korea, Kuwait, Lebanon, Libya, Mauritania, Papua New Guinea, Saudi Arabia, Sudan, Turkmenistan, Venezuela, and Zimbabwe (U.S. Department of State 2011). While not all countries on the Tier 3 list can be considered failed, several rank highly on various indices of failure.

Gender-Based Gaps in Education

Limited access to primary, secondary, and tertiary education is also an issue for females in failing states. Jackie Kirk (2007) notes a tendency among countries in imminent crisis to drastically cut funding to educational programs.

Further, in times of conflict and crisis, governments can spend "ten times more on each member of the armed forces than they are spending on each child in education" (Kirk 2007, p. 187). While this situation can have ramifications for males as well as females, according to the U.K. Department for International Development, girls in fragile states make up the majority of children not enrolled in primary school (Kirk 2007). Education and poverty are deeply entwined. As such, exclusion from basic education will continue to affect women throughout their adult life. However, when levels of education among girls are improved, there are direct benefits in the realm of poverty reduction and other indirect benefits "in terms of the health of their infants and children, family nutrition, immunization rates and educational attainment for their children" (Handley et al. 2009, p. 13).

Worldwide, there are 862 million illiterate people and 600 million (or two-thirds) of these are women (Holsinger and Jacob 2008). Dropout rates are similarly alarming—an estimated 150 million children will drop out of school before finishing their primary education and 100 million will be girls (Holsinger and Jacob 2008). Clearly, gender gaps in education are problematic worldwide, but they are much more prevalent in fragile and failing nations. In part, these gaps are related to nonexistent or limited educational infrastructure.

In Pakistan, which ranks among the most failed nations, the education of girls is particularly inadequate. According to official government statistics, the literacy rate for the Pakistani population is 46%, but among women only 26% are literate (Latif 2012). These numbers may be somewhat inflated, however, as Winthrop (2009) notes, "the women's literacy rate in FATA [Federally Administered Tribal Areas] is only 3% and in the North-West Frontier Province, (NWFP) it is 18%. This is much lower, especially in FATA, than the national level women's literacy rate of 32%." While these gaps could be attributed to recent conflict in the region, it appears that gender-based gaps in female education have been a persistent problem for several decades.

According to Monazza et al. (2008), in Pakistan, between 1985 and 1995, gender gaps in primary education increased 30%, and while recent gaps in primary education have decreased slightly (down to 24% in 2005), they continue to represent a challenge. Gender-based gaps in education have been exacerbated in the region due to high Taliban activity between 2001 and 2009. In the Swat valley of Pakistan, Taliban forces destroyed nearly 400 schools, an estimated 70% of which were schools for girls (Khan 2012). While the Taliban has largely been driven out of the region, gender gaps in education remain. According to the Pakistan Education Task Force (2012, p. 2), "roughly one in ten of the world's primary-age children who are not in school live in Pakistan, placing Pakistan second in the global ranking of out-of-school children." Again, women fare much worse, as "fewer than half of women have ever been to school, and just 35% of those living in rural areas" (Pakistan Education Task Force 2012, p. 6).

Tajikistan, which scores high on the Fragile States Index (number 39 out of 177 countries), provides another example of the exclusion of girls from education. School attendance for girls is not seen as important because the societal expectation is that girls will be wives and mothers who stay within the home, not contributors to the workforce competing for jobs alongside men (Amnesty International 2012). To that end, boys in Tajikistan are more likely to attend school, while girls perform work for the family until they get married (Amnesty International 2012). Family poverty often compounds the issue of education, as many families are too poor to afford the ancillary costs associated with sending a child to school (e.g., books and transportation). If families have to choose between sending their son or daughter to school, they may make the difficult decision to send their male child, partly due to these resource considerations (Amnesty International 2012). The ramifications of this reach well beyond the educational system, influencing opportunities in life, the workforce, and even future health.

Investment in female education is critical in fragile regions and can help improve the overall stability of the entire populace. In Pakistan, Alsam et al. (2008, p. 87) found that increasing educational opportunities for women ultimately led to greater gender equality in the labor force, but those effects are strongly conditioned by cultural norms. Further, increasing female educational opportunities leads to smaller and healthier families (Pakistan Education Task Force 2012), which can have profound effects on future generations.

Gender-Based Gaps in Employment Opportunities

The relationship between employment and state failure is quite complex. Women in failing states do have diminished employment opportunities, but only in some sectors. Gould (2014) found that countries that score high on many indicators of failure actually have a greater percentage of women contributing to the general workforce. Additionally, as states score higher in many dimensions of failure, the relative ratio of female employment in the agriculture industry increases. Notably, countries experiencing economic decline that is sharp or severe or both, have higher relative ratios of female employment in both sectors. Interestingly, the opposite appears to be the case where the service industry is concerned. For example, in countries with widespread violation of human rights, large populations of refugees or IDPs, and suspension or arbitrary application of the rule of law, the relative percentage of female employment in the service sector significantly decreases. These results were further supported by the relationship between indicators of failure and gender gaps in economic opportunity. Higher scores in each aspect of failure contributed to greater gender gaps. Simply put, women have fewer overall opportunities for employment in fragile and failing states. The strongest relationship between gender gaps in employment and failure were found in countries with widespread human rights violations, suspension or arbitrary application of rule of law, and a legacy of vengeance-seeking group grievance or group paranoia. Given these somewhat contradictory results, these findings may seem curious, but employment and economic issues are critical matters for entire populations, therefore gender gaps in employment may not be as critical as the issue of overall employment. This does not appear to be the case when other employment-related issues are considered, as gaps in economic opportunities (measured through gaps in participation, remuneration gaps, and advancement gaps) appear to be greater in failing states. This suggests that while female participation in the workforce may be of diminished import in failing states, gaps in compensation and the ability to advance in one's chosen field both appear to block the advancement of women in fragile and failing states.

Gender-Based Gaps in Health

Women appear to face more hardships in the area of physical health compared with their male counterparts in the same failed states. Life expectancy at birth, health, and survival for women are lower in fragile states. For example, during the 1980s and 1990s in Yemen, the maternal mortality rate was 351 deaths per 100,000, representing nearly 42% of all female deaths in the country (Sunil and Pillai 2010). The situation does not appear to have improved much in recent years, as maternal deaths have remained fairly consistent. Among the factors contributing to maternal deaths are "Early marriage and pregnancy; Malnutrition; Poor quality health services; The large number of women who are anemic during pregnancy; and Poor distribution of health services" (United Nations Development Program 2006, 2011).

Nigeria provides another example of the intersection between state failure and maternal health. The Center for Reproductive Rights (2008) estimates that nearly 60,000 women die each year from pregnancy-related causes that could have been avoided. The center notes significant hardships for Nigerian women. In particular, husbands must accompany their pregnant wives to the hospital, in case a blood transfusion is needed. The hospitals will refuse care in the event that the woman is not married or her husband refuses to donate blood. Additionally, women are required to pay for medical items such as antiseptics and gauze. Lastly, because Nigeria does not have a dependable infrastructure for electricity, power outages are a regular occurrence, which can make labor much more difficult and potentially dangerous (Center for Reproductive Rights 2008).

In addition to concerns arising from maternal mortality rates, female genital mutilation (FGM) is another salient health issue for women worldwide. According to UNICEF (2007), more than 130 million females across the globe have undergone FGM during their lifetime and it is estimated that each year nearly 3 million girls are subjected to FGM (Kaplan et al. 2011). While FGM is conducted in stable nations in North America and Europe, it is far more prevalent in failing states. According to the WHO, there are generally four distinct types of FGM:

1. Excision of the *prepuce* [the fold of skin surrounding the clitoris], with or without excision of part or the entire clitoris;
2. Excision of the clitoris with partial or total excision of the *labia minora* [the smaller inner folds of the vulva];
3. Excision of part or all of the external genitalia and stitching or narrowing of the vaginal opening (infibulation);
4. Unclassified, which includes pricking, piercing or incising of the clitoris and/or labia; stretching of the clitoris and/or labia; cauterization by burning of the clitoris and surrounding tissue; scraping of tissue surrounding the opening of the vagina (*angurya* cuts) or cutting of the vagina (*gishiri* cuts); introduction of corrosive substances or herbs into the vagina to cause bleeding or to tighten or narrow the vagina; and any other procedure that can be included in the definition of female genital mutilation noted above. (UNICEF 2007, p. 2)

Approximately 10%–20% of women in the fragile state of Yemen have undergone the least damaging form of FGM, which involves cuts to the prepuce or hood of the clitoris (Colburn 2002). FGM can cause both physical and psychological problems for women throughout their lives. UNICEF (2007, p. 2) views FGM as a "fundamental violation of human rights. Among those rights violated are the rights to the highest attainable standard of health and to bodily integrity." However, "others view it as an integral part of cultures in which it remained unchallenged for centuries" (Horowitz and Jackson 1997, p. 491). In many countries, FGM is considered an important rite of passage for girls (Kaplan et al. 2011). Cultural debates notwithstanding, some nations have taken steps to end the practice, or at least minimize it. Yemen has outlawed the practice of FGM in hospitals, but this has had little impact on the practice since most FGMs are performed in the home (Colburn 2002).

FGM is also prevalent in many African nations. The top five nations where FGM is most common are Guinea, Mali, Burkina Faso, Mauritania, and the Ivory Coast. Of these, Guinea and the Ivory Coast are among the most failed nations; Mali, Burkina Faso, and Mauritania are all considered fragile. The Ivory Coast banned the practice in 1998 and is a signatory to a number of international treaties that ban its use. Despite the bans, an estimated 40% of women in the Ivory Coast have undergone some form of FGM, with 5% having undergone the most severe type (UNICEF 2007).

Many FGMs are performed outside a hospital setting by individuals with no medical training. Not surprisingly, both the short- and long-term health effects of FGM are myriad and often devastating. During the procedure, girls experience severe pain and bleeding (UNICEF 2007) and complications can arise that include shock, hemorrhage, infections, exposure to HIV/AIDS, and psychological problems (UNICEF 2007; Kaplan et al. 2011). Long-term effects can include "chronic pain, infections, cheloids* formation, primary infertility, birth complications, danger to the new born and psychological consequences" (Kaplan et al. 2011, p. 2). These damaging effects are not limited to the more severe forms of FGM, as shock, hemorrhage, and sexual dysfunction have also been reported with Type 1 and 2 FGM (Kaplan et al. 2011). In a study of FGM in the Gambia (ranked number 63 out of 177 on the Fragile States Index), Kaplan et al. (2011) found that the majority (66.2%) of the 821 women they examined had undergone Type 1 (least severe form) FGM, 26.3% had undergone Type 2 FGM, and only 7.5% had undergone the most severe form of FGM. In all cases, the most common complications were infection, anemia, and hemorrhage (Kaplan et al. 2011). Kaplan et al. (2011, p. 4) go on to note, "even type I FGM/C, the form of FGM/C with least anatomical extent, presented complications in 1 of every 5 girls and women who consulted. Complications in type II FGM/C were observed in 1 of every 2 girls and women examined."

Gender-Based Gaps in Social and Political Participation

When governments enact authoritarian policies (as is typically the case in failing and fragile states), women experience significant barriers to full participation in government and policy-making decisions (Baranyi and Powell 2005). However, it can be argued that all citizens, regardless of gender, are generally excluded from political participation (e.g., voting and holding elected office) in failing states with strong regimes. Thus, the matter of gender and political participation is not necessarily the issue when a country is in the midst of failure; instead, we focus on political participation once state rebuilding efforts have begun.

As Claire Castillejo (2009, p. 1) points out, "it is now widely recognized that women's exclusion from decision making results in state institutions and policies that do not address gender inequalities and are not accountable or responsive to women citizens, thereby perpetuating women's political, social and economic marginalization." Two countries, Sierra Leone and Rwanda, provide noteworthy case studies of state rebuilding and political participation by women.

Sierra Leone is by no means considered a successful state at this time, as it still ranks quite high on the Fragile States Index (number 31), but the situation

---

* Excessive growth of scar tissue.

in the country has improved greatly since 2002. Beginning in 1991, the Revolutionary United Front attempted to overthrow the existing government (United Nations Observer Mission in Sierra Leone 2000). Initially, the army defended the government against the attacks, but in 1992 they overthrew the government (United Nations Observer Mission in Sierra Leone 2000). This marked the beginning of a 10-year civil war that nearly devastated the country. With the help of the United Nations Observer Mission in Sierra Leone (UNOMSIL) and the United Kingdom, order was restored to Sierra Leone and the first free elections were held (United Nations Observer Mission in Sierra Leone 2000). In the first national elections, 124 members of Parliament were elected, and only 18 of them were women (Castillejo 2009). Women were also underrepresented in leadership roles within the government, with just two women (out of 24) holding ministerial positions (Castillejo 2009). At the local level, the situation mirrors the national trend, with few women holding elected office. When the first local elections were held in 2004, just 56 women were elected as counselors out of a possible 456 district seats, though women gained 30 more seats in the 2008 elections (Castillejo 2009).

While there seems to be recognition among some that female participation in the government is a critical issue that requires attention, there has been notable backlash, primarily due to the patriarchal structure of the society. During interviews with women, Castillejo (2009, p. 3) reports that women "say that they can now speak out in ways that they could not before, although they do often face resistance and harassment for taking on a more public role, particularly from customary authorities who argue that it is against tradition."

There have been efforts to establish a 30% quota for women in all levels of political decision-making, as recommended by Sierra Leone's Truth and Reconciliation Commission, but there has been strong resistance from a variety of groups including the political elite and political parties (Castillejo 2009). At present, significant barriers to women's participation in the political process remain. These largely stem from cultural attitudes about proper roles for women, as well as financial limitations for women who attempt to run for political office (Castillejo 2009). While the situation for women has definitely improved since the civil war, full participation in the political process for the women of Sierra Leone has yet to be achieved.

By contrast, the case of Rwanda provides a more successful example of female inclusion in the political process following conflict. In just four months, from April to June 1994, an estimated 800,000 Rwandans (most of them Tutsis) were killed (BBC News 2011). While there has been long-standing tension between the Tutsis and the Hutu throughout Rwandan history, this genocide is considered to be the most brutal manifestation of violence in the nation's history. The genocide was "sparked by the death of the Rwandan President Juvenal Habyarimana, a Hutu, when his plane was shot down above Kigali airport on 6 April 1994" (BBC News 2011). While the issue of genocide in Rwanda is certainly important, it has been discussed at length in the media and by scholars (see, e.g., Prunier 1995; Barnett 2002; Magnarella 2000; Dauge-Roth 2010); therefore, a detailed treatment of the subject will not be provided here. What is most interesting for the purposes of a discussion of gender and political participation is what happened after the genocide ended.

By the time the cease-fire was enacted, Rwanda's population was 70% female, yet they were still largely an excluded group (Remmert 2003). Nine years after the genocide, Rwanda held parliamentary elections and in a somewhat surprising turn, almost half (39) of those elected to the 80 member Chamber of Deputies were women (Burnet 2008). Unlike Sierra Leone, Rwanda embraced the idea of a quota system, such that at least 30% of elected seats were to be held by women (Kudva and Misra 2008). With this move, "Rwanda replaced Sweden as the country with the highest percentage of females in its national legislature" (Burnet 2008, p. 362).

In addition to the quota system, Rwanda's transitional government established a number of policies and programs aimed directly at increasing the inclusion of women in Rwandan politics and society. One large-scale initiative was the establishment of the Ministry for Gender and Woman Development, as well as the establishment of gender posts at all levels of government (Remmert 2003). The purpose of the ministry and the gender posts was to ensure that women's issues were addressed and the government was gender responsive (Remmert 2003).

At first blush, it would appear that Rwanda is heading in a more democratic direction, as well as a more equitable society where women are concerned; however, this may not be the case. As Jennie Burnet (2008, p. 366) explains:

> To quell protest from the diplomatic and international aid communities, the RPF has dressed its increasingly authoritarian governance in democratic clothing by promoting its policies as the best methods to ensure "security" and "good governance". In addition, the regime has increased the participation of all citizens in the political system through an elaborate local level administration, as well as a complicated, tiered electoral system for Parliament and presidency. Finally, the regime has increased the representations of underrepresented groups, particularly women and youth.

Indeed, the inclusion of women in the political process may be a ploy by the government to draw attention away from the more authoritarian aspects of the Rwandan government. Still, there is no doubt that greater inclusion of women in the government has had positive effects. Rwandan women are no longer limited to the role of wife or mother and instead have more agency in their own lives (Burnet 2008).

Gender-Based Gaps in Poverty

Poverty is a central (if not defining) feature of failed states and it is deeply entwined with limited access in other spheres. As Geoff Handley et al. (2009, p. 5) explain, "exclusion from political, social and economic institutions is part of a vicious cycle that leads to low capability levels, which in turn reduces the ability of the people to escape poverty and 'horizontal inequalities' (inequalities between groups …) make up a significant proportion of overall inequality."

Poverty affects virtually every area of life. Handley et al. (2009) state that persistent poverty deprives people of the freedom to live the way that they might want to live (e.g., have basic human rights and income). In other words, people in poverty tend to be "illiterate, have inadequate nutrition, poor human rights, and insufficient income and livelihood opportunities, which taken together drive and maintain their poverty and ensure it passes across generations" (Handley et al. 2009, p. 4).

In addition to its relationship with other sociopolitical exclusions, poverty is also strongly associated with state failure. According to the World Bank (2003), there is a relationship between low levels of income and civil war, both of which contribute to a high likelihood of state failure. Much like other spheres of social life, extreme poverty affects men and women differently in fragile and failing states. In particular, "women are hard hit by poverty where they are excluded from full participation in the labor force or in credit markets, by law or by practice" (Baranyi and Powell 2005, p. 2).

In Sri Lanka (number 29 on the Fragile States Index), women face considerable hardships due to poverty. As evidenced by the country's Gini score (49), there is a large disparity between the rich and poor. The vast majority of the populace (76.4%) live in rural areas and "free trade zones (FTZs), use the labor of the poorest people to create a super-profit for the urban capitalists" (Zavirske and Herath 2010, p. 832). Women are particularly affected by the few employment opportunities in Sri Lanka and often they have little choice but to work for low wages in FTZs (Zavirske and Herath 2010), typically in garment factories, as migrant workers, or in the tourist industry (Mines and Lamb 2010).

Women who work in garment factories can experience both psychological and physical problems, such as "back pain, headaches, dizziness, weight loss, respiratory problems from inhaling cotton dust, or other ailments" (Mines and Lamb 2010, p. 380). Poor working conditions and the exploitation of workers is endemic to factory work in many nations, but Sri Lankan women face additional problems because they can be labeled as being without "lajja-baya," roughly translated as shame-fear (Mines and Lamb 2010). Further, when women are victimized, there is usually a high degree of victim blaming. As Diana Mines and Sarah Lamb (2010, p. 212) explain, women who take jobs in FTZs and other areas outside of their communities are afforded more independence, but they also lose the protection of their community. Moreover, women working outside the home "raise stereotypical notions of their behavior. Reports of widespread sexual harassment, pregnancies, abortions, and sexually transmitted diseases have resulted in female migrant workers, most of whom work as housemaids, as well as women working in the free trade zones being viewed as victims of their own loose moral behavior" (Mines and Lamb 2010, p. 212). Emigration to another country for work is another option for poor women in need of employment. The emigration rate in Sri Lank is 4.7%, with most of those who emigrate staying in Asia and working as domestic help. Much like women in the FTZs, women who emigrate are characterized as promiscuous; and if they are victims of violence or if members of their family are victimized during their absence, they are assumed to be at fault (Zavirske and Herath 2010).

Human Trafficking

While human trafficking is a worldwide crisis and its effects can be found in virtually every nation, it is most pronounced in Africa. Kimberly McCabe and Sabita Manian (2010, p. 10) report "out of a total of 52 countries in Africa, 46 of them (compared to 156 countries worldwide) report adult forced labor"; there are 10 African states that are considered origin countries for forced labor; and 23 out 53 African states are involved with all phases of the trafficking process, origin country, transit country, and destination country. Lastly, there are 76 countries where adults are trafficked for the purpose of sexual exploitation, of which 15 are located in Africa.

Nigeria, which ranks at number 14 on the Fragile States Index (Fund for Peace 2014), has earned the unfortunate distinction of being one of the leading African nations in human trafficking. Nigeria serves as a source, transit, and destination country for women and girls (U.S. Department of State 2014). Some victims stay within the continent and are trafficked to neighboring West and Central African countries, while others are sent to Western European countries (e.g., Spain, the Netherlands, Belgium) (U.S. Department of State 2014). However, South America has increasingly become a destination country for trafficked persons (Truong 2006). For example, in Venezuela, primarily women and girls (but also boys) are trafficked for purposes of sexual exploitation, forced labor, and organ harvesting.

In addition to trafficking in adults, baby harvesting is increasingly problematic in Nigeria. David Smith, a journalist for *The Guardian*, reported that law enforcement in Nigeria discovered a "baby farm," where 32 pregnant teenage girls were locked up in a clinic (Smith 2011). Upon delivery of their children, the teenagers were going to be forced to hand their newborns over to traffickers for illegal adoptions or for use in witchcraft (Smith 2011). While this recent case involved a trafficking network, not all cases of baby harvesting involve criminal networks. Again, the intersection of poverty and trafficking is critical, as there have been reported cases of pregnant girls voluntarily selling (or trying to sell) their newborns. Truong (2006, p. 31) reports that two sisters attempted to sell an unborn child to a doctor in Lagos (the most populated city in Nigeria). The asking price for a baby boy was about US$3875, compared with US$2325 for a baby girl, though they later increased the asking price for a baby girl to about US$3100 to cover cost-of-living increases.

Women and girls are especially vulnerable to trafficking in Nigeria and other parts of the world for a variety of reasons, some of which are endemic to Nigerian society. They are vulnerable to trafficking simply because there is more international demand for them. In some cases, women are viewed as more suitable for some kinds of work (e.g., labor intensive production situations), and there is significant demand for women in the sex industry. In particular, Nigerian women have limited access to education and employment, there are policies in place that limit women's ability to leave the country (which limits potential employment opportunities in other countries), and perhaps most importantly there is a general acceptance/tolerance for violence against women (Truong 2006).

Human trafficking specifically for the purposes of sexual exploitation is a severe problem throughout Sub-Saharan Africa, but especially so in Dijbouti, Eritrea, Ethiopia, Kenya, and Somalia (McCabe and Manian 2010). Somalia, in particular, presents a textbook example of the intersection between state failure and human trafficking. For the 11th consecutive year, the U.S. Department of State has placed Somalia in a "special case" category because the country is without a fully functional central government. Internal trafficking of persons is commonplace in Somalia and the State Department notes, "Somali women and girls may be subjected to sex trafficking in Garowe, Las Anod (Sool region), and pirate towns such as Eyl and Harardheere. Girls are reportedly taken from coastal regions, particularly Bossaso, Puntland and placed in pirates' homes to be exploited in domestic and sexual servitude" (U.S. Department of State 2013, p. 379). Somalia is also a transit country, as many trafficking victims are smuggled into neighboring African nations, Europe, and the Middle East (U.S. Department of State 2013). Internally displaced women are particularly susceptible to human trafficking and traffickers often prey on this population by falsely promising job opportunities outside of Somalia. The U.S. Department of State (2013, p. 379) notes, "Somali women are smuggled, sometimes via Djibouti, to destinations in the Middle East, including Yemen and Syria, as well as to Sudan, Kenya, and South Africa where they are subjected to conditions of domestic servitude and forced prostitution."

In sum, women in fragile and failing states represent an especially vulnerable population because laws are discriminatory, not enforced, or simply do not exist. Research conducted by Laurie Gould (2014) found strong relationships between inequality in family law and human rights violations, progressive deterioration of public services, and criminalization/delegitimation of the state. Similarly, a greater number of human rights violations are found to be strongly associated with the discrepancies between the national law and practice concerning women. A rise in factionalized elites was also found to greatly influence discrepancies between the national law and practice concerning women. Lastly, failing countries do not comply with the TVPA, especially when the following indicators of failure are present: human rights violations, criminalization/delegitimation of the state, and arbitrary application of the rule of law (Gould 2014).

Conclusion

While it is recognized that all citizens in fragile and failing states pay a heavy price, the effects of state failure on women are extreme. The risk of violence both in society and in the home is greater for women in failing states. Similarly, women are often not afforded the right of full participation in social, political, or economic life. Failing states often have societal attitudes that either promote or condone the murder and rape of women, as well as "honor" suicides. Women are especially at risk for violence during times of active conflict. The rape and murder of women as they flee to refugee camps are all too common in failing countries.

Women also face significant barriers to full participation in education. Opportunities in this area are limited for women, which in turn affects their earning potential later in life. This ensures that many women will either remain dependent on men or work for low wages, risking their health and personal safety. Women in failing states are also denied adequate health care and can face numerous health complications from FGMs or die due to complications giving birth. Thus, women are often denied a fundamental right to life in failing states.

All this said, there have been some areas of promise for women, particularly in the realm of political participation. Some African nations have adopted quotas for women in political office, which increases the chance that the aforementioned areas of concern could be addressed. Still, the road to full gender equity in failing states (and in some more sustainable nations) is long and fraught with difficulties. It is critical that these gender issues be addressed as many of these nations attempt to rebuild and stabilize.

References

Alsam, M., G. Kingdon, and M. Söderbom. 2008. Is female education a pathway to gender equality in the labor market? Some evidence from Pakistan. In M. Tembon and L. Fort (Eds) *Girl's Education in the 21st Century: Gender Equality, Empowerment and Growth*, pp. 67–92, Washington DC: The World Bank.

Amnesty International. 2012. Pushed to the edge. http://www.amnesty.org/es/node/17999 (Accessed March 2, 2012).

Baranyi, S. and K. Powell. 2005. Fragile states, gender equality and aid effectiveness: A review of donor perspectives. Report prepared for the Canadian Development Agency, 1–14. http://www.nsi-ins.ca/wp-content/uploads/2012/10/2005-Fragile-States-Gender-Equality-and-Aid-Effectiveness-A-Review-of-Donor-Perspectives.pdf (Accessed February 5, 2012).

BBC News. 2011. Rwanda: How the genocide happened. http://www.bbc.co.uk/news/world-africa-13431486 (Accessed May 19, 2012).

Bilefsky, D. 2006. How to avoid honor killing in Turkey? Honor suicide. *The New York Times*. http://www.nytimes.com/2006/07/16/world/europe/16turkey.html?pagewanted=all&_r=0 (Accessed May 20, 2012).

Burnet, J. 2008. Gender balance and the meanings of women in governance in post-genocide Rwanda. *African Affairs* 107: 361–386.

Caprioli, M. 2000. Gendered conflict. *Journal of Peace Research* 37: 51–68.

Caprioli, M. 2003. Gender inequality and state aggression: The impact of domestic gender equality on state first use of force. *International Interactions* 29: 195–214.

Caprioli, M. 2005. Primed for violence: The role of gender inequality in predicting internal conflict. *International Studies Quarterly* 49: 161–178.

Castillejo, C. 2009. Women's Political Participation and Influence in Seirra Leone. Working paper. FRIDE and the Campaign for Good Governance.

Center for Reproductive Rights. 2008. Pregnant women in Nigeria die due to government negligence, according to center for reproductive rights' new report, 2008. http://reproductiverights.org/en/press-room/pregnant-women-in-nigeria-die-due-to-government-negligence-according-to-center-for-reprod (Accessed June 11, 2012).

Chebogut, J. and G. Ngeno. 2010. The Effects of Domestic Violence in the Family in Kenya. Paper presented at the Kenya Association of Professional Counselors Conference.

Cochintu, I., L. Tutunaru, N. Stoicu, and D. Valea. 2011. International cooperation against human trafficking. *Juridicial Current* 14: 78–86.

Colburn, M. 2002. *The Republic of Yemen: Development Challenges in the 21st Century*. London: Stacey International.

Connell, R. 1987. *Gender and Power: Society, The Person, and Sexual Politics*. Stanford, CA: Stanford University Press.

Dauge-Roth, A. 2010. *Writing and Filming the Genocide of the Tutsis in Rwanda: Dismembering and Remembering Traumatic History*. Lanham, MD: Lexington Books.

Diamond, I. and L. Quinby. 1988. *Feminism & Foucault: Reflections on Resistance.* Boston, MA: Northeastern University Press.

Farr, K. 2005. *Sex Trafficking: The Global Market in Women and Children.* New York: Worth.

Fauveau, V. and T. Blanchet. 1989. Deaths from injuries and induced abortion among rural Bangladeshi women. *Social Science and Medicine* 29: 1121–1127.

Foucault, M. 1977. *Discipline and Punish: The Birth of the Prison.* (A. Sheridan Trans.) New York: Pantheon Books.

Foucault, M. 1988. *The History of Sexuality.* (R. Hurley Trans.) New York: Vintage Books.

Fund for Peace. 2014. The fragile states index. http://ffp.statesindex.org (Accessed March 19, 2014).

Gould, L. 2014. Exploring gender-based disparities in legal protection, education, health, political empowerment, and employment in failing and fragile states. *Women and Criminal Justice* 24: 279–305.

Gould, L. and L. Agnich. 2014. Exploring the relationship between gender violence and state failure: A cross-national comparison. *Violence Against Women* 24: 279–305.

Handley, G., K. Higgins, B. Sharma, K. Bird, and D. Cammack. 2009. *Poverty and Poverty Reduction in Sub-Saharan Africa: An Overview of Key Issues.* London: The Overseas Development Institute. http://www.odi.org.uk/publications/600-poverty-reduction-sub-saharan-africa (Accessed March 19, 2012).

Hausmann, R., L. Tyson, and S. Zahidi. 2008. *Gender Gap Index.* Geneva: World Economic Forum.

Holsinger, D. and W. Jacob. 2008. *Inequality in Education: Comparative and International Perspectives.* Hong Kong: Comparative Education Research Centre, University of Hong Kong/Springer.

Horowitz, C. and C. Jackson. 1997. Female "circumcision." *Journal of General Internal Medicine* 12(8): 491–499.

Hudson, V., M. Caprioli, B. Ballif-Spanvill, R. McDermott, and C. Emmett. 2009. The heart of the matter: The security of women and the security of states. *International Security* 33: 7–45.

Human Rights Watch. 2010. Always on the run. http://www.hrw.org/reports/2010/09/14/always-run (Accessed March 19, 2012).

Idriss, M. and T. Abbas 2011. *Honor, Violence Islam and Women.* New York: Routledge-Cavendish.

Internal Displacement Monitoring Centre. 2012. Gender based violence. http://www.internal-displacement.org/ (Accessed March 19, 2012).

Jaeger, C., T. Webler, E. Rosa, and O. Renn. 2001. *Risk, Uncertainty, and Rational Action.* London: Earthscan.

Kaplan, A., S. Hechavarría, M. Martín, and I. Bonhoure. 2011. Health consequences of female genital mutilation/cutting in the Gambia, evidence into action. *Reproductive Health* 8: 26.

Khan, R. June 26, 2012. Pakistan rebuilds its education network after Taliban are driven out of Swat. *The Guardian.* http://www.theguardian.com/global-development/2012/jun/26/pakistan-education-swat-valley-taliban

Kirk, J. 2007. Education and fragile states. *Globalisation, Societies and Education* 5: 181–200.

Kudva, N. and K. Misra. 2008. Gender quotas, the politics of presence, and the feminist project: What does the Indian experience tell us? *Signs: Journal of Women, Culture & Society* 34: 49–73.

Latif, A. 2012. Alarming Situation of Education in Pakistan. UNESCO, Education for All, Knowledge Sharing, Grassroots Stories, Pakistan. http://www.unesco.org/education/efa/know_sharing/grassroots_stories/pakistan_2.shtml (Accessed October 13, 2012).

Lee, M. 2001. Population growth, economic inequality, and homicide. *Deviant Behavior* 22: 491–516.

Liska, A. 1990. The significance of aggregate dependent variables and contextual independent variables for linking macro and micro theories. *Social Psychology Quarterly* 53: 292–301.

MacKenzie, J. 2012. Afghan women trapped in tribal court system. *Global Post*. http://www.globalpost.com/dispatch/news/regions/asia-pacific/afghanistan/120306/afghan-women-trapped-tribal-court-system (Accessed April 19, 2012).

Magnarella, P. 2000. *Justice in Africa: Rwanda's Genocide, Its Courts, and the UN Criminal Tribunal*. Aldershot: Ashgate.

Marshall, M. and D. Marshall. 1999. Gender Empowerment and the Willingness of States to Use Force. *CSP Publications and Report Series*. http://www.systemicpeace.org/peace.htm (Accessed March 19, 2014).

Martin, B. 1984. *Patriarchy. Uprooting War*. London: Freedom Press. http://www.bmartin.cc/pubs/90uw/uw10.html (Accessed August 2, 2015).

Martin, B. 2002. *Eyewitness to a Genocide: The United Nations and Rwanda*. Ithaca, NY: Cornell University Press.

McCabe, K. and S. Manian. 2010. *Sex Trafficking: A Global Perspective*. Lanham, MD: Lexington Books.

Melander, E. 2005. Gender equality and intrastate armed conflict. *International Studies Quarterly* 49: 695–714.

Messner, S. 1989. Economic discrimination and societal homicide rates: Further evidence on the cost of inequality. *American Sociological Review* 54: 597–611.

Messner, S. 2002. Reassessing the cross-national relationship between income inequality and homicide rates: Implications of data quality control in the measurement of income distribution. *Journal of Quantitative Criminology* 18: 377–395.

Messner, S. and R. Rosenfeld. 1997. *Crime and the American Dream*. Belmont, CA: Wadsworth.

Mines, D. and S. Lamb. 2010. *Everyday Life in South Asia*, 2nd edn, Bloomington, IN: Indiana University Press.

Ming-Jen, L. 2007. Does democracy increase crime? The evidence from international data. *Journal of Comparative Economics* 35: 467–483.

Monazza, A., G. Kingdon, and M. Soderbom. 2008. Is female education a pathway to gender equality in the labor market? Some evidence from Pakistan. In M. Tembon and L. Fort (Eds) *Girls' Education in the 21st Century: Gender Equality, Empowerment, and Economic Growth*, pp. 67–91, Washington, DC: World Bank.

Myint, N. 2008. Migration and trafficking: Putting human rights into action. *Forced Migration Review* 30: 38–39.

Pakistan Education Task Force. 2012. Education emergency Pakistan. http://pakistaneducation-taskforce.com/EER.html (Accessed March 19, 2012).

Poulantzas, N. 1978. *State, Power, Socialism*. London: NLB.

Prunier, G. 1995. *The Rwanda Crisis: History of a Genocide*. New York: Columbia University Press.

Remmert, C. 2003. Women in reconstruction: Rwanda promotes women decision makers. *UN Chronicle* 4: 23.

Russo, N. and A. Pirlott. 2006. Gender-based violence: Concepts, methods, and findings. *Annals of the New York Academy of Sciences* 1087: 178–205.

Sanday, P. 1981. The socio-cultural context of rape: A cross-cultural study. *Journal of Social Issues* 37: 5–27.

Shimko, K. 2005. *International Relations: Perspectives and Controversies*. Boston, MA: Houghton Mifflin.

Smith, D. 2011. Nigerian "baby farm" raided—32 pregnant girls rescued. *The Guardian*. http://www.guardian.co.uk/law/2011/jun/02/nigeria-baby-farm-raided-human-trafficking (Accessed March 10, 2012).

Sunil, T. S. and V. Pillai. 2010. *Women's Reproductive Health in Yemen*. Amherst, NY: Cambria Press.

Truong, T. 2006. *Poverty, Gender and Human Trafficking in Sub-Sahara Africa. Rethinking Best Practices in Migration Management.* New York: UNESCO.

UNICEF. 2007. *Female Genital Mutilation/Cutting: Cote De Ivory.* Abidjan: United Nations Children's Fund.

United Nations. 1996. United Nations declaration on the elimination of violence against women. http://www.un.org/documents/ga/res/48/a48r104.html (Accessed May 2, 2012).

United Nations. 2006. Global initiative to fight human trafficking. Human trafficking: The facts. www.unglobalcompact.org (Accessed May 15, 2012).

United Nations. 2009. Somalia: Another problem in another place. http://www.ohchr.org/EN/NewsEvents/Pages/AnotherProblemInAnotherPlace.aspx (Accessed March 7, 2011).

United Nations. 2012. Report of the special rapporteur on violence against women, its causes and consequences, Rashida Manjoo. http://www.europarl.europa.eu/meetdocs/2009_2014/documents/droi/dv/33_reportspecialrapp_/33_reportspecialrapp_en.pdf (Accessed June 20, 2012).

United Nations Children's Fund. 2000. *Domestic Violence Against Women and Girls.* Innocenti Digest No. 6. http://www.unicef-irc.org/publications/213 (Accessed March 19, 2014).

United Nations Development Program. 2006. *Educational, Scientific, and Cultural Organization, Human Trafficking in Nigeria: Root Causes and Recommendations.* United Nations Educational, Scientific and Cultural Organization. http://www.unesco.org/new/en/social-and-human-sciences/themes/human-rights-based-approach/publications/ (Accessed May 18, 2012).

United Nations Development Program. 2011. Republic of Yemen. http://www.ye.undp.org/yemen/en/home.html (Accessed March 2, 2012).

United Nations Observer Mission in Sierra Leone. 2000. Sierra Leone–UNOMSIL background. http://www.un.org/en/peacekeeping/missions/past/unomsil/UnomsilB.htm (Accessed December 23, 2015).

United Nations Office for the High Commissioner for Human Rights. 1996. Women and violence. UN News Center. http://www.un.org/rights/dpi1772e.htm (Accessed March 19, 2014).

United Nations Office for the High Commissioner for Human Rights. 2012. Special rapporteur on violence against women, its causes and consequences. http://www.ohchr.org/EN/Issues/Women/SRWomen/Pages/SRWomenIndex.aspx (Accessed March 7, 2012).

United Nations Office on Drugs and Crime. 1999. *United Nations Treaty Collection Treaty Reference Guide.* New York: United Nations.

United Nations Office on Drugs and Crime. 2012. World drug report. http://www.unodc.org/unodc/en/data-and-analysis/WDR-2012.html (Accessed January 15, 2014).

United Nations Office on Drugs and Crime. 2014. *Global Report on Trafficking in Persons, 2014.* New York: United Nations Publications.

U.S. Department of State. 2011. *Trafficking in Persons Report, 2011.* Washington, DC: United States Department of State. http://www.state.gov/j/tip/rls/tiprpt/2011/index.htm.

U.S. Department of State. 2013. *Trafficking in Human Beings: 2013 Edition.* Luxembourg: Publications Office.

U.S. Department of State. 2014. *Trafficking in Persons Report, 2014.* Washington, DC: United States Department of State.

Winthrop, R. July 14, 2009. Crisis in Pakistan: Educate women and girls for long-term solutions. Brookings Institute. http://www.brookings.edu/research/speeches/2009/07/14-pakistan-education-winthrop.

WomanStats Project and Database. 2012. The womanstats project and database. http://www.womanstats.org/ (Accessed March 5, 2012).

Woodhull, W. 1988. Sexuality, power, and the question of rape. In I. Diamond and L. Quinby (Eds) *Feminism & Foucault: Reflections on Resistance*, pp. 167–177, Boston, MA: Northeastern University Press.
Zavirske, D. and S. Herath. 2010. I want to have my future, I have a dialogue: Social work in Sri Lanka between neo-capitalism and human rights. *Social Work Education* 29: 831–884.

Case Study Georgia: A State in Crisis

7

They talk about the failure of socialism but where is the success of capitalism in Africa, Asia and Latin America?

—**Fidel Castro**

Though African nations are often considered by many to be among the most fragile nations, many former Soviet bloc countries are on the verge of failing. In this chapter, we examine the former Soviet bloc country, the Republic of Georgia, as it provides an instructive example of how issues of crime and justice are navigated in a fragile state outside of Africa. Georgia is of particular interest because it has successfully addressed many of its systemic problems. While the risk of governmental failure in Georgia remains high, a more nuanced view of state fragility is provided through an examination of Georgia's various social, economic, and political improvements.

Located in the Caucasus region of Eurasia, the Republic of Georgia has a rich history and culture, but this richness has often been overshadowed by protracted war and violence since the dissolution of the Soviet Union. This former Soviet bloc nation currently ranks number 55 on the Failed States Index, placing it on the cusp of failure (Fund for Peace 2013). Improvements in the nation have been unsteady, and at many points the risk of collapse seemed likely. In 2006, the Republic of Georgia ranked at number 60 on the Failed States Index. By 2010, instability in the nation had increased substantially and the risk of failure marched yet higher.* This somewhat desultory path leads us to question three aspects of Georgia's trajectory: (1) What factors have precipitated Georgia's decline into borderline failure? (2) What steps are being taken to increase stability? and (3) What is the nexus between crime, the criminal justice system, and state failure in Georgia?

Recent History and Decline

Georgia became a member of the Soviet bloc during the 1920s and remained under Moscow's rule until the Soviet Union collapsed in 1991. Though the

---

* In 2010, Georgia ranked number 37 on the Failed States Index, placing it in the same category as the violence-plagued nations of Sierra Leone, the Congo, and Lebanon.

nation was forcibly incorporated into the Soviet Union, the result was not entirely disadvantageous. As part of the USSR, Georgia maintained a booming tourism industry and took advantage of the Soviet shadow economy* (sometimes referred to as the "second economy") (Zürcher 2007).† Georgia remained relatively stable during this period, but a series of wars following independence have introduced a persistently destabilizing force into Georgian political and social affairs.

The South Caucasus, which includes Armenia, Azerbaijan, and Georgia, has the dubious distinction of being "the most unstable in the former Soviet Union in terms of the numbers, intensity, and length of its ethnic and civil conflicts" (Nichol 2011, p. 6). The fight for autonomy from Georgia by two South Caucasus regions, Abkhazia and South Ossetia, has been contentious and violent. The desire for autonomy in both areas can be attributed to a number of factors, but the weakening of the Soviet Union was a primary catalyst for the independence movement. As the Soviet Union gradually declined, members of the elite seized the opportunity for South Ossetia and Abkhazia to gain independence. Those in the upper echelon in these regions pushed for political autonomy, driven in part by "the lack of capacity and of political will of the newly ruling nationalist elites in Russia, Georgia, and Azerbaijan to offer credible security guarantees" (Zürcher 2007, p. 50). Governmental weakness has played an influential role in the fight for independence from Georgia and has served to create a vicious cycle, whereby violent conflicts in South Ossetia and Abkhazia serve to increase instability in the region, thus reinforcing a desire for autonomy through violent measures.

Abkhazia's fight for autonomy sparked war and also resulted in a trade embargo, which created a difficult economic situation in the region while also increasing Abkhazia's dependence on Russia. The conflict between the Georgian government and the two breakaway regions, South Ossetia and Abkhazia, is ongoing, and continues to play an instrumental role in Georgia's instability. The source of the conflict in both regions has a long, complex, and (at times) disputed history. As Susan Nan (2010, p. 242) states, "the conflicts over the political status of Abkhazia and South Ossetia involve long histories, multiple interests, ethnic divisions, international politics, social trauma, and war." Some scholars contend that the Soviet Union's "divide and rule tactic" is partly responsible for the current troubles. Linguistic fractionalization was a tool widely used by the Soviets in an effort to create artificial divisions among

---

* A shadow economy is defined as any legal or illegal economic activity that is not included in the calculation of a nation's gross domestic product (GDP; Schneider and Enste 2000).
† In an examination of shadow economies in 76 nations, Schneider and Enste (2000) found that between 1990 and 1993, Georgia had the largest shadow economy (43.6% of GDP) compared with other former Soviet nations.

many groups. Bonner (2008, p. 82) notes, "the Soviets created 'national languages' by distorting and adapting various local linguistic variations. The best example is the creation of Kazakh, Uzbek and other artificially separated Central Asian regions, despite a common Turkic tongue differentiated only by dialects."

Ethnic fractionalization has also played a large role in the ongoing conflict. The South Ossetian people are of Iranian descent and are viewed as a nonnative group by most Georgians (Higgins and O'Reilly 2009). While part of the Soviet bloc, South Ossetia was considered an autonomous region within the Georgian Soviet Socialist Republic (Higgins and O'Reilly 2009). However, following the dissolution of the Soviet Union, South Ossetia lost this status and was absorbed into the newly independent Georgian state (Higgins and O'Reilly 2009). While still part of the Soviet Union, there was no division between North and South Ossetia and both shared a strong connection. The breakup of the Soviet Union did not dissolve the relationship between the North and South. Indeed, the North and South are still strongly connected with no apparent desire to develop a separate South Ossetian state (Higgins and O'Reilly 2009). Rather than two separate nations, "what is seen to exist is one Ossetian nation that is divided into two separate political units. Although North Ossetia is a predominantly Muslim region and South Ossetia is mainly Christian, both regions have many traditional cultural practices in common and these practices are national rather than religious in character" (Higgins and O'Reilly 2009, p. 569).

Attempts by South Ossetia to gain independence began while it was still an autonomous region of the Georgian Soviet Socialist Republic (Human Rights Watch 2009) and intensified after the Soviet Union collapsed (Hoddie and Hartzell 2010; BBC News 2015). The attempted secession sparked a conflict that erupted into a series of wars lasting over 20 years. The dispute began in November 1989, escalated in January 1991, and then flared up again in June 1992 (Zürcher 2007, p. 116). In 1990, South Ossetia declared independence from the USSR and boycotted the election of President Zviad Gamsakhurdia, a move that prompted Gamsakhurdia to revoke the autonomy of the region (Human Rights Watch 2009). This only served to increase instability in the region and ultimately led to a war between South Ossetian separatists, the Georgian police, and paramilitary groups (Human Rights Watch 2009). This war resulted in the de facto secession of South Ossetia and ultimately claimed the lives of thousands of citizens, while displacing thousands more (Human Rights Watch 2009).

The second war, which lasted nearly two years (from December 1991 to November 1993), was triggered by the removal of President Gamsakhurdia from office by opposition groups and warlords (Zürcher 2007). Gamsakhurdia (a former dissident) had become the first elected president of the newly independent Georgia, winning an overwhelming 87% of the vote* (Hash-Gonzalez 2012). Accounts of the election process indicate that it was rife with corruption (Minahan 2013). Opponents of Gamsakhurdia were threatened, many were kept off the ballot, and one political opponent was attacked (Minahan 2013). The lack of an open and free election did not weaken Gamsakhurdia's popularity among the general public; on the contrary, he was viewed as a unifying force for Georgian statehood (Minahan 2013). Gamsakhurdia was able to capitalize on the public's wish to separate from Russia completely and for a very short time public opinion was largely positive (Minahan 2013). His popularity quickly diminished as a result of his dictatorial ruling style and his ethnocentric ideas (Hash-Gonzalez 2012). On taking office, Gamsakhurdia filled government positions with loyal anti-communists, despite the fact that most had no political experience (Minahan 2013). Minahan (2013, p. 121) goes on to observe that Gamsakhurdia viewed "himself as a moral savior of the Georgian nation … [and] backed ethno-centric, anti-Muslim government policies that further alienated many of the republic's non-Georgian groups." Kelly Hash-Gonzalez shares the thoughts of one protester in an interview in 2006. Of ethnic Georgian-ness, the protester noted, "He [Gamsakhurdia] went against social norms and wasn't a reasonable person anymore, but not crazy. It was scary. I remember seeing in [state run] papers around that time, 'Let any women pregnant with a non-Georgian child be cursed'" (Hash-Gonzalez 2012, p. 31).

Amanda Wooden and Christoph Stefes (2009, p. 114) describe Gamsakhurdia's regime "as one of the most short-lived and disastrously failed efforts at authoritarian state building in the former Soviet Union." In just one year, Gamsakhurdia went from being a wildly popular president to an ousted dictator, forced out of the country by a violent coup (Wooden and Stefes 2009). Ironically, his demise as a politician can be partially attributed to his success as a dissident (Hash-Gonzalez 2012). He was an uncompromising and radical dissident, two qualities that usually do not lend themselves particularly well to unifying a nation (Hash-Gonzalez 2012). Rather than build a cohesive Georgian state, Gamsakhurdia instead had opposition leaders arrested and began censoring the media almost immediately after taking office (Wooden and Stefes 2009).

His dictatorial leadership style was partially responsible for his ultimate downfall. With regard to South Ossetia, Gamsakhurdia was predictably unyielding in his position against autonomy for the region. During his campaign, Gamsakhurdia ran on a platform that supported autonomy for both South Ossetia and Abkhazia, but after taking office he quickly reversed

* Non-Georgians in South Ossetia and Abkhazia boycotted the election, as well as a vote on a referendum for Georgian independence put forth by Gamsakhurdia (Souleimanov 2013).

his stance on South Ossetia and wanted it abolished instead (Minahan 2013). The decision to use military force in South Ossetia was extremely unpopular, as many in the nation considered the complete separation of Georgia from Russia to be far more pressing (Wooden and Stefes 2009). The conflict in South Ossetia, coupled with a decree to abolish the position of head of the National Guard, proved to be too contentious for opposition groups and the National Guard. In December 1991, Jaba Ioseliani, a powerful Georgian warlord, and the National Guard (led by Tengiz Kitovani) began to fight Gamsakhurdia's forces and bomb government buildings (Hash-Gonzalez 2012). With his government under attack, Gamsakhurdia hid in a bunker under the parliament building (Hash-Gonzalez 2012; Wooden and Stefes 2009). Efforts to flush him out were unsuccessful, but Gamsakhurdia was permitted to escape to Chechnya during the first week in January (Hash-Gonzalez 2012).* With Gamsakhurdia officially out of office, Kitovani and Ioseliani created the Military Council, which would serve as the tempo-rary government (Hash-Gonzalez 2012). By removing Gamsakhurdia from power, "the rebel coalition had overridden the Georgian constitution. From the perspective of international law, the Georgian government faced grow-ing charges of flagrant human rights abuses directed against not only the minority national groups, but against political groups as well" (Minahan 2013, p. 123).

In an effort to add at least the appearance of legitimacy to the govern-ment, the Military Council worked toward holding elections. However, given the instability of the country at that time, an interim leader was needed. The Military Council brought in Eduard Shevardnadze as the interim head of the State Council. Shevardnadze inherited a country on the verge of com-plete collapse. The military was virtually nonexistent and ill-equipped to handle the violence stemming from militias and paramilitary groups fighting for control of the country (Wooden and Stefes 2009). It took nearly three years for Shevardnadze to form a nominally functional government with an electoral process. On September 23, 1992, Shevardnadze signed a cease-fire agreement with Russian leader Boris Yeltsin to end the conflict in South Ossetia, as well as establish "the Joint Control Commission (JCC), a body for negotiations composed of Georgian, Russian, North Ossetian, and South Ossetian representatives, and the Joint Peacekeeping Forces (JPKFs), a trilateral peacekeeping force with Georgian, Russian, and Ossetian units" (Human Rights Watch 2009, p. 17). Even so, that peace was short-lived, with the most recent conflict occurring in 2008 (Hoddie and Hartzell 2010). In the midst of turmoil throughout the nation, yet another war broke out in 1992 (Zürcher 2007), this time in the Abkhazia region.

---

* Gamsakhurdia later returned to Georgia and attempted to regain power, but he died under suspicious circumstances in 1993.

Located along the Black Sea, Abkhazia was a popular all-Soviet tourist destination (Souleimanov 2013; Zürcher 2007). The principle revenue for Abkhazia came from the tourism industry, as well as the exportation of tea and citrus (Souleimanov 2013; Zürcher 2007). When the Soviet Union declined and finally dissolved, Abkhazia began to face sharp economic decline (Souleimanov 2013). The increasingly dire economic situation in Abkhazia exacerbated existing ethnic cleavages and the population further fragmented into different groups (Souleimanov 2013). There are many similarities between the conflict in South Ossetia and the conflict in Abkhazia, as both regions were striving for the same goal—independence (Hoddie and Hartzell 2010). When Abkhazia declared sovereignty, Georgia retaliated by deploying troops and occupying the region (Hoddie and Hartzell 2010). With the help of volunteers and Russian soldiers, the Abkhazia people launched an assault that lasted a year, and ultimately ended with a cease-fire (Hoddie and Hartzell 2010). According to Human Rights Watch (2009, p. 17), this "military confrontation ... led to some 8,000 deaths, 18,000 wounded, and the forced displacement of over 200,000 ethnic Georgians."

In 1999, Abkhazia officially declared independence, which resulted in an international trade embargo (BBC News 2012). With Russia as their only ally, Abkhazia became increasingly dependent on Russian aid to ensure the region's survival. Recent indicators suggest that without support from Russia, the economy in Abkhazia would be virtually nonexistent. Between direct aid, funding for infrastructure, and pension payments, approximately 70% of Abkhazia's budget flows directly from Russia (International Crisis Group 2013). In a move that further enflamed tensions between Georgia and Russia, Moscow made it easier for the Abkhazian people to become Russian citizens and obtain Russian passports (BBC News 2012). Currently, most residents in Abkhazia and South Ossetia hold Russian passports.

A series of nonviolent demonstrations in Georgia's capitol city, Tbilisi, brought a regime change once again. This came to be known as the "Rose Revolution," which was responsible for removing Shevardnadze from power. A quiet unrest between South Ossetia and Georgia lasted over a decade, but violence flared up again in 2004 when newly elected president, Mikheil Saakashvili, made the restoration of the Georgian territories one of his top priorities (Human Rights Watch 2009). To achieve this goal, Saakashvili deployed law enforcement, military troops, and intelligence personnel into South Ossetia under the guise of "bolstering its peacekeeping contingent up to the limit of 500 troops, as permitted by the cease-fire agreement" (Haro 2010, p. 3). Russia responded in kind by sending several paramilitary groups from Abkhazia, Transnistria, and Russia into the region (Haro 2010).

Military force was not the only tactic employed by President Saakashvili, as he also focused efforts on the elimination of illicit smuggling operations that allegedly involved Russian organized criminal networks and Georgian officials (Haro 2010). The economic impact of disrupting the smuggling operations had a profoundly negative effect on South Ossetia's economy (discussed in detail below).

The last tactic launched by Saakashvili was a campaign aimed at winning the hearts and minds of South Ossetians (Human Rights Watch 2009). The hearts and minds campaign included "economic and cultural projects, including an Ossetian-language television station, pensions, free fertilizer, and humanitarian aid" (Human Rights Watch 2009, p. 18). There were several clashes between Georgian troops and paramilitary groups, but both sides had largely pulled out of the area by late 2004 (Haro 2010).

Tensions remained high in both South Ossetia and Abkhazia, but on July 3, 2008, violence resumed once again. The killing of a South Ossetian police chief and the attempted murder of the head of the pro-Georgian government in South Ossetia provided the catalyst for war (Ryan 2011). Security forces in Georgia and South Ossetia began bombing one another that evening (Ryan 2011). It was clear that Georgia was unable to maintain stability in the breakaway regions and a war with Russia ensued (Hoddie and Hartzell 2010; BBC 2015).

Russian forces became involved in the conflict in August, following an address by Russian President Medvedev during an emergency session of the Russian Security Council (Ryan 2011). In his address, Medvedev condemned the actions of the Georgian government and "he stated that—we shall not allow our compatriots to be killed with impunity. Those who are responsible for that will be duly punished. [He went on to note] historically Russia has been, and will continue to be, a guarantor of security for peoples of the Caucasus" (Ryan 2011, p. 161).

Georgian forces proved to be no match for the Russian military and by August 10, 2008, the Russian military (along with thousands of volunteers) had control of South Ossetia and had bombed airfields and military bases in Georgia (Ryan 2011). A cease-fire agreement, along with a multifaceted peace agreement, was put in place on August 12, 2008 (Ryan 2011). Owing to the fact that Russia has considerable influence in South Ossetia and Abkhazia and has been actively involved in much of the violence, some argue that the conflict in the breakaway regions has gone from separatist/Georgia conflicts to a dispute between Russia and Georgia (Haro 2010). In either instance, the 2008 war provided Russia with the opportunity to increase their military presence in both breakaway regions. After the 2008 war, Russia recognized South Ossetia and Abkhazia as independent states, but the political leadership in Georgia does not recognize the region's independence* and refuses to compromise (BBC News 2015).

---

* Notably, the vast majority of the international community also does not recognize South Ossetian autonomy. Besides Russia, only Venezuela, Nicaragua, and a handful of Pacific Island states recognize South Ossetia as an independent state.

At present, there are approximately 5000 Russian military personnel in Abkhazia, with Russia allocating $465 million to bolster its military infrastructure in the region (International Crisis Group 2013). In 2010, Russia sent S-300 anti-aircraft missiles to Abkhazia purportedly to help protect Abkhazia and South Ossetia. Additionally in 2013, Russia installed a barbed wire fence on the border between South Ossetia and Georgia, a move that has been criticized by the international community. The North Atlantic Treaty Organization (NATO) chief, Anders Fogh Rasmussen, has stated that the fence is a violation of international law and will likely increase tensions in the region (Croft 2013). In both regions, it appears that Russia has plans to stay indefinitely. While there are still no diplomatic relations between Georgia and Russia, the current Georgian president, Bidzina Ivanishvili, has made incremental steps toward opening up the lines of communication between Tbilisi and Moscow (International Crisis Group 2013). Tensions between Georgia and Russia have eased somewhat since 2008, but stability in the region rests heavily on both governments resolving the status of Abkhazia and South Ossetia, as well as returning the hundreds of thousands of internally displaced persons in Georgia (International Crisis Group 2013). A quick resolution of both problems is highly unlikely, as it appears that the "three sets of authorities [Georgian, Russian, and Abkhazia] at least share a common interest to cooperate in incremental confidence-building measures" (International Crisis Group 2013, p. i).

Crime and Criminal Justice Issues

Just as Georgia has struggled to loosen the fetter of post-Soviet domination, it must also confront a criminal justice system racked with problems. While hardly at the crisis stage found in many other corners of the globe, Georgia faces some of the same problems endemic to states in much greater peril. In this section, we will explore several areas that present notable challenges.

Smuggling

The violent conflict in Georgia provided the perfect opportunity for organized criminal networks to flourish without fear of interruptions by law enforcement (Kukhianidze 2006). This situation is certainly not unique to Georgia, as "the criminal world always fills the vacuum in official and legal relations, in... countries plagued by conflict and a fragile state" (Kukhianidze 2006, p. 119). The illicit smuggling of goods was (and to some extent still is) problematic in Abkhazia and South Ossetia. South Ossetia, in particular, has been described as "a nest of organized crime, a smugglers nirvana, where the economy is driven by smuggling in cigarettes, arms, people, and counterfeit U.S. dollars" (Patrick 2011, p. 128). During the conflict in the 1990s, Georgia did not have jurisdiction in Abkhazia or South Ossetia, thereby creating porous borders maintained by a largely corrupted law enforcement presence (Kukhianidze 2006).

On its face, smuggling of goods (such as cigarettes and hazelnuts) may seem somewhat benign, but "smuggling through Abkhazia and the South Ossetia takes place in an atmosphere of rooted violence, innumerable assassinations, kidnappings, hostage takings, and numerous other serious crimes" (Kukhianidze 2006, p. 118). Moreover, smuggling has a detrimental impact on the Georgian economy, which, in turn, renders the resolution of conflicts nearly impossible (Kukhianidze 2006). The most common goods smuggled through and by Abkhazia and South Ossetia are cigarettes, fuel, cars, drugs (principally marijuana), wheat flour, and wheat (Kukhianidze 2006). In addition to smuggling, the Georgian government is concerned with a host of serious issues such as the "illegal arms and drug trade, trafficking in human beings and other transnational organized crimes" (Ryan 2011, p. 18).

The smuggling of nuclear materials is perhaps the most pressing issue, especially where the broader international community is concerned. Weak states, even those lacking biological, nuclear, or chemical weapons, provide an ideal environment to smuggle nuclear materials or parts or both for weapons of mass destruction (Patrick 2011). Georgia provides a clear example of this phenomenon.

The Nuclear Threat Initiative (2012) reports that the Georgian government has conducted 15 nuclear smuggling probes since 2005. In 2006, weapons-grade uranium was transported from Russia to Georgia, despite the presence of radiation detectors at the border crossing (Patrick 2011). Due to the high levels of government corruption that have historically plagued the country, smugglers were able to bribe a border official and successfully smuggle the uranium into the country (Patrick 2011). According to the Nuclear Threat Initiative (2012, para. 2), "four of the six probes made public for the first time by Georgian authorities occurred in 2012, and officials said a 2011 incident was tied to a supply of cesium 137 sufficient to fuel a radiological 'dirty bomb.'"

At least two other incidents in 2012 involved people interested in obtaining uranium (Nuclear Threat Initiative 2012). No reliable data exist about the prevalence of nuclear smuggling, but the instability in Georgia has made the country a key transit site (Nuclear Threat Initiative 2014). Other factors that have helped facilitate the smuggling of nuclear material include unsecured borders, an inability to police almost half of Georgia's coastline (because it is located in Abkhazia), and the geographic proximity to Russia's weapons stockpiles (Patrick 2011; Nuclear Threat Initiative 2014).

Law Enforcement

Prior to the reforms, corruption at all levels of government, especially in law enforcement, was widespread. As such, reining in the police and their policing agencies was a top priority for the Saakashvili government. As the World Bank (2012, p. 8) explains, "the going 'rate' to become a traffic cop was $2,000–$20,000 in bribes in 2003, depending on where the officer would be stationed." Prior to the reforms, it was not unusual for drivers to be stopped and "fined" by law enforcement officers twice during an hour drive (World Bank 2012). Police corruption in Georgia "created a vicious cycle in which money rarely reached state coffers, salaries were not paid regularly, and police turned to crime to make money" (World Bank 2012, p. 13). Not surprisingly, the public's perception of the police was one of negativity and generalized fear (World Bank 2012).

Sweeping law enforcement reforms have been an integral part of reducing corruption. Transparency International (2011) reports that 16,000 police officers were fired immediately and later replaced by 2,300 patrol officers. Additional reductions in law enforcement personnel have been made across the board and there are now approximately 27,000 law enforcement officers, compared with 63,000 in 2003 (Transparency International 2011). To put this in a broader perspective, "before the reforms, Georgia had 1 police officer for every 21 citizens; today, that ratio has fallen to 1 police officer for every 89 citizens. Police also now operate closer to the communities they serve" (Transparency International 2011, p. 27). Though these accomplishments are laudable, Ryan (2011) notes that their sustainability rests in making major changes in law enforcement, such as streamlining and decentralizing law enforcement agencies and services, as well as increasing the level of coordination among state institutions.

Judiciary

According to Lydia Müller (2012, p. 937), "One of the biggest challenges for countries in transition in the process of setting up an independent judiciary is to establish an appropriate system of judicial administration." Georgia provides an excellent example of a nation grappling with exactly this situation. The judiciary in Georgia has been strongly linked and beholden to the executive branch. As the executive has moved into a reform phase, the judicial branch must also follow. Unfortunately, Georgia's history in such matters is less than promising.

As the World Bank (2012) notes, a strong system of checks and balances needs to be implemented. A successful system of checks and balances relies on the presence of an uncorrupted and independent judiciary, both of which are absent in Georgia. There is evidence to suggest that judges have been chosen for their loyalty to the regime in power at the time, rather than their legal and professional qualifications. An examination of the passage rates for judiciary exams reveals that in most years, just 10%–15% of potential judges passed the requisite examination (Transparency International

Georgia 2010). That rate skyrocketed in 1999 to a 40% rate of passage and in 2003, 90% of potential judges passed the exam (Transparency International Georgia 2010).

There is also a belief in some quarters that "judges are pressured by the executive to issue rulings that conform to the prosecution's opinions" (Transparency International Georgia 2010, p. 2). This, along with a zero tolerance policy in law enforcement, helps to explain the reduction in the number of acquittals. In 2005, there were 83 acquittals compared with 30 in 2008 (Kury et al. 2010).

As of this writing, the Georgian judicial system is still plagued with systemic ills and in need of substantial reform. Some of the more salient problems involve: young and inexperienced judges, lack of judicial independence,* and no lifetime appointments (World Bank 2012). On a positive note, the executive branch appears to be cognizant of the problems and has stated that judicial reform will continue (World Bank 2012).

The issue of judicial pay requires special attention, as low pay can result in accepting bribes as a means to supplement income. Georgia began to address this issue by increasing the judicial budget by 8.6% between 2008 and 2010, with the majority of the increase going toward salaries (European Commission for the Efficiency of Justice 2013). While the judicial budget saw an increase, expenditure on training and education for judges decreased by 4% during the same time period (European Commission for the Efficiency of Justice 2013). While an increase in salaries may help address the corruption problem in the judiciary, budget cuts in training and education exacerbate the problems associated with inexperienced judges. Georgia also decreased the number of judges between 2006 and 2010 by approximately 6.3% (European Commission for the Efficiency of Justice 2013). There are now approximately 6.7 judges per 100,000 of the population, which is very low by European standards, but only slightly lower when compared with the United States† (Ramseyer and Rasmusen 2013; European Commission for the Efficiency of Justice 2013).

Similarly, participation in the judicial process is a key element of a fair and functional judicial system. Prior to 2012, Georgia did not use jury trials, but a jury system has been put in place, albeit on a very limited basis (European Commission for the Efficiency of Justice 2013). At present, only Tbilisi City Court and Kutaisi City Court utilize juries and only for aggravated murder cases (European Commission for the Efficiency of Justice 2013).

* Judges can be relocated to remote jurisdictions if they render unpopular judgments.
† The median number of judges in European countries is 21.3 per 100,000 (European Commission for the Efficiency of Justice 2013). In the United States, there are approximately 10.81 judges per 100,000 (Ramseyer and Rasmusen 2013).

During their court observations of high-profile* cases from February through July 2013, Transparency International Georgia (2013) noted that when defendants were offered a jury trial, they refused because they did not believe that the public would give them a fair trial. The most promising observation of the court process was "the principles of equality and adversariality of the parties were observed at court trials. Defense, as well as the prosecution enjoyed equal opportunities for presenting their positions and they could freely exercise the rights safeguarded by procedural legislation" (Transparency International 2013, p. 3).

Reducing Corruption: A Success Story in Progress

Even with all the aforementioned problems, the Georgian government has made measurable strides in reducing crime and corruption. According to the late prime minister, Zurab Zhvania, prior to 2004, Georgia "was a disaster, it was not a state. The only way the previous government viewed the state was as a means to make money. All branches of government were corrupt" (World Bank 2012, p. 6). The previous government had emptied the treasury. This left the government more than GEL 400 million (approximately U.S. $180 million) behind in salary and pension payments (World Bank 2012). Corruption serves as a major roadblock to stability for fragile nations because it "undermines economic growth, jeopardizes financial stability and weakens the ability of the state to deliver basic services" (Phillips 2004, p. 6).

The transformation in Georgia following the Rose Revolution was remarkable. Financial reforms were of particular import between 2003 and 2008, both in an effort to reduce corruption and to stimulate the economy. According to the Organization for Economic Co-Operation and Development (2011), the Georgian government revised the tax code and reduced both the number and the amount of corporate taxes to be collected by the government. As a result, official company registrations rose from 36,000 in 2005 to 51,000 by 2007, thus dramatically decreasing participation in the shadow economy (Organization for Economic Co-Operation and Development 2011). Additionally, the economy became stronger and transnational crime decreased as a result of the efforts of the Georgian government (Ryan 2011). Legal changes were implemented such that both active and passive bribery were criminalized, "criminal responsibility of legal persons for corruption was introduced, and the provisions on money laundering were improved through multiple amendments. Georgia also became a party to the UN Convention Against Corruption in 2008" (Transparency International 2011,

---

* These cases involved current and former government officials.

p. 27). Unfortunately, the August 2008 war effectively halted much of the progress that had been made during the previous five years (Organization for Economic Co-Operation and Development 2011). Improvements in the realm of corruption, however, appear to have continued.

To gain insight into governmental corruption more generally, and the criminal justice system specifically, we turn to Transparency International, which provides a quantitative measure of corruption throughout the world, known as the Corruption Perception Index (CPI). According to their calculations, we see a gradual decrease in the perceived corruption of their government among Georgians (Transparency International 2003–2013). Transparency International uses several secondary data sources (e.g., Freedomhouse and The World Economic Forum) to calculate the amount of perceived governmental corruption. A score closer to 1 indicates a high level of perceived corruption and a score closer to 10 is indicative of less perceived corruption. Their research reflects extremely high levels of perceived corruption in 2003 (1.8), which gradually improved until 2008 (3.9), the year of the most recent violent outbreaks in the breakaway regions. Since that time, the amount of perceived corruption has decreased generally, but compared with many other democracies, Georgians continue to perceive their government as more corrupt than respondents in many other democracies.

In addition to the CPI, Transparency International (2003–2013a) also provides the Global Corruption Barometer, the largest global public opinion survey on corruption. The first survey in 2003 asked a series of questions about the profusion, extent, and future of corruption in a given country. For present concerns, there are three questions that are worth a more detailed consideration.

The first question asks, "How seriously do you believe corruption affects different spheres of life in this country?" Georgian respondents believed that corruption in Georgia very significantly affected political life and culture and values in society. In particular, over two-thirds indicated that corruption very significantly affected the "culture and values" of the nation, whereas over three-quarters said that corruption very significantly affected the political life of the country (Transparency International. 2003–2013a).

When asked, "Do you expect the level of corruption to change in the next three years?" almost 56% expected corruption to increase over the period. Just over 11% of respondents believed corruption would stay about the same. These findings provide an interesting juxtaposition with the previous observation that the average perception of corruption during the 2003–2006 period actually declined (Transparency International. 2003–2013a).

The third question poses an evocative hypothetical, "If you had a magic wand and could eliminate corruption from one of the following institutions, what would your first choice be?"

Criminal justice agencies comprised two of the top three institutions mentioned, while 19.7% of respondents wanted to rid medical services of corruption first, followed by the courts (18.1%) and the police (13.4%) (Transparency International. 2003–2013a).

By 2013, the Global Corruption Barometer survey had been modified to include more questions. Even so, comparisons between current data and the first wave of surveys can still be made. When asked if corruption had increased or decreased during the previous two years, the majority of respondents reported that it had decreased. These results are very promising and help to illustrate the effectiveness of the anticorruption tactics employed by the new administration.

In the 2013 wave, survey participants were asked which institutions they believed were corrupt/extremely corrupt. Once again, the criminal justice system was found to be problematic, with 51% of respondents indicating that they believed the judiciary was corrupt/extremely corrupt, followed by the media (42%), medical and health services (32%), and law enforcement (26%). However, when asked if they had paid a bribe for a service in the last 12 months, just 4% of those surveyed reported bribing the judiciary and 5% had bribed law enforcement. It would appear, at least from the available data, that corruption (or at least the prevailing perceptions thereof) has reduced drastically within the last decade.

Georgia could potentially be on a path toward stability, but Freedomhouse notes a number of systemic roadblocks. In the area of corruption, Freedomhouse (2013, p. 224) observes that a "lack of transparency in business and media ownership still obscures overlap between government and business interests, and many people close to the government have become extremely wealthy." Similarly, the criminal justice system remains questionable. Law enforcement officers have been accused of arresting people for administrative offenses without due process (Freedomhouse 2013). Rates of arrest increased as the 2012 election came closer, suggesting that police were intimidating or silencing those who were not supportive of the current administration (Freedomhouse 2013).

Additionally, the judiciary is still plagued with problems including very low acquittal rates and lingering transparency issues. As Müller (2012, p. 939) states, "In order to regain public trust in the administration of the judiciary, and in its independence in general, it is furthermore necessary to search for new ways of increasing transparency in the daily work of [judicial] councils and in the process of their formation." As with the government more generally, the judiciary has made modest gains, but these are insufficient to fundamentally reorder the public's perception of the institution.

Corrections

The above-referenced low acquittal rates have a latent consequence of grotesque prison overcrowding. According to the International Society for Human Rights (2010), overcrowded and unsanitary conditions have increasingly reached unacceptable levels. For example, Prison Camp Number 7 (located in Ksani) was initially built to hold 1600 inmates, but by 2009 the facility housed 2731 inmates. Conditions inside the facility have been described as "horrifying" and the threat of disease is quite high due to the crude plumbing system in place (International Society for Human Rights 2010). Funding for medical care inside prison facilities has historically been virtually nonexistent, so most inmates go untreated if they fall ill (International Society for Human Rights 2010). The average expenditure on medical care per inmate is $1.00 per month, with Geguthi Prison paying the smallest amount ($0.60) and Rustavi Prison Number 1 spending just $1.75 per month—the largest expenditure compared with the rest of the prison facilities (International Society for Human Rights 2010). Not surprisingly, mortality rates are somewhat high, with 370 of Georgia's 23,995 inmates (1.5%) dying in custody between 2006 and 2009 (Walmsley 2011). By way of comparison, 13,468 (or 0.008%) of the United State's 1.6 million prison inmates died while in custody during the same time period (Bureau of Justice Statistics 2014).

Another informative way to parse differences between Georgian prisons and those in the United States is to examine the leading causes of deaths in custody. In Georgia, inmates most frequently die from respiratory diseases, tuberculosis, coronary heart disease, other infectious diseases, and injury due to violence. In contrast, the primary causes of death for jail inmates in the United States are heart disease and suicide (which account for 61% of all jail inmate deaths) (Bureau of Justice Statistics 2013a). For prison inmates in the United States, the two primary causes of death are cancer and heart disease (Bureau of Justice Statistics 2013b). This comparison demonstrates that abysmal sanitary conditions coupled with substandard health care and a lax culture of inmate security contribute to the swirling cauldron of disease and violence found in this nation's prisons. To be sure, imprisonment in the United States is no panacea—as indicated by the suicide rate—but the basic necessities for human living are more clearly in evidence.

All this said, Georgian inmates are not completely without redress for the conditions inside prison facilities, as there have been a number of successful court cases brought before the European Court of Human Rights. In one such case, *Gorgiladze v. Georgia* (2009), the court declared that the prison conditions were in violation of Article 3 of the Declaration of the European Convention on Human Rights (Article 42 of the Constitution 2012).

Article 3 is a prohibition against torture and states, "No one shall be subjected to torture or to inhuman or degrading treatment or punishment" (European Court of Human Rights 2010, p. 6). The court noted numerous problems with the prison conditions at Prison Camp Number 5, including, "crumbling plaster, peeling paint, windows without panes, floors with broken surfaces, hazardous electric wiring/installations and worn out water systems" (*Gorgiladze v. Georgia* 2009, p. 8).

However, the worst conditions were found in the basement of the prison, which was extremely overcrowded, poorly ventilated, had little light, and was full of piles of garbage (*Gorgiladze v. Georgia* 2009). According to the complaint, the plaintiff, Gorgiladze, was housed in a cell with 35 inmates (it was designed to hold just 24), which forced inmates to sleep in shifts (*Gorgiladze v. Georgia* 2009). Additionally, the cell was reported to be so damp that otherwise healthy inmates routinely became sick (*Gorgiladze v. Georgia* 2009).

Additionally, the court noted that Georgia had violated Gorgiladze's right to a fair trial, as provided for in Article 6, section 1 (Article 42 of the Constitution 2012). Article 6 (1) stipulates, "Everyone is entitled to a fair and public hearing within a reasonable time by an independent and impartial tribunal established by law. Judgment shall be pronounced publicly but the press and public may be excluded from all or part of the trial in the interests of morals, public order or national security in a democratic society, where the interests of juveniles or the protection of the private life of the parties so require, or to the extent strictly necessary in the opinion of the court in special circumstances where publicity would prejudice the interests of justice" (European Court of Human Rights 2010, p. 9). Article 6 was violated in the *Gorgiladze* case, as the court failed to follow the proper procedural rules for the use of lay judges in his initial trial (Article 42 of the Constitution 2012).

The United Nations conducted the first Universal Periodic Review (UPR) of Georgia in 2011. Created in 2006, UPRs provide a mechanism for the United Nations to examine the status of human rights in member nation-states. During the UPR, many of the representatives raised concerns over prison conditions in Georgia. For example, Sweden recommended that Georgia "take effective measures to safeguard the rights of prisoners and to improve the living conditions, including medical and health services, for detainees" (United Nations Human Rights Council 2011, p. 16). Hungary noted that Georgia needed to "carry out effective, impartial investigations into allegations of deaths, torture and ill-treatment caused by excessive use of force by the police and prison officials" (United Nations Human Rights Council 2011, p. 22).

Despite recommendations from the UPR, serious problems with prison conditions appear to remain. Just two weeks prior to the most recent election, Freedomhouse (2013, p. 224) reported "leaked videos showing severe abuse of inmates at a prison outside of Tbilisi were broadcast on television, igniting public outrage and leading to the resignations of the minister of corrections and minister of interior." The government has promised a complete overhaul of the correctional system and it appears that steps are being taken to accomplish this task. Notably, prison populations have been drastically reduced through the use of presidential pardons, amnesty, reductions in time served, and the release of some political prisoners (Bureau of Democracy, Human Rights, and Labor 2013). Based on the most recently available data, the prison population is currently 8,931, down from 19,349 in 2012 (Bureau of Democracy, Human Rights, and Labor 2013).

In summary, Georgia represents a common position along the continuum of relative fragility. It has many structural assets that could afford greater social and economic stability as well as higher levels of public satisfaction with the government. Unfortunately, old demons are being allowed to undermine the nascent positive forces. Until such time as Georgia gains better purchase in the realms of transparency, humane treatment of individuals processed by the criminal justice system, and in the fight against corruption, it is likely doomed to this precarious interstitial existence.

Making Sense of Fragility

In the introduction to this book, we highlighted the work of Monty Marshall and Cole (2009) to help motivate the concept of a state as a complex adaptive system. To briefly reprise their concepts, Marshall and Cole (2009, p. 2) identify four processes through which states come into existence and sustain themselves: self-actuation, self-organization, self-regulation, and self-correction. As they go on to note, these systems, "incorporate multiple, networked and interdependent levels, integrated in cohesive schemes of subsidiarity within which authority is allocated to the level most appropriate to its effects. The analytics focus on the complex relations between dynamics (human agency and environmental forces) and statics (physical and social attributes, conditions, and structures)" (Marshall and Cole 2009, p. 2).

As we consider the future of Georgia, this framework reveals a great deal of useful information about the republic and its capacity to adequately address the needs of its population. In particular, this paradigm speaks directly to a nation's ability to assert its autonomy, respond to threats, provide core goods of state, and deal with both internal and external threats.

With regard to the first criterion, Marshall and Cole (2009, p. 13) describe self-actuation as "the social impetus for establishing state authority to regulate group affairs comes principally from within the social group rather than imposed from outside. This... also suggest that stable (central) state authority should be compatible with and complementary to traditional sources of local authority."

Georgia does not fully meet this criterion. It still exists very much in the shadow of Russia. Moreover, protracted troubles in Abkhazia and

South Ossetia reinforce Georgia's frail grasp on stability. So to do events such as the Rose Revolution and the short tenure of successive regimes.

This volatility also folds into Marshall and Cole's (2009) second criterion, self-organization. This concept speaks both to internal stability and to the presence of emergent structures, the governing question being one of increasing social complexity. Despite the aforementioned troubles, Georgia is both geographically and economically poised to be a much stronger player in world affairs. It attracts substantial foreign investment, particularly in agricultural and transportation sectors (United States Agency for International Development 2015).

The third criterion, self-regulation, is largely a measure as to whether sufficient social structures exist to keep the nation coalesced as a whole. Self-regulation also implies a verticality in the structure of society. One indicator might be whether local governance reflects national priorities and practices. Here again, the situation is complicated. If one were to set aside the substantial issues presented with the Abkhazian and South Ossetian separatists, there still exists an instability in purely Georgian affairs. As above, there are substantial issues with transnational crime and various aspects of the criminal justice system. To this point, the United States Agency for International Development (2015) notes that Georgia needs to "improve the implementation of due process and the protection of human rights by: strengthening the legal framework; improving management of justice system institutions; enhancing the capacity of legal professionals; and improving access to justice of marginalized groups."

The last of Marshall and Cole's (2009) criterion is the capacity for self-correction. The prevailing question here is whether higher-order structures exist that are capable of providing limiting functions to lower-order structures. The prevalence of the rule of national law is a good example of this dynamic.

Echoing earlier themes, the Ferris (2014), a governmental watchdog group, states that since 2003, Georgia "has implemented transformative reforms both in political finance regulation and broader anti-corruption that might just make this small country in the Caucasus the anti-corruption comeback of the century." Of course, few things in this region are so simple. As was also previously noted, corruption remains an important barrier to stability and adaptability. In its most recent report, Transparency International (2015, p. 2), also a governmental oversight organization, casts a grimmer prognosis: "Corruption remains a major problem in … Georgia… threatening economic development and political stability as well as the credibility of governments. While some progress has been made in adopting anti-corruption laws… the capture of important institutions by powerful interests is seriously undermining the effective enforcement of these laws."

References

Article 42 of the Constitution. 2012. 15 years for human rights. http://article42.ge/wp-content/uploads/2015/08/15-years-for-human-rights1.pdf (Accessed January 10, 2014).

BBC News. 2012. Regions and territories: Abkhazia. http://news.bbc.co.uk/2/hi/europe/3261059.stm (Accessed January 25, 2014).

BBC News. 2015. South Ossetia profile. http://www.bbc.com/news/world-europe-18269210 (Accessed June 1, 2015).

Bonner, A. 2008. Georgian losses and Russia's gain. *Middle East Policy* 15: 81–90.

Bureau of Democracy, Human Rights, and Labor. 2013. Country reports on human rights practices for 2013: Georgia. http://www.state.gov/j/drl/rls/hrrpt/humanrightsreport/index.htm?year=2013&dlid=220280 (Accessed May 27, 2015).

Bureau of Justice Statistics. 2013a. *Correctional Populations in the United States, 2012.* Washington, DC: Department of Justice. http://www.bjs.gov/content/pub/pdf/cpus12.pdf.

Bureau of Justice Statistics. 2013b. *Mortality in Local Jails and State Prisons, 2000–2011.* Washington, DC: Department of Justice.

Bureau of Justice Statistics. 2014. *Mortality in Local Jails and State Prisons, 2000–2012.* Washington, DC: Department of Justice.

Croft, A. 2013. NATO faults Russia over South Ossetia fence, also chides Georgia. *Reuters News.* http://www.reuters.com/article/2013/06/05/us-nato-georgia-idUSBRE9541DQ20130605 (Accessed January 10, 2014).

European Commission for the Efficiency of Justice. 2013. *Eastern Partnership Enhancing Judicial Reform in the Eastern Partnership Countries.* Strasbourg: Directorate General of Human Rights and Rule of Law.

European Court of Human Rights. 2010. European Convention on Human Rights. http://www.echr.coe.int/ (Accessed January 2, 2014).

Ferris, L. 2014. Snap shot Georgia: From closed-door corruption to open data. The Sunlight Foundation. https://sunlightfoundation.com/blog/2014/09/03/snap-shot-georgia-from-closed-door-corruption-to-open-data/ (Accessed December 12, 2014).

Freedomhouse. 2013. Nations in transit: Georgia. http://www.freedomhouse.org/report/nations-transit/nations-transit-2013#.Ut2d7Cj0A19 (Accessed January 20, 2014).

Fund for Peace. 2013. Failed States Index. http://fsi.fundforpeace.org/rankings-2013-sortable (Accessed June 6, 2014).

Gorgiladze v. Georgia. 2009. European Court of Human Rights. http://www.humanrights.ge/ (Accessed December 15, 2013).

Haro, F. W. 2010. *Georgia and the Caucasus Region.* New York: Nova Science.

Hash-Gonzalez, K. 2012. *Popular Mobilization and Empowerment in Georgia's Rose Revolution.* Lanham, MD: Lexington Books.

Higgins, N. and K. O'Reilly, 2009. The use of force, wars of national liberation and the right to self determination in the South Ossetian conflict. *International Criminal Law Review* 9: 567–583.

Hoddie, M. and C. Hartzell. 2010. *Strengthening Peace in Post-Civil War States: Transforming Spoilers into Stakeholders.* Chicago, IL: University of Chicago Press.

Human Rights Watch. 2009. *World Report 2009.* New York: Human Rights Watch.

International Crisis Group. 2013. Abkhazia: The long road to reconciliation. http://www.crisisgroup.org/en/publication-type/media-releases/2013/europe/abkhazia-the-long-road-to-reconciliation.aspx (Accessed November 14, 2014).

International Society for Human Rights. 2010. Ishr Georgia report 2010: Prison conditions in the Republic of Georgia. http://www.ishr.org/human-rights/ishr-georgia-report-2010-prison-conditions-in-the-republic-of-georgia/ (Accessed March 3, 2014).

Kukhianidze, A. 2006. Smuggling through conflict zones in Georgia and security in the Caucasus. In U. Gori and I. Paparela (Eds) *Invisible Threats: Financial and Information Technology Crimes and National Security*, pp. 117–125, Amsterdam: IOS Press.

Kury, H., M. Shalikashvili, and E. Phutkaradze. 2010. Georgia. In D. Chu and G. Newman (Eds) *Crime and Punishment Around the World*, pp. 71–76, Santa Barbara, CA: ABC-CLIO.

Marshall, M. and B. Cole. 2009. *Global Report 2009: Conflict, Governance and State Fragility*. Severn, MD: Center for Systematic Peace.

Minahan, J. 2013. *Miniature Empires: A Historical Dictionary of the Newly Independent States*. New York: Routledge.

Müller, L. F. 2012. Judicial administration in transitional Eastern countries. In A. Siebert-Fohr (Ed.) *Judicial Independence in Transition*, pp. 937–969, New York: Springer Science & Business Media.

Nan, S. 2010. The roles of conflict resolution scholars in Georgian–Abkhaz and Georgian–South-Ossetian conflict and conflict resolution. *Cambridge Review of International Affairs* 23: 237–258.

Nichol, J. 2011. Security issues and implications for Armenia, Azerbaijan, and Georgia. In A. Laine (Ed.) *Caucasus Region Political, Economic, and Security Issues: Economic, Political and Social Issues of the Caucasus Region*, pp. 1–44, New York: Nova Science.

Nuclear Threat Initiative. 2012. Georgia conducted 15 nuclear smuggling probes since 2005. http://www.nti.org/gsn/article/georgian-conducted-15-nuclear-smuggling-probes-2005-report/ (Accessed January 20, 2014).

Nuclear Threat Initiative. 2014. Georgia country profile. http://www.nti.org/country-profiles/georgia/ (Accessed January 20, 2014).

Organization for Economic Co-Operation and Development. 2011. *Development in Eastern Europe and the South Caucasus: Armenia, Azerbaijan, Georgia, Republic of Moldova and Ukraine*. Paris: OECD Publishing.

Patrick, S. 2011. *Weak Links: Fragile States, Global Threats, and International Security*. Oxford: Oxford University Press.

Phillips, D. 2004. *Stability, Security and Sovereignty in the Republic of Georgia*. New York: Council on Foreign Relations.

Ramseyer, J. M. and E. Rasmusen. 2013. Are Americans more litigious? Some quantitative evidence. In F. H. Buckley (Ed.) *The American Illness: Essays on the Rule of Law*, pp. 43–68, New Haven, CT: Yale University Press.

Ryan, B. 2011. *Caucasus Region Political, Economic, and Security Issues: Caucasus Region: Economic and Political Developments*. New York: Nova Science.

Schneider, F. and D. Enste. 2000. *Shadow Economies Around the World: Size, Causes, and Consequences*. Washington, DC: International Monetary Fund.

Souleimanov, E. 2013. A wonderful country in the Caucasus… A brief history of Russo-Georgian relations in the pre-Soviet era. *International Journal of Russian Studies* 2: 109–118.

Transparency International. 2003–2013a. Global corruption barometer. http://www.transparency.org/research/gcb/ (Accessed January 20, 2014).

Transparency International. 2003–2013b. Corruption perception index. http://cpi.transparency.org/cpi2013/ (January 20, 2014).

Transparency International. 2011. *Georgia National Integrity System Assessment*. Tbilisi: Transparency International Georgia.

Transparency International. 2013. Georgia releases an interim report on the judicial monitoring of high-profile criminal cases. http://www.transparency.ge/en/node/3311 (Accessed December 15, 2013).

Transparency International. 2015. The state of corruption: Armenia, Azerbaijan, Georgia, Moldova and Ukraine. http://www.transparency.org/whatwedo/publication/the_state_of_corruption_armenia_azerbaijan_georgia_moldova_and_ukraine (Accessed July 1, 2015).

Transparency International Georgia. 2010. Refreshing Georgia's courts—trial by jury: More democracy or a face-lift for the judiciary? http://transparency.ge/en (Accessed January 25, 2014).

Transparency International Georgia. 2013. Interim report on judicial monitoring of high profile criminal cases. http://transparency.ge/en (Accessed January 25, 2014).

United Nations Human Rights Council. 2011. Draft report of the working group on universal periodic review: Georgia. http://www.upr-epu.com/ENG/country.php?id=209 (Accessed December 15, 2013).

United States Agency for International Development. 2015. Georgia: Economic growth and trade. http://www.usaid.gov/georgia/economic-growth-and-trade.

Walmsley, R. 2011. *World Prison Population List*, 9th edn. London: International Center for Prison Studies.

Wooden, A. and C. Stefes. 2009. *The Politics of Transition in Central Asia and the Caucasus: Enduring Legacies and Emerging Challenges*. New York: Routledge.

World Bank. 2012. *Fighting Corruption in Public Services*. Herndon, VA: World Bank.

Zürcher, C. 2007. *The Post-Soviet Wars: Rebellion, Ethnic Conflict, and Nationhood in the Caucasus*. New York: New York University Press.

Case Studies: Weak and Failing States

8

When they say we will go and fight the rebels, they lie. They do not actually go to fight the rebels. Instead they raid the villages and the small scattered communities and seize people's possessions.

—Anonymous Former Janjaweed Recruit

The Murahileen chain People as fisherman chains his catch with a rope. The Murahileen take us into servitude in their land; The Murahileen drag us on the surface of our land. But we will not let go of our land. Sudan is our land.

—Verse from a Dinka Song*

While it is tempting to think of state failure as an atomized and local phenomenon, the nations considered in this chapter demonstrate that state fragility often transcends national borders. To this point, the East African nation of Somalia is often presented as the exemplar of state failure. As such, it is incumbent that this volume should make a detailed consideration of the forces leading to Somalia's deep spiral into the abyss of dysfunction. After a brief examination of Somali history, we will examine a few global consequences including issues of sea piracy, human trafficking, and terrorism.

In addition to Somalia, Sudan and the newly independent Republic of South Sudan will be explored in detail. While the nascent independence of South Sudan could have diminished violence and added stability in an otherwise troubled region, the opposite conditions have materialized. The relationship between the two Sudanese states and how it affects other sub-Saharan countries (in particular, neighboring Chad) holds important lessons for our understanding of state fragility.

Somalia

Located in East Africa, Somalia exemplifies what it is to be a collapsed state. A former British protectorate and an Italian colony, Somalia's path has been a tumultuous one since gaining independence and merging with Italian

---

* The Dinka are an ethnic group in modern Sudan who inhabit the Bahr el Ghazal region of the Nile basin, Jonglei, and parts of the former Kordufan Province and Upper Nile.

Somaliland in 1960 (Fitzgerald 2002; Barrington 2009; Central Intelligence Agency 2013a). Somalia's instability as a nation owes in part to decades of fighting between warlords, fierce interclan enmity, and Cold War politics. Moreover, a number of major natural disasters have claimed the lives of approximately half a million citizens.

The early history of the Somali people has been a point of contention among experts. It was once believed that the Somali people originated from the Red Sea's western coast or southern Arabia, but experts now believe that Somalis trace their origins to the Cushite people who inhabited southern Ethiopia (Fitzgerald 2002). Early Somalis set up villages along the Red Sea coastline, which put them in contact with Arab traders (Permanent Mission of the Somali Republic to the United Nations n.d.; Shelley 2013). As a consequence of this early contact, Arab traders introduced the Somali people to Islam, making them among the first in Africa to convert (Shelley 2013). Archeological digs in Somalia's capital city, Mogadishu, revealed evidence of one of the oldest mosques in all of Africa.

It would be difficult to overstate the role that postcolonial legacy plays in the plight of Somalia. The nation has been repeatedly partitioned to meet the needs and demands of various colonizers, which include Ethiopia, Egypt, Great Britain, France, and Italy (Ibrahim 2013; Fitzgerald 2002). Accordingly, the seeds of long-term instability, infighting, and poverty were deeply sown. Interestingly, European interest in Somalia did not fully materialize until the latter part of the nineteenth century. In 1884–1885, the Berlin conference was held by the major world powers with the goal of carving up Africa in ways that would best serve European colonial interests (Njoku 2013; Ismail 2010). Somalia was of particular significance to colonizers due to its location on the Horn of Africa (Njoku 2013). The British wanted control of the coastal regions of Somalia for purely strategic reasons. Of the colonization, the Foreign Office recommended that Great Britain limit themselves "to securing the utmost possible freedom of trade on that [west] coast, yielding to other the territorial responsibilities ... and seeking compensation on the east coast ... where the political future of the country is of real importance to Indian and imperial interests" (Njoku 2013, p. 55). British interest in the west coast of Somalia was driven by a need to supply meat to their naval port in Aden (now Yemen) (Njoku 2013; Ismail 2010). Additionally, the preservation of this port was vital to Great Britain because it provided a means to protect its interests in India (Njoku 2013).

The French were primarily interested in setting up a coaling station along the Red Sea in an effort to bolster their navy and their ties with their other colonies in Indo-China (Fitzgerald 2002). Additionally, the French were eager to take control of any area in Africa that would weaken Great Britain's dominance in the region (Fitzgerald 2002), as well as thwart Great Britain's plans to build a railway. Italy slowly seized control of various parts of Somalia over a period of many years. Beginning with a claim to southern Somalia in 1888, the Italians eventually seized control over all of southern Somalia, but the process took decades (Fitzgerald 2002). Ethiopian Emperor Menelik II also had plans for the region. With regard to his colonial interests in Somalia, Menelik stated, "I have no intentions at all of being an indifferent spectator, if the distant Powers hold on to the idea of dividing up Africa. For the past fourteen centuries, Ethiopia has been an island of Christians in a sea of pagans" (Njoku 2013, p. 54).

In 1897, the British signed a treaty with Ethiopia, which gave Ethiopia control over the Ogaden region (Ismail 2010). As a consequence of competing colonial interests, "by the turn of the century, the Somali Peninsula, one of the most culturally homogeneous regions of Africa, was divided into British Somaliland, French Somaliland, Italian Somaliland, Ethiopian Somaliland (the Ogaden), and what came to be called the Northern Frontier District (NFD) of Kenya" (Fitzgerald 2002, p. 33).

The Somali people did not slip easily into the hands of foreign colonizers. Rather, they staged a series of protracted violent rebellions. Beginning in 1899, the Somali people, led by religious scholar Mahammad Abdille Hasan, waged a war that lasted until 1920 (Nimtz 1980). The war was primarily directed toward Christian education in the country, but the increasing influence and expansion of colonizers also played a large part (Samatar 1992). The war "was the one of the longest and bloodiest anti-Imperial resistance wars in sub-Saharan Africa, and cost the lives of nearly a third of northern Somalia's population, as well as egregious casualties on the Ethiopian and British sides" (Permanent Mission of the Somali Republic to the United Nations n.d.). The war had a lasting impact on the infrastructure of northern Somalia, primarily because Great Britain did not want to invest money in projects that could be destroyed during the conflict (Permanent Mission of the Somali Republic to the United Nations n.d.). When the country was unified in the 1960s, "the North, which had been under British control, lagged far behind the South in terms of economic development, and came to be dominated by the South. The bitterness from this state of affairs would be one of the sparks for the future civil war" (Permanent Mission of the Somali Republic to the United Nations n.d.).

Present-day Somalia occupies a landmass slightly smaller than the U.S. state of Texas and has a population of approximately 11 million people (Shelley 2013). Infant mortality rates and maternal mortality rates are among the highest in the world, ranking number three and number two, respectively (Central Intelligence Agency 2013a). Life expectancy is quite low, with an average male life expectancy of 48 years and an average female life expectancy of 52 years (World Health Organization 2011). Somali people have limited access to safe water supplies and proper sanitation, thus increasing the risk of food and waterborne infections including hepatitis A and E, typhoid fever, and bacterial diarrhea (Central Intelligence Agency 2013a). Death rates from infectious and parasitic diseases are quite high, with an estimated rate of 504.8 per 100,000 of the population (World Health Organization 2011). Of these, tuberculosis, diarrheal diseases, and childhood diseases (e.g., measles and diphtheria) claim the most lives (World Health Organization 2011). According to the Fragile States Index, Somalia has been among the top failed states since the inception of the index in 2005 (Fund for Peace 2015). From 2005 until the present, Somalia has scored higher on every indicia of failure each successive year. The nation ranked number five on the Failed States Index in 2005 and by 2008 Somalia was classified as number one, a position they continue to occupy (Fund for Peace 2013, 2015).

While Somalia is often presented as the epitome of a failed state, some question whether that label is applicable. Little (2003, p. 14) maintains that there never was a government in the true sense in Somalia. Therefore, he poses the question, "Can we really speak of a failed state, if it is questionable whether a meaningful state ever existed?" He notes that the government provided few services and limited infrastructure to the rural population and a formal means of justice was nominal at best (Little 2003).

Abdullahi Cawsey (2014, p. 2) also provides an interesting counterpoint to the common failed/not failed dichotomous presentation of Somali statehood: "This dichotomy—no state and modern state existence—assumes anarchy in all parts of Somalia since there is no central government, which should impose law and order." Tobias Hagmann and Markus Hoehne (2009, p. 53) argue something similar, "Our analysis of sub-national political orders in the Somali-inhabited territories demonstrates that state formation evolves in contradiction to the 'state convergence.'" Scholars working from this perspective often reference the relative quiescence and erstwhile stability of Somaliland and Puntland, which in their estimation owes to the strength of clan-based customary law, as well as other informal social and political mechanisms at play.

According to I. M. Lewis (2002, p. 11), Somali clan–based customary law employs a contractual type of relationship between individuals and between groups. Clan elders use this system of contractual obligation to negotiate disputes. Resolution may be informed by the social, economic, or political context of the agreements. Lewis points out that the focus of this process is the promotion of social cohesion and the resolution of disputes through consensus building—especially among clan elders. Multiple sources also suggest that a primary way that colonialists were able to gain an effective footing in the region was through a systematic undermining of the clan-based customary system (Bereketeab 2012; Cawsey 2014).

Well-reasoned and factually correct as this perspective may be, it is difficult to set aside the inarguable travesties that have taken place in other sectors of the country. That said, if one wishes to parse relative stability or fragility at a substate or regional level, this paradigm might be especially useful. Unfortunately, for present concerns, the larger international community—rightly or wrongly—tends to regard Somalia as the whole commonly depicted on modern maps, not the clan-based substates these scholars highlight.

Looking to postcolonial Somalia, we see that there was (at least superficially) a working government from 1960 to 1969; and in many ways, Somalia was considered a model postcolonial country (Schraeder 1992). Despite an antagonistic relationship between the Isaaq and Daarood clans, the government appeared to be stable throughout the 1960s; political participation among the populace was high and women received the right to vote in 1963 (Center for Justice and Accountability n.d.). The Somali constitution, drafted in 1960 and amended in 1963, contained many of the rights and safeguards that one would expect to find in any free and democratic society. For example, Article 3 of the Somali constitution calls for the equality of all citizens: "All citizens, without distinction of race, national origin, birth, language, religion, sex, economic or social status, or opinion, shall have equal rights and duties before the law" (Child Rights Information Network 2011, p. 6). Part 2 of the constitution outlines citizen rights, which include the right to vote, the right to hold office, the right to travel freely throughout the country, and the right to join political associations. Part 3 outlines fundamental human rights such as the right to life and liberty, freedom of speech, and freedom of assembly. Additionally, the system of constitutional checks and balances appeared to function as intended and the judiciary operated independently (Grote and Röder 2012). It appears that for a short time, Somalia did have a functional and working government. The logical question then becomes, what went wrong? Or as Clarke and Gosende (2003, p. 132) ask, "How could a state with a strongly cohesive cultural history, a common language and religion, and a shared history of nationalism in opposition to former European colonial masters and non-Somali neighbors collapse so completely?"

There are several key points during the 1960s that hint of the civil war and state collapse to come. First, representatives from various Somali clans were denied the opportunity to participate in the construction of the national constitution (Hashim 2007). In essence, "those who were to be governed by the governing instrument had little if any input into it" (Hashim 2007, p. 204). Additionally, the clan-based structure of Somali society did not lend itself well to a political process that called for proportional representation. The two largest clans (the Isaaq and Daarood) were well-represented in the newly formed government; however, members of smaller clans were largely left out of the process. Members of minority clans and subclans formed ever-smaller groups in an effort to gain a modicum of parliamentary representation (Hashim 2007). In the 1969 election, there were 1002 candidates from 62 different political parties vying for 123 seats in the National Assembly (Hashim 2007; Daniels 2012). Clearly, the imposition of the European notion of proportional representation did not fit into the existing social structure of Somali society (Hashim 2007). This would ultimately become an exemplar of one "of postcolonial Africa's worst mismatches between conventional state structures and indigenous customs and institutions" (Kaplan 2012, para. 2).

When Somalia gained independence in 1960, their economy was largely dependent on foreign aid (Clarke and Gosende 2003). Income generation through taxation was simply not an option at the time, given that the urban population was quite small (Mubarak 1996). From 1960 onward, Somalia's budget remained in a deficit (Mubarak 1996), due in part to the escalating violence with neighboring Ethiopia. In an effort to bolster national security, the Somali government diverted much of their limited resources toward military spending (Mohamoud 2006). The Soviet Union, along with several other countries,* provided training and military equipment such as tanks and MiG-21 bombers (Daniels 2012). Somalia's army became the fourth largest army in Africa by 1970 (Mohamoud 2006), but the growth of the military came at an enormous cost, both financially and socially. Between 1960 and 1990, Somalia allocated approximately 20.45% of the national budget to military spending each year (Osman 2007). High military spending necessitated the diversion of much-needed funds for social programs and infrastructure development. Additionally, the ease with which the Somali government was able to obtain international funding (especially from the Soviet Union) meant "few [governmental officials] gave much consideration to the productive sectors of the economy or to the plight of the average Somali" (Lyons and Samatar 1995, p. 12). Budgetary problems were compounded when a drought from 1963 to 1964 devastated livestock and another drought ravaged the land again in 1969 (Mubarak 1996).

In addition to questionable spending in the military sector, governmental corruption became a serious problem in the fledgling country. In the 1969 election, candidates brazenly offered cash for votes, in some cases as much as £15,000† (Daniels 2012). It is also estimated that from January to October 1969, the prime minister spent nearly £500,000,‡ all of which was the public's money, to buy support on key issues (Daniels 2012). As Jamil Mubarak (1996, p. 11) notes, "the central government was weak and public institutions were suffering from 'excessive democracy' and anarchy. Public confidence in state institutions declined and discontent with the political process and performance of the elected officials grew." Thus, strained relationships between clans, governmental corruption, and a declining economy provided fertile

---

* Italy, France, West Germany, and the United Kingdom also provided support, but their collective contribution was much less than that of the Soviet Union (Daniels 2012).
† This is equivalent to U.S.$23,526 today.
‡ £500,000 is roughly equivalent to U.S.$784,200 today.

ground for the 1969 coup. The events of 1969 provided the first indications that Somalia was on the path toward collapse (Osman 2007).

By the end of the 1960s, it became clear that Somalia's government "had become a travesty, an elaborate, rarefied game with little relevance to the daily challenges facing the population" (Lyons and Samatar 1995, p. 14). The catalyst for governmental change came on October 15, 1969, when President Abdirashiid Ali Shermaake was assassinated by one of his bodyguards (Clarke and Gosende 2003; Barrington 2009). Plans were immediately put in place to install a new president from the same clan as Shermaake (Metz 1992).* However, the prevailing view of many citizens, including the military, was that the existing government was ineffectual (Metz 1992). Just six days after the assassination, the military took control of the government in a bloodless coup. General Siad Barre assumed leadership of the government, organizing his regime into the Supreme Revolutionary Council (SRC) (Lyons and Samatar 1995; Nalbandov 2009). Initially, the populace welcomed the SRC and believed that they would repair the damage caused by the previous Parliament and ultimately fix the nation (Lyons and Samatar 1995; Osman 2007). However, this optimism was short-lived. Following the government takeover, "Somalia's constitution was suspended, the country's 86 political parties were banned, and, promising an end to corruption, Siad Biarre declared himself chairman of a twenty-five member Revolutionary Council" (Clarke and Gosende 2003, p. 134). Barre also set out to abolish "clanism" in an effort to forge one national identity (Freedomhouse 1994). To accomplish this, Barre outlawed clan names and clan political parties and established a one-party system (Freedomhouse 1994). A report prepared for the World Bank (Gajraj et al. 2005, p. 10) casts this effort as being motivated by anything but societal unification: "the leadership skillfully manipulated and politicized clan identity over two decades of divide-and-rule politics, leaving a legacy of deep clan divisions and grievances." The predictable result was a deepening of divisions between clans, thereby fractionalizing the country further (Schlee and Shongolo 2012). By the mid-1970s, it became clear that much like other military dictators who seize power through coups, Barre was not willing to cede power and return Somalia to a democratic nation (Lyons and Samatar 1995). The all-too-familiar situation was one where the Barre government was "oppressive and exploitative" and where interclan factionalism was used by "political leaders to dominate others, monopolize state resources, and appropriate valuable land and other assets" (Gajraj et al. 2005, p. 10).

A variety of reasons have been put forth to explain the collapse of Somalia (e.g., Barre's policies, clan divisions, and postcolonial legacy). We contend

* The Darood.

that myriad forces have coalesced to both cause and perpetuate failure in Somalia. In the first instance, there is a disjuncture between the clan-based organizational structure of Somali society and more Western notions of representative democracy (Gajraj et al. 2005). In the second, Somalia, owing to its geographically important location on the Horn of Africa, was a locus of Cold War proxy battles (Lefebvre 1991; Mantzikos 2010). In terms of Somali society more generally, we see a nation swirling in a perpetual state of anomic chaos, as well as a place of deep social disorganization, rampant poverty, and sustained post-Cold War exploitative intrusion by outside interests.

We turn our attention first to the clan-based social structure. As Paolo Tripodi (1999) notes, clanism runs deep in the Somali culture with the vast majority of the Somali population identifying with one of the four major clans or subclans. Approximately 25% of the population identify with the Hawiya or one of its subclans (Abgal, Ajuran, Degodia, Habr Gedir, Hawadle, and Murosade); 22% of the population identify as part of the Isaaq clan (subclans include Eidagalla, Habr Awai, Habra Tolijaala, and Habr Yunis); 20% of the population are members of the Daarood clan (comprising the Dolbohanta, Majertain, Marehan, Ogaden, and Warsangeli subclans); and 17% of the population identify with the Rahanwein clan (Central Intelligence Agency 2013a). The remaining 16% of the population identifies with the Digil, Dir (Gadabursi and Issa subclans), or as an ethnic minority (Central Intelligence Agency 2013a).

Clans are an especially important part of Somalia's culture, as they are considered to be both the main social and political institution (Clarke and Gosende 2003). A clan-based system is much more cohesive than Western political systems, which are organized according to political party affiliation (Clarke and Gosende 2003). In democratic societies, a person can change his or her political affiliation without modifying or fundamentally changing his or her identity. Clan affiliation is established at birth and according to primordial theory, "cannot be changed, and ... individual choices are permanently defined by these identities" (Osman 2007, p. 48). Though clans were ostensibly eliminated following Barre's rise to power, he deepened clan rivalries in an effort to consolidate his power. As above, Barre employed "a calculated policy of using clan sentiment to exacerbate competition, conflict, and grudges among Somalis" (Kapteijns 2013, p. 2).

A particularly revealing example of Barre's strategic use of clan divisions can be seen in his control of the food supply in ways that would benefit his clan. A series of laws were put in place during the 1970s to reduce food production throughout the country, but the 1975 Land Reform Act proved to be the most detrimental (Osman 2007). In accordance with the act, all land resources became the property of the government and farmers only had "rights as part of government-sponsored cooperatives and associations, and were forced to move from their traditional land to more marginal land with open access" (Suttie et al. 2005, p. 41). As part of the law, all land was required to be registered with the government and farmers were given 50-year leases (McAuslan 1988; Suttie et al. 2005). However, in 1975, most farmland was not legally leased (Suttie et al. 2005); instead, farmers continued to follow tradition and pass their farmland from one generation to the next (Osman 2007). This practice continued because farmers were unaware that failure to register land could be punishable by large fines (Osman 2007) or land seizure (McAuslan 1988). Much of the seized land* was then given to members of Barre's clan (Osman 2007). While most clans suffered under Barre's various anticlan policies, the Isaaq clan was especially targeted. Between May 1988 and January 1990, an estimated 50,000–60,000 members of the Isaaq clan were killed by the Barre government (Freedomhouse 1994).

In 1991, members of the Hawiye rebel group, the United Somali Congress (USC), removed Barre from power and installed Ali Mahdi as the interim president (Freedomhouse 1994). Following the USC takeover, "clan cleansing" (i.e., genocide) began (Kapteijns 2013). In 1991, the Daarood clan was identified as an enemy of Somalia and its members (even those who had not benefited from the Barre regime) were either killed or displaced (Kapteijns 2013). The USC genocide "pitted people against each other on the basis of a particular construction of clan identity: the groups associated with the genealogical construct of Daarood-ness were equated with the hated out-going military regime" (Kapteijns 2013, p. 4).

To be "successful," genocides depend on scapegoating or "othering" a group that is considered to be a threat. According to Newbury (1998, p. 77), when officials want to strengthen their power base, often they will link the difficulties of the people to a "scapegoat: a group to serve as target. With that in mind, it becomes possible to mobilize people on such a scale that the group redefines its own morality. For genocide, if 'everyone' from one group is involved, then killing others becomes not only acceptable but necessary." While Newbury was referring specifically to the 1994 Rwandan genocide, his commentary is equally applicable to the Somali clan cleansing.

On May 17, 1991, the Somali National Movement (composed primarily of members of the Isaaq clan) announced that they were seceding from Somalia and declared sovereignty in the northern part of Somalia (renamed Somaliland Republic) (Schraeder 1992). This move further deepened tensions between the Isaaq and Hawiye clans and intensified violent clashes. The international community has never recognized the Somaliland Republic as an independent state.

In some stead this is a lamentable situation. By most accounts, Somaliland has managed the most difficult of postcolonial feats: democracy. To be sure,

---

* In the event that farmers could not pay the fine (which, in most cases they could not), their farmland would be seized by the government.

the democracy achieved in Somaliland is one balanced on the head of a pin. As many sources suggest, Somaliland should not work. The Barre-era policy of "kill all but the crows"* left the region with little in the way of infrastructure or much else. Journalist Simon Allison (2015) observes, "It was also awash with weapons and militias, and driven by all the traditional fault lines: there were clan rivalries, land disputes, religious and ideological tensions," all of which existed in the shadow of the spiraling Barre regime and related civil war.

Even so, it has managed a tenuous existence for almost a quarter of a century. It has done so through an interesting mix of liberal democracy and traditional clan-based authority. Allison (2015) notes that Somaliland's overburdened court system functions as well as it does because clan structures step in to resolve most low-level criminal matters. Therein lies a somewhat paradoxical danger. Because the government leans heavily on the "values of compromise, consensus-building and egalitarianism, which… are clan traditions," the government also tends to be "stuffed with officials who are there because they have the right bloodline rather than the right qualifications" (Allison 2015).

There is also another perilous development in Somaliland: the rise of Wahhabism, an ultra-orthodox sect of Sunni Islam (BBC News 2012). The people of Somaliland have traditionally followed the relatively moderate Shafi'i school of Sunni Islam, but with growing Sufi influences, Wahhabism has begun to gain dominance. The goal of Wahhabism is the creation of an Islamic state. Necessarily, this orthodoxy tends to attract a certain radical ardor. To put the matter in perspective, Al-Qaeda is rooted in Wahhabism. Moreover, Al-Shabaab and the Islamic State are of Wahhabist origin. The most visible state sponsor of this sect is Saudi Arabia. According to Allison (2015), the Saudis have spent "billions of dollars on spreading Wahhabi dogma throughout the Islamic World—including in Somaliland." The inherent danger of this rising movement comes in its opposition to the region's secular government and Western democratic influences. Whether Somaliland, Puntland, or any other Somali region eventually manages to meaningfully separate itself from the larger morass, one fact remains: the broader outside world sees one contiguous Somalia; and that unitary body is the epitome of state collapse.

The combined forces of governmental corruption, citizen repression, and overwhelming violence have defined Somalia for decades, but the early 1990s is generally regarded as the period in which the nation had "officially" failed. The protracted civil war since 1988 claimed the lives of nearly 700,000 people and displaced an additional three million (Samatar et al. 2010). Many issues of international consequence have emerged both during and after the

* "Kill all but the crows," was an order given by the Somali warlord General Ahmed Warsame in 1988 at the siege of Hargeisa.

collapse of Somalia, but perhaps the most pressing concerns regard human trafficking, sea piracy, and terrorism.

Human Trafficking

Somalia serves as a primary origin country for trafficked persons (McCabe and Manian 2010), as well as a transit and destination country (Meehan 2010; U.S. Department of State 2012). Women and children are primarily trafficked from Somalia for sex purposes or forced labor (U.S. Department of State 2012). Destination areas include countries in the Middle East, Europe, within Somalia, and the rest of Africa (McCabe and Manian 2010). Inside Somalia, victims are typically trafficked from the southern and central regions of the country to northern regions (U.S. Department of State 2012).

The divisive nature of clan relationships is a major driving force behind trafficking within the country (U.S. Department of State 2012). Somali Bantus and Midgaan represent two groups that are often viewed as inferior by other clans. This putative inferiority makes them particularly targeted for forced labor and servitude by more dominant Somali clans (U.S. Department of State 2012). Children represent an especially vulnerable population because there is no governmental system to register births. As a consequence, "it is easier for them to be moved across borders or even for adults to be smuggled outside of Somalia" (McCabe and Manian 2010, p. 17). As mentioned in Chapter 6, the U.S. Department of State compiles an annual list of countries and ranks them according to their degree of compliance with the minimum standards set forth in the Trafficking Victims Protection Act (TVPA). For the 11th consecutive year, Somalia has been placed in the "special case" category owing to the lack of a functioning government since 1991 (U.S. Department of State 2012). With high levels of violence and little centralized government, there is no formal mechanism to attenuate human trafficking or even investigate cases thereof (U.S. Department of State 2012).

It should come as no surprise that reliable data on the extent of human trafficking in Somalia are almost nonexistent, but there is strong evidence to suggest that the problem is widespread (U.S. Department of State 2012). Violence and famine have led to extensive population displacement. Tens of thousands of people have been uprooted by droughts and protracted violence from armed groups (at times these groups have blocked humanitarian aid) (Human Rights Watch 2013a). Many of these refugees have sought relief in internally displaced person camps or in the coastal region of Somalia (U.S. Department of State 2012). An estimated 75,000 internally displaced persons arrived in Mogadishu in 2011 (Human Rights Watch 2013a).

As stated in Chapter 5, traffickers prey on the desire of people (especially displaced persons) to leave the country. As an enticement, they will often make false promises of employment in other countries (U.S. Department of State 2012).* Employment agencies sometimes participate in the process by "targeting individuals desiring to migrate to the Gulf States for employment" (U.S. Department of State 2012, p. 379). As described in Chapter 5, once they are in the possession of traffickers, women and children (particularly girls) are generally subjected to forced sexual servitude in neighboring African nations, Europe, and the Middle East. Somali men are usually forced to work as herdsmen or perform other menial tasks (Meehan 2010; U.S. Department of State 2012). Men trafficked from Cambodia to Somalia are often forced to work on fishing boats off the coast of Somalia (Meehan 2010).

Additionally, there have been reports of children as young as eight years old being abducted by the terrorist group, Al-Shabaab, to become child soldiers (U.S. Department of Labor 2012). Again, reliable data are difficult to obtain, but it is estimated that approximately 2000 children were abducted for military training in 2010 (U.S. Department of State 2012). Child soldiers are forced to perform a variety of terrorist acts including planting roadside bombs and suicide bombing (U.S. Department of State 2012).

In a May 2014 report, the United Nations Office of the Special Representative of the Secretary-General for Children and Armed Conflict documented the recruitment and use of 1293 children, including by Al-Shabaab, the Somali National Army (and allied militia), as well as Ahl al-Sunna wal-Jama'a (ASWJ), the Somaliland Armed Forces, and various other armed groups (United Nations 2014). In the same document, the United Nations also notes that the national army and allied militias were reportedly responsible for 334 child casualties. Child casualties mainly resulted from "crossfire during clashes and indiscriminate shelling." The United Nations (2014) also records the death of 30 children and the injury of 51 others in incidents involving improvised explosive devices.

In early 2015, there was a faint glimmer of hope for child welfare in Somalia. In January, the government in Mogadishu became signatories to the United Nations Convention on the Rights of the Child (CRC). On the occasion, Anthony Lake, executive director of the UN Children's Fund (UNICEF), welcomed the news, "The central message of the Convention is that every child deserves a fair start in life. What can be more important

---

* Trafficking is not the only concern for internally displaced persons as violence is especially prevalent in many of the placement camps. Human Rights Watch (2013a) provides a detailed discussion of violence in displacement camps in their report, "Hostages of the Gatekeepers: Abuses against Internally Displaced Persons in Mogadishu, Somalia."

than that?" (United Nations News Centre 2015). How this symbolic move translates into actual child welfare improvements is yet to be determined, but it stands as an arguably positive sign.

Just to put the matter in a global perspective, the CRC was adopted by the General Assembly in 1989. Since then it has been ratified by 195 countries, making it the most widely ratified international human rights treaty in history. As of today, only two countries have yet to ratify the landmark treaty—South Sudan and the United States (United Nations News Centre 2015).

Sea Piracy

Sea piracy is certainly not a new phenomenon, as it likely emerged at the same time that sea trading began (Monno 2012). While there is no documentation available to pinpoint its exact beginnings, archeologists have uncovered clay tablets from 1350 BC that depict acts of piracy (Monno 2012). While we may be tempted to think of sea piracy as a relic of the past or as fodder for entertainment (i.e., Disney's *Pirates of the Caribbean*), this serious and often deadly crime is still prevalent today.

While the Horn of Africa has long been the locus of piracy, modern piracy in the area has a rather unusual origin. Rather than just the modus of privateers, some sources trace modern Somali piracy to local fisherman besieged by competition from larger foreign commercial fishing fleets working what the Somalis perceived as their rightful domain. Beyond mere encroachment, foreign fleets also dumped toxic waste in the fishing waters (Waldo 2009). While the illegal fishing and dumping was harmful to local fishermen, it proved a huge boon to the foreign fleets. According to the High Seas Task Force (2006), $4–9 billion is generated from this illegal activity with encroachment in sub-Saharan Africa's waters amounting to about $1 billion.

That foreign interests felt free to abuse the Somali coast is consistent with the geopolitical history of the region. Owing to its previously discussed importance in shipping, the Horn of Africa was yet one more victim of the Cold War (Waldo 2009; Schwab 1978). According to Schraeder (1992, p. 571), post-World War II U.S. foreign policy toward the Horn of Africa was "guided by a series of Cold War rationales that viewed the region as a means for solving non-African problems." Schraeder (1992, p. 571) goes on to state that Western interests did not regard countries and peoples of the region as having their own intrinsic value but "rather, as a means of preventing the further advances of Soviet communism."

In a rather precarious game of shifting alliances, the mid-century fates of Somalia and Ethiopia exemplify all that was wrong with Cold War politics. The United States wanted to build third-world stopgaps against socialist expansion. This first led to American financial and military support of Haile Selassie in Ethiopia. Playing both sides of the table, U.S. President John F.

Kennedy attempted to forge alliances with Somalia as well (Lefebvre 1998). The Soviet bloc pursued a similar strategy by offering Somalia $30 million in military aid (Lefebvre, 1998). In 1963, a Russian military aid agreement was established, including the training and arming of Somalia's army.

This all changed in the wake of the 1974–1977 Ethiopian revolution that produced a Soviet-backed regime headed by Mengistu Haile Mariam (Schraeder 1992). The Ethiopian revolution also propelled a shift in U.S.-Somalia relations, support of the Siad Barre regime in particular. This owed to the fact that Washington regarded Somalia as an important "access country from which the United States could counter militarily any perceived Soviet threat to Middle Eastern oil fields" (Schraeder 1992, p. 571). Building on the long-standing enmity between Somalia and Ethiopia, the United States (principally through Saudi Arabia) began to provide Somalia with arms. For their part, Ethiopia was assisted by the Soviet Union and Cuba (Lefebvre 1998). After the 1991 fall of the Soviet Union, the dynamic changed markedly.

With the withdrawal of Cold War–driven interests, Somalia's fortunes took a decidedly poor turn. In 1992, the government of Siyad Barre coupled with the disintegration of the Somali Navy and police coastguard services provided a significant element necessary for state failure (Rozoff 2009; Waldo 2009). Nomadic people were robbed of their livestock (and livelihoods), and in the wake of the 1974 and 1986 droughts, were resettled along the extensive Somali coast. These groups developed into inshore fishing communities (Waldo 2009). This might have been a practical and sustainable transition, save for the aforementioned epidemic of foreign poaching and pollution, which spurred the rise of piracy.

As to the dumping itself, a United Nations Environmental Program (2006) report confirmed that industrialized nations have been illegally disposing of hazardous waste in Somali territorial waters since the outbreak of the Somali civil war. The main reason is cost. In 2009, it cost a European country around $2.50 per ton to dump its toxic waste in Somalia, compared with $1000 per ton to legally dispose of it in Europe (Ewing 2008). Taking advantage of the fact that there was no meaningful governmental interdiction mechanism in place to stop them, the practice boomed.

Ahmedou Ould-Abdallah, the United Nations envoy for Somalia, observes, "There is no government control … there are few people with high moral ground … people in high positions are being paid off, but because of the fragility of the TFG [Transitional Federal Government], some of these companies now no longer ask the authorities—they simply dump their waste and leave" (Ewing 2008). This in turn further imperiled the livelihood of Somali fishermen (Waldo 2009). When fishermen first attempted to intervene they were repulsed, often violently, by the encroachers. In response, they started arming themselves. The encroachers then began carrying more sophisticated weapons to overpower the fishermen. The fishermen responded in kind. What emerged was a cycle whereby fishermen would attack or reciprocate against the foreign vessels. They soon discovered that they could turn defense and retribution into profit, and thus began the modern wave of Somali piracy (Waldo 2009).

The United Nations Convention on the Law of the Sea (UNCLOS) defines piracy as:

> a. Any illegal acts of violence or detention, or any act of depredation, committed for private ends by the crew or the passengers of a private ship or a private aircraft, and directed:
>   i. On the high seas, against another ship or aircraft, or against persons or property on board such ship or aircraft;
>   ii. Against a ship, aircraft, persons or property in a place outside the jurisdiction of any State;
> b. Any act of voluntary participation in the operation of a ship or of an aircraft with knowledge of facts making it a pirate ship or aircraft;
> c. Any act of inciting or of intentionally facilitating an act described in subparagraph (a) or (b). (United Nations Convention on the Law of the Sea (UNCLOS) 1982, Article 101)

Somali piracy has received extensive media attention in recent years and has emerged as an especially problematic issue for the international community. According to Samatar et al. (2010), there are four necessary conditions that must be in place for piracy to thrive: (1) favorable geographic features; (2) the presence of ungoverned spaces; (3) a lack of effective law enforcement/government or a cultural environment that is unwilling to combat piracy; and (4) the rewards need to be high and the risks relatively low. Somalia meets all of these criteria. Notably, the second and third can be directly linked to state failure (Wilson 2009). Indeed, the failure of the state was necessary to pave the way toward piracy (Samatar et al. 2010) because as criminological research has revealed, "weakened, failed or states in conflict provide criminogenic environments that further facilitate opportunistic criminality due to the resultant socially disorganized communities and anomic conditions" (Rothe and Collins 2010, p. 333).

Somali sea piracy has been on the rise since 2008, with the West Indian Ocean and the Gulf of Aden being especially targeted (Geib and Petrig 2011; Rothe and Collins 2011; Figliomeni 2012; Ece 2012). For years, the violence associated with the failure of Somalia was largely contained within Africa. As such, the international community did not feel the full effect of governmental collapse for at least a decade. However, sea piracy brought Somalia's state failure to the attention of the international community. As Geib and Petrig (2011, p. 1) note, "ignoring state failure is not an option. Sooner or later the absence of effective governmental control will lead to intolerable problems, forcing the international community to act."

This is precisely what has happened. The international community has been forced to act because 90% of goods and resources moving from the Red Sea to the Gulf of Aden and beyond must travel through narrow shipping lanes en route to their destinations (Tuerk 2012; Ece 2012). In the Gulf of Aden alone, it is estimated that 22,000 ships must navigate this chokepoint each year while carrying nearly 8% of the world's traded goods and 12% of the world's petroleum (Chalk 2008, 2010; Geib and Petrig 2011).

Piracy represents a grave threat to vessels throughout the region. According to the International Maritime Organization (2012), 341 piracy incidents were reported to the organization in 2012, representing a decrease from the 544 incidents that were reported in 2011. The majority of these incidents (99) were committed by Somali pirates, followed closely by attacks in the South China Sea (90) (International Maritime Organization 2012). Governmental improvements, such as the ability to oust pirates from certain areas, have been partially attributed to the decline in attacks (Oceans Beyond Piracy 2013). While these numbers appear to demonstrate a decline in piracy, they only tell part of the story.

According to Oceans Beyond Piracy (2013) and the International Maritime Organization (2012), the overall rate of Somali pirate attacks has decreased in recent years, but the success rate has improved. In 2011, Somali pirates attacked approximately 286 ships, but only successfully hijacked 33 ships, representing a success rate of 11.54% (International Maritime Organization 2012). Of the 99 Somali pirate attacks in 2012, 13 ships were successfully hijacked, thus increasing the success rate to 13.13% (International Maritime Organization 2012). These figures should be interpreted with caution, as there appears to be significant underreporting of incidents to international organizations (Huggins and Kane-Hartnett 2013). As Chalk (2008) observes, only about half of all pirate attacks are reported to the proper authorities.

Generally, there are three types of piracy, ranging from low risk to high risk: (1) armed robbery of anchored ships or ships that are preparing to anchor; (2) armed robbery of ships in open territorial waters (usually in very narrow passes)*; and (3) the "phantom ship" phenomenon (Chalk 2008; Ece 2012). With the exception of the phantom ship phenomenon (which will be discussed later in the chapter), most pirate attacks are conducted for the purpose of kidnapping crewmembers and holding both the ship and crew for ransom (Rothe and Collins 2011). For example, in November 2011, Somali

---

* These attacks tend to be more sophisticated than type one. They typically involve a well-armed mother ship and the armed robbery is usually preceded by armed conflict, which can be deadly (Ece 2012).

pirates released the M/T *Gemini** and 21[†] crewmembers in exchange for a multimillion-dollar ransom (Maritime Bulletin 2013). It is estimated that between 2005 and 2012, Somali pirates were paid between $339 and $413 million in the form of ransoms, making piracy an extremely lucrative enterprise (Yikona 2013).

The duration of captivity for some hostages is especially long, with more than half of the hostages held in captivity for more than two years (Oceans Beyond Piracy 2013). In the case of the M/T *Gemini*, the ship and crewmembers were held captive for 19 months (Maritime Bulletin 2013). Ransoms tend to increase the longer a ship and its crewmembers are held, creating a greater financial reward for pirates and a more dangerous situation for hostages (Yikona 2013). Hostages held for long periods of time are generally considered to be at high risk. Oceans Beyond Piracy (2013) classifies hostages as high risk if two of the following conditions are in place: (1) being held hostage for more than one year; (2) being held hostage on land; (3) failure of ship owners or insurance companies to negotiate for release; and (4) being kidnapped while on land.

The human cost of piracy is high. Of the 23 vessels captured and released between 2010 and 2011, all of the hostages interviewed reported threats of violence or psychological abuse or both; half of the hostages reported some type of physical abuse (punched, slapped, etc.); and 10% reported extreme physical abuse (e.g., having fingernails pulled out with pliers) (Oceans Beyond Piracy 2013). The treatment of hostages appeared to worsen between 2012 and 2013 as reports from hostages indicated that all interviewed had suffered threats of abuse, all reported actual physical abuse, and 15% reported extreme physical abuse (Oceans Beyond Piracy 2013).

Beyond the grim human toll, there are profound economic consequences associated with Somali piracy. The situation is so bad that many shipping companies have begun to take the longer route through the Cape of Good Hope off the coast of South Africa to avoid encounters (Sheikh 2009). Other business sectors also bear the brunt of piracy. For ships travelling through the region, insurance premiums have become extremely high. This has led to a bourgeoning industry of private military contractors hired out to accompany ships and their cargo as they pass through the Gulf of Aden (Sheikh 2009).

When piracy takes the form of the phantom ship, the process is much more complicated than with ransom negations. Chalk (2008, p. 6) describes a

---

* At the time of capture, *Gemini* was transporting 28,000 tons of crude palm oil to Indonesia (Maritime Bulletin 2013).

[†] Initially, the pirates did not release four South Korean crewmembers because they planned to obtain additional ransom money from the South Korean government (Maritime Bulletin 2013). The South Korean government paid an undisclosed amount of money to the pirates in exchange for the crewmembers.

typical scenario, "a vessel is first seized and its cargo offloaded into lighters at sea. The ships are then renamed and reregistered under flags of convenience (FoCs) and issued with false documentation to enable them to take on fresh payloads. The new cargo, which is never delivered to its intended destination, is taken to a designated port where it is sold to a buyer who is often a willing participant in the venture."

With an estimated loss of between $13 and $16 billion each year, the monetary costs associated with sea piracy are enormous. The staggering cost of sea piracy presents a serious problem for the international community, but there is also substantial evidence that the profits from sea piracy are being used to fund conflicts within Somalia (Tuerk 2012). While the majority of the funds are used to pay investors, provide salaries for pirates, laundered through various businesses, or transported across the porous borders between Somalia and bordering countries, some of the money is reinvested within Somalia (Yikona 2013). Through interviews with 30 Somali pirates, Yikona (2013) found that most pirate financiers (19) utilized their illicit proceeds to develop militias or other avenues of gaining political power*; financing legitimate businesses such as hotels or restaurants was the second-most common form of monetary investment (with 18 financiers reportedly engaging in these endeavors); lastly, investment in the transportation business was the third-most commonly reported type of spending (with an estimated 15 financiers believed to be participating in this financial activity). Investment in the transportation industry typically takes the form of "renting" boats that will be used in pirate attacks, but there are reports of investments being made in the trucking industry (Yikona 2013).

The relationship between state failure and piracy can be viewed as a feedback loop, wherein a lack of governmental control leads to illicit economies (such as the pirate economy) and the funds obtained through piracy help fund efforts to further destabilize the region and promulgate violence (Tuerk 2012). Indeed, it is troubling that many piracy financiers hold considerable assets throughout Somalia, "raising concerns over a criminal influence on the economy especially at a time when peace and security start returning to Somalia, further allowing economic growth to develop" (Yikona 2013, p. 60). Combating piracy in Somalia is extremely costly and the funds that are used to deter and catch pirates often divert much-needed resources away from other areas that might be more beneficial for the nation as a whole. For example, the cost to send one frigate to the Gulf of Aden for six months could fund salaries for nearly 100,000 police officers for six months (Chalk 2010). The international community has spent an enormous amount of money to

* According to Yikona (2013, p. 64), "the networks investing the most in militias are reportedly located in Puntland, where individual cases of operational cooperation between pirate financiers and Al-Shabaab were reported to the team."

combat piracy at sea,* but most experts contend that a land-based approach designed to address the underlying social conditions that continue to promote piracy is a much more promising approach (Chalk 2010). In other words, piracy is merely symptomatic of the larger problem of failure; therefore, international efforts that focus mainly on acts of piracy serve only as Band-Aids for the larger problem of failure (Rothe and Collins 2011). Until state failure is fully addressed, the international community will continue to bear the financial burden of sea piracy.

Terrorism

With the collapse of the Somali government, it is not surprising that a number of internal terrorist groups have emerged inside its borders. Al-Shabaab ("The Youth"), a terrorist group with links to Al-Qaeda, has had considerable involvement in recent violence throughout Somalia (Masters 2013). In just two years, Al-Shabaab went from a relatively unknown group to a major international terrorist group (Gartenstein-Ross 2009). The group has its roots in Al-Ittihad Al-Islami (AIAI), a group partially funded by Al-Qaeda and Osama bin Laden. Following the coup that removed Siad Barre from power, AIAI had plans to set up an Islamic state in Somalia (Masters 2013). After suffering heavy losses during confrontations with Ethiopia, AIAI formed the Islamic Courts Union (ICU) and Al-Shabaab emerged as the militant wing of the ICU (Davis 2010).

The ICU fought various warlords for control of Somalia's capital city, Mogadishu, and by June 2006 they had gained complete control (Gartenstein-Ross 2009; Masters 2013). By October 2006, the ICU was in control of key cities throughout Somalia and had set their sights on Baidoa, one of the last strongholds of the Somali transitional federal government (TFG) (Gartenstein-Ross 2009). The previous ICU victories stoked fears from neighboring Ethiopia that violence might spill over the border, prompting the Ethiopian government to respond with military force (Masters 2013). During the short war, Ethiopian forces, along with support from the U.S. military, defeated the ICU and drove them out of Mogadishu and into neighboring Eritrea (Gartenstein-Ross 2009; National Counterterrorism Center 2013). However, Al-Shabaab remained in Somalia, where they took over the resistance movement and continued recruiting new members (Dagne 2011b).

Recruiting efforts were wildly successful because as Wise (2011) points out, Al-Shabaab was able to capitalize on anti-Ethiopian sentiments after

---

* For example, in 2009, a naval task force headed by the European Union's "Operation Antalanta," placed ships on patrol in or near the Gulf of Aden. These included both unilateral deployments and coalition forces operating under the auspices of the United States' Combined Task Force 151 and NATO's Operation Ocean Shield. The purpose of these operations was to lure out and interdict Somali pirates (Chalk 2010).

the Ethiopian victory in Mogadishu. The leadership of the organization was largely secretive and many of the nationalist volunteers were unaware of Al-Shabaab's overarching objectives (Dagne 2011b). Also during this time, Al-Shabaab continued to radicalize and began to "employ militant 'crusader' language to exploit and evoke primitive fears of powerful outsiders, claiming the TFG relied entirely on protection provided by foreign infidels" (Ibrahim 2013, p. 284). The Ethiopian invasion may have been successful at driving fundamentalist ICU forces out of the capital, but it also helped transform Al-Shabaab from a largely obscure Islamic organization to one of the most powerful terrorist groups in Somalia (Wise 2011).

By 2008, Al-Shabaab had thousands of fighters and had carried out numerous terrorist attacks, both in Somalia and in other African nations (Masters 2013). Before establishing close ties with Al-Qaeda, Al-Shabaab did not have a central mission; however, most members of Al-Shabaab believed that their primary enemy was the TFG, thus many of their attacks directly targeted the government. The group claimed responsibility for bombing various targets in Mogadishu, as well as the central and northern regions of Somalia (National Counterterrorism Center 2013). It is also believed that Al-Shabaab was responsible "for a wave of five coordinated suicide car bombings in October 2008 that simultaneously hit targets in two cities in northern Somalia, killing at least 26 people, including five bombers, and injuring 29 others" (National Counterterrorism Center 2013, para. 2).

The group received international attention in 2011 when they blocked foreign aid workers from delivering food, a move that cost the lives of tens of thousands of people, including 29,000 children (Dorell 2011; National Counterterrorism Center 2013). There have been some reports that humanitarian agencies paid Al-Shabaab as much as $10,000 in "taxes" to gain access to areas where aid was critically needed (Saul 2014). The following year, Al-Shabaab banned the International Red Cross Committee from distributing supplies, claiming that the food provided was spoiled and not fit for human consumption (Saul 2014).

After allying with Al-Qaeda,* the groups' ideology purportedly became more aligned with Al-Qaeda's globalized war against the West. As a consequence, Al-Shabaab's attacks were no longer exclusively directed toward internal targets (Wise 2011; National Counterterrorism Center 2013). For example, in 2010, Al-Shabaab was responsible for bombings in Uganda that killed 76 people and injured more than 80 people (Dagne 2011a). Despite carrying out attacks outside Somalia, some question whether Al-Shabaab is truly committed to a more globalized mission of terror. It is probably more appropriate to describe Al-Shabaab as a "glocal" terrorist organization. The concept

---

* The two groups did not officially merge until February 2012 (National Counterterrorism Center 2013).

of "glocalization" is primarily associated with the increasingly entwined spheres of local issues and global dynamics (Toft et al. 2011). As Toft et al. (2011, p. 122) observe, "today there exists a vast network of local groups with global ties that share ideas, resources, and personnel to wage their terrorist campaigns." Al-Shabaab clearly fits within this characterization, as it is affiliated with Al-Qaeda, but most of their efforts are still directed inside Somalia.

Ideological issues notwithstanding, Al-Shabaab's tactics have changed since their alignment with Al-Qaeda. The war waged against the TFG was largely based on guerilla tactics; however, Al-Shabaab is increasingly making use of incendiary devices and suicide bombings, the preferred attack methods of Al-Qaeda (Wise 2011). Though Al-Shabaab was driven out of Mogadishu in August 2011, their attacks have continued (Human Rights Watch 2013a). In April 2013, suicide bombers attacked a court complex in Mogadishu, leaving 20 dead (Ibrahim 2013). Just after the attack, members of Al-Shabaab detonated a car packed with explosives outside a government building, killing at least three aid workers (Ibrahim 2013; Human Rights Watch 2013a).

The failure of Somalia's government can be directly linked to the success of Al-Shabaab. As Wise (2011, p. 2) rightly points out, the absence of effective governmental opposition permitted Al-Shabaab to operate unchecked throughout the south-central region of the country:

> Al-Shabaab exploited this operating space by building a secure network of camps to train fighters and establishing a system of taxation and extortion to raise funds... by providing ... basic governmental services, Al-Shabaab gained a great deal of goodwill and popular support, which bolstered its recruiting.

An estimated 3000 African Union peacekeepers have been killed during efforts to drive Al-Shabaab out of Somalia (Reuters 2013). In June 2013, Al-Shabaab staged an attack on a United Nations compound in Mogadishu (Ibrahim and Kulish 2013), dampening hopes that the recent relative calm in Mogadishu would continue. However, efforts to drive Al-Shabaab out of several key areas in Somalia have been successful and the TFG, along with the African Union Mission in Somalia, is currently in control of the capital (Amnesty International 2013a). Additionally, Al-Shabaab is no longer in control of the port city Kismayu (Ibrahim and Kulish 2013). While this would seem to be a positive step, Kismayu has not experienced peace since the removal of Al-Shabaab because their exodus left an enormous power vacuum, prompting rival clans to fight for control of the city (Ibrahim and Kulish 2013). At least 71 people have been killed and 300 wounded since the withdrawal of Al-Shabaab and fighting among factions, the use of land mines, and hand grenade attacks have increased (Ibrahim and Kulish 2013).

On September 21, 2013, members of Al-Shabaab stormed a shopping mall in Nairobi, Kenya, killing 62 people and injuring another 175 (BBC News

2013). The involvement of Al-Shabaab was not clear until the group claimed responsibility for the attack by tweeting, "The Mujahideen entered #Westgate Mall today at around noon and are still inside the mall, fighting the #Kenyan Kuffar (infidels) inside their own turf" (BBC News 2013). Al-Shabaab has issued numerous threats against the Kenyan government in response to their continued military presence in Somalia.* The standoff, which lasted three days, was finally resolved by Kenyan Security Forces.

Fractured Justice in Somalia

Given Somalia's ineffectual if not wholly failed government, the absence of a formal and fair criminal justice system in most parts of the nation should come as no surprise. Put simply, the current criminal justice system in Somalia is badly broken and the uniform application of due process rights does not exist (U.S. Department of State 2013). The United Nations (2012, p. 4) provides a detailed assessment of the state of criminal justice in Somalia by noting, "proper administration of justice is still lacking, respect of law and order is often compromised, and the overall capacity of members of the justice sector to ensure that the justice system is accessible to the population is very limited or often non-existent."

This does not mean, however, that a criminal justice system does not exist in Somalia, but much like the rest of the government it is simply not dependable or truly functional. Still, people are routinely processed through the Somali criminal justice system; and based on accounts from the United Nations and various human rights organizations, treatment within the system is characterized by the absence of even the most basic human rights protection.

The basis for the legal system in Somalia is a combination of English common law, Shari'ah law, customary law, and Italian law (Meehan 2010). The legal system currently in place has three important features, "(1) each system is sanctioned by a charter which proclaims the supremacy of Islamic Shari'ah (law); (2) a three-tier judicial system has been established, including a supreme court, a court of appeals, and courts of first instance; (3) the laws of the period prior to 1991 remain applicable until and unless they are amended" (Grote and Röder 2012, p. 566). The law provides that suspects can only be arrested if a warrant is obtained or if they are caught committing the crime (Meehan 2010). Additionally, suspects are supposed to have the right to see a judicial official within 24 hours of their arrest (Meehan 2010). However, it is extremely unlikely that these rights are actually upheld. To this

---

* There are an estimated "4,000 Kenyan troops in the south of Somalia, where they have been fighting the militants since 2011 as part of an African Union force supporting Somali government forces" (BBC News 2013).

point, Human Rights Watch (2013a) describes Somalia's judicial system as being in a dire state. Of particular concern is the ongoing use of military tribunals to prosecute military officials, civilian police officers, and members of Al-Shabaab. Despite modest improvements in some areas of the judicial system (i.e., access to basic legal counsel and the reinstatement of the supreme court in late 2012), "concerns remain over the right to be tried by an independent and competent tribunal, the right to prepare a defense, and especially the use of military courts to try civilians" (Bader 2014, para 4).

Unfair and secretive tribunals represent a serious threat to citizens and the stability of the country. As a result of one military tribunal, three men (two soldiers and one civilian law enforcement officer) were shot by firing squad after being found guilty of murder (Bader 2014). The executions took place in public on a football field as children watched (Bader 2014).

Female crime victims appear to fare even worse in the justice system. The UK Foreign and Commonwealth Office (2013) described a case of a female rape victim in Somalia who attempted to seek justice. Following her rape, the victim reported the incident to the police and shortly thereafter she was taken by government officials and given to African Somalia troops at the Union Mission. Once in their custody, she was gang-raped by troops and then left in the street (UK Foreign and Commonwealth Office 2013). Authorities took nearly three months to investigate the allegations (UK Foreign and Commonwealth Office 2013), but the police investigation was secretive and so rife with mismanagement that the Somali authorities have ordered a new, open, and impartial investigation (Human Rights Watch 2013a). At present, the outcome of the case is still pending.

Unfortunately, this case does not appear to be an isolated occurrence. Human Rights Watch (2014) reports that sexual assaults committed by government soldiers and allies are common in Mogadishu. During the first half of 2013, there were nearly 800 reported cases of sexual assault and gender violence in Mogadishu (Muscati 2013). If anything, this figure should be treated as an underestimate, as many women do not report attacks for fear of reprisal by the police or other security forces. Women interviewed by Human Rights Watch (2014) reported that no place was safe for women; they live in a perpetual state of fear because attacks are common and justice is virtually nonexistent.

The prison system in Somalia is in dire need of reform. An independent expert from the United Nations visited several prisons in Puntland and Somaliland and described the inhumane conditions. In particular, the inspector found, "in a significant number of cases, detentions were either unlawful or arbitrary, with prisoners detained without a legal basis. He was also shocked to find women and girls detained for disobeying their parents or husband. Detention conditions were close to inhumane, and water and sanitation were frequently lacking" (United Nations 2012, p. 15).

In the capital city, Mogadishu, the conditions appear to be even worse. A total of 950 prisoners are held at Mogadishu Central Prison; of these, approximately 135 inmates are awaiting trial and 61 males are on death row (United Nations Political Office for Somalia 2012). While male and female inmates are kept separately in accordance with Somali law, there is no separation of adults and juveniles (United Nations Political Office for Somalia 2012). The United Nations Political Office for Somalia (2012) also notes an absence of a clearly defined separation of inmates sentenced by military courts versus civilian courts, as well as a lack of separation between inmates according to the seriousness of their offense.* As in more stable nations, proper classification and housing of prisoners is vital to the safety of the inmates and prison guards. Additionally, rehabilitation efforts are hampered when inmates are not separated appropriately. In the event that rehabilitation programs were available in the Mogadishu Central Prison, it would be almost impossible to ensure that inmates were participating in the appropriate rehabilitative program.

Overcrowding at the facility is also problematic for male inmates. Each prison room is designed to house 50 inmates; however, at present, the rooms are almost three times over capacity, holding 120 male inmates per room (United Nations Political Office for Somalia 2012). In the prison, there is no source of clean water, no electricity, and there is currently one functioning toilet and washing station per room (United Nations Political Office for Somalia 2012). Relatedly, health conditions at Mogadishu Central Prison are cause for serious concern. The daily food budget for each inmate is $1, leading to issues of malnutrition and poor health outcomes (United Nations Political Office for Somalia 2012). Further, the overcrowded nature of the facility, as well as the lack of proper light and ventilation, have created an environment where communicable diseases such as tuberculosis and cholera flourish (United Nations Political Office for Somalia 2012). These medical problems are further compounded by a lack of prison doctors and acceptable health care (United Nations Political Office for Somalia 2012). A staff of five nurses, working with outdated and unsanitary equipment, provides the only medical care for the 950 inmates at the prison (United Nations Political Office for Somalia 2012).

Somalia's treatment of prisoners is especially problematic, given that they are signatories to the following international covenants and conventions: the International Covenant on Civil and Political Rights; the International Covenant on Economic, Social and Cultural Rights; the Convention against Torture and Other Cruel, Inhuman or Degrading Treatment or Punishment; the Standard Minimum Rules for the Treatment of Prisoners (1957); the

---

* Inmates or those awaiting sentencing for typical crimes are not properly separated from inmates who have committed serious national security offenses.

Body of Principles for the Protection of All Persons under Any Form of Detention or Imprisonment (1988); the Basic Principles for the Treatment of Prisoners (1990); the Standard Minimum Rules for the Administration of Juvenile Justice (1985); the UN Rules for the Protection of Juveniles Deprived of their Liberty; and the Convention on the Rights of the Child (2015). At present, it appears that the Somali government has violated virtually all of these covenants and conventions.

Somalia's story is far from over. While violence and bloodshed have come to define the nation, there is hope that a more stable government will bring much-needed governance to the country. In August 2012, a new Parliament was put in place, a president was appointed, and a new constitution was drafted (though not amended) (Amnesty International 2013a). In September, the Parliament elected Hassan Sheikh Mohamud (2009) as president and he selected Abdi Farah Shirdon Saaid to be his prime minister (Amnesty International 2013a).

In a positive step toward women's rights, the first female minister of foreign affairs was selected (Amnesty International 2013a). All this said, violence by militia groups, a flourishing shadow economy, the government's inability to maintain or build meaningful infrastructure, and a fractured justice system still represent serious problems throughout the nation. Moreover, radical Islamists and the profusion of terrorist organizations pose serious impediments to the assistance that the international community might otherwise grant. Even so, many state actors and nongovernmental organizations (NGOs) are actively engaged in trying to rebuild Somalia. Until the people of Somalia address the internal issues dogging its stability, it may be decades before Somalia becomes anything more than the exemplar of state failure.

Sudan and South Sudan

Building on themes similar to the case of Somalia, Sudan and the newly formed South Sudan have a tumultuous history that includes civil war, famine, and genocide. At first blush, there are many obvious similarities between Sudan and Somalia. Both countries were adversely affected by colonization, and both nations are the locus of fierce intergroup rivalries. However, there are some important differences between the two nations that warrant discussion.

While cultural cleavages are evident in both nations, the division in Sudan stems largely from religion, social class, and postcolonial legacy, and not from clan-based rivalries, as is the case in Somalia. A second key difference between Somalia and Sudan can be seen in how each country has responded to the failure of their government. In both cases, civil wars raged on for years, but in Sudan, civil war quickly turned into one of the worst cases of genocide in the twenty-first century. Additionally, failure in Somalia has translated into a general state of lawlessness and an environment where transnational crimes flourish. This is not the case in Sudan. The failure of the government and the civil war that has engulfed the nation has been contained within Africa, with little transnational crime originating from Sudan.* In this case study, we will explore the religious conflict in the Sudan, as well as the genocide in Darfur. Additionally, we will discuss the development of the new country, South Sudan, and examine whether the optimism that surrounded its creation was deeply misplaced.

Sudan has a rich history that has been complicated by matters of border changes, religious clashes, and postcolonial legacy. Given its geographical location, Sudan has been strongly influenced by Egypt and at various points in its history has been ruled by Egypt. In the interest of focusing our examination on contemporary issues of failure, we will not discuss the very early history of Sudan, but rather begin our historical discussion with the European colonization that began during the nineteenth century.

Beginning in the 1890s, European interest in Sudan began to take hold. The British, French, and Belgians all wanted to stake claim to parts of Sudan (Metz 1992). Britain was especially interested in Sudan because they had a strong desire to exclude the other colonial powers from gaining control in the region (Abushouk 2010), while also safeguarding their interests in Egypt, notably "control over the Nile to safeguard a planned irrigation dam at Aswan" (Metz 1992).

In an effort to gain control of the region, Great Britain aided Egypt in reconquering Sudan (Metz 1992). What resulted was joint Egyptian and British rule from 1899 to 1936 (Metz 1992; Collins 2008). Initially, only North Sudan was colonized, because South Sudan was largely inaccessible (Collins 2008). In 1904, after several successful swamp clearing expeditions, South Sudan became accessible to the military and the process of conquering the southern area of the nation began (Collins 2008). It would take 30 years to fully conquer South Sudan, but by the 1930s, South Sudan was under the control of the British.

Northern and southern Sudan have remained divided since the country's inception, but the rift between the two regions was exacerbated by British rule. Efforts at building infrastructure and modernizing Sudan were largely directed to the north, in part because the British did not believe that the southern region was ready for modernization (Metz 1992). The prevailing view of the British, which was also shared by the Sudanese in the north, was that the south was "primitive and backward" (Deng 1995, p. 134).

---

* Human trafficking is an issue in Sudan and to a lesser extent in South Sudan. According to the CIA (2013c), Sudan is listed as a "Tier Three" nation with regard to trafficking. As the agency observes, "Sudan does not fully comply with the minimum standards for the elimination of trafficking and is not making significant efforts to do so." That said, levels of transnational crime are still far below that of Somalia.

Adding fuel to the north/south division, the two regions were administered in two very different ways by the British (Johnson 2012). In the north, Great Britain was heavily invested in the political structure, educational system, and social system. However, in the south, Great Britain favored an indirect approach, whereby the country was governed by traditional institutions, essentially "cutting it off, as it were, from the rest of the country" (Khalid 2010, p. 19). Christian missionaries were permitted to spread Christianity in the south, but were barred from entering the north because the British did not wish to become embroiled in religious conflict (Khalid 2010). Khalid (2010) notes that the spread of Christianity was not necessarily encouraged in the south, but the British did little to hinder the work of the missionaries.

In the 1920s, the British enacted a radical policy that further deepened the rift between the north and south. The British enacted several "closed door" policies that severed any existing ties between the north and south (Fadlalla 2004, p. 32). In particular, the British banned all northern Sudanese from the southern region. Additionally, "the British gradually replaced Arab administrators and expelled Arab merchants, thereby severing the South's last economic contacts with the north."

The colonial administration also discouraged the spread of Islam, the practice of Arab customs, and the wearing of Arab dress. At the same time, the British made efforts to revitalize African customs and tribal culture that the slave trade had disrupted. "Finally, a 1930 directive stated that blacks in the southern provinces were to be considered a people distinct from northern Muslims and that the region should be prepared for eventual integration with British East Africa" (Collins 2005, p. 369). In effect, the British created two countries, a move which would heavily influence the social standing of the southern Sudanese people.

During World War II, the policy of north/south separation was questioned and in 1946, representatives at the Sudan Administrative Conference agreed that the north and south should be merged into one country (Metz 1991; Collins 2008). In 1947, the Juba Conference was held and the policy toward the south was clearly articulated. The civil secretary presiding over the conference indicated that the future of South Sudan was to be found in merging with the north, rather than with Uganda or the Congo (Collins 2008). The civil secretary went on to note,

> The policy of the Sudan Government regarding the Southern Sudan is to act upon the fact that the peoples of the Southern Sudan are distinctly African and Negroid, but that the geography and economics combine (so far as can be foreseen at present) to render them inextricably bound for their future development to the Middle East and the Northern Sudan: and therefore to ensure that they shall through education and development be equipped to take their places in the future as socially and economically the equals of their partners of the Northern Sudan in the Sudan of the future. (Collins 2008, p. 199)

The merging of these two distinct regions did not go smoothly. The policy of keeping the north and south separate meant that politicians in the north had very few dealings with the southern population and, as a consequence, did not understand the unique issues and problems of the southern population (Johnson 2012). Similarly, the south had very little interaction with the north and had difficulties relating to the northern political class (Johnson 2012). Separate administration is not entirely to blame, but it was certainly instrumental in exacerbating the divisions between the two regions. As Johnson (2012, p. 25) notes, "it is not necessarily the case that Northerners and Southerners would have developed a common national understanding had the policy of administrative segregation never been imposed, but the gulf of misunderstanding which separated the North and South was all the greater as a result of that segregation."

Further complicating relations between the north and south was a long-standing negative view that northern politicians held of the south. Deng (1995, p. 135) notes that politicians in the north had an "attitude that was condescending at best and contemptuous at worst" and this view continued even as South Sudan gained its independence. Southern Sudanese politicians were largely excluded from the government (only four southern Sudanese were put in positions of authority) and there was also resentment in the south that Arabic had become the national language (Metz 1992). The merging of the two regions and the development of an autonomous Sudan was not supported in the south. Rather than feeling that they had gained independence from Great Britain, the prevailing sentiment in the south was that they were being colonized once again, this time by the north (Deng 1995). This response was not necessarily unwarranted. In the mid-1950s, the south saw a dramatic increase in the number of northerners taking positions of power as administrators, army officers, police officers, and teachers, thus stoking fears of colonization (Johnson 2012).

Because northern politicians did not share political power with the south, they attempted to control the region through force (Deng 1995). In doing so, the northern Sudanese applied the same tactics and techniques that they had observed during British rule (Deng 1995). That is to say, "they resorted to the ruthless suppression and repression of local resistance and attempted assertion of law and order by crude military and police forces reminiscent of the early British administration in the South" (Deng 1995, p. 135).

In August 1955, southern army troops reacted violently to the decision that they would be placed under the command of northern officers (Metz 1992). Southern troops killed hundreds of northern Sudanese, including members of the military and government officials (Metz 1992). Reaction from the north was swift and severe—70 southern soldiers were executed for their part in the mutiny (Metz 1992). The future was clear: even with an independent state, Sudan would not be united. The cleavage between the north and the south simply ran too deep and the division would lead to numerous civil wars (the first lasting from 1947 until 1972), ultimately culminating in one of the greatest humanitarian crises of the twenty-first century.

Initially, Sudan's government was a parliamentary democracy, but that changed on November 17, 1958, when General Ibrahim Abbud took control of the government in a bloodless coup (Collins 2008). The unification of the country became one of the primary goals of the new military regime, and the spread of Islam to the south became the primary mechanism for unification (Collins 2008). According to Collins (2008, p. 33), with Parliament dissolved, southern representatives were forced to return to the south to find employment, a move that created a power vacuum, "which the military government promptly filled with their concept of Sudanese nationalism in which the strength of the Arab language, Arab culture, and the Arab past fused with the powerful traditions of Sudanese tribal history and the deep emotions of Sudanese Islam." These ideals, which were long held by the northern Sudanese, did not mesh well with the south because "Arabization and Islamization ... were anathema to the Africans with their own very different linguistic, cultural, and religious traditions" (Collins 2008, p. 33).

Open rebellion against the new policies was almost immediate in the south. By the mid-1960s, it became clear that Islam would not find much purchase in the south (Collins 2008). This paved the way for a civilian transitional government led by Muhammad Majub, whose policies toward the south were even more draconian than the previous regime (Collins 2008). Under Majub, the army was directed to eliminate educated Africans, thus leading to mass killings and massive flows of refugees to bordering countries (Collins 2008). This too would prove to be a failure as it only strengthened the resolve of the south and caused many southern Sudanese to take leadership positions in guerrilla movements (Collins 2008).

After another bloodless coup in 1969, a new military regime took control of the government. For a time, it looked as though north/south relations could be restored. On March 28, 1972, Major-General Joseph Laug announced that southern Sudan would be given more autonomy and allowed self-governance, as well as a greater voice in the united Sudan (Collins 2008). The Addis Ababa agreement, while popular in the south, was abhorred by many in the north; however, for a short time there was relative peace (Collins 2008). Peace began to break down in 1976, when large deposits of oil were discovered in South Sudan (Collins 2008). By 1983, the north and south were once again at war and the country would remain at war until 2005 (Yongo-Bare 2009).

While the first civil war was confined to the south, the second civil war expanded into some parts of the north and east (Yongo-Bare 2009). The importance of oil in the perpetuation of Sudanese violence cannot be overstated. Jok (2001, p. 46) notes that "the Sudanese government has forcibly removed thousands of civilians from the region in order to protect the oil producing areas, burning several villages to the ground and using bombers and artillery to clear a 100-kilometer area around the southern oil fields." In short, the exploitation of oil has only served to intensify the existing conflict (Human Rights Watch 2003).

After a very brief period of democracy in Sudan, the National Islamic Front (now called the National Congress Party) took control of the government and installed Omar al-Bashir as president of Sudan (Brosche and Rothbart 2012). The coup was largely instigated by Hassan al-Turabi, a Sunni Muslim and Shari'ah law proponent (Brosche and Rothbart 2012). While al-Bashir publicly stated that the "reason for the coup was to save the country from rotten political parties," the actual reason stemmed from a desire for further Islamization of the country (Brosche and Rothbart 2012, p. 76). In addition, al-Bashir wanted to maintain a unified Sudan, comprising both the north and south (BBC News 2015). As will be discussed later, this goal was not achieved and South Sudan officially separated from Sudan in 2011. Al-Bashir ultimately agreed to a divided Sudan, but his "attitude to Darfur, where a conflict has raged since 2003 when rebels took up arms at alleged government discrimination, has been characterized by belligerence" (BBC News 2015, para. 12).

Darfur

The genocide in Darfur began in 2003, but the roots of the violence reach back to the 1960s. The conflict was not entirely based on religion because in some cases Muslims were attacking Muslims (Johnson 2012). Religion did play some role, however, as those who identified themselves as Africans (not Arabs) bore the brunt of the brutality. In addition to religious differences, the conflict can also be attributed to linguistic fractionalization (Arab-speaking vs. non-Arab-speaking populations), as well as livelihood (pastoralists, farmers, and the urban population) (Osman El-Tom 2009). Because of the numerous divisions in the region, many have erroneously concluded that the crisis in Darfur was not related to the north/south rift (Johnson 2012). However, as Johnson (2012, p. xviii) notes, "Darfur was not unrelated to the war in the South, or to the wars in the Nubia mountains, Blue Nile or eastern Sudan." Problems in Darfur began during the civil war between the primarily Islamic north and the predominantly Christian/Animist south (Zissis 2006). In an effort to restructure the political system in a way that would benefit the south, as well as the population that was marginalized in the north, the Darfur Development Front formed alliances with the New Forces Congress (Yongo-Bare 2009). This alliance, along with the Beja Congress, was responsible for the overthrowing of the Ibramim Abboud military regime (Yongo-Bare 2009). Conflict between Darfur and the northern government intensified and in 1981, Darfur rejected the appointment of a northern governor in the region (Yongo-Bare 2009). Darfur, along with South Sudan, continued to be marginalized by the government (Osman El-Tom 2009). Twenty percent of the Sudanese population lives in Darfur, yet from 1989 to 2000, only 11% of ministerial positions and just 15% of state governorships were held by politicians from Darfur (Osman El-Tom 2009). Comparatively, 16% of the Sudanese population lives in the southern region, yet 13% of ministerial positions and all state governorships were held by southern Sudanese politicians during the same time period (Osman El-Tom 2009). While the southern region has historically been marginalized by the ruling government, the Darfur region has been treated similarly, if not slightly worse than the south. Stability in the region gradually decayed and finally culminated with a war that began in 2003 (Yongo-Bare 2009).

In 2003, the Sudan Liberation Movement/Army (SLM/A) and the Justice and Equality Movement (JEM) rebels attacked government targets in Darfur in a bid for more autonomy, better infrastructure, and a share in the oil wealth (Zissis 2006). After a failed cease-fire, the government used the Janjaweed to attack African Masalit, Fur, and Zaghawa villages (each of these groups are primary supporters of the SLM/A and JEM) (Zissis 2006). Though the African Masalit, Fur, and Zaghawa are technically Muslim, they practice a form of Islam that is mixed with Sufism and Animism (Zissis 2006). Thus, it is slightly misleading to indicate that the violence was not religiously based because the Janjaweed are Muslim and the population of Darfur was not viewed as being entirely adherent to the Islamic faith. As such, the mixing of faiths in Darfur was viewed contemptuously by the Islamic Sudanese government (Zissis 2006). However, the crisis in Darfur was not entirely based on differences of religious ideology, as bias against farmers and a fight for land both played an integral role in the conflict. In Darfur, tribes are differentiated on the basis of "Africans" (settled farmers) and "Arabs" (cattle or camel herders). This divide was perpetuated by colonial policies, which created a false chasm between the "farmers and herders by dividing them into settled peoples… and nomads… Issues of survival were rendered in terms of ethnic and racial divisions. As such, pitted 'Fur [the people of Darfur] against Arabs in a civil war… 1987–89, both sides claiming that one side was trying to empty the land of the other'" (Gelot 2012, p. 73).

As part of the war efforts, the Sudanese government "funded Darfur's Arab militias—which came to be known as the 'Janjaweed,' or 'armed horsemen'—to keep the rebels at bay" (Zissis 2006, para. 2). Human Rights Watch (2005) reports that some of the worst atrocities have been committed by the Um Jalul of Musa Hilal (camel herders) against the Fur and Zaghawa (farmers).

The quote at the beginning of this chapter from an anonymous Janjaweed recruit, "When they say we will go and fight the rebels, they lie. They do not actually go to fight the rebels. Instead they raid the villages and the small scattered communities and seize people's possessions," illustrates that the Janjaweed were not fighting rebels. Survivor accounts from combined Janjaweed and government attacks tend to correspond with the recruit's account. One anonymous survivor recounted planes, trucks, and armed soldiers on horses and camels all descended upon her village (Totten and Parsons 2013). She goes on to note, "as we were running I saw men from our village shot. They killed 27 men ... We didn't have any guns in our village and they [the Government of Sudan troops and the Janjaweed] did all the shooting" (Totten and Parsons 2013, pp. 564–565).

In 2008, the Sudanese government launched a series of strategic attacks against civilians in an effort to drive civilians out of the northern corridor of Darfur before they launched attacks on JEM rebels (Human Rights Watch 2008). Janjaweed soldiers and government forces launched a joint attack that destroyed villages and killed, assaulted, kidnapped, and raped civilian villagers (Human Rights Watch 2008). Thousands of civilians who survived the 2008 attacks fled to refugee camps in neighboring Chad (Human Rights Watch 2008). In total, the United Nations estimates that 300,000 people were killed during the war and an estimated 2.6 million people were displaced to refugee camps in Sudan and Chad (BBC News 2010).

President Omar al-Bashir has denied allegations that he deployed the Janjaweed, but on July 12, 2010, the International Criminal Court (ICC) issued an arrest warrant for al-Bashir for the genocide that took place in the Darfur region (Human Rights Watch 2010). A year prior, the ICC issued an arrest warrant for al-Bashir for crimes against humanity (Human Rights Watch 2010). At the time of this writing, al-Bashir has not been arrested and there is substantial doubt that he will ever face trial for his crimes. Al-Bashir has traveled to numerous countries within Africa since the two arrest warrants were issued, but some "African countries rallied behind Bashir and issued resolutions stating that they would not cooperate with the ICC in apprehending the Sudanese leader even if Bashir visits countries which have ratified the Rome Statue" (Sudan Tribune 2013a, para. 6).* Unrest in the Darfur region is ongoing, with no clear end in sight. Most recently, on July 4, 2013, a curfew was imposed in the South Darfur capital following an outbreak of violence between tribal militias and security forces (Sudan Tribune 2013b). For some, the solution to the violence in Darfur may be found in seeking an independent state for Darfur. South Sudan took this approach and many had hoped that with the creation of South Sudan, tension in the region would abate. In the next section, we will explore the development of

* The Rome Statute established the ICC, its jurisdiction, administration, and criminal procedures.

South Sudan and examine whether relations have improved between Sudan and South Sudan.

South Sudan

On July 9, 2011, South Sudan officially gained its independence from the north (BBC News 2013). South Sudan encompasses 644,329 km², making it slightly smaller than the U.S. state of Texas (Central Intelligence Agency 2013b). The country's population is just over 11 million and the majority of its citizens live in rural areas (Central Intelligence Agency 2013b). South Sudan ranks 18th in the world for infant mortality (69.97 deaths per 1000 live births) and it is estimated that 27% of the population over age 15 are literate (Central Intelligence Agency 2013b).

The first year of independence did not go smoothly for South Sudan (Human Rights Watch 2013b). Violence between the North and South continued, especially along the border between the two countries (Human Rights Watch 2013b). Additionally, the country suffers from a grossly inadequate criminal justice system, which has (at a minimum) hampered efforts to administer justice and, at worst, has resulted in human rights violations (Human Rights Watch 2013b). Due to a lack of trained criminal justice personnel, the South Sudanese have resorted to using military force to quell disturbances (Human Rights Watch 2013c). According to Human Rights Watch (2013c), the military has unlawfully detained over 130 civilians since February 2013. Suspects have been held for weeks, and in some cases months, without charge, and many allege that they were beaten during their detention (Human Rights Watch 2013c).

The Jonglei state is an area of particular concern due to violence, population displacement, and abuses by security forces (United Nations News Centre 2013). The UN Mission in South Sudan notes that there has been significant population displacement (United Nations News Centre 2013), with some organizations such as the International Committee of the Red Cross (2013) estimating that thousands of residents in the Jonglei state have been displaced. Aid organizations in the area have reported numerous incidents of uniformed personnel breaking into homes and shops for the purpose of looting while the residents are away (United Nations News Centre 2013). The provision of food, clean water, and shelter has been problematic in many parts of South Sudan for quite some time. The International Committee of the Red Cross (2013) notes that poor harvests, flooding, and violence have taken a toll on thousands of people in Jonglei. Elsewhere in South Sudan, the situation is little improved. The International Committee of the Red Cross is providing basic necessities (e.g., food, farming tools, and household goods) to an estimated 25,000 people located on the west bank of the Nile (International Committee of the Red Cross 2013).

South Sudan is still in its infancy, so it is far too early to predict the ultimate success or failure of the nation. However, the Fund for Peace (2015) currently ranks South Sudan as the most fragile state, followed closely by Somalia, the Central African Republic, and Sudan.* Haken and Taft (2013, para. 6) propose two scenarios that help explain the current failure in South Sudan: either the government cannot properly control the violence that is quickly escalating, or the violence may be "spurred on by politicians and power brokers who are interested in land, money, and revenge." Neither scenario bodes well for the future of South Sudan.

There is also evidence of widespread corruption in the government. In 2012, government officials either "misplaced" or stole $4 billion (Haken and Taft 2013). While it may be tempting to label South Sudan a failed state, we must remember that the country is just four years old and is still recovering from a civil war that killed two million people and nearly obliterated the infrastructure. Clearly, changes are badly needed and "South Sudan has a long road ahead of it to create a democratic and prosperous nation, and it will undoubtedly take time and the efforts of many" (Haken and Taft 2013, para. 10). Absent substantial improvements in the government, especially in the criminal justice system, South Sudan will likely continue the same cycle of violence that has defined the nation for decades.

International Implications of Sudanese Conflicts

As stated at the beginning of this section, Sudan has responded to violence and governmental failure in ways that are vastly different from Somalia. While comparatively little transnational crime has been exported outside of Africa, human trafficking is an important concern in Sudan and South Sudan. Additionally, the spillover of violence from Sudan into neighboring Chad has caused enormous problems with stability in the entire region.

Within Sudan, human trafficking is most concentrated in the eastern region. The principle targets in the east are asylum-seeking refugees from Eritrea (Amnesty International 2013b). Amnesty International (2013b) reports that refugees from the Shagarab refugee camps (near the Eritrean border) have been kidnapped and taken to Egypt, where Bedouin criminal groups hold them for ransom. In addition to the immigrant population, large numbers of women and girls from rural regions in Sudan are trafficked internally for the purposes of domestic servitude or sexual

---

* Scores in each area of the Failed States Index range from a low of 1 (indicating stability/ success) to a high of 10 (indicating instability/failure). The highest score that a country can receive is 122.0 points. Currently, Sudan scores 110.8 points and South Sudan scores 114.5 points (Fund for Peace 2015).

exploitation. The U.S. Department of State (2013) notes that thousands of Dinka women, as well as girls from the Nubia tribe, were abducted during the 20-year civil war that began in 1983. Some are still in the custody of their captors. Women and children are also exported by traffickers to countries in the Middle East (e.g., Qatar, Egypt, and Saudi Arabia) for domestic servitude or to various European countries for sexual exploitation (U.S. Department of State 2013). In some countries, such as Saudi Arabia, Sudanese children are forced by criminal gangs to beg on the street (U.S. Department of State 2013).

Until recently, the Sudanese government had done little to combat human trafficking; however, on July 11, 2013, the Sudanese cabinet endorsed a law that would address this growing problem (*Sudan Tribune* 2013a). According to the *Sudan Tribune* (2013a, para. 2), "the proposed law details human trafficking offenses and penalties while specifying measures aimed at protecting victims and witnesses and maintaining information confidentiality." The law, if passed, would possibly move Sudan from the State Department's Tier Three list for human trafficking (a country currently not in compliance and not taking any steps toward compliance with the TVPA), to the Tier Two watch list (a country that is not in compliance with the TVPA, but is taking substantial steps to ensure compliance).

South Sudan has a slightly better record in the area of human trafficking compared with Sudan. They are currently on the State Department's Tier Two list, which indicates that they are taking steps to ensure compliance with the TVPA. Nevertheless, human trafficking remains a problem in South Sudan. The trafficking patterns in South Sudan are similar to those of Sudan, as women and girls from rural areas are particularly targeted for victimization, either by being forced to work in domestic servitude or by being sexually exploited (U.S. Department of State 2013). The large number of displaced persons in South Sudan has exacerbated problems with human trafficking, making the situation for potential victims in South Sudan somewhat similar to those in Somalia.

The government in South Sudan has taken steps to address certain types of human trafficking. According the U.S. Department of State (2013), the government has been working to eliminate the use of child soldiers in its military. Specifically, the government "identified and demobilized 72 children from the [Sudan People's Liberation Army] SPLA, improved efforts to vet new recruits for age verification, and, in partnership with UN agencies, increased its provision of reintegration services to demobilized children" (U.S. Department of State 2013, p. 337). While this is a positive step, there is still more work to be done in this area. The government has yet to address other types of trafficking that are especially problematic in the country, such as children who are trafficked for the purposes of sexual exploitation (U.S. Department of State 2013).

Effective law enforcement is severely lacking in South Sudan, which hampers efforts to bring perpetrators to justice. However, if traffickers are arrested and prosecuted, Article 282 of the Penal Code calls for "up to seven years imprisonment for the sale of a person across international borders. The Penal Code Act also prohibits and prescribes punishments of up to seven years imprisonment for abduction (Article 278) and transfer of control over a person (Article 279) for the purpose of unlawful compulsory labor ... up to two years imprisonment for compulsory labor without aggravating circumstances ... Article 276 criminalizes buying or selling a child for the purpose of prostitution and prescribes a punishment of up to 14 years imprisonment" (U.S. Department of State 2013, para. 7).

As previously noted, Sudanese troubles have a profound spillover effect into neighboring Chad, which has had its own war-related issues over the past several decades. With decades of armed conflict (and the violence in Darfur in particular), Sudan's problems have become Chad's. According to Human Rights Watch (2004), many of the Janjaweed attacks have crossed the border into Chad. The attacks began as simple cattle raids, but quickly escalated to include attacks on civilians (Human Rights Watch 2004). Tensions have been further escalated because many Chadian ethnic groups share bloodlines with Darfurians (Human Rights Watch 2004). Given the shared bloodlines between Chadians and Darfurians, as well as the close geographical proximity of the two areas, it is not surprising that war and political upheaval in both areas would have a negative influence on the region. Chadian rebels have used Darfur as a base of operations and vice versa (Human Rights Watch 2007). In the midst of the crisis in Darfur, rebels in Chad working to oust the Deby regime were doing so in Sudan (Human Rights Watch 2007).

Sudanese rebels were working out of Chad during the same time period (Human Rights Watch 2007). The Chadian rebels attempting to remove the Deby regime from power were thwarted with the help of France and the Sudanese rebel group, JEM (Gebrewold 2009). Human Rights Watch (2007) reports that in 2006 and 2007, Saudi Arabia and Libya brokered an agreement between Sudan and Chad that would put an end to governmental support of opposing militias in each country. The primary enforcement mechanism for this accord is the Tripoli Agreement, which stipulates the deployment of joint patrols from Chad and Sudan along the border region (Human Rights Watch 2007). As Belachew Gebrewold (2009) observes, adherence to this agreement is questionable, as there were reports of Chadian rebels receiving support from the Sudanese government in 2008. Gebrewold (2009) also notes the government support of opposing militias has made the peace process extremely tenuous. As he goes on to state, "Chadian rebels supported by Sudan almost toppled the government of Chad in early 2008 ... Sudanese rebels supported by Chad went as far as Khartoum.... This shows that Chad and Sudan are fighting a proxy war using each other's rebels to achieve their military objectives. As a result, Chad is caught in the Darfur crossfire" (Gebrewold 2009, p. 198).

In addition to problems stemming from the support of militias in each country, the crisis in Darfur drastically increased the number of displaced Darfurians seeking refuge in Chad (Human Rights Watch 2007). The Office of the United Nations High Commissioner for Refugees (2013a) estimates that 368,290 Sudanese refugees are currently living in Chad. There are an additional 97,550 displaced persons from the Central African Republic and an estimated 86,929 internally displaced persons (Office of the United Nations High Commissioner for Refugees 2013a,c). The large number of both internally and externally displaced persons in Chad (especially in Eastern Chad) has placed an enormous strain on already limited resources (Office of the United Nations High Commissioner for Refugees 2013a,c). In Southern Chad, problems with flooding in the region have destroyed crops and homes, making life even more difficult for displaced persons (Office of the United Nations High Commissioner for Refugees 2013a,c). In addition to basic necessities, such as food, shelter, and water, the Office of the United Nations High Commissioner for Refugees (2013c) reports "providing education is equally important in order to protect boys from forced recruitment and discourage early marriage for girls."

Providing even rudimentary necessities for refugees has proved challenging. In the case of safe water for drinking and cooking, the Office of the United Nations High Commissioner for Refugees (2013b) reports that the recommended minimum of 15 liters of water per person per day is currently not being met in a new refugee camp in Southeast Chad. The absolute minimum daily allotment needed for survival is seven liters per day and human rights workers have been struggling to provide 10 liters per day (Office of the United Nations High Commissioner for Refugees 2013b). The steady flow of refugees into Chad does not appear to be slowing down and will likely increase, as Nigerians have begun to seek refuge from the conflict with Boko Haram (Office of the United Nations High Commissioner for Refugees 2015).

Whether Sudan will ultimately follow Somalia's ill-fated path has yet to be determined. Even with the humanitarian nightmare that is Darfur, there are signs that Sudan and South Sudan are on a relatively better footing. The tenuous stability is of course subject to the influences and vicissitudes of regional neighbors and the broader international community.

Making Sense of Failure

As has been well discussed in this volume, the path to failure is a complex one. Therefore, it is incumbent that we frame Somalia's failure and the Sudanese fragility in terms larger than the mere political and economic motives previously elaborated. At the outset of this work, we asked the reader to adopt a complex systems paradigm when considering the life course of a state. The cases of Somalia and Sudan demonstrate why this analytical perspective is particularly useful.

In the introduction to this book (and again in Chapter 7), we use the work of Monty Marshall and Cole (2009) to better understand state capacity to function. By thinking of the state as a complex adaptive system, we have a series of functional reference points that reveal critical insights into a given state's vitality. To briefly reprise their concepts, Marshall and Cole (2009, p. 2) identify four processes through which states come into existence and sustain themselves: self-actuation, self-organization, self-regulation, and self-correction. As we have done with Georgia, in looking at Somalia and Sudan we can apply a more generalized version of Marshall and Cole's process model and build on it with an additional theoretical vocabulary.

In the first instance, Marshall and Cole (2009, p. 13) observe that a state should be "self-actuating." In Somalia, we see attempts at this process, but little in the way of systemic stability or sustainable claims of actuation. Once free of the colonial fetter and the Cold War hegemonic shuffle, Somalia scratched out an arguably relevant and somewhat stable existence for a very brief time. Unfortunately, the international community poisoned that nascent dynamic with a series of inputs (and withdrawals) that merely perturbed the system without shifting it into a new epoch of stability. The separatist movements in Puntland and Somaliland also go to this point. Unlike South Sudan, whose claim of actuation is in some stead valid, the full separation of these regions from Somalia appears to have stalled under the pressure of Islamist hegemony. Even so, the seeds of putative stability still exist within Somalia, vis-à-vis the traditional clan structure. Similarly, the frail grasp of democracy is also still in evidence. What Somalia likely requires is a blended approach to representative government that melds traditional sensibilities into formal representative structures.

Sudan and South Sudan fare better along this axis, but by the slimmest of margins. Like Somalia, the crisis in Sudan and South Sudan largely emanates from a legacy of colonial rule. Even though the governments of these nations are easily among the most ineffectual, brutal, and dysfunctional on Earth, they are technically self-actuating. While it would be ludicrous to frame the protracted war and eventual division of the country as any kind of success, these events demonstrate that the two dominant cultural and social groups have exerted claims on territory based on traditional and internal differences, rather than being solely an artifact of European division.

The second criterion is the capacity to self-organize (Marshall and Cole 2009). As previously explained, this means that the state exhibits an observable steady condition of existence or functioning that emanates out of hierarchical or specialized structures within it. As an example, one might see a stable nation hold regular elections, seat the winners, and convene a governmental assembly that makes policy decisions. The institution arises as an expression of individualized sentiments; and while it may vary in its composition and priorities, it exists as a continuing construct within the nation.

For the first time in two decades, Somalia established a transitional government in 2004. Eight years later, it completed the transition with the election of a new federal Parliament and speaker, the national constituent assembly's adoption of a provisional constitution, the election of a new president, and the naming of a new prime minister and cabinet (U.S. Department of State 2013). This hybrid system accords the president and prime minister with equal powers. Some onlookers suggest that this builds tension and power struggles into the system (Wasuge 2015). Somalia's future is also dependent on the successful implementation of its plans for "Vision 2016," a program to ensure free and fair national elections. In addition to preparing the country for elections, the government has a mandate to finalize the national constitution and establish the federal member states (U.S. Department of State 2013). Whether that happens, or how well it happens, will likely be determinative of Somalia's near future.

In considering the differences between Somalia and Sudan, one is often forced into a comparison between what went wrong and what went worse: chaos and famine or genocide and violent oppression. Since its 1956 independence, Sudan's political arrangements have yielded ineffectual governments that fail to guarantee the rule of law (Mbaku 2015). This has, according to senior fellow at Brookings Institution, John Mukum Mbaku (2015), allowed those atop the power structure, "to behave with impunity and engage in activities (e.g., corruption) that have constrained economic growth and development, endangered the peaceful coexistence of the country's diverse population groups, alienated the international community, significantly reduced foreign investment, and endangered the country's international standing."

With respect to the criterion of self-regulation, the Sudanese government is capable of disseminating its will through a tenuously stable hierarchy. Unfortunately, that will is regularly drenched in the blood of innocents. As above, there is a great deal of factionalized fighting and a general lack of cohesion between regional ethnic concerns and the central government.

While the long-term independence of nascent South Sudan is still an undecided issue, horrible internal conflict is well-documented. The political struggle between President Salva Kiir and his former Vice President Riek Machar has become fully fletched ethnic violence. Each turned to their respective constituencies: President Kiir mobilized his Dinka ethnic group and Machar turned to his Nuer ethnic group for support. The South Sudanese people have paid dearly for the struggle. Ten thousand people have been killed and more than 1.8 million have been internally displaced since civil war broke out in South Sudan in December 2013 (International Crisis Group 2014). A series of cease fires and talks have proved futile. Instead of holding an election in 2015, the nation's lawmakers have extended Kiir's term until 2018.

Both South Sudan's upheaval and Somalia's ill-fated trajectory speak to the third criterion: capacity for self-regulation. The central proposition here is whether the hierarchy effectively mediates lower-order functions in the system. To ask it more plainly: Do the priorities and actions of local governments reflect those of the national government? Is there a vertical ordering in the system?

For many decades, Somalia existed largely at the whim of a colonial power. Once free of that fetter, it became just one more pawn in the Cold War. Since that time, it has been largely a dysfunctional swirl of chaos. To worsen matters, Somalia experienced violence between deeply divided clans and a series of droughts caused famine and disease to run rampant (Shane and Leiberman 2009; Chalk 2010). As Shane and Leiberman (2009, p. 8) state, these conditions resulted in an anomic society largely void of "social and moral norms that regulate behavior plunging the country into lawlessness... [representing] a regression to a 'state of nature'—a hypothetical social state similar to anarchy that existed before the rule of law and the state's monopoly on the use of force." Viewed in this way, illicit trafficking, piracy, and terrorism are an extension of the land-based violence caused by anomic tensions (Chalk 2010).

Regarding their capacity for self-regulation, Sudan and South Sudan pose an interesting question. On the one hand, that the former contiguous Sudan experienced a secession suggests a gross incapacity for self-regulation. On the other, the cleavage may actually represent a more honest existential reckoning of the Sudanese borders; and as such, be testament to the more "natural" partition of the country. Of course, few things in global politics are that cleanly sliced. Nowhere is that more evident than in the twined fates of these two countries. Moreover, the genocide and displacement suggest that whatever the new phase into which this struggle has shifted, it does not bode well for either side, the people, economic stability, or the interests of justice. Whatever verticality of bureaucratic communication may exist is damped by the grisly violence used to actuate it.

The last of Marshall and Cole's (2009) criteria, "self-correction," almost warrants no discussion. Somalia is the exemplar of a society unable to right itself or respond positively to perturbations. Much like a spinning top that careened off the table, whatever momentum that may still exist only serves to sharpen the mercurial swings of chaos, rather than recenter the toy. In fact, this complete absence of self-correction might be one of the defining features of failure.

As the preceding discussion confirms, Sudan and South Sudan paint a similar picture. The nation reached a tipping point and divided. In some measure, this can be considered a self-correction; a slipping into a new stasis. Unfortunately, the sound from Sudan and South Sudan is less the clarion of freedom's new trumpets than the howls of Tennyson's nature: red in tooth and claw.

References

Abushouk, A. 2010. The Anglo-Egyptian Sudan: From collaboration mechanism to party politics, 1898–1956. *The Journal of Imperial and Commonwealth History* 38: 207–236.

Allison, S. 2015. Somaliland: Losing patience in the world's most unlikely democracy. *The Daily Maverick*. http://www.dailymaverick.co.za/article/2015-04-07-somaliland-losing-patience-in-the-worlds-most-unlikely-democracy/#.VXRtnmA2VfY (Accessed June 30, 2015).

Amnesty International. 2013a. Somalia. http://www.amnesty.org/en/region/somalia/report-2013 (Accessed June 1, 2014).

Amnesty International. 2013b. Egypt, Sudan: Kidnap and trafficking of refugees and asylum-seekers must be stopped. https://www.amnesty.nl/nieuwsportaal/pers/egypt-sudan-kidnap-and-trafficking-refugees-and-asylum-seekers-must-be-stopped (Accessed June 3, 2014).

Bader, L. March 13, 2014. Dispatches: Somalia—Firing squad on the football field. Human Rights Watch. http://www.hrw.org/news/2014/03/13/dispatches-somalia-firing-squad-football-field (Accessed December 5, 2014).

Barrington, L. 2009. *After Independence: Making and Protecting the Nation in Postcolonial and Postcommunist States.* Ann Arbor, MI: University of Michigan Press.

BBC News. 2010. Darfur death toll rises to two-year high in Sudan. http://www.bbc.co.uk/news/10259604 (Accessed June 3, 2014).

BBC News. 2012. Sufism re-emerges in Somalia as Al-Shabab's control wanes. http://www.bbc.com/news/world-africa-18467464 (Accessed June 20, 2015).

BBC News. 2013. Kenya stand off: As it happened. http://www.bbc.com/news/world-africa-24200990 (Accessed December 23, 2015).

BBC News. 2015. Profile: Sudan's Omar Al-Bashir. http://www.bbc.com/news/world-africa-16010445 (Accessed July 2, 2015).

Bereketeab, R. 2012. *The Horn of Africa: Intra-State Inter-State Conflicts and Security.* London: Pluto.

Brosche, J. and D. Rothbart. 2012. *Violent Conflict and Rebuilding: The Continuing Crisis in Darfur.* New York: Routledge.

Cawsey, A. 2014. The success of clan governance in Somalia: Beyond failed state discourse. http://somalithinktank.org/wp-content/uploads/2014/05/Latest-1.pdf (Accessed June 20, 2014).

Center for Justice and Accountability. n.d. Somalia: Colonial legacy. http://www.cja.org/article.php?id=436 (Accessed June 5, 2014).

Central Intelligence Agency. 2013a. World factbook: Somalia. http://www.cia.gov (Accessed June 1, 2014).

Central Intelligence Agency. 2013b. World factbook: South Sudan. http://www.cia.gov (Accessed June 1, 2014).

Chalk, P. 2008. *The Maritime Dimensions of International Security: Terrorism, Piracy, and Challenges for the United States.* Santa Monica, CA: Rand.

Chalk, P. 2010. Piracy in the Horn of Africa: A Growing Maritime Security Threat. *Combatting Terrorism Center Sentinel*. https://www.ctc.usma.edu/posts/piracy-in-the-horn-of-africa-a-growing-maritime-security-threat (Accessed May 7, 2013).

Child Rights Information Network. 2011. Inhumane sentencing of children in Somalia. Draft report prepared for the Child Rights Information Network. www.crin.org (Accessed June 1, 2014).

Clarke, W. and R. Gosende, 2003. "Somalia: Can a collapsed state reconstitute itself?" In R. Rotberg (Ed.) *State Failure and State Weakness in a Time of Terror*, pp. 129–158, Cambridge, MA: World Peace Foundation.

Collins, R. 2005. The Ilemi triangle. In R. Collins (Ed.) *Civil Wars & Revolution in the Sudan: Essays on the Sudan, Southern Sudan, and Darfur, 1962–2004*, pp. 367–376, Hollywood, CA: Tsehai.

Collins, D. 2008. *A History of Modern Sudan*. Cambridge: Cambridge University Press.

Dagne, T. 2011a. The Republic of South Sudan: Opportunities and challenges for Africa's newest country. Congressional Research Service. http://fpc.state.gov/documents/organization/170506.pdf (Accessed June 9, 2013).

Dagne, T. 2011b. Somalia: Current conditions and prospects for a lasting peace. Washington, DC: Congressional Research Service. https://www.fas.org/sgp/crs/row/RL33911.pdf (Accessed December 23, 2015).

Daniels, C. 2012. *Somali Piracy and Terrorism in the Horn of Africa*. London: Scarecrow Press.

Davis, J. 2010. *Terrorism in Africa: The Evolving Front in the War on Terror*. Lanham, MD: Lexington Books.

Deng, F. 1995. *War of Visions: Conflict of Identities in the Sudan*. Washington, DC: The Brookings Institute.

Dorell, O. 2011. Terror group blocking aid to starving Somalis. *USA Today*. http://usatoday30.usatoday.com/news/world/2011-08-14-somalis-famine-terrorists-block-aid-groups_n.htm (Accessed December 23, 2015).

Ece, N.J. 2012. The maritime dimensions of international security: Piracy attacks. NATO Science for Peace and Security Series—E: *Human and Societal Dynamics, Maritime Security and Defence Against Terrorism*, pp. 33–49. IOS Press. http://ebooks.iospress.nl/publication/25845 (Accessed December 23, 2015).

Ewing, B. 2008. Is toxic waste behind Somali piracy. *Digital Journal*. http://www.digitaljournal.com/article/261147#ixzz3dBSy9PrT (Accessed June 30, 2015).

Fadlalla, M. 2004. *A Short History of Sudan*. Bloomington, IN: iUniverse.

Figliomeni, V. 2012. Countering piracy and other organized illicit activities in East Africa: Piracy, illicit activities of organised crime and failed states. In S. C. Gallett (Ed.) *Piracy and Maritime Terrorism: Logistics, Strategies, Scenarios*, pp 148–169. Amsterdam: IOS Press.

Fitzgerald, N. 2002. *Somalia: Issues, History, and Bibliography*. Hauppauge, NY: Nova Science.

Freedomhouse. 1994. *Freedom Around the World: The Annual Survey of Political Rights and Civil Liberties*. Lantham, MD: University Press of America.

Fund for Peace. 2013. Failed States Index. http://ffp.statesindex.org/rankings-2013-sortable (Accessed June 6, 2014).

Fund for Peace. 2015. Fragile States Index. http://fsi.fundforpeace.org/rankings-2015 (Accessed July 2, 2015).

Gajraj, P., S. Sardesai, and P. Wam. 2005. *Conflict in Somalia: Drivers and Dynamics*. Washington, DC: World Bank. http://documents.worldbank.org/curated/en/2005/01/18107249/conflict-somalia-drivers-dynamics (Accessed June 6, 2014).

Gartenstein-Ross, D. 2009. The strategic challenge of Somalia's Al-Shabaab: Dimensions of jihad. *Middle East Quarterly* 25–36. http://www.meforum.org/2486/somalia-al-shabaab-strategic-challenge?gclid=CLT-qeawsKMCFYxi2godo0-W3w (Accessed May 1, 2010).

Gebrewold, B. 2009. *Anatomy of Violence: Understanding Systems of Conflict and Violence in Africa*. Farnham: Ashgate.

Geib, R. and A. Petrig. 2011. *Piracy and Armed Robbery at Sea: The Legal Framework for Counter-Operations in Somalia and the Gulf of Aden*. Oxford: Oxford University Press.

Gelot, L. 2012. *Legitimacy, Peace Operations, and Global-Regional Security: The African Union-United Nations Partnership in Darfur*. New York: Routledge.

Grote, R. and T. Röder. 2012. *Constitutionalism in Islamic Countries: Between Upheaval and Continuity*. New York: Oxford University Press.

Hagmann, T. and M. Hoehne. 2009. Failures of the state failure debate: Evidence from the Somali territories. *Journal of International Development* 21: 42–57.

Haken, N. and P. Taft. 2013. *The Dark Side of State Building: South Sudan*. Washington, DC: The Fund for Peace. http://library.fundforpeace.org/fsi13-southsudan (Accessed June 2, 2014).

Hashim, A. 2007. Somalia: State failure, state collapse, and the possibilities for state reconstruction. In G. Kich (Ed.) *Beyond State Failure and Collapse: Making the State Relevant in Africa*, pp. 201–220, London: Lexington Books.

High Seas Task Force. 2006. Closing the net: Stopping illegal fishing in the high seas final report of the ministerial led task force on illegal, unreported and unregulated fishing on the high seas. http://www.high- seas.org/docs/HSTFfinal/HSTFFINAL_web.pdf (Accessed June 1, 2014).

Huggins, J. and L. Kane-Hartnett. 2013. Somali piracy—Are we at the end game? Oceans Beyond Piracy. *Working Paper*. http://oceansbeyondpiracy.org/sites/default/files/attachments/- Jon%20Cleveland%20Document%20_final.pdf.

Human Rights Watch. 2003. *Sudan, Oil, and Human Rights*. New York: Human Rights Watch.

Human Rights Watch. 2004. *Darfur in Flames: Atrocities in Western Sudan*. New York: Human Rights Watch. http://www.hrw.org/reports/2004/sudan0404/6.htm (Accessed May 15, 2013).

Human Rights Watch. 2005. *Entrenching Impunity: Government Responsibility for International Crimes in Darfur*. New York: Human Rights Watch.

Human Rights Watch. 2007. *Darfur 2007: Chaos by Design*. New York: Human Rights Watch. http://www.hrw.org/reports/2007/09/19/darfur-2007-chaos-design-0 (Accessed May 15, 2013).

Human Rights Watch. 2008. They shot at us as we fled: Government attacks on civilians in West Darfur in February 2008. https://www.hrw.org/reports/2008/darfur0508/index.htm (Accessed November 8, 2013).

Human Rights Watch. 2010. Sudan: ICC warrant for Al-Bashir on genocide. http://www.hrw.org/news/2010/07/13/sudan-icc-warrant-al-bashir-genocide (Accessed May 14, 2013).

Human Rights Watch. 2013a. Hostages of the gatekeepers: Abuses against internally displaced in mogadishu, Somalia. https://www.hrw.org/report/2013/03/28/hostages-gatekeepers/abuses-against-internally-displaced-mogadishu-somalia (Accessed December 23, 2015).

Human Rights Watch. 2013b. Human rights in South Sudan. http://www.hrw.org/africa/south-sudan (Accessed December 15, 2013).

Human Rights Watch. 2013c. South Sudan: 'rough justice' in lakes state. http://www.hrw.org/news/2013/06/24/south-sudan-rough-justice-lakes-state (Accessed December 15, 2013).

Human Rights Watch. 2014. 'The power these men have over us': Sexual exploitation and abuse by African union forces in Somalia. https://www.hrw.org/report/2014/09/08/power-these-men-have-over-us/sexual-exploitation-and-abuse-african-union-forces (Accessed December 15, 2014).

Ibrahim, M. 2013. Coordinated blasts kill at least 20 in Somalia's capital. *The New York Times.* http://www.nytimes.com/2013/04/15/world/africa/deadly-attacks-strike-somalias-capital-mogadishu.html?_r=0 (Accessed June 1, 2014).

Ibrahim, M. and N. Kulish. 2013. Militants attack U.N. compound in Somalia's capital. *The New York Times.* http://www.nytimes.com/2013/06/20/world/africa/un-compound-in-somalia-is-attacked.html (Accessed June 1, 2014).

International Committee of the Red Cross. 2013. South Sudan: Tens of thousands continue to suffer the effects of violence. http://www.icrc.org/eng/resources/documents/update/2013/04-05-south-sudan-people-suffering.htm (Accessed May 13, 2013).

International Crisis Group. 2014. South Sudan: A civil war by any other name. http://www.crisisgroup.org/en/regions/africa/horn-of-africa/south-sudan/217-south-sudan-a-civil-war-by-any-other-name.aspx (Accessed December 23, 2015).

International Maritime Organization. 2012. Reports on acts of piracy and armed robbery against ships, Annual Report. http://www.imo.org/en/OurWork/Security/PiracyArmedRobbery/Reports/Pages/Default.aspx (Accessed December 23, 2015).

Ismail, I. 2010. *Governance: The Scourge and Hope of Somalia.* Victoria, BC: Trafford Publishing.

Johnson, D. 2012. *The Root Causes of Sudan's Civil Wars: Peace or Truce.* London: James Curry.

Jok, M. 2001. *War and Slavery in Sudan.* Philadelphia, PA: University of Pennsylvania Press.

Kaplan, S. 2012. *Somalia's Complex Clan Dynamics.* The Fragile States Resource Center. http://www.fragilestates.org/2012/01/10/somalias-complex-clan-dynamics/ (Accessed May 1, 2013).

Kapteijns, L. 2013. *Clan Cleansing in Somalia: The Ruinous Legacy of 1991.* Philadelphia, PA: University of Pennsylvania Press.

Khalid, M. 2010. *War and Peace in Sudan.* New York: Routledge Books.

Lefebvre, J. 1991. *Arms for the Horn: U.S. Security Policy in Ethiopia and Somalia, 1953–1991.* Pittsburgh, PA: University of Pittsburgh Press.

Lefebvre, J. 1998. The United States, Ethiopia and the 1963 Somali–Soviet arms deal: Containment and the balance of power dilemma in the Horn of Africa. *The Journal of Modern African Studies* 36: 611–643.

Lewis, I. 2002. *A Modern History of the Somali.* Oxford: James Curry.

Little, P. 2003. *Somalia: Economy without State.* Bloomington, IN: Indiana University Press.

Lyons, T. and A. Samatar. 1995. *Somalia: State Collapse, Multilateral Intervention, and Strategies for Political Reconstruction.* Washington, DC: The Brookings Institute.

Mantzikos, I. 2010. U.S. foreign policymaking toward Ethiopia and Somalia (1974–1980). *African Journal of Political Science and International Relations* 4: 241–248.

Maritime Bulletin. 2013. Statistics of pirated and released vessels and crews 2010–2012. http://www.odin.tc (Accessed January 4, 2014).

Marshall, M. and B. Cole. 2009. *Global Report 2009—Conflict, Governance and State Fragility.* Arlington, VA: Center for Systemic Peace and Center for Global Policy.

Masters, J. 2013. Al-Shabaab. Council on Foreign Relations. http://www.cfr.org/somalia/al-shabaab/p18650#p5 (Accessed May 23, 2014).

Mbaku, J. 2015. Sudan: Elections 2015. *Africa in Focus.* http://www.brookings.edu/blogs/africa-in-focus/posts/2015/04/01-sudan-election-2015-mbaku (Accessed June 20, 2015).

McAuslan, P. 1988. Land policy: A framework for analysis and action. *Journal of African Law* 31(1 & 2): 185–206.

McCabe, K. and S. Manian. 2010. *Sex Trafficking: A Global Perspective.* Lanham, MD: Lexington Books.

Meehan, N. 2010. Somalia. In G. Newman (Ed.) *Crime and Punishment Around the World,* pp. 198–205, Santa Barbara, CA: ABC-CLIO.

Metz, H. 1992. *Somalia: A Country Study.* Washington, DC: Library of Congress.

Mohamoud, A. 2006. *The Case of Somalia (1996–2001)*. West Lafayette, IN: Purdue University Press.

Monno, A. 2012. Piracy and terrorism, Threats to maritime security: A brief analysis. In S. C. Gallett (Ed.) *Piracy and Maritime Terrorism: Logistics, Strategies, Scenarios*, pp. 52–83, Amsterdam: IOS Press.

Mubarak, J. A. 1996. *From Bad Policy to Chaos in Somalia: How an Economy Fell Apart*. Westport, CN: Praeger.

Muscati, S. 2013. Here, rape is normal: A five-point plan to curtail sexual violence in Somalia. Human Rights Watch. https://www.hrw.org/report/2014/02/13/here-rape-normal/five-point-plan-curtail-sexual-violence-somalia (Accessed December 5, 2014).

Nalbandov, R. 2009. *Foreign Interventions in Ethnic Conflicts*. Farnham: Ashgate.

National Counterterrorism Center. 2013. Al-Shabaab. http://www.nctc.gov/site/groups/al_shabaab.html (Accessed May 23, 2014).

Newbury, D. 1998. Understanding genocide. *African Studies Review* 41(1): 73–97.

Nimtz, A. H. 1980. *Islam and Politics in East Africa*. Minneapolis, MN: The University of Minnesota Press.

Njoku, R. 2013. *The History of Somalia*. Santa Barbara, CA: Greenwood Press.

Oceans Beyond Piracy. 2013. *The Human Cost of Maritime Piracy, 2012*. The One Earth Future Foundation.

Office of the United Nations High Commissioner for Refugees. 2013a. 2013 UNHCR country operations profile—Chad. http://www.unhcr.org/pages/49c3646c2.html (Accessed May 23, 2014).

Office of the United Nations High Commissioner for Refugees. 2013b. Liquid treasure: The challenge of providing drinking water in a new refugee camp. http://www.unhcr.org/51d5443f9.html (Accessed May 19, 2014).

Office of the United Nations High Commissioner for Refugees. 2013c. UNHCR starts moving displaced families from Darfur to safer areas of Chad. http://www.unhcr.org/51769fdf9.html (Accessed May 19, 2014).

Office of the United Nations High Commissioner for Refugees. 2015. 2015 UNHCR country operations profile—Chad. http://www.unhcr.org/pages/49e45c226.html (Accessed July 2, 2015).

Osman, A. 2007. *Could be the Book: Governance and Internal Wars in Sub-Saharan Africa: Exploring the Relationship*. London: Adonis & Abbey.

Osman El-Tom, A. 2009. Darfur people: Too black for the Arab-Islamic project of Sudan. In S. Hassan and C. Ray (Eds) *Darfur and the Crisis of Governance in Sudan: A Critical Reader*, pp. 84–102, Ithaca, NY: Cornell University Press.

Permanent Mission of the Somali Republic to the United Nations. (n.d). Country facts. https://www.un.int/somalia/somalia/country-facts (Accessed May 19, 2014).

Reuters. 2013. Somalia: Thousands of peacekeepers have died during mission, U.N. says. *New York Times*. http://www.nytimes.com/2013/05/10/world/africa/somalia-thousands-of-peacekeepers-have-died-during-mission-un-says.html?_r=0 (Accessed May 17, 2014).

Rothe, D. and V. Collins. 2010. An exploration of system criminality and arms trafficking. *International Criminal Justice Review* 21(1): 22–38.

Rothe, D. and V. Collins. 2011. Got a band-aid? Political discourse, militarized responses, and the Somalia pirate. *Contemporary Justice Review: Issues in Criminal, Social, and Restorative Justice* 14(3): 329–343.

Rozoff, R. 2009. Cold War origins of the Somalia crisis and control of the Indian ocean. http://rickrozoff.wordpress.com/2009/08/28/cold-war-origins-of-the-somalia-crisis-and-control-of-the-indian-ocean/ (Accessed May 19, 2014).

Samatar, A. 1992. Destruction of state and society in Somalia: Beyond the tribal convention. *The Journal of Modern African Studies* 30: 625–641.

Samatar, A., M. Lindberg, and B. Mahayni. 2010. The dialectics of piracy: The rich versus the poor. *Third World Quarterly* 31: 1377–1394.

Saul, B. 2014. *Research Handbook on International Law and Terrorism*. Cheltenham: Edward Elgar.

Schlee, G. and A. Shongolo. 2012. *Islam & Ethnicity in Northern Kenya & Southern Ethiopia*. Martlesham: James Currey.

Schraeder, P. 1992. *Intervention into the 1990s: U.S. Foreign Policy in the Third World*. Boulder, CO: Lynne Rienner Publishing.

Schwab, P. 1978. Cold War on the Horn of Africa. *African Affairs* 77(306): 6–20.

Shane, J. and C. A. Lieberman. 2009. Criminological theories and the problems of modern piracy. In M. R. Haberfeld and A. von Hassell (Eds) *Maritime Piracy and Maritime Terrorism: The Challenge of Piracy for the 21st Century*, pp. 271–290, Dubuque, IA: Kendall Hunt.

Sheikh, A. 2009. Ransom paid as Somali pirates free supertanker. *The Independent World*. http://www.independent.co.uk/news/world/africa/ransom-paid-as-somali-pirates-free-supertanker-1270796.html (Accessed May 17, 2014).

Shelley, F. 2013. *Governments around the World: From Democracies to Theocracies*. Santa Barbara, CA: ABC-CLIO.

Sudan Tribune. 2013a. Sudan's Bashir to visit Chad, Libya despite ICC warrant. http://www.sudantribune.com/spip.php?article45488 (Accessed May 14, 2014).

Sudan Tribune. 2013b. Curfew imposed in South Darfur capital after deadly clashes with tribal militias. http://www.sudantribune.com/spip.php?article47187 (Accessed May 14, 2014).

Suttie, J. M., S. Reynolds, and C. Batello. 2005. *Grasslands of the World*. Rome: Food and Agriculture Orfanizations of the World.

Toft, M., D. Philpott and T. Shah. 2011. *God's Century: Resurgent Religion and Global Politics*. New York: W. W. Norton.

Totten, S. and W. Parsons. 2013. *Centuries of Genocide: Essays and Eyewitness Accounts*. New York: Routledge.

Tripodi, P. 1999. *The Colonial Legacy in Somalia*. New York: St. Martins.

Tuerk, H. 2012. *Reflections on the Contemporary Law of the Sea*. Leiden: Martinus Nijhoff.

UK Foreign and Commonwealth Office. 2013. Human rights and democracy: The 2012 foreign and commonwealth office report—Country updates: Somalia. http://www.ecoi.net/local_link/244475/386790_en.html (Accessed January 2, 2014).

United Nations. 2012. Report of the independent expert on the situation of human rights in Somalia, shamsul bari. http://www.ohchr.org (Accessed June 1, 2014).

United Nations. 2014. Annual report of the secretary general on children and armed conflict. http://www.securitycouncilreport.org/un-documents/children-and-armed-conflict/ (Accessed December 23, 2015).

United Nations Convention on the Law of the Sea (UNCLOS). 1982. http://www.un.org/depts/los/convention_agreements/convention_overview_convention.htm (Accessed December 23, 2015).

United Nations High Commissioner for Refugees. 2013. Country report: Chad. http://www.unhcr.org/pages/49e45c226.html

United Nations News Centre. 2013. South Sudan: UN reinforces peacekeeping presence in Pibor town amid violence. http://www.un.org/apps/news/story.asp?NewsID=44929&Cr=pibor&Cr1#.UeLi_xbIa2w (Accessed June 1, 2014).

United Nations News Centre. 2015. UN lauds Somalia as country ratifies landmark children's rights treaty. http://www.un.org/apps/news/story.asp?NewsID=49845#.VnqeIZMrLdQ (Accessed December 23, 2015).

United Nations Political Office for Somalia. 2012. Assessment of the prison system in Mogadishu/South Central Somalia. http://www.ohchr.org/EN/Countries/AfricaRegion/Pages/SOIndex.aspx (Accessed June 3, 2014).

U.S. Department of Labor. 2012. 2012 findings on the worst forms of child labor. https://www.dol.gov/ilab/reports/child-labor/findings/2011TDA/somalia.pdf (Accessed December 23, 2015).

U.S. Department of State. 2012. *Trafficking in Persons Report*. Washington, DC: U.S. Department of State.

U.S. Department of State. 2013. Somalia: Country specific information. http://www.travel. state.gov/content/passports/en/country/somalia.html (Accessed October 21, 2015).

Waldo, M. A. 2009. The two piracies in somalia: Why the world ignores the other? http:// wardheernews.com/Articles_09/Jan/Waldo/08_The_two_piracies_in _Somalia.html (Accessed June 3, 2014).

Wasuge, M. 2015. Public policy challenges: Somalia behind the world—Reflection. https:// mahadbile.wordpress.com/tag/policy-issues-in-somalia/.

Wilson, B. 2009. Effectively confronting a regional threat: Somali piracy. *Conflict Trends* 1(1): 11–12.

Wise, R. 2011. Al-Shabaab. Center for Strategic and International Studies. http://csis.org/ publication/al-shabaab (Accessed June 3, 2014).

World Health Organization. 2011. World health statistics 2011. http://www.who.int/whosis/ whostat/EN_WHS2011_Full.pdf.

Yikona, S. 2013. *Pirate Trails: Trafficking the Illicit Financial Flows from Pirate Activities off the Horn of Africa*. Washington, DC: The World Bank.

Yongo-Bare, B. 2009. Marginalization and war: From the South to Darfur. In S. Hassan and C. Ray (Eds) *Darfur and the Crisis of Governance in Sudan: A Critical Reader*, pp. 68–83, Ithaca, NY: Cornell University Press.

Zissis, C. 2006. Darfur: Crisis Continues. Council on Foreign Relations. http://www.cfr.org/ sudan/darfur-crisis-continues/p10600 (Accessed May 3, 2014).

Concluding Thoughts 9

The history of any nation follows an undulatory course. In the trough of the wave we find more or less complete anarchy; but the crest is not more or less complete Utopia, but only, at best, a tolerably humane, partially free and fairly just society that invariably carries within itself the seeds of its own decadence.

—Aldous Huxley

This volume bears strong testament to Huxley's sage words. Nations, even under the best of circumstances and led by the noblest of intentions, are a messy business. Seldom do they collapse into absolute chaos. More often there is just enough heat in the ember of hope to encourage pockets of stability. To this point in our story, we have labored the details of fragility. Without an enumeration of preceding issues, the reader is likely able to construct his or her own "how to ensure failure" theoretical scenario. We have explored, in its full redness of tooth and claw, myriad ways to run the ship of state aground.

As we have seen, fragility manifests from a constellation of system inputs and responses. Sometimes these inputs are pregnant with malice, sometimes they are just a sad artifact of natural disaster. Fragility takes many forms, the effects of which can be seen in the economic vitality, political/governmental stability, geographical integrity, public health, public infrastructure, criminal justice system, and just about any other aspect of life in society.

There is, however, one dimension of failure that we have yet to fully elucidate: failure as contaminant and its associated stigma. Time and again throughout this book, we have shown that fragility is many things, but seldom is it an atomized condition. Like a tumor, fragility may begin as a localized phenomenon (even if that locale is an entire nation or region), but unchecked the tumor can spread throughout the entire host. Even if it is excised, there is a lasting imprint. Much in the way that Americans use the term *felon*, to permanently inscribe deeds onto a person convicted of serious crimes, the moniker of "failed" when applied to nations has a similar set of consequences.

Michèle Lamont and Virag Molnar (2002, p. 168) discuss the process through which humans erect "symbolic boundaries" between themselves and others. As they state, symbolic boundaries are "conceptual distinctions made by social actors to categorize objects, people, practices, and even time and space." Placing things in categorical hierarchies or "diagnostic packages" helps us psychologically sort through all the information that we encounter in daily life (Massey 2007; Simmel 1971; Schneider 2005; Zelizer and Tilly 2006). As Luc Boltanski and Laurent Tévenot (2006) observe, this sorting of new people emerges through a series of implicit social agreements about the relative symbolic worth or dissimilarity of other people. The ensuing nomothetic categorizations are ultimately reinforced through a process of "relational identifications and feedback" (Castaneda 2012, p. 161).

There exists a substantial body of criminological theory that examines the social and psychological process of delineating criminogenic neighborhoods (e.g., Fagan and Davies 2000; Sampson and Raudenbush 1999; Sampson et al. 2002; Wacquant 1993, 2007, 2008; Wilson and Kelling 1982; Wilson 1987). As an extension of this work, we suggest that an apt metaphor can be constructed: if the Earth is a city, then failed and fragile nations are its ghettos.

A few years ago, one of us (Pate 2010) conducted a study on the ways in which segregated settlement patterns can endogenously evolve in modern societies. While that research focused on neighborhood-level phenomenon, the dynamics are fully applicable to a larger stage. At the national scale, this "tragedy of the commons" may be regarded as the collective impact of "rational" but atomized individuals attempting to maximize their personal utility without a view toward broader social consequences (Hardin 1968). The goals of this utility-maximizing behavior might take the shape of a warlord capturing an oil field; or it might be a mother trying to hoard food against a coming famine. At the community level, it could be a greater or lesser tolerance for mercurial governance.

Poverty and affluence are necessarily strong drivers of this dynamic. Just as affluent citizens may cordon themselves behind gated communities (Atkinson and Blandy 2005) or work in secured office parks and take recreation in similarly protected environs (Davis 1990), so too do more affluent nations secure, seclude, trade, and travel more among themselves. Andreas Wimmer (2008, p. 975) helps us to understand the consequences of these delineations thusly: "a boundary displays both a categorical and a social or behavioral dimension ... how to relate to individuals classified as 'us' and 'them' under given circumstances."

For more affluent individuals and nations alike, physical separation from the disruptive "other" may seem the most rational choice. Not only is this choice rational, but it is often undergirded with moral justifications supportive of any inequalities that may exist (Lamont 2000). Once these beliefs are internalized, it is difficult to humanize "the other," and stigmatization appears "natural" (Bourdieu 1991). In such cases, an increased reliance on protective measures and a growing emphasis on "law and order" or military strength in capitalist democracies (characterized by significant levels of inequality) can lead to heightened levels both of unease and fear (Low 2003;

Atkinson 2006) and of crime itself (Sutton et al. 2008). These forces combine to create a feedback loop that at once promotes a "need" for protective action and "legitimates" the increased and economic social distance.

For members of stigmatized and excluded "communities of fate" (Sutton et al. 2008), or in the present case, "nations of fate," generated by such choices, an equally rational response may be to strike out through crime and other predatory behavior (i.e., terrorism) (Jordan 1996; Wilkinson 2005). Absent overt rebellion or crime, the relative "order" of stigmatized spaces may become the focus of formal social control. As Fagan and Davies (2000) observe, the competing social structure of (disadvantaged vs. affluent) spaces reinforces the notion that disorder is a phenomenon more common to poor and minority communities. This in turn promotes a "durable spoiled identity" for the modern American ghetto (Wacquant 1993; Sampson and Raudenbush 1999). This spoiled identity subsequently "legitimates" differential modes and intensities of formal social control. We hold that the world's fragile and failed states have also been pushed into the yoke of their own durable spoiled identity.

In his landmark study, *Place and Placelessness*, geographer Edward Relph (1976) provides us with an informative perspective as to the mechanisms through which failed states are consigned to the ranks of the irreparable and incorrigible. Relph argues that space is neither a void nor a container into which places are situated. Rather, we must look on space and the places therein as a more experientially derived construct. The principle question is one of how people experience the place. Relph (1976, p. 9) contends that there are many different types of experience that exist in "a continuum that has direct experience at one extreme and abstract thought at the other." For Relph, place may be experienced in many different ways, but there are two primary divisions relevant to this discussion. There is one kind of experience that is more physical and direct and another that is more cerebral, emotive, and abstract.

Given that the vast majority of people in the developed world have very limited direct experience with fragile places, the primary global estimation of them is largely an abstraction, fed by nuanced media portrayals and stereotypes. This caricature then feeds an affective and indelible pastiche of national identity, which in turn gives the outside world "permission" to dismiss these places' potential and trivialize their plight. Allen Pred's (2000) study of racism in Sweden goes straight to this point, namely, that one need not have any direct experience with a place to have very strong negative feelings about it. This then suggests an analogy with regard to racial and cultural stereotypes.

In one of his studies of communal disorder, Robert Sampson and Raudenbush (2009) discusses implicit bias, "The use of racial and ethnic context to encode disorder does not mean that people are necessarily prejudiced in the sense of group hostility. The power of cultural stereotypes is that they

can operate beneath the radar screen of our conscious reasoning, forming...
[an] implicit bias".

Wacquant et al. (2014) help pull this into clearer focus with their work
on "territorial stigmatization." Blending the work of Erving Goffman and
Pierre Bourdieu, they develop a highly instructive concept of a ruined
and inaccessible land, square in our midst, replete with all the social, economic, and moral baggage of the aforementioned tumor. Quoting the work
of Dominique Kalifa (2012, pp. 61–62), they describe the dominant public
image of the post-industrial urban ghetto: "...vortexes and vectors of social
disintegration, fundamentally dissolute and irretrievably disorganized,
whereas the 'counterworld' of the classic industrial *bas-fonds* was seen as
'a powerful and hierarchized counter-society,' an 'inverted double, a counterfeit and caricatural version of the organized society' surrounding it"
(Wacquant et al. 2014, p. 5).

The applicability of this vivid pronouncement is axiomatic with regard
to fragile and failing states, but their next observation shines perhaps the
harshest light on the stigmatized and spoiled state. With respect to how more
affluent and stable environs differentiate themselves from their ruined neighbors, Wacquant et al. (2014, p. 5) discuss the "racialization [of residents and
place] through selective accentuation or fictive projection." As they state, the
populations of these ghettos, "are nearly always painted in darker and more
exotic hues than their demography warrants" (Wacquant et al. 2014, p. 5).
Cultural differences are exaggerated and violence becomes sensationalized,
"and referred back to the allegedly intrinsic sociocultural traits of the residents fit to brand them as outcasts" (Wacquant et al. 2014, p. 5).

At the level of nations, we also see a lingering postcolonial taint in the
form of infantilizing the people of fragile states. The developed world often
looks on as a parent watching his or her toddler attempt wobbly first steps,
dotted by regular trips and falls. Extending the logic of Wacquant et al. (2014),
even if the child manages a few steady strides we always keep the "ready to
tumble at any minute" narrative close at hand.

Perhaps nowhere do we see better evidence of a complex adaptive system
at work than here. So many of the world's fragile states have a postcolonial
fetter. To have been colonized in the first place is to encumber some degree of
moral or intrinsic failing—at least that would seem a prerequisite emotional
neutralization for a colonizer to extend its paternal hand. With that paucity
of "right" national "stuff," the colonial master is free to manage, manipulate,
and exploit as fits its desire. This then sets in motion a national tempo of
governance that may be far out of step with indigenous sensibilities. The population, no matter how besieged, learns to adapt. They assent to new national
boundaries. They get a new or second national language. They learn to take
tea and dress in Western attire. They ascribe to (or at least feed) the appetites
of their colonial masters.

When the master withdraws the erstwhile order, they are left at a difficult crossroads: carry on, turn back, or blend then and now. All too often, the native elite (usually the military) steps in to play the role of new master. Again, society must decide the course. This might be a fairly tidy exercise save for one fact: the technical exit of one controlling outside interest does not mean that all parties withdraw. Corporate interests, who have been fatted on the tight tether of colonial control, still jealously protect their investments. States, who by fiat of geography, occupy a space deemed strategically important, do so both before and after colonial egress. Somalia comes to mind. Lastly, no nation is a complete loss, as they can always serve as host to a proxy battle.

It is tempting to make an analogy to a ball in a pinball machine, but such characterizations only rob these nations of their social agency. It suggests that they are helpless to right their own ship—that they somehow really do lack that "right stuff" required to join the ranks of the "civilized" world. A self-fulfilling prophesy of inevitable failure is carefully curated. "They" are not the same as "us." Therefore, differential treatment is "permissible." In the words of Charles Tilly (2008, p. 7) "The act of giving credit or (especially) assigning blame draws us-them boundaries: We are the worthy people, they the unworthy."

While we coined the term to frame the contours of corporal punishment (Pate and Gould 2012, p. 152), the concept of *subjugative shaming* applies in the context of failed states as well. The modern global economy is united by a power distribution (reflected in economic disparities) designed in the words of Foucault "to render docile" the social, economic, geographical, and political "other." This is accomplished through differential resource allocation, paternalism, atavism narratives, and disengagement, which function to permanently marginalize and stigmatize fragile states. A necessary component of this process is the creation of highly visible hierarchies that venerate some nations while branding others with a subjugative shame. Participation in global affairs is contingent, temporary, and amenable to revocation.

What Then Can Be Done?

By way of final summary, one might turn to the famous logic puzzle, the Prisoners' Dilemma. The Nobel Prize–winning economist, Thomas Schelling (1978, p. 224), describes the essential feature of the exercise, "There is one way that everybody can act so that everybody is doing what is in his own best interest given what everybody else is doing, yet all could be better off if they all made opposite choices." Of the Prisoners' Dilemma generally, Schelling (1978, p. 224) says, "Its fascination is that it generates an inefficient equilibrium."

The systematically reinforced disadvantage and social maladaptation of chronically impoverished and crime-plagued communities also arguably fits the definition of "inefficient equilibrium." As Schelling (1978, p. 230) frames it, "We still have the original problem of inducing the Right choices that maximize the collective outcome." As policy implications go, few are greater.

To a large extent, the more prosperous and stable nations of the world act as though the pathway to state failure is a mystery. In some ways, this detachment echoes Adam Smith's "invisible hand." In a globe of self-interest-maximizing international actors, the rising tide just somehow forgot to raise a few ships. Failed nations are the vestigial farriers in a world full of supersonic jets.

That these struggling nations have not met the expectations of modernity does not mean that they may be cast off as the global *lumpenproletariat*. Neither does it mean that the developed world should regard them as miscreant children. Nor does it mean that their plight should only be remembered when a sudden influx of terrorists or an undiscovered cache of oil is revealed. Rather, it means that the developed and stable world had a hand in fostering the conditions now manifest in many of these forlorn places; and as a consequence of that very visible hand, now has an onerous moral and ethical responsibility it must fulfill.

References

Atkinson, R. 2006. Limited exposure: Social concealment, mobility and engagement with public space by the super-rich in London. *Environment and Planning*, pp. 1–16. http://epn.sagepub.com/content/early/2015/08/06/0308518X15598323.full.pdf (Accessed February 12, 2013).

Atkinson, R. and S. Blandy. 2005. International perspectives on the new enclavism and the rise of gated communities. *Housing Studies* 20(2): 177–186. (Special issue on gated communities.)

Boltanski, L. and L. Tévenot. 2006. *On Justification: Economies of Worth*. Princeton, NJ: Princeton University Press.

Bourdieu, P. 1991. *Language and Symbolic Power*. Cambridge, MA: Polity Press.

Castaneda, E. 2012. Places of stigma: Ghettos, barrios and banlieues. In R. Hutchinson and B. D. Haynes (Eds) *The Ghetto: Contemporary Global Issues and Controversies*, pp. 159–190, Boulder, CO: Westview Press.

Davis, M. 1990. *City of Quartz: Excavating the Future in Los Angeles*. New York: Verso.

Fagan, J. and G. Davies. 2000. Street stops and broken windows: Terry, race, and disorder in New York City. *Fordham Urban Law Journal* 28: 457–504.

Hardin, G. 1968. Tragedy of the commons. *Science* 162(3859): 1243–1248.

Jordan, B. 1996. *A Theory of Poverty and Social Exclusion*. Cambridge, MA: Polity Press.

Kalifa, D. 2012. *Les bas-fonds. Histoire d'un Imaginaire*. Paris: Seuil.

Lamont, M. 2000. *The Dignity of Working Men: Morality and the Boundaries of Race, Class, and Immigration*. New York and Cambridge, MA: Russell Sage Foundation and Harvard University Press.

Lamont, M. and V. Molnar. 2002. The study of boundaries in the social sciences. *Annual Review of Sociology* 28: 167–195.

Low, S. 2003. Towards a theory of urban fragmentation: A cross-cultural analysis of fear, privatization, and the state. *European Journal of Geography*, p. 349. https://cybergeo. revues.org/3207 (Accessed February 12, 2013).

Massey, D. 2007. *Categorically Unequal: The American Stratification System*. New York: Russell Sage Foundation.

Pate, M. 2010. *Segregation and Social Control: An Agent Based Simulation*. Dissertation. University at Albany, State University of New York.

Pate, M. and L. Gould. 2012. *Corporal Punishment Around the World*. Santa Barbara, CA: Praeger.

Pred, A. 2000. *Even in Sweden: Racisms, Racialized Spaces, and the Popular Geographical Imagination*. Berkeley, CA: University of California Press.

Relph, E. 1976. *Place and Placelessness*. London: Pion.

Sampson, R. and S. Raudenbush. 1999. Systematic social observation of public spaces: A new look at disorder in urban neighborhoods. *American Journal of Sociology* 105: 603–651.

Sampson, R., J. Morenoff, and T. Gannon-Rowley. 2002. Assessing "neighborhood effects": Social processes and new directions in research. *Annual Review of Sociology* 28: 443–478.

Schelling, T. 1978. *Micromotives and Macrobehavior*. New York: W.W. Norton.

Schneider, D. 2005. *The Psychology of Stereotyping* (Distinguished Contributions in Psychology). New York: The Guilford Press.

Simmel, G. 1971. The metropolis and mental life. In D. Levine (Ed.) *Georg Simmel on Individuality and Social Forms*, pp. 324–339, Chicago: University of Chicago Press.

Sutton, A., A. Cherney, and R. White. 2008. *Crime Prevention: Principles, Perspectives and Practices*. Cambridge, MA: Cambridge University Press.

Tilly, C. 2008. *Credit and Blame*. Princeton, NJ: Princeton University Press.

Wacquant, L. 1993. Urban outcasts: Stigma and division in the black American ghetto and the French urban periphery. *International Journal of Urban and Regional Research* 17: 366–383.

Wacquant, L. 2007. Territorial stigmatization in the age of advanced marginality. *Thesis Eleven* 91(1): 66–77.

Wacquant, L. 2008. *Urban Outcasts: A Comparative Sociology of Advanced Marginality*. Cambridge: Polity Press.

Wacquant, L., T. Slater, and V. Borges Pereira. 2014. Territorial stigmatization in action. *Environment and Planning A* 46: 1270–1280. http://www.loicwacquant.net/assets/ Papers/Recent-Papers/TERRITORIALSTIGMAINACTION-final-proofs.pdf (Accessed February 11, 2015).

Wilkinson, R. 2005. *The Impact of Inequality: How to Make Sick Societies Healthier*. New York: New Press.

Wilson, J. and G. Kelling. 1982. The police and neighborhood safety: Broken windows. *The Atlantic Monthly* 127: 29–38.

Wilson, W. J. 1987. *The Truly Disadvantaged: The Inner City, the Underclass, and Public Policy*. Chicago, IL: University of Chicago Press.

Wimmer, A. 2011. A Swiss anomaly? A relational account of national boundary making. *Nations and Nationalism* 17(4): 718–737.

Zelizer, V. A. and C. Tilly. 2006. Relations and categories. In A. Markman and B. H. Ross (Eds) *The Psychology of Learning and Motivation*. 47. *Categories in Use*, pp. 1–32, San Diego, CA: Elsevier.

Index

Stockman, Jamilia, 140
Stolow, Jeremy, 92
Structured group, 116
Subjugative shaming, 271
Sudan Administrative Conference, 245
Sudan and South Sudan, 243–248
 civil wars in, 247–248
 conflicts and international implications
  of, 252–255
 European interest in, 244
 human trafficking in, 252–253
 Islamization of, 248
 Juba Conference, 245
 Penal Code Act, 254
 Sudan Administrative Conference, 245
 violence, 247–248
Sudanese Islam, 247
Sudanese nationalism, 247
Sudan Liberation Movement/Army
  (SLM/A), 249
Sudan People's Liberation Army
  (SPLA), 253
Sudan Tribune, 253
Sufism, 249
Suicide, 175
Sunni Islam, 228
Sunni Muslims, 86
Supreme Revolutionary Council (SRC), 225
Sutherland, Stuart, 144
Sweet, William, 28
Sykes–Picot Agreement, 79
Syria
 in historical context, 79–82
 Islamic State in, 84–88
 modern, 82–84
 sovereignty, 81
 terrorism in, 79–84
Syrian Ba'thist regime, 82

T

Takfir, 100
Taliban, 132, 135, 136, 151, 180
Targeted killings, 31
Ta'zir, 96
Technology, and economic order, 16
Terrorism
 anomie, 75–78
 Boko Haram, 101–107
 defined, 74–75
 economic inequality, 7
 former prisoners, 66–67

instability of states, 6
Islamic State, 84–101
 marginalization, 7
 radicalized religious groups, 73–74
 in Somalia, 237–240
 in Syria, 79–84
 transnational crime and, 132–133
 ungoverned spaces in Middle
  East, 78–79
Teschke, Benno, 4
Tévenot, Laurent, 268
Thein Sein, 62–63
Tiananmen Square massacre, 64–65
Tilly, Charles, 7–8, 10, 271
Tlass, Mustafa, 139
Tlass Foundation, 139
Torture
 People's Republic of Bangladesh, 44–47
 psychological effects of, 46
*Toward a Theory of Minority-Group
  Relations* (Blalock and
  Wilken), 18
Trafficking Victims Protection Act (TVPA),
  229, 253
Training Human Rights Association for
  Afghan Women, 169
Transnational crimes
 cocaine production, 124–127
 defined, 115
 drug trafficking, 121–122
 FBI on, 115–116
 globalization, 117
 illegal activities, 116–117
 legal instruments for combating,
  119–120
 opium production, 122–124
 organizations, 116–117
Transnational criminal networks, 117
Transnational organized crime, 115
 state fragility, 155–157
Transparency International, 131, 206, 209, 214
 Corruption Perception Index (CPI), 209
 Global Corruption Barometer, 209–210
Transparency International Georgia, 208
Tribe, Keith, 71
Trinkunas, Harold, 76
Tripodi, Paolo, 226
Truman, Edwin, 157
Truman, Harry, 30
Tumblr, 91
Turabi, Hassan al-, 248
Twitter, 91